I0084559

D.G. van der Keessel

Select Theses on the Laws of Holland and Zeeland

Being a commentary of Hugo Grotius' Introduction to Dutch jurisprudence, and

intended to supply certain defects therein, and to determine some of the more

celebrated controversies on the law of Holland

D.G. van der Keessel

Select Theses on the Laws of Holland and Zeeland
Being a commentary of Hugo Grotius' Introduction to Dutch jurisprudence, and intended to supply certain defects therein, and to determine some of the more celebrated controversies on the law of Holland

ISBN/EAN: 9783337310080

Printed in Europe, USA, Canada, Australia, Japan

Cover: Foto ©Suzi / pixelio.de

More available books at **www.hansebooks.com**

SELECT THESES

ON THE

LAWS OF HOLLAND AND ZEELAND,

BEING A COMMENTARY OF

HUGO GROTIUS' INTRODUCTION TO DUTCH JURISPRUDENCE,

AND INTENDED

TO SUPPLY CERTAIN DEFECTS THEREIN, AND TO DETERMINE SOME
OF THE MORE CELEBRATED CONTROVERSIES ON
THE LAW OF HOLLAND;

BY

DIONYSIUS GODEFRIDUS VAN DER KEESSEL,

ADVOCATE, AND PROFESSOR OF THE CIVIL AND MODERN LAWS
IN THE UNIVERSITY OF LEYDEN.

LEYDEN: S. & J. LUCHTMANS, 1800.

TRANSLATED FROM THE ORIGINAL LATIN BY

CHARLES AMBROSE LORENZ,

OF LINCOLN'S INN, BARRISTER-AT-LAW; ADVOCATE OF THE SUPREME COURT
OF THE ISLAND OF CEYLON.

SECOND EDITION,

WITH A BIOGRAPHICAL NOTICE OF THE AUTHOR,

BY

PROFESSOR J. DE WAL,

OF LEYDEN.

CAPE TOWN: J. C. JUTA.

1884.

TO

JOHN DRIEBERG, ESQ.,

PROCTOR OF THE SUPREME COURT OF CEYLON,

AND NOTARY PUBLIC OF COLOMBO,

THIS WORK IS DEDICATED,

IN GRATEFUL REMEMBRANCE OF MANY KINDNESSES RECEIVED,

BY HIS LATE PUPIL,

THE TRANSLATOR.

DEC. 1854.

TRANSLATOR'S PREFACE

TO

THE FIRST EDITION.

THE following Translation of Van der Keessel's *Theses Selectæ* will, it is hoped, be found acceptable to the Profession, in those British colonies where the Roman-Dutch Law still obtains. The treatise of Grotius, a translation of which has been published by Mr. Herbert, of British Guiana, required, after the lapse of nearly two centuries, much comment and alteration ; and the present Work, together with the *Rechtsgeleerde Observatien*, published in 1778 by a Society of Dutch Advocates, of whom the celebrated Van der Linden was one, is perhaps indispensable as a companion to the *Introduction to Dutch Jurisprudence*. Some portions of it will necessarily be found inapplicable to the colonies at the present day ; but it has been thought advisable to publish a translation of the entire book, in order to avoid the risk of omitting any portions, which, though not applicable to one colony, may be of use in another.

The Translator has spared no pains in endeavouring to render the translation correct and reliable : and has indeed deferred its publication for nearly a twelvemonth, in order to compare it with the various authorities cited throughout the book, and by submitting some portions of it to the judgment of others, to assure himself of the general correctness of his renderings.

He is not, however, quite confident but that under the peculiar difficulties of translating from modern law-Latin into an acquired language, some errors might have escaped his observation; but these, it is believed, are not of a grave nature, and will no doubt be excused, equally perhaps with the general want of elegance in the language,—a fault which he believes he has frequently fallen into, in endeavouring to be precise in his translation.

A different mode of arranging the citations has been adopted, which will be found more convenient than that of incorporating them with the text, as in the original. Most of those laws or treatises of which no Latin translations exist, but which the author has quoted by the Latin titles, have been cited in the translation by their proper Dutch titles.

It is to be regretted that there exists no complete biography of the author of a treatise held in such high estimation, and who is still remembered in his native country with respect and admiration. The high testimony borne to his talents by his pupil and friend, Van der Linden, in the Dedication of his *Judicieele Practycq*, is by no means a solitary proof that among the most eminent men of that time, Van der Keessel was esteemed a great scholar and jurist. The Translator has had the pleasure of receiving a communication from another pupil and a relative of the author's (Mr. J. T. Bodel Nijenhuis, of Leyden), a translation of a portion of which may not prove uninteresting as the reminiscence, at the distance of nearly half a century, of one—perhaps the last—of that great body of writers on the Roman and Dutch Laws, whose works are still read and studied throughout Europe, and in the remotest parts of the world, and whose labours are among the evidences of the greatness and glory of the Old Netherlands.— "It is to me, and will hereafter, when more generally known, be to the Old Netherlands, a matter of great satisfaction, that the *Theses* of Professor Van der Keessel are still held to be of such great authority in Ceylon, as to require, after a period of more than forty years, translation into the English language. I am, perhaps, the only survivor of his pupils, having, during the years 1814-1816, studied the Institutes of the Roman Law under him, and been presented by him to the Prætorship of the University. He died on the 7th of August 1816, in the 78th year of his age. You will find mention made of him in Siegenbeek's *Leidsche Hooge-School*, in Te Water's *Narratio*, and more particularly in the Annual Oration delivered in the year after his death by the Rector J. van Voorst, and published in *Annales Academiæ Lugd. Bat.* for the year 1816-1817. We have no personal account of him in a separate form. Such a thing would be of more likely occurrence at the present day. But during the last forty years many men of note amongst us have died, without being particularly mentioned. He was an excellent jurist of the old style; and during the fifty years of his labours, sent forth many eminent pupils. He was also a sincere Christian, as you may judge from his Oration *de Advocato Christiano*."

The Translator has seen several copies of the Author's *Dictata ad Grotii Introductionem*, being the lectures delivered by him at the University of Leyden, according to the plan spoken of in his preface to the present work, where he proposes to treat in the printed Theses of such points only as were omitted by Grotius, or have since undergone alteration, or become subjects of controversy, and to reserve for oral lectures such points as may tend to the explanation of the text or the fuller development of these Theses. But as these *Dictata* have never been published, and the MS. copies, originally not very numerous, are at present, from the small demand there has existed since 1806 for works on the ancient law, very rare, and belong only to such private individuals as from a knowledge of their great value, or from the nature of their studies at the University, have taken care to provide themselves with copies, the Translator has not hitherto been able to become the possessor of one. He had, however, been enabled, through the kindness of Professor de Wal, of Leyden, to take very full extracts from some of the most important portions, and these he proposes to publish at some future time as an Appendix or Supplement to the present volume, incorporating with them the valuable comments of Professor Schorer on the text of Grotius. The original MS. of the *Dictata*, bequeathed by the Author to the Public Library of Leyden, still exists there, and is readily produced to students who may be desirous of consulting it. It is a valuable work, and contains very full comments on almost every point of any importance in law; and in fact constitutes in itself a complete treatise on the Law of Holland up to the year 1800.* A treatise of this nature would, if attainable, be of the highest importance in the

---

* The Translator was so fortunate as to become the possessor, in 1855, of the Author's copy of these *Dictata*, together with his annotated copy of Grotius; and a collection of Addresses and Prayers with which he appears to have inaugurated or closed his annual Lectures.—(Tr. 1868.)

colonies, being the last work on the subject of the Law of Holland as it still obtains in the Dutch ceded colonies; for with the exception of Van der Linden's Institutes, a treatise of a very elementary nature, there is hardly another work of any authority which brings the law down to the period immediately preceding the cession of these colonies.

It is not perhaps too much to expect that translations of treatises such as those of Grotius, Van der Linden, and Van der Keessel, and such works as those of Burge and Story, in addition to their utility as books of reference to the Colonial Practitioner, will be of use in pointing out to the Colonial Legislator the general superiority of the system of Dutch Jurisprudence over the English, in point of simplicity and completeness, as well as in its freedom from anything approaching to technicality or refinement. But without presuming to bespeak for the present translation any share in a result so desirable, the Translator trusts merely that it will tend to supply the want, which, in Ceylon at least, has not unfrequently been felt, of an available Commentary on Grotius' Introduction, bringing the Law down to recent times.

Amsterdam, 19th *December*, 1854.

A BIOGRAPHICAL NOTICE

OF

DIONYSIUS GODTFRIED VAN DER KEESSEL;

BY

MR. J. DE WAL,

Professor of Law in the University of Leyden.

Dionysius Godtfried van der Keessel,* who has acquired an immortal reputation as an author by writing the work of which a translation was recently offered to the English reader, deserves to be better known in his life and professional career by every one under whose notice his work is likely to come. It is in the hope of affording such information that I have written the few pages following.†

He was the son of a Protestant clergyman of some literary fame, and was born in 1738 at Deventer, a town which had been renowned from of old as a nursery of literature and science. The Gymnasium of his native place afforded him ample opportunities to prepare himself for his university career. The vocation of his father enabled him to make the Hebrew language, as well as Latin and Greek, an object of his

---

* Not *G. D. van der Keesel*, as, among others, his anonymous biographer in the "*Woordenboek van Kunsten en Wetenschappen*" writes. Nor, *Van der Keesel*, as *Von Ditmar* speaks of him frequently in a treatise we shall mention later ; though this mistake is to be imputed to *Oelrichs*.

† Some few notices only of the life and writings of this Lawyer are given by *Te Water* in his *Narratio*, p. 231 ; and *Van Voorst* in the *Annales Acad. Lugd. Batav.* 1816-17, pp. 30-33.

studies. At length being well prepared, he set out for Leyden, where Rucker, Scheltinga, and Weisse at that time taught jurisprudence.

Rucker (1702—1778) had become known by his treatise "*De naturali et civili temporis computatione*" (1749,) and by his extensive acquaintance with the *Literary History of Jurisprudence*. Scheltinga, who in the same year in which Van der Keessel first saw light was called to the professorial chair at Leyden, supported alone (as the great Ruhnkenius somewhere observes)* at that time the fame of "*Elegantior Jurisprudentia*." Weisse was not unfavourably known as a publicist.

Instructed by these teachers, and perfectly versed in the spirit of the Roman Law, Van der Keessel on leaving the University gave the first brilliant proof of his eminent talents by the defence of his dissertation *De usucapione partus et foetus rei furtivae*," published at Leyden in 1761. This very excellent academical essay was favourably judged of, not only at home and abroad, but was also reprinted by Oelrichs in his Thesaurus. Later writers,† especially Von Ditmar, a Livonian lawyer, who published a separate treatise on the *Lex Atinia*, have used this dissertation with much profit.‡ ;

As soon as he had left the University, Van der Keessel began to practise as an advocate at the Hague.

---

* *Hugo Civil. Magazin*, v. 350. See also *Bergman, Adnot. ad Wyttenbachii Vitam Ruhnkenii*, p. 402, 410.

† *Ger. Oelrichs, Thesaur. Dissert. Jurid. Select. in Acad. Belgic. habitarum*, vol. I—II. p. 179, 264.

‡ *Wold. Frid. Car. a Ditmar, Comment ad Legis Atiniae hist. et interpret.* Heidelb. 1818.

Seldom has it fallen to the lot of any one to obtain so speedily a distinguished reputation as a pleader. And as the chair of Roman Law at Groningen was vacant, the hereditary Stadtholder, Prince William V, and the Curators or Council of the University of that town could not do better than invite the youthful Van der Keessel (then only 24 years of age) to fill up the vacancy.

If this task must have appeared difficult to him in a place in which he was wholly a stranger, to all around him it doubtless appeared more so, from the circumstances in which he first took his position as a public teacher of jurisprudence.

At that time Professor van der Marck, a man of acute wit, but at the same time imperious, and firmly attached to his once-conceived opinions, had just published his *Institutiones Juris Civilis privati, communis, et reipublicæ Groningæ Omlandicæ proprii.** The campaign against the preponderate influence of the Roman Law, the struggle for the German element of our *popular* institutions, the defence of a practical law of Nature,—all were undertaken. Numerous disciples ranged themselves under the banner of the overbearing Professor. And Van der Keessel,—was he to commence his professional career by a polemical contest with the opponents of that course of Jurisprudence, the teaching of which was to be thenceforth the business of his life? "*Magna,*" as I have written elsewhere,† *viri Juvenis eruditionis fama non minus expectationem civibus adfere-*

---

* t. I. Gron. 1761, 8vo.

† *Orationes Academicæ de historia Juris Nerlandici Studio,* Lugd. and Amst. 1852, p. 113 sq.

*bat, quam ipsa quæstionis tunc agitatae gravitas.
Oratione inaugarali in Oct. Anni 1762, disquisivit ' an
capita illa Juris Romani, quae in usu hodie non esse
dicuntur, in academiis doceri expediat.' Modeste, ut
juvenem decet, atque ex animo suam exposuit de gravissimo
argumento sententiam. Nec tamen ' minus vereor,' inquit
' ne in hac parte viris doctissimis displiceam, qui materiam
dicendi non minus quam ipsam orationem suo probare
calculo non poterunt. Vereor et illud maxime, ne vel
arrogantiae vel pravis adfectibus tribuant qui sinistris
suspicionibus indulgent, quod tale orationis elegerim thema,
quod hoc tempore aliquatenus controversum est."*

We see that he perfectly understood the difficulty of
his future position. With youthful courage, but at the
same time with a generous modesty, he pointed out the
way which, in his opinion, lawyers should follow. He
showed clearly, that no one could know the Roman Law
unless he investigated *the whole* Roman Law in its
intimate connection and dependence, and examine the
organic construction of its parts, whether obsolete or
still continuing in use. But with all that, there was
no show or shadow of anger or contempt against those
who loudly preached up another doctrine.

The *Historia Juris Literaria* of that time has not, in
my opinion, been sufficiently studied. Materials
abound. Here let it be sufficient to observe that the
storm which had long threatened at last broke out,
when at Groningen, in 1765, was published the
*Dissertatio Politico-Juridica, qua disquisitur num et
quatenus prudentiae conveniat civili, in rem publicam
Groninganam jus recipere peregrinum, praesertim Roma-
num.* This diffuse performance, published in the name
of Dr. Feddo Hovingh, and dedicated to the celebrated

S. H. van Idsinga, was soon known to have flowed from the pen of Professor van der Marck. Not without malice was reference made* to a passage from the oration of Van der Keessel, to make him appear as a supporter or abettor of the same principles.

It is not my purpose to mention here the legion of pamphlets to which this tract gave rise. I need only mention a " *Brief van een Groninger Rechtsgeleerde over zekere dissertatie onlangs te Groningen uitgegeven,*"† which appeared in the same year, 1765, and was by many attributed to the pen of Van der Keessel. Scarcely, I must confess it, can I give credence to this opinion (though I was lately informed of it by the Nestor of Dutch jurists, Professor Tijdeman); the more so as Van der Keessel himself in his inaugural speech at Leyden declared—" *in alma Groningana, laetissime florente, per septem et quod excurrit annos, jus civile non sine fructu docueram, procerum favore suffultus et* COLLEGARUM AMICITIA *ornatus* "‡—an expression which the upright man would certainly have omitted, if he had been engaged in an underhand controversy with one of the most celebrated of his colleagues. The words just quoted are taken from a discourse with which he entered upon a new career. An honorary pension had been accorded to Rucker on account of his advanced age, and Van der Keessel was elected to succeed him. On the 12th March, 1770, Leyden saw him ascend the professorial chair, discoursing "*De legislatorum Belgarum in recipiendo jure Romano prudentia.*" The subject was

---

* Gron. 1765, p. 91 et seqq.

† A Letter from a Groningen Lawyer on a Dissertation lately published at Groningen. ‡ p. 38.

chosen from the very centre of the polemics of those days, and was so handled that no one could possibly think himself personally offended.

That he met Van der Marck and his school in an open vizor we cannot doubt, as we hear him develop the reasons which led him to choose this subject. "*Aliam viam ingressi sunt nonnuli, et cum de aequitate legum Romanorum atque certissima in foro receptione disputari amplius non posse intelligerent, per cuniculos hanc arcem Romanam subvertere, callide conati sunt. Agnoverunt quidem juris nostri, in se spectati, praestantiam; non etiam, in foro illud receptum esse, sunt inficiati; sed hoc posterius temporis iniquitati, juris naturalis ignorantiae, et sanioris politices neglectui tribuendum esse dixerunt. Parum igitur prudenter receptam jurisprudentiam Romanam, in hoc emendatiore juris naturalis statu, ex tribunalibus nostris exterminandum esse, quavis data aut studiose quaesita occasione, apud quosvis harum rerum saepe imperitos sed arbitrium illud satis temere suscipientes, rationibus veri quadam specie non destitutis, efficere allaborarunt.*"[*]

Van der Keessel's fame increased from day to day. By the side of Pestel and Voorda, he formed a school here from which have sprung the most eminent jurists that have shed a lustre on our Fatherland. The zeal with which his Dictations on the Roman-Dutch Law were noted down by his pupils affords us an opportunity of judging of the excellence of his instructions. He always followed the method then in use, of having all his remarks to the students committed to papers.

There is no University, in which one of his pupils has

---

[*] ll. p. 6.

not taught,—no Court or tribunal at which one of them has not gathered the fruits of his instructions, either as a judge or a pleader. "*In splendidissimorum virorum orgine* (says Van Voorst on this subject in his Eulogium), *qui ipso praeceptore usi sunt, ipse Rex noster* (William I.) *principatum tenet, qui cum in hoc universitate studiis operam dabat juris civilis, criminalis et hodierni principia, et legum de jure privato ferendarum praecepta* explicantem audivit.*" Sparing was he in the publishing of his writings; and whose who have tested the few fruits of his literary labours complain only that they have not been more abundant. Whenever he appeared as a speaker at the Academical Festivities, it was either to sharpen in the youth the true love of their country,† or to consider the inviolability of judicial power as the palladium of society in troublous times,‡ or at another time to sketch the vocation of pleaders as Christians.§

Perhaps the ideas of Political Economy developed in the discourse first mentioned may not at present be generally honoured as correct; but every one will

---

* *Van Voorst*, Oratio, p. 31. These words of *Van Voorst's* are incorrectly interpreted by the biographer of *Van der Keessel* in the Dictionary of *Nieuwenhuis*, who here speaks of the discourses concerning the particular right to propose laws. In other respects he has copied Van Voorst's words almost literally.

† *Oratio de Amore Patriae in juventute Belgica exitando prudenterque dirigendo.* L. B. 1774.

‡ *Oratio de aequitate judicantium, optimo turbatae reipublicae remedio.* L. B. 1785.

§ *Oratio de Advocato Christiano.* L. B. 1792. The picture of the true Christian, sketched in the first part of this work, is not wanting in vivacity; but the examples by which he, in the second, explains the duties of Christian advocates are perhaps less justly chosen.

b

especially recognize in them the thoughts of a noble and clear-thinking man and citizen.

Particularly is this to be observed in the oration which he pronounced on the 23rd April, 1790, when he *more majorum* conferred the degree of *Doctor Juris Utriusque* on *Johannes Cornelis van der Kemp ;* at which ceremony the Prince himself was present.* Nowhere can it be shown more forcibly and more justly how in the Roman Law the principles of morality, honour, virtue, and conscientiousness are applied and maintained.

But the chief work that Van der Keessel permitted to see the light is doubtless the " *Theses Selectae Juris Hollandici et Zeelandici.*" It is true that Hugo de Groot's *Inleiding tot de Hollandsche Rechtsgeleerdheid,*† was often reprinted, and explained by many notes ; but no one had ever, in a continued commentary, developed the questions of law to which many provisions of the law of the land gave rise,—no one had considered the book in relation to the many later laws and regulations passed in this country. Some commentators had only paid attention to the antiquarian part of the much-praised work. Others had only indicated a few loose remarks and suggestions on disputed points, by notes and queries. Van der Keessel endeavoured to explain and amplify in his lessons the whole of the Dutch Law practically. The Theses give not only a clue by which to follow that commentary, but at the same time an uninterrupted chain of decisions on the very questions of law which

---

* *Oratio de Studio Juris Civilis ad bonos mores formandos et virtutem colendam aptissimo.* L. B. 1790.

† Introduction to Dutch Jurisprudence.

require answering. The aim Van der Keessel had in view is strikingly set forth in his preface. The grounds of proof by which he confirmed his propositions, he communicated in his lectures with exceeding care and by a fixed method.* The manuscript of his lectures is, at his express request, desposited in the Academical Library at Leyden for general use, but with the definite condition that it shall never be made public in print.†

In domestic happiness Van der Keessel lacked nothing. Till 1811 he was happy in the possession of an excellent spouse, CATHERINE ADRIANA BODEL. His life was an example of moderation, uprightness, piety, and virtue. In 1808 he resigned his professorship. He saw Kemper and Tijdeman succeed him, to continue, with his colleague Smallenburg, the work to which he, with the eminent Pestel, had consecrated his life.

At length, advanced in years, wearied with his

---

* For a long time *Van der Keessel* was involved in a sharp dispute with his colleague, *Bavius Voorda*, concerning the instruction in Modern Law at the University of Leyden. In 1798 *Voorda* brought the matter before the Government. It appears never to have been decided, *Voorda's* death having (9th July, 1799) intervened. Comp. *Gab. de Wal, de Claris Frisiae Jurisconsultis.* Leovard : 1825, p. 405.

† " *Quæ insuper, ad uberiorem hujus præstantissimi libri Grotiani pro juris disciplinae usum, scripta, reliquit ex optimi viri voluntate Bibliothecae Academiae dono data sunt,*" says Prof. *van Voorst* very justly, p. 32. But quite otherwise did the anonymous biographer translate, when he wrote,—"His other writings, which he left for a profitable use of the excellent work of Grotius, are at his own request given to the Academic Library at Leyden." Cf. *Geel, Catalogus Libr. MSS. qui inde ab anno* 1741 *Bibliothecae Lugduno-Batavae accesserunt* (L. B. 1852) p. 233. No. 832. The same Library is possessed of *Van der Keessel's Novae Praelectiones Institutionum Autographae,* 1771, *sive Commentarius ad Böckelmanni Compendium.* (No. 799.)

b 2

labours, full of faith, he laid his head to rest on the 6th August, 1816. No child of his shed tears over his grave; but therefore is not the man forgotten, whose work even now, almost a century since the beginning of his career, appears in a youthful form for the advantages of the present generation.

J. D. W.

Leiden, May, 1855.

AUTHOR'S PREFACE.

WHEN in the year 1792 I commenced a series of lectures on Dutch Jurisprudence in the University of Leyden, for the benefit of the students, who at that time had no public interpreter of the Modern Law, I resolved upon adopting the same plan which, in 1767 and the following years, I had followed in my lectures on the Laws of Groningen, delivered in the University there. I proposed to myself to trace, with the guidance of some good compendium, our local laws to their true sources, and to give full explanations of these laws; to apply to our own law those portions of the Roman Law which have been adopted by us; and to point out accurately what portions of the Code of Justinian, or of the Canon Law, might or might not be adopted, in order to supply the defects of the local law, preserving the analogy as well of the primary as of subsidiary law.

For no one can, I think, properly fulfil the office of an advocate in our courts, unless, in addition to an accurate knowledge of the Civil Law and its necessary subsidiaries extending through the whole system of the Digests, he possesses a practical acquaintance with the entire body of laws which obtains in the Court to which he has attached himself. And if he does not find it possible to acquire this knowledge in the course of his university studies, he ought to follow the example of the celebrated Bynkershoek, who, after he had left the University, framed for himself, by personal application, an entire system of the Jurisprudence of Holland and Zeeland. For those who think themselves sufficiently able to acquire a knowledge of the Modern Law solely from practice and at particular emergencies, and by occasionally consulting the commentators, commit a serious error, and thereby alone afford a proof that they are acquainted neither with the definite principles, nor the true analogy of the Law, and are wont, in pleading or defending causes, to rely on the mere authority of the Doctors and on precedents, and indeed more on some imaginary system of equity, than on sound principles.

But since it may be difficult for the young student who passes from the University to the Bar (for all students are not like Bynkershoek) to form for himself by his unaided study and industry, a proper compendium of the Dutch Law, out of so large a body of laws and statutes as those prevailing in Holland; and since few persons at that age are gifted with so mature a judgment as to be able by natural genius to reduce these principles as it were into harmony : it both is, and indeed the Directors of this University have felt it to be a matter of the greatest importance, that persons should be appointed by public authority to deliver lectures and afford instruction in Modern Jurisprudence with the same diligence with which the Civil Law, since the revival of Literature and the foundation of this University, has with great advantage to the State been cultivated and taught, by celebrated jurists.

And this task having been intrusted to me by the Directors of the University, I cannot but narrate here in a few words the plan which, in my opinion, ought to be pursued in the interpretation of the Modern Law.

And, indeed, I at once observed that it would not be

possible to reduce into absolute accordance or harmony all the statutes and received customs prevailing throughout Belgium (which was at that time under the League, but some provinces of which possessed independent legislative authority) ; and which laws and customs were in many respects not only different from, but plainly contradictory to, each other. For who is not aware, for example, that the free right of disposition by testament had already been for a long time permitted in Holland and Zeeland, being considered favourable to commerce (in which pursuit the people were zealously engaged), and to the promotion of industry among the citizens in the acquisition of property, which they should know they might freely dispose of for the benefit of their wives and friends ; when, on the other hand, the people of Groningen, and especially of Omlandt, who were rather devoted to agriculture, were desirous of perpetuating their property in their families, and scarcely permitted any, even the most restricted, testamentary disposition ?

Since, then, these and many other principles of law, so discordant with each other, are not capable of being reduced to the proportions of a strict system ; and since the fertility of statutes at some places is so great, that if you desire to omit nothing, but to follow up carefully the streams which flow from different sources, you ought either to touch lightly upon each, and say something of all and nothing of the whole ; or to spend several years in the University in discoursing upon the modern law of our country ; under these circumstances it will not appear surprising that I should have adopted the method of those eminent authors who have undertaken to illustrate the statutory laws of their country by means of commentaries, or to reduce them into a compendium (such as Schrassert, de Timmerman, Van Wezel, Hammerster, Nessink, and Laman, and others whom I need not name); and should have undertaken to write a commentary on the Jurisprudence of that province wherein the University of Leyden is situated.

And it is well that as regards our own portion of Holland (for in the *Jus Privatum* the old distinction between the States of Holland has been hitherto observed) there exists such an excellent compendium of Dutch Jurisprudence as that of the eminent Hugo Grotius; which, in a very small compass, treats of a vast number of subjects, arranged and digested in a most accurate method, and so explains them, that by tracing each subject to its original sources and to the Civil Institutes, it exhibits the admirable harmony and analogy of the laws; so that it is justly entitled to be considered the model of a proper compendium of the Laws of Holland, and to be read, studied, and remembered by all who acknowledge the Jurisprudence of our country.

Moreover, this book of Grotius, having been written expressly for Holland (which being at that time almost exclusively devoted to the pursuit of commerce, was already fully provided with laws, both ancient and recent, relating to Navigation, Insurance, Average, Exchange, and the like), contains, as it were, an epitome or summary of all these subjects, and is therefore a book so necessary to all citizens of the States of Holland who are engaged in trade or commerce, or at least to the advocates who give opinions in cases of this kind, that even lawyers practising beyond Holland are at present frequently compelled to send their clients to advocates in Holland.

And this is indeed the reason why professors of the

Modern Law at Leyden, such as Voet and Scheltinga, have selected this excellent treatise of Grotius as a guide and text-book in their explanations of the law. I followed, therefore, the example of these authors, and purposed to explain the Laws of Holland from the text of Grotius in such a manner that I might at one and the same time enumerate and expound the Laws of Zeeland, which in many cases agree with and have often preceded those of Holland, sometimes supply defects in them, and at other times are slightly different from them.

This book having been written in the year 1619,[*] all the laws and the decisions of both the Courts since that year, as well as the more recent statutes of various places, are wanting in it. And hence the first duty of a commentator on Grotius is to supply those alterations which have been introduced by subsequent legislation up to the present time, and to correct in those points whatever rules he thought should be adopted out of the more ancient laws.

Moreover, throughout this treatise, which the author has modestly entitled an " *Introduction* to Dutch Jurisprudence," there is admirable brevity and an admirable shrewdness in the employment of vernacular terms in law. This is, however, frequently accompanied by so much doubt and obscurity, that it becomes the duty of a careful commentator to explain them, and therefore, in the first place, to enlarge in his commentaries whatever Grotius, in accordance with the plan of his work, supposed required brevity ; and whatever he expressed in the vernacular, by terms plain indeed, but now

* See Book. II. Chap. xxiii. Sec. 13.

mostly obsolete and less understood, to explain in Latin by the use of terms and phrases with which those who have, as it behoves them, previously studied the Roman Law are more conversant.

It should also be observed that in some places Grotius refers to the Roman Law, but so as either expressly or tacitly to set it in opposition to the Law of Holland; that in other places he simply supplies those doctrines from the Civil Law which might now be in practice; and that in other places, again, by simply explaining a Roman Law, he tacitly indicates that that should be taken as the Law of Holland, and supplied from the more copious source of the Civil Law. It should be the care of the commentator not to include all these passages under the same rule, but to assign to each its proper weight and authority.

He should further be careful to note those portions of his treatise wherein Grotius, as a witness, makes any assertion with reference either to the ancient Laws of Holland, or to the customs of his time (on which assertion we ought to place the reliance due to the authority of a man of great learning and integrity); and also those portions wherein he states that any Roman Law has been adopted in Holland, but subject to controversy, so that it has been thought by many that if in such a case there should happen to be an opinion contrary to the true spirit of the Civil Law, we should modestly differ from Grotius, no less than from Cujacius, Jacob Godfried, Schulting, and the other jurists of former times. There is a notable instance of this in the common but doubtlessly erroneous opinion that succession *ab intestato* should be restricted to the tenth degree.

Lastly, we should not omit to observe that Grotius

has at times either adopted some portions of the Roman Law, which seem at variance with the principles of the Law of Holland, or omitted some which are by no means inconsistent with the analogy of the local law.

Since, therefore, all these subjects require the care and attention of the commentator, and since it appears necessary that in the first place he should, upon a similarity of principles, lay down certain definite and fixed rules (founded on the reason of the law, the authority of legislators, and the history of Roman Jurisprudence as adopted in our Courts), whereby the true and proper use of the Roman Law and of the statutes of the neighbouring States in supplying the defects in the Law of Holland, might be defined; and as, since the time of Grotius, some of the doctrines laid down by him have either been called into question, or been altered, in the works and opinions of eminent jurists of Holland, and by various decisions of the two Courts, it will not appear surprising that the commentary I had written on this treatise of Grotius should have swelled out into so large a volume as to require two entire academic terms and six lectures every week for its delivery; though I had studiously endeavoured to avoid dwelling too fully on those points which had already been treated of since the year 1776 by the learned and industrious authors of the *Rechtsgeleerde Observatien.**

But the course of study in the University hardly allows of commentaries on any subject being prolonged for a space of two years, if we would consult the conve-

---

* *Rechtsgeleerde Observatien,—tot opheldering van verscheidene duistere passagien uit de Inleidinge tot de Hollandsche Rechtsgeleerdheid van Mr. Hugo de Groot, 4 fascic. in 8vo.' s. Hag. 1778.*

nience of those who are either desirous themselves, or are pressed by domestic affairs, to complete their university studies in a few years.

Since, then, I was anxious to attend to these circumstances, and at the same time to omit nothing which might be considered useful towards supplying the defects in this treatise of Grotius, I purposed, by means of printed commentaries, to touch upon such points as had been, for the sake of conciseness, omitted by him, or had undergone alteration since the publication of the work, or had hitherto been the subject of controversy ; but to reserve for oral discussion whatever would tend to the better explanation of the text, and to the fuller development of the printed Theses. In these Theses I have avoided all reference to the public Law of Holland, now repealed ; or to the antiquities of our Law ; a task which has been most diligently performed by the learned authors of the Observations just cited.

On these principles have I laboured, not, I trust, in vain, to benefit the students of the University encouraged and animated in this hope by the example of most of those who attended zealously and assiduously my Lectures on Grotius, and have given public evidence of their advancement in their profession.

But, then, methinks I hear some inexperienced person remark,—Why these labours, at a time when by command of the Supreme Court of the States of Holland, several learned jurists are engaged in the preparation of a new code of laws, by which all the statutes and customs of every State shall be repealed ?

If such there be, let him consider that before such an undertaking can be fully accomplished and approved of by the legislators, no little time will have elapsed, and that in the meanwhile our young men require instruction in the present laws in order to practise in the Courts of Holland; unless we would imitate the folly of those who would rather remain hungry than eat the green nuts before they can find the ripe fruits.

Besides, since the laws and customs, which prevail in Holland, have been to a great extent borrowed from the Law of Nature and the Civil Law, tempered by the principles of Equity, and have at the same time been adapted as well to the nature of those transactions which obtain almost throughout Europe, as to the necessities of commerce and navigation, and in the next place established with the recommendations of public utility and with the consent of the people; it need not be feared that from this circumstance alone, namely, that they have been pleasing to our ancestors, these eminent men, who are no less distinguished for prudence and experience than for learning, would on this point, of all others, depart from them. Indeed, if I may be permitted to anticipate events, I should say that most of those laws which now prevail amongst us will be left unaltered in the new code; and those only which are doubtful and contested will be more clearly elucidated and defined; but that those portions of the ancient laws which yet remain will be expunged. Our students will hence derive from a commentary on the works of Grotius the same benefits which students of the Civil Law derive from a study of the *Jus Antejustinianeum;* they will learn both to understand more correctly the origin of the laws and their true meaning, and to illustrate the practice of the laws by precedents. They will also be more precise in investigating the reasons even of each single word which the new framers of our laws might employ in the laws which are to be shortly introduced. And more; students of law will, if I am not mistaken, be able to obtain from our Theses this additional advantage—that they will attend more carefully to those portions of the new code wherein those points of the Law of Holland which are remarked upon as doubtful or contested will have to be more precisely defined, and reduced, as it were, to an exact harmony. In a word, the diligent student of Grotius will as much excel in the new local law as the advocate who is read and skilled in the Civil Law excels the pettifogger, who has never learnt to understand and interpret the present laws from the sources whence they have derived their origin.

In these Theses I have followed the division of sections adopted in the latest edition of the *Introduction.* I have frequently cited those decisions of the Court which have been selected and printed in the Appendix to the third and in the sixth volume of the *Hollandsche Consultatien,* and which are considered as of great authority amongst us, a more correct edition of which, however, though not sufficiently known to the public, has been published under the title of *Decisien en Resolutien van den Hove van Holland.** There is also a MS. copy of these decisions in the public library of the University, in some parts of which, as well as in another MS. in my possession, some excellent emendations of the printed edition may be found; of which there will be found some instances in the following Theses. I have quoted the works of those who have written on our laws in the native tongue, as well as the

* S. Hage, 1751, 4to.

statutes by their proper Dutch titles, in order to prevent any difficulty in the way of beginners not well versed in the Laws of Holland. But the Placaats, Resolutions, and Programma of Holland and Zeeland, which are to be found in the *Groot-Placaat Boek*, I have referred to simply by their dates; as they may be easily found in the copious Index of that work, which we owe to the industry of the learned jurist, Johannes van der Linden.

D. G. VAN DER KEESSEL.

Leyden, 8th September, 1800.

SELECT THESES,

ETC.

BOOK I.—CHAPTER II.

SEC. 1.

I. GENERAL Laws should be promulgated in all places where it is customary to make promulgation ; for they are not binding at a place where promulgation has not been made. There is a notable instance of this in a decision of both the Courts, cited by *Merula.*[1]

II. Privileges granted to particular places, as well as other particular laws, when promulgated in those places for which they are passed, constitute the law there.

III. But judgments, and authorized interpretations of the law, provided they have been publicly recorded. have the force of law, even without promulgation.

SEC. 9.

IV. Justice is not administered in Holland according to the Laws of *Moses.*[2]

SEC. 21.

V. Ancient customs of Holland, provided they have not been abrogated by subsequent law, have the force

[1] *Manier van Proced* p. 1. lib. i. t. 4. c. 5. n. 3. not. 28, last edit.
[2] *Decr. Holl.* 19 Mar 1735.

B

of law, although they may not have been registered among the acts of the Court.[3]

Sec. 22.

VI. There are many proofs of the *Roman* Law having been received *in subsidium* by us:—1. Various portions of the Law of Holland, wherein the principles of the Civil Law have been *tacitly* adopted: 2. Those portions of our law wherein technical *terms*, borrowed from the Roman Law, are so employed as render it evident that the doctrines comprehended under these terms have themselves been adopted in our Courts: 3. Similar parts of our law, wherein our Legislators expressly adopt or confirm certain prints of Roman Law: 4. Many maxims, rules, and precepts of our legislators, wherein they either acknowledge that the Civil Law has been adopted to its full extent, or direct that, in the adjudication of causes, the judges should determine disputes by that law.[4]

VII. But the question—to what extent the Roman Law has been adopted in our Courts, and in what cases the laws of neighbouring states should be resorted to—may, it seems, be almost fully determined by the following rules, illustrated by some examples.

Rule 1: In every province, town, or district, that law should before all others be resorted to, which is

---

[1] The *Pol. Ord. Holl.* 39. is not opposed to this; see Van de Wall, *Handv. van Dordt,* p. 1328, sqq. Bynkershoek (*Q. J. Priv.* 1. iii. c. 13) is, however, of a different opinion.

[2] See, for instance, *Decis. Holl.* 25 May, 1785; and Dissertt. H. Fagel *de Orig. et usu Jur. Rom. in Hollandia,* and J. C. van der Hoop, *De Necessario Romani Juris, et subinde quoque Canonici Juris in Hollandia studio,* Edit. 1779, 8vo.

proper to that place, and has been expressly promulgated or framed for it by the legislator, or by him who
has the power of passing statutes.[5]

VIII. *Rule* 2 : Those special customs also, which
have been adopted in any place or city, ought to be
observed there.[6]

IX. *Rule* 3 : On those points of *Roman* Law, which
have been expressly adopted into the *Dutch* Law, we
should have recourse at once to the Roman Law.[7] There
are instances of this in the laws cited below, and in similar
laws of Holland, which prohibit alienations in fraud of
creditors.[8] Many instances may also be found in connection with those matters, the names or terms of
which having been employed in our laws, prove that the
doctrines of the Roman Law designated by those terms,
have been adopted amongst us ; as in the terms
Testament, Legacy, Fidei-commissum, Substitution, the
Legitimate, Falcidian, and Trebellianic portions; the
*Senatusconsultum Vellejanum ; Beneficium ordinis,
divisionis,* &c. If, however, any alteration has been
made on these points by modern law, either by enact-

---

[5] See *examples* in *de Unie tusschen Holland & Zeeland van* 15 April
1576, art. 9 ; *Provis. Accord. van* 7 Mar. 1607, art. 13 ; *Nader Provis.
Accord. van* 11 Jun., 1674, art. 30 ; in the law of *Amsterdam,* passed by
the States of Holl. 8 Mar. 1594; and of *Rotterdam,* 23 Dec.,
1604 ; and in the Law of Succession *ab intestato,* of *North Holland,*
18 Dec. 1599.

[6] See instances in *de Costum. van Rhynland,* art. 1, and in Grotius.
B. ii. chap. 20. § 12 ; and B. iii. ch. 16. § 9 ; and ch. 28. § 5.

[7] See instances in *Polit. Ord. Holl.* art. 4, 13, 18, 35 ; *Zeeland,* art.
11, 12, 22, 23, 33 ; in the Law of *Holland,* 18 Dec. 1599, art. 14 ; 5 Febr.
1665 ; *Decr. Holl.* 15 Nov., 1719 ; in the Law of *Zeeland,* 27 Nov., 1654,
art. 8; of *Middelburg,* 7 Jul., 1708, art. 26.

[8] As the law of *Amsterdam,* 1644, art. 14 ; of *Haarlem,* 1656, art. 15,
of *Leyden,* 1656, art. 14.

B 2

ment or by custom, the latter ought, according to the 1st and 2nd rules, to be observed.[1]

X. *Rule* 4; When a question arises as to the interpretation of any rule of *Dutch* Law, especially concerning an *extensive* or *restricted* interpretation,[2] every such law ought to be explained from its own original source. Those laws, therefore, which have been taken from the Roman Law, ought to be explained from the Roman Laws.[3]   On the other hand, those laws which have originated in local customs or ancient laws, ought to be explained from these sources; such as the laws relating to succession by antenuptial contract, and the community of property between husband and wife.[4]

XI. If the principles of the Roman Law and those of the Law of Holland have been intermixed in any statute, such a mixed law should be interpreted, each part from its own proper source.[5]

XII. If it be doubtful from which Law any particular rule of Dutch Law has derived its origin, but if in the practice of the Court it has received a particular construction with reference to the *Roman* Law, we ought not to depart from such construction, though it may be at variance with the analogy of our own law.[6] In like manner, if the terms of such a rule of Dutch Law may conveniently receive an interpretation from the more copious sources of the *Roman* Law, such an inter-

---

[1] There is an instance in Grotius, B. i. ch. 6. § 3.

[2] [See Van der Linden's Institutes, p. 62.—Tr.]

[3] See an instance in the *Placaat of Charles V.* of the 4th Oct. 1540, art. 6, in fin.

[4] Ibid. art. 17.   See Grotius. B. ii. ch. 11, s. 8, fin.

[5] There is an instance in the *Ord. Zeeland*, cap. ii. art. 22.

[6] As in the example in Grotius, B. i. ch. 5. s. 25.   Comp. with s. 21-23.

pretation should also be adopted: as in the instance of the prohibition of donations as between husband and wife.[7]

XIII. Where these *subsidia*, of which we have spoken, fail, we should carefully guard against falling into the common error of those commentators, who would have deficiencies in the Law of Holland, even in matters of local origin, supplied from the laws of those neighbouring states which were formerly united by the Treaty of *Utrecht*.* For on these very points, some of these states have adhered more closely to the analogy of the ancient law; whilst others, having adopted the rules of the Roman Law, have derogated from the ancient law; so that the corollaries which some of them have drawn from the ancient laws, do not seem to have been in every instance approved of by their neighbours: for instance, the marital authority in regard to alienating the immovable property of the wife, is greater in *Holland*[8] than in *Zeeland*;[9] and by the laws of *Groningen*,[10] *Omlandt*,[11] and *Oldampt*,[12] antenuptial contracts require the consent of the *familia*, being considered as *pacta familiæ*, whilst by the Law of *Holland* they may be legally entered into by persons who have attained majority, without the consent of the *familia*.

XIV. It must also be laid down as a rule, though contrary to the opinion of most commentators on our laws, that the common or general Law of Holland cannot be made up or proved out of the particular laws of particular cities or parts of Holland.

[7] See Grot. B. iii. ch. 2, s. 9.   * [Ao. 1579.—Tr.]
[8] Grot. B. i. ch. 5. § 22.   [9] Ord. Zeeland, cap. iii. art. 46.
[10] Of 1689; tit. *van Houwl. Voorw.* art. 18, 19.
[11] L. 3. art. 9.   [12] L. 4. art. 22.

XV. The laws of neighbouring states are, however, of some use in interpreting and supplying the Law of Holland ; as will appear from the following rules :

Rule 5 : When our laws, in matters of local origin or entirely of more recent origin, have adopted and still preserve the same principles as are found in the laws of our neighbours, they ought to be interpreted and supplied from the latter ; as in the instance of the community of goods between husband and wife ; in the question discussed by *Boel* in his notes on *Loenius* ;[1] in succession by antenuptial contract ; in *retractus*, exchange, insurance, bottomry, &c.

XVI. Yet, even in these matters of local origin, the equity of the Roman Law has not unfrequently superseded the innate principles of the ancient law.[2]

XVII. *Rule* 6 : In matters of *Roman* origin, or in those which occur in the *Roman* Law as well, we ought, in the absence of any statute, to have recourse at once to the Roman Law, and not to the statutory laws of our neighbours. Of this there are very many instances, in connection with testaments, contracts, property, servitudes, pledges, &c.

XVIII. *Rule* 7 : Laws and local customs, whether general or particular, entirely failing, we ought to recur to the *Roman* Law and seek a decision thence.[3] Nor could it properly be required that the use or adoption

---

[1] *Decis.* 99, p. 625, sqq.

[2] There are instances given by Bynkershoek, *Q. J. Priv.* l. ii. c. i. p. 192, sq. and l. ii. c. 2. p. 199 ; l. 2. c. 9. p. 280. Grotius *in responso*, A. 1610, in Van Leeuwen's *Pract. der Notar.* d. ii. cons. 18 ; and in a decision of both Courts, A. 1768 and 1771, in *de N. Nederl. Jaarb.* 1775, p. 1127, sqq.

[3] Loen. *Decis.* 55 ; Bynkersh. *Q. J. Priv.* l. ii. c. 14. p. 327, 329, 333, 334.

of the Roman Law on that particular point should have been confirmed by some decision.

XIX. *Rule* 8: Inasmuch as the Roman Law has only been received *in subsidium*, it follows that it should not only give place to the Law of Holland, but also that it cannot be admitted whenever it is at variance with the analogy of our law.[4]

XX. *Rule* 9: Those rules of Roman Law which depend on the peculiar constitution of the *Roman State* possess no authority in our courts.

XXI. *Rule* 10: Whenever any rule of Roman Law has been abrogated by the general custom of the neighbouring countries, it is presumed, in a doubtful case, to have been abrogated here also.

XXII. *Rule* 11: He who cites the Roman Law, so far as it is not at variance either with express laws, well-known customs, or the analogy of the Dutch Law, and does not manifestly depend on a different system of government, has a good case, and is not bound to prove that the rule has been expressly adopted.

XXIII. In the Rules we have above laid down, we do not use the terms *a rule of Roman Law* or *the Roman Law*, in their common or general meaning, but in their true and original signification ;[5] and we therefore have not hesitated to dissent, as we have done in *Thes.* 299 and 364, from some opinions of *Grotius*.[6] If, however, the constant practice of the Courts has altered the true intention of the Roman Law (as in the renunciation

---

[4] There are instances in Grot. B. i. ch. 6. § 3 ; B. ii. ch. 18. § 15, and § 21.

[5] See not. (a) ad Heinecc. *Histor. Jur.* l. i. § 417. (Edit. argentor. 1751) ; Bynkersh. *Præf. Obs. Jur. Rom.*

[6] B. ii. ch. 17. § 29, n. 33, and ch. 30. § 1. f.

of the *Setum Vellejanum*); or if any recent rule of the Roman Law has never been adopted (as in the instances cited by *Vinnius*[1] and *Groenewegen*),[2] we ought not to depart from the practice of the Courts.

XXIV. *Rule* 12 : In the total absence of local law, of custom, and of the subsidiary law of which we have spoken, we ought to have recourse to Natural Equity.

XXV. In the Courts of Holland, however, some use is made also of the *Canon* Law, so far as some of its provisions have either been borrowed, though with alterations, from the Civil Law, or have been tempered by principles of Equity ;[3] or having been incorporated with the Civil Law, have likewise been adopted amongst us; as in matrimonial causes,[4] the year of mourning,[5] espousals, and separation from bed and board.[6]

SEC. 27.

XXVI. All persons, whether citizens by birth, or merely residents, who, though born elsewhere, have taken up their domicile in Holland, are bound by the Laws of Holland.

XXVII. In the consideration of any difficult question concerning conflicting statutes, it seems necessary to draw a distinction between *personal, real,* and *mixed* statutes.

Personal statutes are not only those which define the *status* of a *person,* but those also which, by reason of

---

[1] *Select. Q.* l. 2. c. 15, in fin.
[2] *De Leg. Abrog.* ad. l. 27. § 1. Cod. iv. 32.
[3] As in the instances in Grot. B. ii. ch. 16. § 6 ; and ch. 20. § 10.
[4] Bynkersh. *Q. J. Priv.* l. iii. c. 10, init.
[5] Ib. l. ii. c. 4, p. 220, sq. and p. 223.
[6] Huber, *Hedend. Rechtsg.* l. iii. c. 22. § 49.

such *status*, pronounce any one qualified or unqualified for the performance of any *personal* act.

XXVIII. *Real* statutes are those which treat of *things*, or which treat of them in such a manner that, though mention is made of the person also, yet the enactment is intended to affect the *thing*, and not the *person*; such as the laws concerning donations between husband and wife, the community of property between them; the right to make a will, whether permitted or prohibited to *filii familias*; concerning the alienation and usucaption of the property of minors, &c.

XXIX. *Mixed* statutes are those which prescribe the *ceremonies, forms*, and *mode* of acts and transactions.

XXX. The force and effect which statutes have *within* the territory of the legislator are different from that which they have *beyond* the territory.

Within the territory, they are binding on those who are subjects,

1. In respect of their *domicile*; and this holds true also of those who have been exempted from the ordinary jurisdiction; but not of foreigners residing there temporarily for study or any other purpose;

2. In respect of their *immovable property*; which is regulated by the law of the place where it is situated;

3. In respect of their *residence* there; for those who reside in a country are bound to observe, in the management of their affairs, the laws of that country, and to abstain from those offences which are prohibited there;

4. In respect of their *movable* property, which, wherever found, is subject to the laws of that place.

XXXI. *Beyond* the territory of the legislator, the statutes are also binding on those who are perpetual subjects. But there are two modes of considering this subject:

Firstly, as regards a legislator or judge adjudicating in his own territory on an act or matter which a fellow-citizen has done elsewhere. He may legally decide thereon, according to his own laws, whether the question concerns a personal, real, or mixed statute; though, as it will shortly appear, in respect of a mixed statute, a different rule has in most places been adopted by Comity.

XXXII. *Secondly*, as regards the legislator and judge of another country adjudicating on a similar act of a foreigner, not a citizen. And in a question of this kind (viz., concerning the force and authority of a foreign statute in the territory of another supreme power), a distinction should be drawn between that which obtains in *strictness of law*, and that which has been adopted by the *mutual comity* of nations.

XXXIII. In *strictness of law*, statutes are not binding beyond the territory wherein they have been enacted; and magistrates and judges are not therefore bound, in adjudicating, to observe foreign statutes. And this, as regards *real* statutes, is a fixed rule, and has been adopted everywhere. Thus a will relating to immovable property, though permitted by the law of the place where the testator had his domicile, has no force in the place where the property is situated, if prohibited there; and succession *ab intestato* to immovable property is regulated not by the law of the testator's domicile, but by the law of the country where the property is situated.

XXXIV. The same rule should hold as regards *personal* statutes; for in strictness of law the judge of any

place is not bound to acknowledge the quality of a
person which the law of his domicile has assigned him,
since this law is not binding on the judge.*

XXXV. Nor, if we observe the strictness of law, is
the rule otherwise in regard to *mixed* statutes.

XXXVI. By *courtesy*, however, and *mutual comity*,
nations have departed from this strictness, not indeed in
respect of real statutes, as regards immovable property ;
but certainly as regards *movable* property, since these are
supposed to be found in the place of domicile ; excepting,
however, in the case of arrest, and sometimes the case
of taxes (*tributa*).

XXXVII. Incorporeal things also, being referable
either to movable or immovable property, are governed
by the law which affects the property with which they
are classed.

XXXVIII. If the definitions in statutes vary, in
classifying incorporeal things with movable or immovable
property, as in the case of debts, those statutes should
be observed which have been enacted by the legislator
of whom the debtor is a subject.

XXXIX. In respect of *mixed* statutes, it has been
received as a rule by the consent of almost all legislators
and by mutual comity, that contracts, testaments, and
other acts duly executed, in accordance with the laws of
the place where they were executed, should be valid in
every other place, unless there be an express law to the
contrary, or they have been executed elsewhere in fraud
of the law of the domicile.

---

* [For a singular illustration of this rule as regards Legitimacy,
see *Birthwhistle* v. *Vardell*, 9 Bligh, R. 75 ; and Story on *Conflict of
Laws*, § 87a; and as regards Marriage, *Brook* v. *Brook*, 7, W. R.
110, 451.—Tr.]

XL. This rule applies also to judicial acts; which should be executed with the solemnities required by the law of the place where the proceedings are carried on. The law, however, which is administered as between the parties, is not always the law of the latter place.

XLI. We should be careful not to infer from the rule in *Thes.* 39, that acts not executed according to the law of the place of their execution, are valid nowhere else.

XLII. In respect of *personal* statutes, the comity of nations has in a similar manner permitted that the *status*, quality, and capacity of a person should depend on the law of his domicile, and accompany him everywhere.

XLIII. In contracting, and in other transactions, we may expressly depart from statutes, unless they be prohibitory.

XLIV. We may also *tacitly* depart from statutes; as is done in contracting a marriage, if the law of the place where the bridegroom resides differs from the law which prevails in the bride's domicile; unless the real statute, which is departed from, be prohibitory.

CHAPTER III.—SEC. 4.

XLV. Children yet unborn are considered as already born, whenever their advantage is in question; and they may therefore succeed *ab intestato*, though they may not have been conceived at the time when the person, whose succession is in question, died.[1]

CHAPTER IV.—SEC. 2.

XLVI. Although slaves who are found on Dutch ground are, as a rule, free; yet fugitive slaves from our

[1] As in the case in § 7. Inst. iii. 1.

colonies do not come under this rule, but may at any time be claimed by their owners; and the law of the States General of the 23rd May, 1776, has made full provision in this respect.

CHAPTER V.

XLVII. *Espousals** may legally be entered into subject to conditions; which, if honourable, suspend the effect of the espousals; unless by subsequent cohabitation, a condition such as the law does not deem necessary to the validity of the marriage, should appear to have been tacitly waived.

XLVIII. Immoral or impossible conditions vitiate the espousals.[2]

XLIX. The distinction between espousals *de præsenti* and espousals *de futuro* has not been received in Holland; for prior espousals *de futuro* are preferred to subsequent espousals *de præsenti*; and there is nothing to prevent parties from withdrawing by mutual consent from espousals *de præsenti*.[3]

L. Espousals contracted clandestinely by persons below 25 or 20 years, without the consent of those whose consent is necessary to the marriage, are indeed invalid, but the parties are not liable to the punishments under the *Placaat* of the 4th October, 1540,[4] if, previous to cohabitation, the consent of the parents had been obtained.

LI. As public espousals, or rather espousals declared publicly, *i.e.*, in the presence of magistrates, ought not

* [*Trouw-Beloften.* Van der Linden's Inst. p. 71.]
[2] Voet *ad Pand.* lib. xxiii. tit. 1. § 8; nor is this opposed to cap. ult. X. *de. condit. appos. in despons.*
[3] Loen. *Decis.* cas. 43.
[4] Art. 17.

to be dissolved without their knowledge, lest the *status* of the espoused persons might remain in uncertainty; so by mutual consent, and with the knowledge of the magistrates, they may be dissolved; nor has the magistrate regularly any power over unwilling parties (as rightly enacted at Amsterdam in a law respecting matrimonial causes of the 29th January, 1754[1]), unless where it has been otherwise provided.[2]

LII. Espousals cannot be effectually contracted by minors without the authority of the parent or guardian, nor by the parents on behalf of children who are minors or under years of puberty.

LIII. The espousals of minors, entered into without the consent of their guardians, are not binding on themselves if unwilling, even though they may not have obtained *restitutio in integrum*.[3]

LIV. Males, above the age of 25 years, and females above 20, may enter into espousals without the consent of their parents,[4] and if contracted after they had attained 25 years, they cannot withdraw from them, in order to submit to the wishes of their parents who do not show a just cause of dissent.[5]

LV. A daughter, however, who, being above the age of 20, but not having as yet attained legal majority, has entered into espousals without the consent of her parents, to whose authority she is subject, may even without obtaining relief alter her intention; as decided

---

[1] Art. 15.

[2] *Polit. Ord. Zeeland.* art. 23 ; *Ord. Leyden.* art. 101. § 16.

[3] Brouwer *de Jur. Connub.* l. i. cap. 15. n. 2 ; Bynkersh. *Q. J. Priv.* l. ii. c. 3 ; Loen. *Decis.* 4.

[4] Arg. *Polit. Ord. Holl.* art 3.

[5] Boel *ad Loen. Decis.* cas. 55. p. 343.

by the Court of Holland in a case reported by *Loenius*,[6] who herein correctly refers to the Roman Law,[7] the application of which on this point is by no means precluded by the rules of Dutch Law.

LVI. An orphan girl, below the age of 25, who, after attaining her 20th year, has contracted espousals without the consent of her guardian, may likewise withdraw from them ; and may obtain relief even against espousals to which the guardian has added his consent. The rule is different as regards a widow who is a minor.

LVII. Upon espousals an action is maintainable to compel performance ; and if a condemnation to perfect the marriage follows thereon, there will be no marriage until the judgment has been carried into execution. The party condemned, who may desire antenuptial contracts to be previously prepared with equitable conditions, should therefore have a hearing.[8]

LVIII. Of two espousals, whether absolute or conditional, the prior one should have preference, unless the latter has been confirmed by marriage celebrated in due form. The latter bride, however, who had consented in good faith and was disappointed in her expectations of marriage, may sue for damages even in respect of the marriage; or, if the former bride happens to have died or is unwilling to marry, she may legally sue even for the perfecting of the marriage.

LIX. The punishment of *Infamy** does not seem to have been adopted by the customs of Holland as against a person who has contracted two espousals.

---

[6] 8 Jul. 1632 ; see Loen. *Decis.* cas. 55.   [7] Cod. v. 4. 20.

[8] Schrassert, *Obs. Pract.* 229, n. 3, & 4 ; Boel *ad Loen. Decis.* cas. 55 p. 357, sqq.

* [See Voet. *ad Pand.* iii. 2. tot. tit.]

The rule in Zeeland is different, if the espousals have been publicly declared;[1] and by the law of that country a fine or other discretionary punishment has also been ordained. So also in some of the Dutch statutes, as in that of *Leyden*.[2]

LX. As espousals may be dissolved by mutual consent, so also they may at any time be dissolved at the desire of either party, on just grounds, such as those enumerated by *Boehmer* in his treatise *de Jure Ecclesiastico Protestantium ;*[3] to which may also be referred the case in the Code *de Repudiis ;*[4] and the case of a father, who, having promised a dowry, made cession of his property,—as decided by the Court of Holland in the year 1640.[5]

LXI. Relief may be granted against espousals entered into by minors even with the parents' consent, if *læsio* can be proved to have been sustained in consequence of youthful imprudence. This rule is based on the general law, whereby a *filiusfamilias* who has sustained *læsio*, may be relieved against an obligation contracted by him even with the father's consent. Nor do the decisions cited in opposition hereto by the Jurists in *de Regtsgeleerde Observatien*[6] prove the contrary ; since these decisions relate to cases where no *læsio* had been alleged as a ground for relief.

SEC. 2.

LXII. In Holland the crime of Bigamy, if accompanied by cohabitation, is by the Criminal Code of *Philip*

---

[1] *Pol. Ord. Zeeland.* art. 23.   [2] Art. 101. § 5.
[3] *L.* iv. t. 1. § 162, sqq.   [4] Cod. v. 17. 2.
[5] See Bort. *Nagelat. Werken,* l. ii. t. 20. in not. p. 133.
[6] Part. i. obs. 99.

II.[7] to be punished by severe corporal castigation and transportation for life, even since the passing of the Political Ordonnance.[8]   If it has not yet been consummated by cohabitation, lighter corporal punishment, or transportation with infamy,* is to be decreed. A married person who, during marriage, has contracted new espousals, especially if they have already been publicly proclaimed, should, it appears, be exposed as infamous, deprived of his dignity, and fined.

LXIII. The new law of Zeeland has defined this more precisely.[9]   The first part of *art.* 13 of this law decrees against a bigamist who has publicly contracted espousals the punishment of infamy under the Roman Law, and in addition thereto the punishment against adultery decreed by the 9th and 10th articles of the same law, *viz.,* loss of dignity, a fine of 600 florins and temporary civil imprisonment on bread and water.

The latter part of the law decrees public corporal punishment against those who consummate this crime by cohabitation.

LXIV. If the second marriage has been contracted in good faith by both parties, the former spouse being supposed to be dead, it is so far valid as a putative marriage, that the children born thereof are legitimate under the Canon Law[10] (which has herein been adopted by the Court, and by the States of Holland[11]); and the marriage will hold good as between such parties themselves, if, in addition to the consent of the former spouse

---

[7] Art 60.   [8] Art. 15, 16, 17.

* [This, according to Van der Linden, would imply *public exposure on the scaffold.* Inst. p. 355.]

[9] *Pol. Ord. Zeeland,* A. 1666, art. 13.

[10] C. 14, X. *qui. fil. sint legit.*   [11] 19 Jul. 1637.   Loen. *Decis.* 78.

who renounces his right, there be the sentence of a judge, declaring the former marriage dissolved.[1]

LXV. And even if the second spouse alone has acted *bonâ fide*, having been deceived by the bigamist, a son born of such a union shall also be legitimate.[2]

SEC. 3.

LXVI. Although persons under the age of puberty cannot contract a marriage, and the public proclamation of espousals is denied them by law; yet if either of them, erroneously taken to have attained puberty, has contracted a marriage in public form, it will become valid upon his or her attaining puberty.[3]

LXVII. The Roman definition of the *annus luctus*, or year of mourning, has, according to the example of the Canon Law,[4] been abrogated amongst us, but the duration of it is left to the just discretion of an honest judge; except in those places where a period of six months, or other such period of mourning, has been fixed by statute; from which, however, we should take care not to infer a general law of Holland.[5]

LXVIII. A woman marrying within the year of mourning is not subject to infamy, nor to the punishments decreed by the Code *de secundis nuptiis;*[6] as decided by the Court in 1586.[7]

---

[1] Van Alphen. *Papeg.* t. i. p. 60 & 61, and t. ii. p. 589.

[2] C. 14, X. last cited ; Hert. *de Matrim. Putat.* § 7 & 17. As to the other effects of a putative marriage, see Hert. d. l. § 21 & sqq.; Stockmans, *Decis. Brabant.* 62 ; Sande, *Decis. Fris.* l. ii. t. 5 def. 2.

[3] Arg. Dig. xxiv. 2, 4.   [4] Cap. pen. & ult. X. *de secund. nupt.*

[5] *Supra*, Th. 14.

[6] Cod. v. 9. 1 & 2.

[7] *Decis. & Resol. van den Hove van Holland*, n. 247.

LXIX. But the punishments against second marriages enacted by the same Code in favour of the children of the former marriage,[8] are not, from the reason of the law, deemed to have ceased, as properly decided by the Court on the 24th February, 1586;[9] nor is it surprising that Bynkershoek, who had not seen the entire passage in the *Decisien en Resolutien*, should have erred in explaining the decision.[10] It may, however, be reasonably doubted whether the more correct opinion of the Court has been adopted in practice.

LXX. The marriage of an adulterer with the adulteress is prohibited as an offence by the Law of Holland of the 18th July, 1674; and the punishment decreed by the written law[11] (which directs that the hereditary benefits acquired by such a person should be forfeited to the Treasury) is to be so construed, in connection with the intention of this new law (whereby the forfeiture of the property has been abolished), as that the property left should pass to the co-heirs, substitutes, or legitimate heirs.[12]   The Law of Zeeland of the 18th March, 1666,[13] similarly declares such a marriage void.

LXXI. The crime of Rape prevents marriage.[14] The new Law of Holland of the 25th February, 1751, draws a distinction between the two offences—*Abduction* and *Rape*, *i.e.*, the *violent abduction* of a virgin; and leaves the latter subject to all the severities of the Civil Law.

---

[8] Cod. v. 9. 3 & 5.

[9] See the above Collection of *Decisions*, in append. sub. litt. B. p. 239.

[10] *Quæst. J. Priv.* l. ii. c. 4. p. 229.

[11] Dig. xxxiv. 9, 13.   [12] See Th. 19.   [13] Art. 12.

[14] Cod. ix. 3. l. unic. § 1, junct. *Ord. Pol. Holl.* art. 18, *Zeeland*, art. 33, and *Resol. Holl.* 25, Febr. 1751, in fin.

LXXII. The former, from the intention of the law, may be defined to be the *abduction of a youth or virgin, whether a major or a minor, and having a father or mother, accomplished with his or her consent, but without the knowledge or consent of the parent or guardians, for the purpose of marriage.* This crime does not, indeed, hinder a marriage, with the consent of the parent or guardian,[1] but is so surrounded by various penalties, most wisely appointed, that the abducer cannot hope for any pecuniary benefit therefrom.

LXXIII. Marriages between Protestants and Catholics were also formerly restricted by the Law of Holland of the 24th January, 1755, on account of the difference of religion. This law has, indeed, been abrogated by a Resolution of the Delegates of the people of Holland;[2] but its effect in excluding the community of property is yet observed in respect of marriages contracted before the passing of the new law.

LXXIV. Although many commentators on the Laws of Holland agree in considering the marriage of a guardian or his son with the ward as lawful, yet the reasons on which they proceed are very frivolous; and the opposite doctrine of Bynkershoek[3] appears to me more reasonable; and is supported by the rules we have laid down in *Thes.* 17 and 18, and by the Placaat of the 4th of October, 1540.[4] The same rule has been enacted by the Law of Flushing.[5] It has also been decided by

---

[1] [*Resol. Holl.* 26th June, 1783; *Groot Plac. B.* d. ix. p. 375.]
[2] 6 Mar. 1695.
[3] *Q. J. Priv.* l. ii. c. 3. p. 218, seq.
[4] Art. 12, arg.   [5] A. 1763, art. 48.

..ae *Schepenen* of Amsterdam[6] that, after the tutelar accounts have been rendered, the prohibition ceases.

SEC. 14.

LXXV. Marriages contracted by minors without the consent of the parents are, *ipso jure,* void;[7] but if the other requisites have been complied with, their subsequent consent confirms the marriage retrospectively; but not so as to discharge the parties from the penalties decreed by the Placaat of 1540.[8]

SEC. 15.

LXXVI. The public proclamation of banns or espousals should not be permitted by the Commissioners of Matrimonial Causes to minors, without the consent of the parents.[9] The minors should not, however, be wholly precluded from appearing before the judge with a just complaint against the abuse of the paternal authority.[10]

LXXVII. Under the term *parents,* without whose consent the proclamation of espousals is not permitted to minors under twenty-five or twenty years of age, who may be desirous of entering into marriage at once,[11] are not included grandfathers and grandmothers, uncles, or guardians.[12] In Zeeland the rule is different.[13]

---

[6] 23 May, 1749; see Lybrechts, *Reden Vertoog. over het Notar. Ampt,* tom. i. p. 144, seqq.

[7] *Pol. Ord. Holl.* art 3, junct. 13.   [8] Art. 17.

[9] *Polit. Ord.* art. 3.

[10] Dig. xxiii. 2. 19; and Voet *ad Pand.* d. t. § 22,

[11] *Pol. Ord. art.* 3.   [12] *Plac. Holl.* 31 Jul. 1671.

[13] *Poll. Ord.* 153, art 7.

LXXVIII. The proclamation of espousals between parties above this age is certainly allowed, after intimation thereof has been given to the parents by the Commissioners appointed for such causes : and their silence for a period of fourteen days is taken as consent, so far as concerns the Commissioners (for such seems to be the purport of the general words of the Ordonnance above cited[1]) ; but this does not hinder them from opposing the marriage before it has been celebrated.

LXXIX. Parents expressing their dissent to these Commissioners may at the same time explain the grounds of such dissent ; but are not bound to submit them to their decision ; though at Amsterdam this right is so limited, that the Commissioners may, if the grounds do not appear just, permit the proclamations.[2]

LXXX. Disputes between the parents and the children who are desirous of contracting a marriage are not taken cognizance of by the *Schepenen* but by the whole Court of Magistrates, two thirds at least of the judges being present ; and if their judgment be in favour of the parents' dissent, no appeal lies against it.[3] If there be a less number of judges, an appeal will lie.

LXXXI. If the dispute regarding the parents' unwillingness to consent to the marriage is carried on not with the children, but with their suitors, the matter comes under the jurisdiction of the ordinary judge ; and therefore an appeal is not refused, except in a case where the ordinary judge is at the same time a magistrate having jurisdiction over the matter (such as the

---

[1] *Pol. Ord.* art. 3.

[2] *Plac.* 1754, art 5 & 6.

[3] *Resol. Holl.* 9 Aug. 1646, and 27 Sept. 1663 ; Bynkershoek *Q. J. Priv.* l. ii. cap. 5.

Court), and has consulted with the competent number concerning the matter, and given judgment in favour of the parents.[4]

LXXXII. The consent of a parent who is of unsound mind is not, by the Law of Holland, to be supplied according to the rule laid down in Cod. v. 4. 9; but in contracting a marriage the children adopt the same rule with those who have no parents.

SEC. 16.

LXXXIII. By the general Law of Holland it is only necessary that proclamation of the espousals should be made at the place of domicile of both the parties espoused.[5] The laws of some places require also that proclamation should be made at the place of domicile quitted within a year and a day,[6] or even within three years.[7]

LXXXIV. Besides the solemnity of proclamations, a solemn celebration of the marriage is also required. This was in former times performed either by a priest or a magistrate, but now, by the Law of Holland of the 7th May, 1795, it must necessarily be by a magistrate. If these requisites be neglected, the marriage is, by the Law of Holland, void;[8] but not so by the Law of Zeeland.[9]

LXXXV. A prior *sponsus*, who has not appeared upon these proclamations, loses his action for damages; unless he was really ignorant of them.

---

[4] Bynkersh. d. l. p. 241. seqq.
[5] *Pol. Ord.* art. 3.
[6] *Ord. Leyd.* art. 101, § 10.
[7] *Ord. Amstefd.* A. 1754, art 10.
[8] *Polit. Ord.* 13.
[9] *Pol. Ord. Zeeland,* art. 6. in f. junct. art. 22.

LXXXVI. By the Law of Holland espousals are proved in the same manner as other acts. A half-full proof, however, cannot be supplied by oath tendered to the plaintiff by the judge although it may make place for the purgatory oath.[1]

SEC. 17.

LXXXVII. A marriage, after it has been publicly celebrated (which may be done even by procuration), is held as perfected, although the parties may not have retired to the nuptial bed.

SEC. 18.

LXXXVIII. Either of the married parties may sue for a divorce, and the forfeiture of the rights resulting from marriage, on the ground of adultery, as decided by the Supreme Court.[2] The commission of a heinous crime is an equally good, and even stronger ground. Malicious desertion also determines a marriage; as has been decided frequently in Holland, and in Zeeland enacted by law.[3]

LXXXIX. It has also been decided by the Supreme Court[4] that the marriage of a person who has been condemned to death, and has evaded the punishment by flight, or on whom the severest punishment short of death, or that of transportation for life, has been

---

[1] Brouwer de Jur. Connub. l. i. c. 23. § 24, 26, seqq.

[2] 19 Feb. 1743; see Lybrechts, Reden. Vertoog, t. i. p. 169.

[3] New Pol. Ord. Zeeland, art. 17.

[4] Nov. 12, 1793.

inflicted, may, at the petition of the innocent spouse, be dissolved.*

XC. Separation from bed and board cannot, even by mutual consent, be effected without just cause. If in addition to a separation from bed and board, a separation of property has taken place, no community of property exists any longer between the parties. The innocent party is, however, entitled to the dowry at the proper time.†

SEC. 19-21.

XCI. The power of the husband over the wife, being a more extensive species of guardianship, constituted *ipso jure*, is such, that he may manage her property according to his own discretion, free from the necessity of preparing an inventory, rendering accounts or answering for mismanagement (*culpa*).

. SEC. 22.‡

XCII. A husband may legally alienate the property of his wife without her consent, even where all community of property has been excluded.‖ In Zeeland, however, the law is different.[5]

---

* [This decision will be found reported in a collection of cases published by *Van der Linden,—Verzameling van Merkwaardige Gewijsden der Gerechtshoven in Holland;* Leyd. 1803; d. i. cas. 32, p. 247. A previous case will be found cited in *de Groot Plac. Boek*, d. vi. p. 540.—Tr.]

  † [See Bynkersh. *Qu. Jur. Pr.* lib. ii. c. 8.—Tr.]

  ‡ [Grot. B. i. ch. 5, § 22, line 3, in Mr. Herbert's Translation, for "*and whatever he has held*"—read "*even such property as she has held.*"—Tr.]

  ‖ [See Schorer, Aanteeken over de Inleid. van H. de Groot. (Middelb. 1797) ad b. ii. d. 48. § 2, p. 374.—Tr.]

  [5] *Ord. Zeeland*, cap. iii. art. 46.

XCIII. The wife is liable to the extent of one half on all contracts of the husband, and hence also on his engagements as a surety, and even on donations; unless all community both of profit and loss has been excluded.

XCIV. As it is evident from several charters and statutes of Holland and Zeeland, that the property of the wife is not subject to confiscation for the offences of the husband, but that a half of the common property should be reserved to her, so also it follows from reasonable interpretation, from the equity of the Roman Law,[1] and from the very words of certain statutes,[2] that even lighter pecuniary penalties paid on account of any crime committed by the husband should be deducted from his share in the common estate, and should by no means be charged against the wife.[*]

SEC. 23.

XCV. A married woman has no legal character or standing *in judicio;* not even where she carries on a trade; except in those places where it has been otherwise

[1] Dig. xvii. 2. 1. 52, § 18, and 1. 56. See Th. xvi.

[2] See *Ord. Zeeland,* cap. iii. art. 45.—*Privileg. Voorn.* A. 1477, art. 16. p. 20; *Ord. Vlissing.* cap. vi. art. 2. p. 66.

[*] [The distinction suggested by Groenewegen (*de Leg. Abrog.* ad. Cod. iv. 12.) and Voet (*ad Pand.* xxiii. 2. § 56) between *delicta graviora* and *delicta leviora* is refuted by Rodenburg, *de Jur. Conj.* part ii. tit. 2 § 3. See also Boel's note on Loen. *Decis.* cas. 103, p. 670, ed. 1712, and the authorities there cited. The Supreme Court of Ceylon (Creasy, C. J., and Temple and Thompson, J. J.), have held that the wife's moiety of the common estate was not liable to satisfy damages recovered in a civil action in respect of a theft committed by the husband. *Coére* v. *Fernando;* 29 Oct. 1861.—Tr.]

enacted; from which, however,[3] we cannot infer a general law.[4]

XCVI. So also a married woman cannot, without the consent or confirmation of the husband, be made civilly liable on her own contracts; but she is in all respects naturally liable; so that the suretyship of a third person who has joined in the contract is valid, and the *condictio indebiti** is not maintainable for any sum which the woman may since the dissolution of the marriage have paid in respect of it.

Sec. 24.

XCVII. Among the stipulations in antenuptial contracts by which the power of the husband may be legally restricted, may be mentioned that one whereby the husband is deprived of the right of alienating the wife's property; and this prevents the alienation of immovable property, or of debts payable to a particular creditor (*obligatien die op naam staan*), although such stipulations may not have been made public; notwithstanding the law of the 30th July, 1624, which has never been adopted in practice.

XCVIII. The alienation of movable property, however, and of notes payable in blank or to the bearer, when effected by the husband in his own name, contrary to such a stipulation, seems to be valid; reserving to the wife an action for indemnity against the husband.

XCIX. The wife may also legally stipulate that she should not be liable for debts contracted during the

---

[3] Th. xiv.

[4] Other exceptions may be found in the *Rechtsgel. Observ.* part iv. obs. 7, and in Voet *ad Pand.* lib. v. tit 1, § 16, 17, and lib. ii. tit. 4, § 34, 36·

* [See defin. Grot. b. iii. ch. 30, § 4.]

marriage, provided all community of property and of profits has been excluded. But whatever has been supplied to them on credit for domestic purposes may be claimed to the extent of a half from the wife, she having her recourse against the husband.[1] Nor is the publication of such an agreement required in Holland.

SEC. 25.

C. As a married woman may without her husband's knowledge or consent make a testament, so also she may make a donation *causâ mortis*, provided the *dominium* or property in the thing given passes only after her death.

SEC. 26.

CI. The marital power is not determined, but only suspended, by the insanity of the husband.[2] The wife may, however, justly claim to be allowed the administration of her own property, as if the husband were absent.

CHAPTER VI.—SEC. 1.

CII. Although the adoption of children has not been practised in Holland, yet there is nothing to prevent not only arrogation, but even adoption, properly so called.[3]

CIII. An inheritance bequeathed to children by a stranger is not administered by the father in right of

---

[1] Neostad. *de Pact. Antenupt.* obs. 9, in not. (d.)—*Decis. & Resolut. van den Hove van Holland. n.* 396.

[2] Dig. xxiv. 1. 22, § 7, with Dig. i. 5. 20, and i. 6. 8.

[3] See Stockmans, *Decis. Brabant,* 69.

his paternal power, but as guardian, or by some one else to whom the guardianship has been committed either by the testator or the pupillary magistrates.[4]

CIV. That which children acquire in either Service, they should have solely for themselves, by right of *peculium castrense,* even after the death of the father; but that which they acquire by their own industry passes, by right of *peculium profectitium,* to the father, and even to a mother by whom they are maintained. In the latter class, however, gifts made to the children by their sponsors cannot properly be included, as decided by the Supreme Court.[5]

Sec. 3.

CV. Although a father has no usufruct in the *adventitious* property of a minor son, yet he may legally claim to have his children maintained therefrom. Nor is a precedent wanting on this point; for the Court on the 5th December, 1736, adjudicated to a surviving parent all the revenues of a large inheritance left to her child by his grandfather.[6]

CVI. Pupillary substitution has not indeed been practised amongst us; and the Court on the 10th November, 1632, held that the property which had devolved on an *impubes* from his father was subject to the deduction of the legitimate and Trebellianic portions in favour of the heirs *ab intestato.* But the residue of the property belongs to the substituted heir (as correctly stated by

---

[4] *Leg. pupill. (Weeskeuren van) Leyd.* art. 30; *Rotterd.* art. 30, 31; *Vlissing.* art. 33; and the same has also been expressly provided by the Law of *Middleburg,* of the 10 Aug. 1765.

[5] See Van Leeuwen, *Comm.* B. iii. ch. 16, § 7.

[6] See Lybrechts, *Reden. Vertoog.* tom. i. p. 316 in not.

Loenius),[1] not indeed in right of *fidei commissum,* but, as it would appear, by that quasi-military substitution, which is permitted to every testator by the Law of Holland.[2]

Sec. 4.

CVII. The direct emancipation of children, which was evidently not unknown amongst us in former times,[3] is hardly in use at the present day, since in place thereof it is usual to obtain *Venia Ætatis.*

Sec. 5.

CVIII. The paternal power is determined upon the attaining of 25 years, but not in respect of contracting a marriage. The same rule should hold in respect of obtaining a higher rank.[*]

CIX. As by the Roman Law the paternal power was determined by deportation, so the reason of our law requires that upon a punishment similar to deportation, or upon exile, the children should pass from the power of the father to that of the mother, or should be educated and controlled by guardians; and the pupillary laws of most places are in favour of this rule.[4]

Chapter VII.—Sec. 3.

CX. Although the legal age or majority, which at

---

[1] See Decis. 57.   [2] See *infra,* under B. ii. chap. 18, § 21.

[3] See Roseboom, *Cost. van Amst.* cap. 39. art. 3.

[*] [See Groeneweg. *de Leg. abrog.* ad Dig. xiv. 6. 1. § 3; Voet *ad Pand.* i. 7. § 10. Utrechts. Consult. vol. i. cons. 109.—Tr.]

[4] *Weeskeuren van Alkmaar,* t. iv. art. 13; *Monnickendam, Purmerend, Enkhuisen, Graft, de Zype,* ibid. *Briel,* art. 70; *Vlaardingen,* art. 52; *Gouda,* art. 92; *Leyden,* art. 60; *Medemblick,* art. 50; *Gorinchem,* art. 46; *Amsterdam,* art. 33; *Rotterdam,* art. 33; *Dordrecht,* art. 48; *Middelburg,* art. 50, 51.

present discharges a child from tutelage, has by the more recent laws been fixed at 25 years, yet these laws have permitted the magistrates, upon the advice of the near relatives, to discharge good and prudent youths from tutelage at an earlier age.[5] The more usual practice has however been to obtain *Venia Ætatis* ; of which alone therefore mention is made in the Laws of Gorinchem.[6]

CXI. Most of our pupillary laws expressly testify that the distinction between the *tutela* of *impuberes* and the *cura* of minors has been abrogated amongst us.

SEC. 6.

CXII. Persons under the age of 25 years, though they may have obtained *Venia Ætatis* or have become *sui juris* by contracting marriage, are not admitted to the guardianship of others ;[7] and this rule is also adopted by various pupillary laws.[8] The Law of *Middelburg* excuses them, if they desire it.[9]

CXIII. Soldiers are to be excused from undertaking a guardianship ; as evident both from a reasonable construction of the law, and from those pupillary laws which allow of the substitution of another guardian in place of a dative guardian who changes his domicile.[10]

---

[5] *Ord. Leyd.* 1583, art. 104; *Weeskeur. van Amsterd.* art. 24 ; *Rotterd.* art. 38; *Haarlem,* 1596 ; *Dordr.* 1639, art. 59 ; *Costum. Middelb.* rubr. xv. art. 10, 11 ; *Weesk. van Middelb.* art. 52, 53, 54.

[6] *Weeskeuren van Gorinchem,* art. 42.

[7] *Voet ad Pand.* xxvi. 5.

[8] *Weeskeuren van Alkmaar, Monnickendam, Purmerend, Graft, de Zype,* tit. vii. art. 13 ; *Briel,* art. 11.   [9] Art. 4.

[10] *Weeskeuren van Rotterd.* art. 12 ; *Enkhuis.* t. vii. art. 2 ; *Medembl.* art. 19 ; *Alkmar.* tit. vii. art. 5, &c., *Vlaarding.* art. 20.

CXIV. A mother or grandmother may be guardian of the children or grandchildren (except perhaps in the town of Vlaardingen[1]); but not, it would seem, if she be below 25 years of age.[2] Nor does the decision in the celebrated case of *Staat* and *Oorlog*[3] prove the contrary.

CXV. Most of those who are not admitted to the office of guardian, are enumerated by the Jurists in the *Rechtsgeleerde Observatien*.[4]

Sec. 11.

CXVI. In some places it is necessary that testamentary guardians should be confirmed by the pupillary magistrates;[5] and may even be rejected, if they be not fit persons.[6] At other places, however, when the Orphan Chamber is excluded, the guardians are merely bound to produce the *grosse* of the last will by which they have been appointed, and to undertake the guardianship.[7]

Sec. 8.

CXVII. Although the general Law of Holland does not recognize legitimate guardians, who are *ipso iure*

---

[1] *Weesk. van Vlaard.* art. 17.

[2] Arg. Cod. v. 35. 2; Nov. cxviii. cap. 5.

[3] Aitzema, tom. iii. p. 554, 556.

[4] Part. i. obs. 14; and *Supplem.* part iv. p. 196.

[5] *Weeskeuren van Alkmaar.* t. vii. art. 2, 8; *Monnick. Purmer. Graft. Zype* d. 1. *Briel*, art. 106, sqq. *Enkhuis*, t. vii. art. 4; *Middelb.* art. 20.

[6] *Weesk. van Enkhuis.* t. vii. art. 8; *Alkmaar.* t. vii. art. 12; *Monnick.* &c. *Briel*, art. 110.

[7] *Weesk. van Rhynl.* art. 11; *Leyd.* art. 10; *Vlaarding.* art. 8 f.; & art. 10. f.; *Medembl.* art. 27.

admitted to the guardianship; yet the pupillary magistrates should appoint the nearest relatives as guardians, provided they be fit persons.[8] *Grotius* is, however correct in stating that in the territory of *Voorn*, the guardianship was formerly committed *ipso jure* to the nearest cognate; which rule obtained in other places also, viz., in *Zeeland*,[9] in *South Holland*,[10] and in the city of *Dordrecht*.[11]

SEC. 9.

CXVIII. A guardian may be appointed over a person who already has a guardian, by any one who bequeaths any property to the ward; but the guardian who has been appointed by a predeceased father will jointly with the mother have the care of the *person* of the ward, and if after the death of the mother a colleague is given him under her testament, both of them will jointly discharge the duties of guardian.

CXIX. The frequent and daily use of the clause whereby a guardian is permitted to substitute another, proves that an uncertain person may at present be appointed guardian by testament,[12] contrary to the rule of the Civil Law.[13] But it may reasonably be doubted

---

[8] The *Weeskeuren van Alkmaar* (t. vii. art. 2) should be understood in this sense, and the punctuation corrected according to those of *Monnickendam, Purmerend, Graft*, tit. vii. art. 2; *Briel*, art. 100.

[9] *Ord. Zeeland.* cap. ii. art. 27.

[10] Van der Eyck, *Handv. van Zuid-Holl.* p. 131.

[11] *Costum. Dordr.* art. 65.   See van de Wall, *Handv. en Priv. van Dordr.* p. 1351.

[12] See *Weesk. van Leyden*, art. 21; *Gouda*, art. 51.

[13] Dig. xxvi. 2. 20; Inst. ii. 20. § 27.

D

whether security is to be dispensed with in the case of an uncertain appointment.[1]

CXX. As regards testamentary guardians, it makes a great difference whether they have been appointed generally, or with exclusion of the Orphan Chamber. In the former case, they may administer without giving security, but are bound to render accounts to the Orphan Chamber: in the latter, having exhibited that part of the testament whereby they have been appointed guardians, and the Orphan Chamber has been excluded, they are clearly independent of its supervision. In Zeeland, however, such an exclusion can neither be made without the leave of the magistrates, nor when duly made does it release the guardians from the duty of depositing the *grosse* of the testament and the inventory, properly stamped, at the Orphan Chamber.[2]

SEC. 11.

CXXI. In some places, a father who has been appointed guardian by the Orphan Chamber, if he contracts a second marriage, forfeits the office;[3] or after rendering the accounts, may be reappointed as guardian.[4]

CXXII. One or more guardians from the side of the father should, if possible, be associated with a mother whom the Orphan Chamber has appointed guardian.

[1] Inst. i. 24. arg. pr.

[2] *Weeskeuren van Vlissing.* art. 57–64; *Middelb.* art. 64–74; and *Interpret.* 10. Dec. 1689, art. 9–13.

[3] *Weesk. van Amsterd.* art. 37; *Medembl.* art. 14; *Alkmaar,* tit. x. art. 2; *Monnick., Purmerend, Enkhuis., Graft, Zype,* d. 1; *Briel,* art. 151.

[4] *New Ord. Dordr.* 1768, art. 33.

As regards a father, the same provision has not been everywhere made.[5]

SEC. 13.

CXXIII. A surviving parent, who does not claim the guardianship over his children, does not indeed forfeit the succession, as under the Civil Law;[6] but is subject to other pecuniary penalties, and may even be compelled, under pain of civil imprisonment, to appear. Nominating a proper person is also, amongst us, equivalent to claiming the guardianship;[7] but so, that a person who acts *bonâ fide* is not subject to the responsibilities of guardianship.[8]

SEC. 14.

CXXIV. A guardian desirous of excusing himself, should within fourteen days (to be computed from the day on which he became aware of his appointment), or within such other time as may be fixed by law, submit his excuse to the Orphan Chamber, or, upon appeal, to the ordinary judge, supported by good reasons, which, however, are to be left to the decision of the judge.[9] The executors of a testament need not allege any such excuse.[10]

[5] But see (v. c.) *Weesk. van Rhynl.* art. 17; *Leyden,* art. 13; *Goud.* art. 42; *Dordr.* art. 33.

[6] Cod. vi. 58. 10.

[7] Arg *Weesk. van Rhynl.* art. 12 & 15.

[8] Dig. xxvi. 6. 4. § 4.

[9] Some of these reasons are enumerated in some of the laws. See *Weesk. van Goud.* art. 68; *Middelb.* art. 14; *Vlissing.* art. 10.

[10] *Weesk. van Rhynl.* art. 20, in f.

CHAPTER VIII.—SEC. 3.

CXXV. In the difficult question of Dutch Law respecting the power of guardians or relatives over the marriage of a ward, we must distinguish between various parts of Holland.

In some places the registration and proclamation of espousals is not permitted to wards, without the consent of the guardians ;[1] but on the other hand, the guardians are obliged to state their reasons for dissenting,[2] and the judgment of the relatives is preferred to that of the guardians.[3]

In many parts of Holland the marriage of a ward, contracted without the consent of the relatives and guardians, does indeed remain in force, but is subject to the penalties of the Placaat of 1540 ;[4] and in this sense should the *art.* 17 of the Political Ordonnance be understood ; as clearly declared by the States in the pupillary laws passed by thom, wherein they have subjected such marriages to the above penalties.[5]

In the remaining parts of Holland, the consent of the relatives to the marriage of a ward is necessary ; and where this has been neglected, it falls within *art.* 17 of the Placaat, which has been expressly adopted by *art.* 13 of the Political Ordonnance.

---

[1] *Ord. Leyden,* art. 101. § 3; *Ord. Amsterd.* of 1754 concerning marriage, art. 3.

[2] d. art. 3. [3] Arg. Placaat of *Charles V.* of 1540, art. 17.

[4] Art. 17.

[5] *Weesk. van Alkmaar,* t. v. art. 12 ; *Monnickend. Purmerend, Graft,* ibid; *Enkhuis.* t. v. art. 10 ; *Briel,* art. 84; *Zype,* art. 9 ; and similar others, if any.

Nor is this affected by *art.* 3 of the Political Ordonnance, declared by the Resolution of the 9th August, 1646, and the 31st July, 1671; the purport of which is that that prerogative of parents, whereby they may absolutely prevent, by their dissent, the marriage of their minor children, without being bound to explain the grounds of such dissent, belongs neither to guardians nor to relatives, even in the ascendant line, but to the father and mother alone.

CXXVI. The Law of Zeeland renders the marriage of wards, contracted without the consent of the relatives and guardians, not only subject to the penalties of the above Placaat, but also declares them absolutely void,[6] and restrains them also in other ways.[7]

SEC. 4.

CXXVII. A ward cannot appear in court, either as plaintiff or defendant, without his guardians, even in respect of civil offences. But in criminal causes, at least in cases of extraordinary process, it has been the rule, contrary to the Criminal Ordinance of King *Philip,*[8] that they ought to defend themselves without guardian or curator.[9]

SEC. 5.

CXXVIII. The contract of a ward who, even after attaining puberty, has bound himself without the consent of his guardian, is clearly invalid; nor is it so confirmed

---

[6] *Ord. Pol. Zeeland.* art. 7, 8, 22.
[7] *Weesk. van Vlissing.* art. 47, 49.
[8] *Styl van Proc. in Crim. Zaaken,* art. 61.
[9] *Weesk. van Alkmaar,* t. v. art. 9; *Monnick. Purmer. Graft.* ibid; *de Zype,* t. v. art. 8; *Briel,* art. 81.

by an oath as to render it necessary to obtain *restitutio in integrum* against it.

CXXIX. Although the movable property of a ward may for good reasons, and with the consent of the pupillary magistrates, be alienated, yet the more valuble things should be retained, according to the discretion of the relatives, for his own use;[1] and the ward himself, if he be above 18 years, should be consulted on the subject.[2]

SEC. 6.

CXXX. As the immovable property of a ward, and other things which are reckoned as immovables, may not be alienated without a decree of the superior magistrates, or of the Court of Holland; so also it is evident from Law 22 of the Code v. 37, and from the practice of inventorising those movables which may legally be sold under the authority of the Orphan Chamber (such as furniture, articles of clothing, jewellery, and other things, namely, which bring no income),[3] that the same rule ought also to be laid down in respect of public Dutch or foreign securities.

CXXXI. In order to such a decree being duly pronounced, the advice of the Orphan Chamber should be taken. In some places the nearest relatives of the ward should also be heard; but this is not everywhere required.[4]

CXXXII. This decree should be given by the magistrate who had assigned the guardian over the ward; as

---

[1] *Weesk. van Alkmaar*, t. iii. art. 5 & 6, and similar others.

[2] *Weesk. van Haarlem*, art. 12.

[3] *Weesk. van Alkmaar*, t. iii. art. 5, 6, with art. 7 & 8, in fin. &c.

[4] *Weesk. van Rhynl.* art. 35; *Enkhuis.* t. iv. art. 9; *Rotterd.* art. 25; *Leyden*, art. 38.

evident not only from 1. 5. § 12 of the Digest xxvii. 9, but also from the circumstance of its being necessary to have the advice of the Orphan Chamber (over which no other magistrate possesses any command or control), and a statement of the reasons for alienation from the guardian: unless, perhaps, the question concerns the alienation of immovable property situated elsewhere, which has devolved on the ward from a stranger, and is administered by a guardian residing elsewhere ; in which case it is advisable to obtain a decree from the magistrates of both places.[5]

SEC. 8.

CXXXIII. The acts of a guardian done or contracted on behalf of the ward are binding on the latter, reserving to him his right to *restitutio in integrum*. The law which has been enacted in the town of *Vlaardingen*[6] is therefore anomalous, viz., that if a guardian has done anything ill or needlessly on behalf of the ward, without the advice of the Orphan Chamber, the pupillary magistrates may rescind or annul it.

CHAPTER IX.—SEC. 1.

CXXXIV. As regards the security to be given by guardians, the same rule has not been prescribed at all places. Some laws expressly require personal security ;[7] others lay down no rule regarding security ;[8] others,

---

[5] Voet *ad Pand.* xxvii. 9, § 5.　　　[6] *Weesk. van Vlaard.* art. 74.
[7] *Weesk. van Rhynl.* art. 21 ; *Vlaarding.* art. 22 ; *Leyden*, art. 17 : *Gouda*, art. 46 ; *Vlissing.* art. 30.
[8] *Weesk. van Enkhuis.* tit. viii. ; *de Zype*, d. t. viii.

again, leave it to the discretion of the pupillary magistrates whether to require security or be satisfied with a juratory bond.[1]   And to these latter does Grotius seem to refer in the text: but they cannot[2] be properly taken to constitute the general Law of Holland.

SEC. 3.

CXXXV. As regards the preparation of an inventory of the minor's property, there are three distinct cases to be considered.   The *first*, on the death of either of the parents; in which case the surviving parent (and not the guardian or the Orphan Chamber), and even the step-father or step-mother, should at the request of the guardian prepare (and may, if necessary, be compelled by the Orphan Chamber to prepare) an accurate inventory of the whole estate, which the law, as regulated by custom, considers to have been in common between the married persons, and produce it for the examination and approval of the guardians and the Orphan Chamber.[3]   In some places, however, the surviving parent prepares the inventory jointly with the pupillary magistrates or the guardians.[4]

CXXXVI. Although where the Orphan Chamber has been excluded, its authority in this respect ceases,[5] yet the reason of the law imposes on the guardian the

---

[1] *Weesk. van. Alkmaar.* tit. viii. art. 2 ; *Purmerend, Graft,* ibid, *Briel,* art. 118 ; *Medembl.* art. 23 ; where, however, the authority of the Burgermeesters is required.   [2] Voet *ad Pand.* xxvi. 7. § 2.

[3] *Weesk. van Amsterd.* art. 4 ; *Rotter.* art. 14, 15, 16 ; *Medemblick,* art. 34 ; *Alkmaar,* t. ii. art. 7 ; *Enkhuis.* t. ii. art. 7 ; *Rhynl.* art. 26 ; *Leyden,* art. 27 ; *Goud.* art. 58 ; *Vlissing.* art. 5, 6, 14, 15.

[4] *Weesk. van Dord.* art 38 ; *Middelb.* art. 22.

[5] *Weesk. van Rotter.* art. 16, in fin.; *Leyden,* art. 10 init.

duty of requiring an inventory from the parent; and
by the new Law of *Dordrecht* this has been expressly
enjoined on a guardian.[6]

CXXXVII. By the general Law of Holland, which
is also expressly approved of by some statutes, the first-
dying parent cannot dispense with the inventory, which
it is the duty of the surviving parent to prepare. At
some places, however, such a remission may be approved
of by the Orphan Chamber, either solely,[7] or with the
consent of the town magistrates.[8] At *Middelburg*, notwithstanding such a remission, an inventory should be
prepared, but must be delivered, duly stamped, to the
Orphan Chamber;[9] unless either parent having left a
definite sum on account of the legitimate portion, and
declared it to be equal in amount to such portion, had
thereupon discharged the survivor from the obligation
of making an inventory, and the survivor in addition
thereto, has, since the death of the first-dying parent,
confirmed this declaration on oath;[10] in which case
it is also necessary that the testament, as well as the
declaration of both the parents as to the amount of the
legitimate portion, should not have preceded the death
of the predeceased parent by a period of more than
four years.[11]

CXXXVIII. With the consent, however, of the
relatives and guardians, even where nothing has been
said in the testament, the surviving parent may on just
grounds be discharged from the duty of preparing an

---

[6] *Ord. Dordr.* 29 Dec. 1764: *Nederl. Jaarb.* 1764, p. 940, sq.

[7] *Weesk. van Vlaarding.* art. 35.   [8] *Weesk. van Rotter.* art. 16.

[9] *Weesk. van Middelb.* art. 59-62.   [10] *Ibid.* art. 75, 76, seq.

[11] *Keur. van Middelb.* 1645. art. 8.

inventory;[1] and at some places this may even be done by consent of the guardian alone.[2]

Sec. 4.

CXXXIX. A surviving parent who in preparing the inventory fraudulently conceals any property forfeits his share therein.[3] *Voet*[4] incorrectly denies this, and cites *Groenewegen*,[5] whose opinion cannot, however, have any weight against a subsequent decision, which is mentioned by *Van Leeuwen*,[6] or against a law which has since been enacted.

Sec. 5.

CXL. The *second* case in which an inventory is prepared on behalf of the wards, is where during the lifetime of both or either of the parents, any property has devolved on the children, in which case the executors or guardians who have been appointed over such property by the testator himself, or if there be none, then the parents are bound to produce to the Orphan Chamber the *grosse*[7] of the testament and an inventory of the property: and this, lest the parents (though they might, in the absence of an appointment of guardians, administer the property) might without the knowledge

[1] *Weesk. van Amsterd.* art. 4, 5; *Alkmaar, &c.* t. ii. art. 9.

[2] *Weesk. van Rotter.* art. 14; *Leyden*, art. 25; *Goud.* art. 56.

[3] *Weesk. van Alkmaar*, t. ii. art. 8, and others cited in *de Rechtsgel. Observ.* part iii. obs. 9.

[4] *Ad Pand.* xxvi. 7, § 5.

[5] Ad ibid.

[6] *Comm.* B. i. ch. 16, § 7.

[7] *Weesk. van Leyden*, art. 29.

of the Orphan Chamber appropriate to themselves the profits thereof which were not left to them.[8]

CXLI. The same duty of preparing or adding to an inventory is incumbent on the guardians of a ward who has lost either of his parents, and to whom any property has been given or bequeathed without any provision as to the guardianship. This property should be administered by the guardians whom the ward already has.[9]   ·

SEC. 6.

CXLII. The object of requiring an inventory to be made by a surviving parent,[10] is to secure a division of the common property between the parent and the wards in the presence of the Orphan Chamber;[11] that is, to have that share assigned to each which each is entitled to;[12] which assignment is generally made in the presence of the nearest relatives,[13] within a short period, fixed by law, but certainly before a second marriage has been contracted,[14] the proclamations whereof are in most places not permitted until the assignment has taken place; pecuniary penalties being also in some places enacted in this respect,[15] or the penalty, namely, that a

---

[8] *Weesk. van Rotter.* art. 30, 31; *Rhynl.* art. 46; *Leyden,* art. 30; *Goud.* art. 61; *Alkmaar,* tit. ii. art. 19–21, &c.; *Vlaarding.* art. 41; and see *Weesk. van Alkmaar,* t. iv.; *Amsterd.* art. 31.

[9] *Weesk. van Amsterd.* art. 13, 14; *Medembl.* art. 46; *Vlaarding.* art. 40; *Leyden,* art. 31; *Rhynl.* art. 30; *Goud.* art. 62; *Alkmaar,* tit. ii. art. 22; *Rotter.* art. 29; *Dordr.* art. 50, 51; *Haarl.* art. 10; *Middelb.* art. 49.   [10] Th. 135.   [11] *Weesk. van Vlissing.* art. 19.

[12] *Weesk. van Alkmaar,* t. ii. art. 10.

[13] *Weesk. van Alkmaar,* t. ii. art. 5, 6; *Monnick. Graft. Purmer.* 1 c. *Enkhuis.* t. ii. art. 2; *Briel,* art. 26, 27; *Amsterd.* art. 3, 10.

[14] *Rechtsgel. Observ.* part i. obs. 15.

[15] *Weesk. van Rotter.* art. 28; *Briel,* art. 50.

surviving parent, who may acquire any property after the dissolution of community by the death of the other parent, is obliged to share the same in common, but without community of loss, with the children, to whom an assignment has not been made at the proper time:[1] which penalty is, however, in certain respects limited by some laws as regards property in ships.[2]

CXLIII. The movable property thus assigned is kept in the custody of the Orphan Chamber: and the immovable property is registered, unless the Chamber has upon good cause permitted the surviving parent to have the administration thereof, under proper security.[3]

CXLIV. The necessity of making an assignment of the property to the children ceases, in three cases: 1. Upon the consent of the nearest relatives; in which case the community of property between the surviving parent and the children continues, but not if the former contracts a second marriage;[4] 2. At the desire or disposition of the first-dying parent, to be proved to the Orphan Chamber within six weeks; in which case, however, the Chamber has the power, if circumstances render it necessary, notwithstanding such disposition, to direct the assignment to be made;[5] and 3. If the

---

[1] *Weesk. van Amsterd.* art. 21, 22; *Leyden*, art. 24; *Goud.* art. 55; *Vlissing.* art. 17; *Alkmaar*, t. ii. art. 27, 28, and similar others; *Briel*, art. 48, 49; *Vlaarding.* art. 31; *Dordr.* art. 42, 43.

[2] *Weesk. van Medembl.* art. 53: and *Vlaarding.* art. 32.

[3] *Weesk. van Medembl.* art. 45; *Grootebroek*, art. 7; *Alkmaar*, t. iii. art. 1–4; *Enkhuis.* &c. d. 1.; *Vlaard.* art. 60; *Briel*, art. 52–55; *Amsterd.* art. 12; *Middelb.* Interpr. art. 14.

[4] *Weesk. van Enkhuis.* t. ii. art. 2; *Amsterd.* art. 3; *Gorinchem*, art. 33; *Rhynl.* art. 31; *Haarlem*, art. 8; *Alkmaar*, tit. ii. art. 12, and similar others.

[5] *Weesk. van Alkmaar*, tit. ii. art. 13; *Purmer. Monnick. de Zype*, ib.

estate is not solvent; which is in most instances to be proved by the inventory,[6] and should even be confirmed by oath;[7] excepting where, with the consent of the Orphan Chamber, the inventory has been dispensed with by the relatives and guardians.[8] The second of these exceptions is not made in some pupillary laws, except where the Orphan Chamber has been excluded,[9] and in others it is disallowed.[10]

SEC. 7.

CXLV. As regards the three modes in which an assignment may be made, see the *Rechtsgeleerde Observatien, Part.* iii. *obs.* 10.

The redemption of the common estate by the surviving parent, which is not disallowed at *Middelburg* and *Flushing*,[11] may be effected by the consent of the relatives and the Orphan Chamber, provided the creditors are neither defrauded,[12] nor affected in their rights, by the discharge of the wards,[13] whose interests, however, are in some places protected by allowing them a prescription of eighteen months[14] or three years[15] as against the creditors.

[6] *Weesk. van Alkmaar,* t. ii. art, 14, and similar others; *Vlaarding.* art. 38; *Briel,* art. 35.

[7] *Weesk. van Gorinchem,* art. 34; *Enkhuis.* t. ii. art. 5.

[8] *Weesk. van Medembl.* art. 40; *Dord.* art. 45.

[9] *Weesk. van Haarlem,* art. 3.   [10] *Weesk. van Amsterd.* art. 8.

[11] *Weesk. van Middelb.* art. 28, 29 ; *Vlissing.* art. 22–24.

[12] See decision of the Court, 23 Mar. 1615; *Decis. & Resol. van den Hove,* n. 106.

[13] Ibid. n. 83. *Sent. van den Hoogen en Provinc. Raad.* dec. 129.

[14] *Ord. Amsterd.* 31 July, 1656.

[15] *Ord. Leyden,* 24 Sept. 1659, inserted in *Weesk. van Leyd.* art. 26, which has been adopted also in *Gouda, Weesk.* art. 57.

A voluntary division of the property appraised by common consent between the surviving parent and the guardians of the ward, under the authority of the Orphan Chamber, and made at the residence of the deceased, passes both property and debts in due proportion to each; so that those movables only which have passed to the wards (and not all the goods, as is generally but erroneously believed) are to be publicly sold in order to pay their share of the debts.[1]

If a division cannot be effected by mutual consent, that kind of division may be resorted to which is effected without the parent's consent, namely, by dividing the property into equal shares, and drawing lots for the same.[2]

SEC. 8.

CXLVI. The *third* case in which an inventory should be made is when the surviving parent dies either with or without having made an assignment of the property. And the duty of making such inventory rests either with the relatives or guardians, or with the Orphan Chamber, unless the latter has been excluded; the guardians being, however, in every case bound to make the inventory in the presence of some public officer.[3] The Law of *Medemblick* requires that it should be produced to the Orphan Chamber duly stamped and confirmed by the oath of the guardians, and be preserved by it during the continuance of the guardianship.[4]

[1] *Weesk. van Leyden*, art. 33; *Medembl.* art. 36; *Goud.* art. 64.
[2] *Weesk. van Rhynl.* art. 32; *Vlaarding.* art. 29, in fin.
[3] *Weesk. van Enkhuis.* t. ii. art. 12; *Medembl.* art. 27, 28.
[4] *Weesk. van Medembl.* art. 29.

The same rule has been enacted at *Middelburg* and *Flushing*.[5]

SEC. 9.

CXLVII. The instrument which testifies to the assignment of the property having been made by the surviving parent, as well as all chirographs or notes for money due to the wards, are kept in the custody of the Orphan Chamber. The latter are secured against alienation by a note made on them, and are not allowed to remain in the hands of the guardian for a longer time than will enable him to collect the interest.[6] But the books of accounts left by the surviving parent, after a note has been taken of those debts which have not been scored out or receipted, remain with the guardian.[7]

CXLVIII. Movable property or notes belonging to a ward in common with another who is a major, although in most instances kept in the custody of the Orphan Chamber, unless when delivered under proper security to the person having the larger share therein, should rather, according to the law of some places, be divided.[8]

CXLIX. Property belonging in common to several wards, who have been instituted heirs by the parents, ought rather to remain undivided, unless the parents have directed otherwise, or it appears to the Orphan Chamber more advantageous that a division should be made; or the attainment of majority or marriage of one of the

---

[5] *Weesk. van Middelb.* art. 60; *Vlissing.* art. 63.

[6] *Weesk. van Rhynl.* art. 39, 40; *Rotter.* art. 27; *Alkmaar*, tit. iii. art. 1-3, and similar others; *Gorinchem*, art. 36; *Medembl.* art. 45; *Haarlem*, art. 13; *Leyden*, art. 48, 49.

[7] *Weesk. van Leyden*, art. 48; *Goud.* art. 80.

[8] *Weesk. van Leyden*, art. 33; *Goud.* art. 64; *Dordr.* art. 50.

wards renders a division necessary ;[1] and by the Law of *Flushing*,[2] even in the last case, the community amongst the remaining minors should, it is said, be continued,

CL. The wards are to be educated by the person to whom the predeceased parent has committed this duty (unless the Orphan Chamber thinks it unadvisable) ;[3] even if such person be the widow or widower of the parent's second marriage.[4]

CLI. If the testament has made no provision in this respect, the parent who by an assignment of the property has delivered in full the portions of the wards cannot regularly be compelled to educate and maintain them: but, if he desires it, he should be preferred to others, and should be allowed out of the income of the property the necessary funds for their maintenance ;[5] and if such income be insufficient, something should either be deducted out of the property[6] or supplied by the parent.[7]

CLII. If, however, the assignment of the property has been made by the parent by way of redemption, he is bound, in lieu of the profits of the portion which belongs to the children, to maintain them himself (even if such profits be insufficient),[8] and not from the income of property which may have devolved on the

---

[1] *Weesk. van Amsterd.* art. 43; *Gorinchem,* art. 41; *Medembl.* art. 51; *Alkmaar.* t. iv. art. 15; *Monnick. Purmer. Graft. Zype,* ibid; *Vlaarding.* art. 63; *Haarlem,* art. 17; *Dordr.* art. 53; *Middleb.* art. 45, 46.   [2] *Weesk. van Vlissing.* art. 28, 29.

[3] *Weesk. van Alkmaar, Monnick. Enkhuis. Graft. Zype, Purmer.* tit. iv. art. 8.

[4] Voet *ad Pand.* xxvii. 2. § 1.   [5] Dd. ll. art. 5, 9, 12.

[6] Ibid. art. 10.   [7] Art. 11.

[8] *Weesk. van Alkmaar,* &c. tit. iv. art. 2 ; *Amsterd.* art. 31; *Gorinch.* art. 45 ; *Medembl.* art. 48; *Vlaard.* art. 49 ; *Dordr.* art. 46.

children from other sources, unless it has been otherwise provided by the testator or donor or by the Orphan
Chamber.[9] The children should be maintained by the
parent not only up to their 18th, or 15th, or 16th year,
as provided by some laws, but even up to majority,[10] or
till the time fixed by agreement between the Orphan
Chamber and the parent.[11] And this burthen of main-
taining the children attaches, even after the death of
the surviving parent, to his estate ; unless the portions
assigned or allotted to the children in the redemption
are restored,[12] or an equitable compromise is made in
this respect.[13] At some places, however, the estate of
the parent is not subject to this burthen.[14]

SEC. 10.

CLIII. A guardian may legally invest the moneys
of the ward in the purchase of profitable estates in the
country.[15] But in *Gorinchem, Haarlem, and Flushing* it
has been enacted otherwise.[16]

CLIV. In respect of the purchase of annual rents with
the money of the ward, certain peculiarities have been
adopted by the Law of Holland of the 12th Sept., 1592 ;
as that these obligations should properly be contracted
in the presence of the Orphan Chamber, and should

[9] Dd. 11. art. 4 ; *Rhynl.* art. 46 ; *Amsterd.* art. 31.
[10] *Weesk. van Alkmaar,* &c. tit. iv. art. 2.
[11] *Weesk. van Dordr.* art. 46 ; *Medembl.* art. 48.
[12] *Weesk. van Alkmaar,* tit. iv. art. 3.
[13] *Weesk. van Leyden,* art. 28 ; *Goud.* art. 59.
[14] *Weesk. van Vlaarding.* art. 49 ; *Vlissing.* art. 25 ; *Middelb.* art. 30.
[15] See the laws cited in the *Rechtsgel. Observ.* part iii. obs. 13 ; and
Weesk. van Gouda, art. 71.
[16] *Weesk. van Gorinch.* art. 37 ; *Haarlem,* art. 14 ; *Vlissing.* art. 42.

E

have the same right of preference as the rents established by authority of the Schepenen,[1] which right should be held to subsist even after the ward has attained majority (contrary to the opinion of *Voet*,[2] who proceeds on the authority of an opinion given before the law last cited was passed) :[3] and, further, that the debtor cannot pay off or redeem such rents before three months' notice, but that the ward-creditor may, on attaining majority or contracting a marriage, demand the redemption thereof after six months' notice. These and other advantages seem to have been tacitly held out by the laws of *Leyden and Gouda*, in respect of debts due to wards, if contracted through the Orphan Chamber.[4]

CLV. The money of the ward may (not so much under the Resolution of the States of 1608, which was temporary, as under those of the 23rd May, 1635, and the 11th December, 1642) be safely lent to the Dutch States or to the Public Treasury of Holland : and this has been permitted also by several subsequent laws. The same rule has been enacted in Zeeland by the Placaat of the 31st May, 1679. It does not, however, follow from this that such money cannot be either invested in the purchase of country farms, or lent out at interest to private parties on good mortgage and personal security. Without this security it cannot properly be lent out either to private citizens or to

---

[1] Law of the 24th May, 1656 ; *Handv. van Amsterd.* p. 643.

[2] *Ad Pand.* xx. 2. § 14 in f.

[3] As to this right of preference, see *Weesk. van Amst.* art. 28, 29 ; *Vlaarding.* art. 64 ; *Leyden,* art. 42 ; *Goud.* art. 47 ; *Enkhuis.* tit. vi. art. 6 ; *Alkmaar,* tit. vi. art. 7, and similar others. *Gorinchem,* art. 26 ; *Briel,* art. 92.

[4] *Weesk. van Leyden,* art. 43-47 ; *Goud.* art. 75-79.

foreigners, and if lent by the parent or testator, it is not at the risk of the guardian, who is free from gross fault.[5]

SEC. 11.

CLVI. Guardians may claim remuneration in respect of their administration of the guardianship, unless they be relations in the ascendant line, to whom it is not in some places allowed. The amount of such remuneration varies in different places; but in the absence of any statute, it has been the custom to allow them a 40th part on the receipts, an 80th on expenses, and a 100th on money found in the estate, on property sold and on capital paid up.[6]

SEC. 12.

CLVII. The annual accounts which guardians are by various laws required to render to the Orphan Chamber, generally in the presence of the relations of the ward, should not be confounded with those accounts which ought to be rendered to the ward himself, at the termination of the guardianship;[7] and the laws which require that an account should be rendered of a remission justly and equitably made by the parent, should be understood as referring to the above annual or biennial rendering of accounts.[8]

[5] Cod. v. 51. 2. *Decis & Resol. van den Hove van Holland*, n. 332; *Weesk. van Alkmaar*, and similar others, t. viii. art. 6; *Enkhuis.* t. viii. art. 4; *Zype*, t. viii. art. 5; *Briel*, art. 122.

[6] Upon a decision of the Supreme Court, 28th July, 1725, in Lybrechts *Reden. Vertoog, Append.* tom. ii. lit. Z, p. 508.

[7] This distinction is expressly made in the *Weesk. van Gouda*, art. 8, and *Leyden*, art. 53.

[8] *Weesk. van Alkmaar*, tit. ix. art. 2, and similar others; *Briel*, art. 142; *Middelb.* art. 69.

Sec. 14.

CLVIII. The privilege attaching to debts due to a ward, namely, that they may be recovered by parate execution,[1] does not attach to old debts which have devolved on the ward from other sources, as by inheritance.[2]

Chapter X.—Sec. 1.

CLIX. On the death of the ward, his property should be delivered up and the accounts rendered to his heirs; and if there be any doubt as to the right of the heirs, the Orphan Chamber has no power to retain the property, but it should be delivered to them under proper security on their summarily proving their right.[3]

CLX. Although it has been the custom in many places that the guardianship should terminate *ipso jure* at the age of 25 years, yet many pupillary laws either do not discharge the wards from guardianship until they have with the consent of the surviving parent or the nearest relatives applied for such discharge,[4] or they empower the magistrates to retain under guardianship those whom they do not consider sufficiently competent to administer their own property ;[5] and from a decree of this kind (granting that the guardianship does not terminate *ipso jure* at majority), an appeal can hardly be allowed.

[1] *Rechtsgel. Observ.* part iii. obs. 17.

[2] Dig. xlv. 1. 2. § 2, and *Weesk. Van Alkmaar*, tit. vi. art. 6, and t. viii. art. 6.

[3] *Weesk. van Vlaarding.* art. 71 ; *Medemblick*, art. 65.

[4] *Weesk. van Medembl.* art. 58, 59 ; *Vlaarding.* art. 66 ; *Alkmaar*, tit. x. art. 4, 6 ; *Monnick. Purmer. Graft. Enkhuis. de Zype*, ibid ; *Briel*, art. 153, 155 ; *Rotterd.* art. 38, 39 ; *Middelb.* art. 52, 53.

[5] *Weesk. van Amsterd.* art. 24, 25 ; *Gorinchem*, art. 42, 43 ; *Leyden* art. 65, 67, 68 ; *Gouda*, art. 97, 98.

SEC. 3.

CLXI. In order to obtain *Venia Ætatis*, it is necessary that the minor, if a male, should have attained the age of 20, or if a female, 18 years. The application is made to the Supreme Power (in former times, to the States), by petition, wherein the above age should be stated and proved; and on this petition the pupillary magistrate and the Orphan Chamber, after having heard the guardians and relations, give their advice: after which *Venia Ætatis* is granted by rescript.[6] This proceeding should be carefully distinguished from that emancipation (as it were) of the wards, or discharge from guardianship, which some laws allow the magistrates to grant: and of which we have already spoken.[7]

SEC. 4.

CLXII. When guardians, whether testamentary or dative, are suspected, the superior magistrates, and in some places even the pupillary magistrates, may, after hearing the relatives of the ward, remove them, either upon a complaint made to them, or *ex officio ;* but in most cases without injury to the guardians' reputation.

SEC. 5.

CLXIII. In case of a ward's continued absence for a period of 16, 18, or 20 years, or even a shorter period, his property should, after diligent inquiry has been made

---

⁶ *Weesk. van Gorinch.* art. 42; *Alkmaar*, tit. x. art. 7, 8; *Monnick. Purmer. Enkhuis. Graft. Zype*, ibid.; *Resol. Holland*, 9 and 14th Dec. 1669.

⁷ Th. 110; and see *Weesk. van Dord.* art. 57, junct. art. 56.

in this respect, be delivered over to the next heirs under personal or real security.[1] Where the period has not been defined by law, it should be left, as well as the matter itself, to the determination of the judge.

CHAPTER XI.—SEC. 1, 2, 3.

CLXIV. Those who through infirmity of body or mind are incapable of administering their own property, may either retain their guardian or curator, or accept one appointed by the Orphan Chamber or (as in some places) by the superior magistrates; a decree from whom would also seem to be necessary, where the incapacity arises after the attainment of majority.[2]

SEC. 4.

CLXV. A prodigal may, whether the relatives apply for it or not, be interdicted by the superior magistrates (not, regularly, by the Court of Holland) from the administration of his property; and a curator may, after due investigation into the matter, be appointed, reserving, however, an appeal to the Court, after the charges have been heard and rejected.[3] The effect of such a decree when duly promulgated is that, like a ward, the person so interdicted cannot bind himself, and his property is kept in the custody of the Orphan Chamber.

[1] *Rechtsgel. Observ.* part i. obs. 16; and *Supplem.* part iv. p. 197, and New Law of Amsterd. 30th Jan., 1777.

[2] See *Weesk. van Rhynl.* art. 50; *Haarlem,* art. 11; *Dordr.* art. 59; *Vlaarding.* art. 67; *Medembl.* art. 60.

[3] *Weesk. van Leyden,* art. 69; *Gouda,* art. 100; *Rhynl.* art. 48; *Alkmaar,* t. xi. art. 3, and similar others; *Briel,* art. 162; *Medembl.* art 60; *Vlaarding.* art. 67; *Dordr.* art. 59; *Haarlem,* art. 11; and see Resol. of the Court, 17 Jun., 1722.|

CLXVI. The force of this decree is cancelled and the prodigal discharged from curatorship, by a counter-decree of the same magistrates; against which no appeal can be taken; as contended by the Amsterdammers and established by them before the States on the 27th August, 1750, whilst deliberating on the general Law of the 24th February, 1751.

SEC. 5.

CLXVII. The rule laid down in respect of the property of insane persons, prodigals, and the like, viz., that it should be under the control of the Orphan Chamber, has been most wisely extended by the laws of *Leyden* and *Gouda*[4] to property devolving, as, for instance, by inheritance, during their absence, on persons who have gone abroad without leaving a procurator at home.

SEC. 7.

CLXVIII. Our laws do not allow of a married woman being appointed curator over her husband if insane or prodigal.[5]

CHAPTER XII.—SEC. 2.

CLXIX. Legitimate children are not only those who have been conceived in wedlock, but those also who though conceived *before* were born *after* marriage,

---

[4] *Weesk. van Leyden,* art. 32; *Goud.* art, 63.

[5] See *Rechtsgel. Observ.* part i. obs. 17: and Supplem. part iv. p. 198; and see *Weesk. van Rhynl.* art. 53; *Leyden,* art. 72; *Gouda,* art. 100. [But see Voet *ad Pand.* xxvii. 10. § 10; and xxiii. 2. § 48.—Tr.]

and whom the father by having married the mother during pregnancy has acknowledged to have been conceived to him.[1]

SEC. 3.

CLXX. Where the marriage has been dissolved, a child in order to be deemed legitimate should be born within 10 months, *i.e.*, 300 days after the dissolution; notwithstanding the decision of the Court of the 11th July, 1537.[2]

SEC. 9.

CLXXI. Dotal instruments are not required in a legitimation by subsequent marriage; but a registration of it amongst the public acts (which is necessary in all cases of marriage) is sufficient.[3] At Amsterdam it is required by the ancient local law, and even now by custom, that the children who are to be legitimized should be present at the celebration of the marriage, and that the father should in the presence of the magistrates acknowledge them to have been procreated by him.[*]

CLXXII. Legitimation by rescript from the Sovereign neither deprives a third person of the property which, in consequence of the illegitimacy of the children, has already been acquired by him or is to devolve

---

[1] Cod. v. 27. 11.

[2] See *Sentent. van den Hoogen en Provinc. Raad*, dec. 93.

[3] This is sufficient under the *Roman Law* also: see Code ii. 7. 4. § 4.

[*] [A curious case is reported by Stockmans in his *Decis. Brabant.* (dec. 66), where the legitimacy of a child who had been legitimated by subsequent marriage was upheld even as against the declaration of the mother (made after the husband's death) that the child was conceived to another.—Tr.]

on him under a *fidei-commissum ;*† nor confers on the children so legitimized the right of succession to the property of those paternal relatives who have neither expressly nor tacitly consented to the legitimation : except as regards persons born after such legitimation upon a new marriage, to whom the legitimized children may succeed.

CHAPTER XIII.—SEC. 1.

CLXXIII. Foreigners, according to *Grotius* and to the ancient laws, are all those who are born out of Holland, unless born of a Dutch father during his absence on affairs of State, or in the service of the India Companies, or of a mother whilst casually travelling beyond the limits of the country.

SEC. 3.

CLXXIV. Although relatives born and domiciled out of Holland may be heirs to foreigners residing in Holland, yet under the former law such inheritance was subject to a tax called *Recht van Exue,* established either by charters or even by ancient custom, and wont to be levied by the Dutch cities even as against each other ; unless it had been remitted by agreement entered into between them.   But by a recent law of Holland[4] this tax has been wholly abolished.

CLXXV. In judicial proceedings the condition of foreigners residing elsewhere is sometimes more and

† [But see *Holl. Cons.* d. i. cons. 150.   The authorities on this point are collected in La Leck's *Register,* d. i., p. 495, sqq. (edit. 1778, *Utrecht*), tit. *Legitimatie.*—Tr.]

[4] *Publ.* 6 April, 1797.

sometimes less advantageous than that of citizens and inhabitants. It is less advantageous in a case of arrest for establishing jurisdiction, and in respect of security to appear in court and to satisfy the judgment: more advantageous in respect of the speedy termination of the former proceeding within three days (which period is at some places termed *dwars-nagt*), and of a prompt decision upon an arrest whereon they may be detained.[1]

Sec. 4.

CLXXVI. The right to tolls, as well as the exemption from them, which was in former times granted to citizens only, and not to foreigners, has been abolished by a recent law of Holland.[2]

Sec. 6.

CLXXVII. Letters of Naturalization simply granted to strangers do not confer on them the right of attaining to dignities.[3] They are not, however, as supposed by Bynkershoek, useless[4] (although magistrates may, even in the absence of such letters, treat foreigners in the light of citizens), for even where a foreigner may not have obtained the citizenship of any place, these letters allow him a defence as against a foreign people, and exempt him from being summoned away, whether in civil or criminal matters, by the ordinary and competent judge.

The advantages of Letters of Naturalization *ad honores* are greater, for thereby an opening is afforded to

---

[1] *Keur van Leyden*, art. 114

[2] *Placaat*, 5 March, 1795.

[3] *Resol. Holland*, 25 Sept., 1670.

[4] Bynkersh. *Q.J. Publ.* l. ii. cap. ii. p. 265.

persons born out of Holland of acquiring most of our dignities, though not in contravention of the laws prevailing in the different cities.

BOOK II.

CHAPTER I.—SEC. 14.

CLXXVIII. By the Law of Holland, as under the Roman Law, incorporeal things, where the law or the will of the owner has given no direction to the contrary, are not comprehended under movables or immovables ; as in the case of legacies, agreements, and mortgages.

CLXXIX. But when it becomes necessary to refer them to one or other of these classes, then prædial servitudes and actions *in rem* should be considered as immovables ; and actions *in personam*, although for the recovery of immovable property, or though immovable property may have been mortgaged for the debt, should be reckoned as movables ; excepting the action arising on the instrument called *Kusting-brief*, by which immovable property which has been sold is, by the same formal instrument of cession, mortgaged to the seller for the price, so as to give the latter a preferent right as against prior general mortgages.[5]

CLXXX. The right of tithes, fines,* and emphyteutic or ground-rent, and annual real rents,† and even

[5] Boel erroneously dissents from this opinion ; *ad Loen. Decis.* cas. 50. p. 316-318.

* [See Grot. B. ii. ch. 46, and Van der Linden, *Instit.* p. 171, 172.—Tr.]

† [*Canon ;* see Grot. ii. 40 § 2.—Tr.]

mixed rents imposed on land (viz., such as cannot be redeemed), seem referable to the class of immovables.

CLXXXI. Bonds or securities (*obligatien*) whether public or private, given for money lent, although they be secured by mortgage, as well as annual mixed rents (such as the Dutch rents), which are redeemable, are unquestionably included among movables.[1]

CHAPTER II.—SEC. 12.

CLXXXII. The possession of *res hereditariæ*, or the property composing an inheritance, does not pass *ipso jure* to the heir upon his adiating the inheritance, but a new taking or apprehension thereof is necessary ; for the maxim *Le mort saisit le vif* does not hold in Holland.[2]

CHAPTER III.—SEC. 5.

CLXXXIII. The true owner of property, movable as well as immovable, which has been alienated without his consent, not only by one who has stolen it, but even by one to whom it has been lent, or let, or given in deposit, or by any other person not having a mandate to sell, may legally claim it from any one who is in possession of it, without making restitution of the price paid by him.[3] This rule obtains in the Law of Holland,

[1] Van Alphen, *Papeg.* d. ii. p. 480. [See also Boel *ad Loen.* cas. 50.—Tr.]

[2] *Holl. Consult.* d. ii. cons. 305.

[3] See decisions in Van Leeuw. *Cens. Forens.* part i. book iv. ch. 7. § 17; *Nederl. Adv.* tom. ii. cons. 68 ; De Haas, *Nieuw Holl. Consult.* cas. 25 ; Boel *ad Loen.* cas. 50, p. 321, sq. Nor does the dissent of Groenewegen (*LL. Abrog. ad Instit.* iv. i. § 16. n. 3) and of Matthæus (*Paroem.* vii. n. 7), or the decision in Neostadt (*Dec. Supr. Cur.* 86) and Loenius (cas. 9 & 80) on a case not similar, affect to the contrary.

even in respect of public Dutch securities sold without the owner's consent;[4] but not so in the Law of Zeeland.[5]

Sec. 6.

CLXXXIV. The exceptions to this rule are : 1st, in respect of goods which have been *bonâ fide* sold in public market,—the price whereof should be restored;[6] 2nd, in respect of goods, even though stolen, which have been given in pledge to public pawnbrokers;[7] 3rd, at some places, in respect of goods sold by old-clothes merchants, after having been publicly exposed for eight days (which is not, however, the general Law of Holland, since the purport of the law of the 17th March, 1563, and of similar other laws is different); and 4th, in respect of gold or silver sold to a goldsmith for a just price, and by him openly exposed.[8]

Chapter IV.—Sec. 7-26.

CLXXXV. The old distinction between the nobler and other birds and beasts seems to be no longer recognized by the recent Laws of Holland, since every owner of land is now [9] permitted to hunt *any* game on his own land though prohibited from doing so on another's land.[10]

---

[4] See *Resol. Holl.* 25 Feb., 1683.

[5] *Ord. Zeeland.* 31 May, 1679 ; 25 Sept., 1695.

[6] *Decis. Cur.* 26 Jan., 1674 ; *Bell. Jurid.* cas. i. p. 3. [Matth *Paroem.* vii. 17.—Tr.]

[7] *Rechtsgel. Observ.* part ii. obs. 28. See also *Ord. Haarlem* of the 17 March, 1750, art. 5 ; *Keur. van Haarlem,* t. i. p. 294.

[8] *Plac.* 9 Dec., 1661, art. 51. [See *Gr. Plac. Boek* d. ii. p. 2775.—Tr.]

[9] *Publ. Holl.* 28 July, 1795. art. 1, 2.

[10] *Ibid.* art. 1, 2.

SEC. 27.

CLXXXVI. The privileged right of Hunting on the lands of private parties,[1] or even in public places, does not any longer belong to particular persons ;[2] unless any one has acquired the right of hunting from those to whom such right belongs.[3]

SEC. 8 & 28.

CLXXXVII. By the most recent law, hunting and fowling with any kind of weapon is permitted to every one on his own property or leasehold ;[4] provided he does not discharge such weapon in the direction of the high-way or of another's land ;[5] but it is not lawful either to hunt on or to send forth dogs into another's land without the consent in writing of the owner.[6]   Disputes arising in respect of hunting are entertained by the judge of the place, reserving an appeal to the Court; the forestal jurisdiction being now wholly abolished.[7]

SEC. 23.

CLXXXVIII. A new law has also been passed in respect of the right of Fishing [8] which has again been in certain respects altered and added to by a later law.[9]

SEC. 32.

CLXXXIX. Things lost continue to belong to the owner; and after he has been summoned by the public crier to claim them, but does not appear, they pass to

---

[1] Art. 2.   [2] Art. 1.   [3] Art. 1.
[4] Art. 1 & 2.   [5] Art. 3.   [6] Art. 2, 4, 6.   [7] Art. 9.
[8] *Publ. Holland*, 18 Aug., 1795.   [9] *Publ. Holl.* 10 Feb. 1796.

the finder, not to the Treasury.[10] When wood and timber have been detached and carried away from rafts by the force of the stream, notice thereof should forthwith be given to the chamber which presides over this kind of trade.[11]

SEC. 33.

CXC. Uninhabited lands and islands, discovered in the sea, pass to the discoverer, notwithstanding the law of the States General of the 27th March, 1614.*

SEC. 34.

CXCI. An enemy's ship, captured by a merchant vessel which had not been sent out for the purpose of capture, belongs to the masters and sailors capturing it, not to the owner of the vessel or of the merchandise conveyed therein.[12]

CXCII. A ship captured by the enemy becomes, by the reason of law, the property of the enemy capturing it, even though it may not have been taken into a port or to the place where the fleet is lying;[13] and therefore if it be recovered or recaptured by a citizen of Holland it passes to him who has so recaptured it, and not to the original owner. But this rule has been tempered by the laws of the States General, and more recently by the laws of the 13th April, 1677, 31st May, 1697, and 6th June, 1702.[14] If, however, it has been taken into a

[10] Voet ad Pand. xli. i. § 9, in med.

[11] Publ. Holl. 22 July, 1677, and 18 January, 1698. [See Gr. Pl. Boek, d. iii. p. 629, and d. iv. p. 605.—Tr.]

* [Gr. Pl. Boek, d. i. p. 563.—Tr.]

[12] Bynkersh. Quæst. Jur. Publ. lib. i. c. 20.

[13] Voet ad Pand. xlix. 15, § 3.   [14] Voet d. 1. § 4.

hostile port and confiscated, the right of the owners becomes wholly extinct ;[1] nor, if sold to the citizen of a friendly nation, can it be seized as hostile property, though it may not as yet have reached the port of such friendly nation. The decree of the States General of the 27th November, 1666,[*] is, however, at variance with this doctrine.[2]

SEC. 36.

CXCIII. Although the Treasury of the Sovereign might take possession of shipwrecked goods cast upon the shore, the owner whereof had not appeared, and which in former times passed to the Sovereign after the lapse of a year; yet it does not appear from the very ancient Law of Holland, at least as tempered by the practice of the Civil Law, that the true owner should be shut out by the Treasury by the brief period of a few weeks.[3] In course of time, however, the right of the Treasury seems to have been so improperly construed that it was to be preferred to the owner who might appear; and hence it became necessary to grant various charters or privileges in order to support the right of the owner to the shipwrecked goods, and to protect them from others who might seize upon the wreck. The principal enactment of this kind is the

[1] Bynkershoek, *Q. Jur. Pub.* l. i. c. 4, in f.
[* See Van den Berg. *Nederl. Advys Boek*, d. ii. cons. 61.—Tr.]
[2] See Bynkersh. d. l.
[3] Phil. a. Leidis, *de Cura Reipubl.* &c., cap. i. p. 3; Old Stat. of Zeeland, of 1256, art. 35, 36; and of 1495, cap. iv. art. 13; Decis. of the Court in *de Memor. van 't Hof over Strand-roof* of 9 Jan. 1764 in *de Byvoegs. op de Nederl. Jaarb.* d. xxii. p. 1742–1747, and *'t Bericht van den Bailluw Testart*, van 4 July, 1768, § 54, in *de N. Nederl. Jaarb van* 1769, p. 634, sqq.

Law of Charles V. of the 16th March, 1529,[4] and of Philip II. of the 15th May, 1574.[5] Several laws of the States of Holland relating to this subject may be found in the *Groot Placaat-Boek*[6] (the latest of them being the law of the 2nd December, 1663[7]), and most of them have frequently been reviewed by the Court of Holland.

CXCIV. And on these laws two controversies have arisen in our own times: *firstly*, whether under *art.* 8 of the *Instructions*, the Court possesses sole jurisdiction not only civilly as regards the right to the shipwrecked goods, but also criminally in respect of the plunder of wrecked vessels; and not only as against those who may have been apprehended in the criminal act or have taken to flight, but also against thos+ who, whilst residing in their place of domicile, may have been suspected of such crime. The latter question the Court has held in the affirmative;[8] but Testard[9] has, correctly as I think, denied the preceding proposition.

CXCV. The other question was, whether these goods were so far under the care and supervision of the Treasurer of domanial property that no one, not even the owner himself, could take, collect, or have the custody of them, but ought to obtain them from the Treasurer after paying the salvage. And on this question the Court was in favour of the affirmative. But would it

---

[4] Transcribed by the Court in the above decision, *Byvoegs. op de N. Nederl. Jaarb.* d. xxii. p. 1760, seqq.
[5] *Groot Plac. Boek*, d. ii. p. 2117.   [6] d. i. p. 1072, sqq.
[7] Ibid. d. ii. p. 3082.
[8] In the treatise above cited, *Byvoegs. op de Jaarb.* d. xxii. p. 1731, sqq.
[9] *'T Bericht op den Brief van 't Hof; N. Nederl. Jaarb. van* 1769, p. 578, sqq.

be competent for the owner or his agent, as, for instance, the master of the vessel, to collect the shipwrecked goods on his own authority, and to carry them to his own residence or to the place to which they were consigned? The celebrated Testard in his treatise above cited, and subsequently the magistrates of Amsterdam also,[1] have contended in favour of the proposition.

CXCVI. The latter controversy has been decided, and the whole subject has been definitely settled by a new law of the States of Holland ;[2] whereby the owners, if present, are prevented neither from collecting the wrecks nor, if absent, from reclaiming the shipwrecked goods within fourteen days; nor the magistrates of the place from keeping them in the meanwhile in their custody.[3] In Zeeland a law no less full and equitable had already preceded this.[4]

CXCVII. Although shipwrecked goods, the owner whereof is not known, may be sold by the Treasury after the lapse of a year and six weeks, yet it seems that by the more recent law of Holland, the owner may claim them even after that time.[5]

Sec. 38.

CXCVIII. Treasure found by a person on his own land, passes by the law of Holland wholly to the finder; but if found on another's land, it is divided between the

---

[1] In an excellent treatise entitled *Harmonie of Overeenstemming tusschen de Priviligien en Placaaten op 't stuk van de Strand en Zeevonderyen*, in *de N. Nederl. Jaarb. van* 1772, p. 286, sqq.

[2] *Plac.* 22 July, 1772.

[3] See *Groot Plac. Boek*, d. ix. p. 811, sqq.

[4] *Plac.* 14 Jun. 1751: *Groot Plac. Boek*, d. viii. p. 907, sqq.

[5] Boel *ad Loen. Decis. cas.* 94 p. 595 ; *Bericht van Testard*, § 56 & 59

owner and the finder; notwithstanding the law of the 8th January, 1487,[6] which only relates to shipwrecked goods, whereof the owner is not known.[7]

CHAPTER V.—SEC. 3.

CXCIX. Various particular laws of Holland,[8] and also the general law of Zeeland,[9] have carefully provided against alienations in fraud of creditors (which if made by one who has already made cession to the Court, are by the Placaat of the 4th October, 1540,[10] declared *ipso jure* void), being made shortly before cession, say, to one creditor, to the prejudice of the others; and by all these laws such alienations are declared void, unless they have preceded the cession to the Court by two months, or six or four weeks (for the periods fixed by the several laws are various), and the other precautions prescribed by these laws have been also observed.

SEC. 4.

CC. But alienations in fraud of creditors made at any time, by one who is insolvent but has not yet made cession to the Court, are not *ipso jure* void; but may be rescinded within one year by means of the *actio Pauliana* (which has in this respect been adopted by our laws), without the necessity of *restitutio in integrum*: and a purchaser who has been privy to the fraud is not entitled to restitution of the price paid by him, if not

---

[6] Art. 15; *Groot Plac. Boek*, d. iv. p. 1213.
[7] *Memor. van 't Hof*, p. 1758; Testard, *Bericht*, p. 626, sqq.
[8] For which see *Groot Plac, Boek*, d. iv. p. 468, sqq.
[9] *Plac.* 27 Jun. 1776, art. 18, 22–24.   [10] Art. 3.

F 2

found in the debtor's estate.[1] But a payment to one of
the creditors not made for the purpose of procuring
any benefit for the debtor, is valid.[2]

SEC. 11.

CCI. Although movable property, as well as public
securities (*obligatien*), may, even under the law of
Holland, be legally alienated by simple delivery, yet
there is an exception in respect of larger ships and
those instruments wherefrom annual returns are derived;
which, to provide against the duty of two and a half
per cent. being fraudulently avoided, are required to be
delivered or transferred in the presence of a judge. At
Amsterdam, however, the larger ships are usually transferred in the presence of a notary and witnesses.[3]

SEC. 13.

CCII. The alienation of immovable property, as well
by the ancient law,[4] as by the Placaat of the 10th May,
1529, cannot be effected without a solemn cession in
law, in the presence of the judge of the place; nor,
under various laws of the States,[5] without the payment
of a fortieth part of the price to the Public Treasury.
When the cession has been made, it passes the *dominium*
or property in the thing sold, though the instrument of
cession may not have been delivered.[6]

[1] Voet *ad Pand.* xlii. 8. § 19.   [2] Ibid. § 17.
[3] See Lybrechts, *Reden. Vertoog*, d. i. p. 10.
[4] *Rechtsgel. Obs.* part iii. obs. 32.
[5] The latest of which is the *Ordonnance* of the 9th May, 1744.
[6] See *Boel. ad Loen. Decis.* cas. 17, p. 157, sqq. [See also Neostad.
Decis. Supr. Cur. 70; and not. to *Decis. Cur. Holl.* n. 32, Matth.
Paroem. part v. n. 13.—Tr.]

In respect of legal mortgages, however, and of alienations under title of dowry, community by marriage, antenuptial contract, testament and division of inheritance* (provided the value of the thing does not exceed the hereditary share), there is no necessity for this cession.†

Both these rules have been adopted by the Law of Zeeland also.[7]

Sec. 14.

CCIII. The mere sale and delivery of the thing sold, if the price has not been paid or credit given in respect thereof,‡ does not pass the property therein to the purchaser, although it may not have been stated that the thing was sold for ready money.[8] At *Middelburg*, however, the rule is different.[9] At *Amsterdam* a demand should be made of the purchaser within six weeks, and he should be sued for the price within the six days next following, or the thing purchased be put under arrest within six weeks ;[10] and at *Leyden* the price should be demanded within fourteen days, and the action instituted on the next following Court day, and prosecuted without interruption.[11]

* [See an exception in *Nederl. Advysb.* d. i. cons. 285, p. 658.—Tr.]

† [See Groenew. *ad* leg. abrog. Inst. iii. 23. 8; Wassenaer. *Pr. Jud.* c. ix. § 9. 10.—Tr.]

[7] *Keur. van Zeeland,* cap. ii. art. 11; *Costumen van Middelburg,* rubr. viii. art. 2.

‡ [As to what amounts to *giving credit,* see Voet *ad Pand.* xix. 11 § 11.—Tr.]

[8] *Rechtsgel. Obs.* part 3. obs. 33 ; *Handv. van Amsterd.* p. 502, 520; and the new *Ordonn.* of the 27th Jan., 1741, ibid.

[9] *Costum. van Middelb.* rubr. viii. art. 3.

[10] *Keur. van Amst.* 31 Jan., 1658, and 10 Feb., 1682, and 18 Sept. 1697 ; and 27 Jan., 1741; *Handv.* p. 503.

[11] *Keur. van Leyd.* 13 Sept. 1659 ; Mieris, *Handv. van Leyden,* p. 251.

CCIV. A person who, knowing himself to be insolvent, has fraudulently purchased anything from another, and has shortly after made cession to the Court, though credit may have been given him for the price, is bound to restore the thing to the seller claiming it :[1] and this rule seems to have been adopted in the decisions of both Courts, upon a statute of *Antwerp*,[2] contrary to the custom of *Amsterdam*,[3] as well as to the reason of the law, which is relied upon by *Bynkershoek*.[4]

CHAPTER VI.—SEC. 2.

CCV. A *bonâ fide* possessor, who is in possession of the property of another by a particular title, acquires the fruits by gathering, as under the Roman Law, and is not bound to restore them even to the owner on his appearing. This has also been provided at *Voorn*,[5] and in Zeeland,[6] and has been generally adopted.*

CHAPTER VIII.—SEC. 7.

CCVI. Although previous to the publication of this work of *Grotius*, both the Courts had frequently acted on the principles of the Civil Law respecting the doc-

[1] *Decis. & Resol. van den Hove van Holland*, n. 118 ; Neostad. *Decis. Supr. Cur.* 5.

[2] *Costum. van Antwerp*, t. lviii. art. 7. See also *Costum. van Vlissing.* cap. vii, art. 6. p. 70.

[3] Of which see Evidence given on the 15th April, 1617 : *Handv.* p. 505.

[4] *Quest. J. Priv.* l. iii. cap. 15. p. 499, sqq.

[5] *Keuren van Voorn*, A. 1519, art 56.

[6] *Keuren van Zeeland*, cap. ii. art. 3.

* [See also *Nederl. Advysb.* d. i. cons. 108. p. 280; Sande. *Decis. Fris.* iii. 15 def. 1., P. Voet *ad Inst.* ii. 1. 36. § 5. Vinn. *ad. Inst.* ii. 1. 35. § 10. 11; Groenew. *ad LL. abr.* cod. iii. 32. 22.—Tr.]

trine of prescriptions,[7] yet it has since become the practice, on his authority, and in 1637 was held by the
Court of Holland as a rule (as *Loenius*, who was present
at the discussion, testifies,[8]) that prescription is com-
pleted, in respect of immovable property and annual
rents, by the third of a century, but that in respect of
actions *in personam* a prescription of thirty years is
sufficient;[9] and this rule most authors have with good
reason adopted in respect also of movable property.
And even in respect of the hypothecary action for
immovable property against a third party in possession
Grotius allows the same term of prescription.[10]   He has
also adopted some of the shorter prescriptions of the
Civil Law, as that of a year in an action for injury,[11] of
two years in respect of the exception of the non-receipt
of consideration (*non numeratæ pecuniæ*);[12] and of four
years in cases of relief on the ground of minority.[13]

CCVII. But since in these prescriptions of a third of
a century and of thirty years, neither *bona fides* nor a
just title is required,[14] and since the recovery of movable
property from one who is in possession of it by a just
title is commonly considered more difficult amongst us
than it was amongst the Romans, the reason of the Law
of Holland is by no means opposed to the usucapion of
a movable thing in three years.[15]

---

[7] Neostad. *Decis. Cur. Holl.* iii. § 10; decis. viii. § 2; dec. xiii. and
dec. xv. *Decis. & Resol. van den Hove.* n. 356.

[8] *Decis.* 76.

[9] And see Bynkersh. *Q. J. Priv.* l. ii. cap. 15. init.

[10] Book ii, ch. 48. § 44.   [11] Book iii. ch. 35. § 3.

[12] B. iii. ch. 5. § 3.

[13] B. iii. ch. 48. § 13, &c.; and see *Costum. van Rhynl.* art. 102.

[14] Matth. *Paroem.* ix. § 2 and 3.

[15] Of which see *Costum. van Rhynl.* art. 102; Matth. *Paroem.* ix. § 6.

Sec. 8.

CCVIII. Although the ancient prescription of one year (which required both *bona fides* and a just title, and the cognizance of the *Schepenen*, and confirmed either *dominium* or possession),[1] was still in use about the middle of the seventeenth century,[2] yet it seems to have since passed into disuse, in consequence of the more frequent use of the interdict for retaining possession.*

Sec. 9.

CCIX. In Zeeland, as regards immovable property, the prescription of twenty years has been adopted against parties present, and of thirty against parties absent;[3] and this prescription requires neither *bona fides* nor a just title, but possession only. Nor does the reason of the Law of Zeeland allow of the doctrine that as regards movable property, the longer prescription, namely, that accomplished in thirty years, is there necessary; but as regards these, the usucapion of three years, and in respect of incorporeal property the prescription of thirty years, seem to have been adopted from the Roman law.

CCX. Prescription, even *longissimi temporis*, fails to run by our law not only against wards who are under puberty, as under the Roman Law, but also against those who have already attained the age of puberty.[4]

---

[1] Of which see Van de Wall, *Handv. van Dordrecht*, p. 141, sqq.

[2] Van de Wall, ib. and Groeneweg. *ad. Cod.* vii. 39, § 10 and 11.

* [*Mandament van Maintenue.* Van der Linden, Inst. p. 185.—Tr.]

[3] *Keur. van Zeeland*, cap. ii. art. 2; *Costum. van Vlissing.* cap. xxi. art. 2.

[4] *Weeskeur. van Alkmaar*, t. vi. art. 8; *Graft, Purmerend, Monnickend.* ibid.; *Enkhuis.* t. vi. art. 7; *Briel*, art. 93; *Medembl.* art. 67; *Grootebroek*, art. 11.

CHAPTER IX.—SEC. 26.

CCXI. It has been decided by the Court of Holland that when a fidei-commissary estate is augmented by alluvion, such augmentation is not subject to the *fidei-commissum*.[5]

CHAPTER X.—SEC. 8.

CCXII. He who has built on another's land of which he was in possession *bonâ fide*, may by the Law of Holland, on losing possession, recover the *useful* expenses incurred by him, even by action.[*]

CCXIII. But a lessee who has built with the consent of the owner, may recover only the value of the materials; but cannot on this ground retain the land, although it is bound to him by way of legal mortgage, until he should receive the value.[6] If he has built without such consent, he may before the termination of the lease remove that which he has built. Not so in Zeeland.[7]

CCXIV. Many authors maintain, contrary to the opinion of *Grotius*, who has followed the rule of the Civil Law, that a *malâ fide* possessor may deduct the useful expenses also. Their opinion cannot, however, be admitted.[8]

---

[5] 23 Octob., 1647; see Bort. *Holl. Leenr.* d. v. t. 3. c. 10. qu. 3. n. 10, p. 178.

[*] [*i.e.* Not only by way of exception to the original action, founded on the right to retain the property until compensation, but (according to the text) by action against the owner, even after eviction.—*MS. Dictata.*—Tr.]

[6] *Ord. Holl.* 26 Sept., 1658, art. 10, 11, 12.

[7] *Ord. Zeeland.* 26 Jan., 1664: art. 5; and see art. 10 & 11.

[8] Arg. d. *Ord. Holl.* (26 Sept., 1658), art. 12.

SEC. 9 & 11.

CCXV. Trees planted on a leasehold estate pass with the land; and an owner who has not directed them to be planted is not bound to restore the value of them.[1] At *Middelburg*, plants, properly so called, may be removed by the lessee;[2] which, however, is not, it seems, to be understood of trees, nor extended to other, even *bonæ fidei*, possessors.

CHAPTER XI.—SEC. 7.

CCXVI. The Confusion or Merger of the estates of two persons, which results from their marriage, takes place *ipso jure*, and brings into community not only the right, but also the possession, without delivery or cession in law; and affects not only present, but also future property.[3]

SEC. 8.

CCXVII. Authors are not agreed as to the origin of this Community, which obtains in Holland and Zeeland.[4] Perhaps ladies who brought their own property in marriage, not content with the statutory portion which would devolve on them, in place of the ancient dowry, after the death of the husband, were wont to stipulate for themselves by antenuptial contract an equal share in the property; and this, which was at first effected by a contract duly entered into, afterwards in process of

---

[1] Ibid. art. 13.   [2] *Costum. van Middelb.* rubr. ix. art. 12.
[3] See *Costum. van Middelb.* rubr. xii. art. 2.
[4] *Rechtsgel. Obs.* part ii. obs. 32: *Supplem.* part iv. p. 238; and *Ord. Dordr.* art. 49, in Van de Wall, p. 1348.

time, and through their frequency, passed into a custom.[5] But lest this custom might be extended farther, or be adopted also between parents and children, the ancient statutes of Zeeland[6] expressly provided that it should be allowed only between husband and wife.[7] And not without reason has it been observed between husband and wife up to the present time; since those who marry are mostly persons of equal condition, whom the law presumes to be equal also in substance.

CCXVIII. This community takes place between the married couple as soon as the marriage has been celebrated, except in the town of *Schoonhoven* and *Vianen*,[8] and at *Middelburg*, where it is required that the parties should have previously retired to the nuptial bed.[9] It does not however obtain—1stly, in a marriage contracted by a minor, without the knowledge of the parents or relatives[10] (and the laws last quoted[10] seem to exclude both parties from the community); and 2ndly, in a marriage which has originated in the abduction of one of the parties, effected even with his or her consent, but without the knowledge of the parents, in contravention of the law of the 25th February, 1751.[11]

SEC. 9.

CCXIX. Community of property between husband and wife takes place on a second marriage, although there

---

[5] Neostad. de *Pact. Antenupt*. obs. ix. in not. p. 33.
[6] A. 1256, art. 82 and 1290, art. 91.
[7] See the New Statutes, cap. ii. art. 20.
[8] *Rechtsgel. Obs.* part ii. obs. 32.
[9] *Costum. van Middelb.* rubr. xii. art. 1 ; where see *De Timmerman*.
[10] *Placaat* of the 4 Oct. 1540, art. 17; *Polit. Ord.* art. 13.
[11] See *supra* Thes. 71, 72.

may be children of the first bed; as decided by the Court[1] and Supreme Court.[2] Nor is the custom under the *Lex hac edictali*, which had then been already adopted in Holland, opposed to this rule : and the arguments urged by *Bynkershoek*[3] and *Barels*[4] do not prove it to be absurd or to require alteration.

SEC. 10.

CCXX. Neither *direct* nor *hereditary feuds* come into the community of property (*Voet*[5] and others apparently dissenting without good reason); though the party, who has brought such property in marriage, ought to keep the other indemnified in respect of a hereditary feud.

Voet has correctly laid down[6] that money realized by the sale of a feud becomes common property.

CCXXI. It is agreed amongst all authors that property subject to a *fidei-commissum*, and even the Trebellianic portion (if the party burthened has not deducted it), do not become common.[7]

SEC. 12.

CCXXII. By virtue of this community of property, even debts contracted before the marriage become common between the husband and wife, as evident both

---

[1] 20 Mar. 1612 & 8 Oct. 1614: see *Decis. van den Hove van Holland*, n. 422.

[2] 31 Jul. 1620. ibid. n. 155.

[3] *Q. J. Priv.* l. ii. c. 2 pr.

[4] *Aanmerk. over eenige onzer aloude gebruiken in de Rechts-oeffeninge*, cap. l.

[5] *Ad Pand.* xxiii. tit 2. § 71.   [6] Ibid § 79.

[7] See Neostad. *Decis. Cur.* v. § 12 and *de Pact. Anten.* obs. 14. p. 46.

from the nature of community and from the express words of the statutes and customs hereon,[8] and confirmed by the evidence of the *Schepenen* in 1677, recorded by *Boel*,[9] who without sufficient reason dissents from an opinion entertained everywhere and by almost every one.

SEC. 13.

CCXXIII. Upon the dissolution of the marriage, the common property, together with the debts, are equally divided between the husband and wife, or their successors; those children, however, who have received any thing out of the common estate, under title of dowry or otherwise, are obliged to bring the same into collation, not only in favour of a mother, but sometimes even of a step-mother.[10]

SEC. 15.

CCXXIV. Although from the nature of the statutory community, each party is on the dissolution of the marriage liable to the extent of a half in respect of the debts contracted before the marriage, as enacted in some places, yet in Holland, since the year 1597, a contrary rule seems to have been followed, on the authority of the Supreme Court,[11] and which the Court has also approved of since,[12] and the Lawyers (including *Grotius*) have adopted. They add, however, less correctly, that a married person who has paid the whole

---

[8] See *Rechtsgel. Obs.* part. iii. obs. 37; *Costum. van Middelb.* rubr. xii. art. 1.

[9] Boel *ad Loen Decis.* cas. 99. p. 640.

[10] De Haas, *Nieuwe Holland. Consult.* cas. 28.

[11] Neostad. *de Pact. Antenupt.* obs. 12, 13.   [12] Loen. *Decis.* cas. 99.

of a debt contracted by himself before the marriage, may reclaim a half share thereof from the heirs of the other party ; a doctrine wholly repugnant to the reason whereon this right is founded, and which *Grotius* seems to have purposely omitted here.

SEC. 17.

CCXXV. The rule is different as regards debts contracted during the marriage; but not as regards debts which arise *ex delicto.*[1]

SEC. 18 & 19.

CCXXVI. The right of abandoning the common estate by a solemn ceremony previous to the interment of the husband is granted to the Widow by several statutes.[2] It does not affect those debts which she herself contracted during the marriage, with the authority of her husband, as decided by the Court on the 6th July, 1633,[3] and much less those which arise in respect of a trade carried on by her.

CHAPTER XII.—SEC. 1.

CCXXVII. It stands to reason that the community of property between husband and wife may be excluded by antenuptial contract, not only expressly, but even tacitly ;[4] and this is confirmed by an opinion given by *Grotius,* in *de Hollandsche Consultatien.*[5]

[1] See the Evidence of the *Schepenen* of *Amsterdam ;* of which *supra,* Th. 222.

[2] *Rechtsgel. Obs.* part ii. obs. 34; and *Supplement.* part iv. p. 240; and see Boel *ad Loen.* cas. 65. p. 434, sqq.

[3] Loen. *Decis.* 65.   [4] Dig. ii. 14. 2. [See *infra,* Th. 247.]

[5] D. iii. st. 2. cons. 182; and see d. ii. cons. 198, and d. iv. cons. 54, 362.

Sec. 3.

CCXXVIII. Antenuptial contracts, in their widest signification, seem hardly capable of being otherwise defined than as *agreements between future spouses or others concerned, regarding the laws or conditions by which the marriage should be regulated.* Whence it appears that they cannot properly be entered into where the spouses, even if minors, are unwilling, and that the consent of the relatives is not necessary to the contracts of majors; and that relatives, and even strangers, who may be disposed to exercise any liberality towards them, are not prohibited from becoming parties thereto; and lastly, that it is competent for the parties, in case of a diversity of statutes, to choose either specifically or generally one or other of the statutes whereby the marriage should be regulated. But contracts or stipulations which are contrary to any prohibitory law, or to morals, or to the nature of marriage, are not valid; amongst which, however, should not be classed the stipulation that the husband may not change his domicile without the consent of the wife, though *Voet*[6] is of a different opinion.*

Sec. 4.

CCXXIX. Antenuptial contracts may be legally entered into *ab initio* without writing; but care should be taken that nothing be done in fraud of the duty imposed on documents requiring the public stamp, or that

---

° Voet *ad Pand.* v. i. § 101. [See Loen. *Decis.* cas. 54.—Tr.]

[* As regards two antenuptial contracts of different dates, see *Nederl. Advijsb.* d. iv. cons. 240.—Tr.]

if such a fault has been committed, it be rectified;[1]
though *De Haas* in his notes on *Van Leeuwen*,[2] and
also the Jurists in *de Rechtsgeleerde Observatien*,[3] vainly
maintain the contrary. In order, however, to render these
nuptial contracts, even when in writing, effectual as
against creditors, they should be entered into either
publicly or in the presence of a notary and witnesses, or
of the relatives of both parties, or before respectable
witnesses.

CCXXX. If in an antenuptial contract reference is
made to an inventory to be separately prepared of the
goods brought in marriage, such inventory shall be valid
if duly and formally made; if not, the contract itself, as
regards the property, shall not be vitiated, but the
quantity or value of such property will have to be proved
by other evidence.[4]

SEC. 5.

CCXXXI. Where no dotal contract has been entered
into before marriage, the statutory community of property comes into force; and this cannot subsequently
be excluded by any act *inter vivos*, unless a separation
not only from bed and board, but also from property
has taken place upon the decree of a judge.[5]

SEC. 6.

CCXXXII. The doctrine in *Thes.* 219, as to the
community of property subsisting in a second marriage

[1] *Plac. Holl.* 30 Sept. 1744, and of 1794, art. 49.
[2] *Cens. Forens.* part i. lib. i. c. 12. § 9.   [3] Part ii. obs. 35.
[4] *Holl. Consult.* d. iii. cons. 164.
[5] Neostad. *de Pact. Antenupt.* obs. 7, 8; and not. (a) ibi.

notwithstanding the *Lex hac edictali*, should also hold in respect of that kind of community which is expressly introduced by antenuptial contract, and which is to be taken in place of the statutory community, and not as a universal partnership; as *Bynkershoek* has correctly laid down and supported by decisions.[6] And hence in such a case, also, a married person will become liable for debts contracted before marriage,[*] although on this point, also, the Court was formerly of a different opinion.[7]

SEC. 8.

CCXXXIII. In establishing this kind of disposition, which by the Law of Holland may be done by ante-nuptial contract, two rules are to be observed: 1. That the will of the parties contracting (whether it be the future spouses, or those who promise or stipulate any-thing in such contracts), should be left entirely free; and 2. That the right of disposing of the property, as well *inter vivos* as *causâ mortis*, should also be left free, and independent of the consent of relatives.

The subjects of a dotal contract are chiefly three: 1. The property of the parties marrying; 2. The pro-perty of the children; and 3. The property of some third party.

CCXXXIV. *First:* As regards the property of the spouses themselves, the more usual stipulations, and indeed those *inter vivos*, are the following:

1. That the property of the parties, either wholly (in which case there will be a universal community of fruits or profits) or in part (the fruits of the residue

---

[6] *Q. Jur. Priv.* l. ii. c. 2.
[*] [1 h. 222.]
[7] Neostad. *Decis. Cur.* 5; and *de Pact. Antenupt.* obs. 14.

G

being reserved to the party stipulating), shall contribute towards sustaining the burthens of the marriage, which by our law attach no less to the wife than to the husband.[1]

2. That the property of the parties shall be in common, either absolutely and immediately, or under condition; which condition whilst it is in force, acts retrospectively. This stipulation has this peculiarity, namely, that it may be extended to immovable property situated at a place where the statutory community is not known, but not at a place where it is prohibited.[2] In other respects it is similar to the statutory community.

3. That the property of the parties shall not be in common.[3]

4. That one party may acquire from another.[4]

CCXXXV. The succession to the property of both or either of the parties may also be defined by antenuptial contract (as established by the testimony on two occasions of a great number of witnesses,[5] and admitted in the Political Ordinance[6]); in which case the succession will be conventional, and cannot be revoked at the will of one party, and is to be preferred not only to the legitimate, but also to testamentary succession;[7] though at the same time a testamentary disposition, revocable at the will of the disposing party, may also be made in an antenuptial contract.[8]

---

[1] See an instance in 't Nederl. Adv. Boek, d. i. cas. 169, sqq.
[2] See Thes. 43.   [3] Of which under sec. 9.
[4] Of this stipulation, see under sec. 9, 10, 16.
[5] 22 Sept., 1574 and 7 May, 1592, in Bort, post Tract. Notabele Poincten van Leenen, p. 362.
[6] Art. 29.   [7] Rechtsgel. Obs. part ii. obs. 36.
[8] Costum. van Rhynland, art. 92; Roseboom, Costum. van Amsterdam, ap. 42. art. 7.

CCXXXVI. The *first* species of these successory contracts or stipulations, which provides that the one party should succeed to the whole estate of the other first-dying, is neither cancelled by the birth of children nor admits of the *querela inofficiosi testamenti*, but from the reason of law it cannot deprive the children born of such marriage of the legitimate portion, which should be paid to them.

CCXXXVII. The *second* species allots to the survivor a *filial* or child's portion ; which, if there be children of a former marriage, is to be determined strictly according to the rule of the law *hac edictali* ;[9] and if there be no such children, it should be liberally construed, according to the intention of the contracting parties, as a *virile* share in the property left by the first-dying spouse.

CCXXXVIII. If a filial portion has been left to the surviving spouse under the condition " if children be born," then, failing such condition, the share is clearly not due on this *casus omissus* ; [10] but if it has been left absolutely, and if no children be born, then, from the reason of law, it includes the entire inheritance, and not a half, as *Van Leeuwen*,[11] *Voet*,[12] and others have without sufficient reason maintained.

CCXXXIX. The *third* species admits strangers, either certain or uncertain, to succeed to the property of the parties. In the former case, such a disposition, if made without a regular contract entered into with them, is like a testament, revocable ;[13] but if promised

[9] See Voet *ad Pand.* xxiii. 2. § 120, 125, sqq.
[10] Dig. xxiv. 3. 22.
[11] *Cens. Forens.* part. i. lib. i. cap. 12. § 15.
[12] *Ad Pand.* xxiii. 2. § 129.
[13] Roseboom, *Costum. van Amsterd.* cap. xlii. art 9.

to them, they joining in the stipulation, it cannot be revoked;[1] contrary to the rule which obtains in respect of the other kind of successory contracts.[2]

CCXL. In the latter case, or where it has been declared that the property should revert to the side from whence it came, a new succession *ab intestato* would seem to be introduced, which if not confirmed by the mutual promises of the spouses, will not prevent a contrary disposition by testament,[3] nor affect a prior disposition in favour of relatives ; and in this sense I approve of the doctrine of *Voet*.[4] If such prior disposition has been made in favour of a stranger, it seems to be a question of will.

CCXLI. *Secondly:* In antenuptial contracts, disposition may be made concerning the succession to the property of the children ; as—

1. By electing a particular rule of legitimate succession which obtains at any place by statute.[5]

2. By admitting to the succession of the first-dying children the remaining survivors ; and to the succession of the last survivor the relatives of that side from whence the property came. Such a disposition neither prevents the spouses from making a different disposition by testament, nor burthens the children themselves with a *fidei-commissum ;* but it excludes the parent who has so contracted, from the succession, and even the legitimate succession.[6]

---

[1] Schrassert, *Practic. Obs.* 270 ; Voet *ad Pand.* xxiii. 4. 64.

[2] Cod. ii. 3. ult. See Coren, *Consil.* xiii. n. 12 ; Voet *ad Pand.* ii. 14. § 16.

[3] Roseboom, d. 1, art. 7 ; Neostad. *Decis. Supr. Cur.* 78, vers. " *haud secus, &c. ;* " Coren, *Observ. Rer. Jud.* xx. n. 22.

[4] *Ad Pand.* xxiii. 4. 65.   [5] Of which see *Infra.* on B. ii ch. 29.

[5] *Holl. Cons.* d. iv. cons. 4 ; Neostad. *de Pact. Antenupt.* obs. 3.

CCXLII. The bond of *fidei-commissum*, however, may unquestionably be annexed even by the antenuptial contract to such a disposition ;[7] but in such a case the children so burthened may legally deduct their legitimate and Trebellianic portions, and the parent will also be entitled to succeed thereto.[8]

CCXLIII. 3. By admitting a particular third person, to the succession to the property of the last surviving child. And if such third person has not, by stipulation in the dotal contract, acquired a right to such succession, a contrary disposition may be made in favour of the children.[9] If, however, he has acquired this right, they cannot exclude him by testament, but are not prohibited from alienating the property *inter vivos*.

CCXLIV. *Thirdly :* Antenuptial contracts may be made respecting the property of any third consenting party. Of this kind are :

1. The contract of the parent, who gives the dowry ; and which is unquestionably effectual. Such a dowry however, if it be immoderate, leaves room for a *querela inofficiosæ dotis.*[10]

CCXLV. 2. The contract of a stranger, who by the antenuptial contract promises a dowry either absolutely or after his death. And such a contract is, from the reason of the law, irrevocable.[11]

3. A condition or *modus* may be annexed to either of these promises of dowry, to the effect that such dowry should be restored, upon the dissolution of the marriage,

---

[7] Voet *ad. Pand.* xxxvi. 1, § 9.
[8] Voet (*ad Pand.* v. 2. 40 in f.) *dissentiente.*
[9] Voet *ad Pand.* xxiii. 4, 66.
[10] Schrassert, *Obs. Practic.* 255.   [11] *Holl. Cons.* d. iii. cons. 27.

either to the donor or to any other person, or should
revert to the side from whence it came. The former of
these conditions does not exclude the donor himself
from reclaiming the dowry, even if there be children
of such marriage.[1] The latter condition, if made even
generally in favour of the relatives of the side whence
the property came, seems nevertheless to exempt the
dowry, where there are no children, from testamentary
disposition by the spouses; though many authors think
otherwise.[2]

CCXLVI. 4. To this class may be referred those
contracts, whereby, in order to encourage a marriage, a
disposition is made concerning the future succession to
the property of a third consenting party; of which
there are various kinds; such as that one or both of the
spouses may succeed wholly or in part to the person
promising; or that the spouse may succeed in equal
shares with the children, to a parent so promising; or
that in consideration of a handsome dowry, he will
renounce the inheritance of the parent; or that the
parent will renounce his legitimate share in favour of
the bride, whom the espousing son should institute as
heir. Such stipulations may legally be entered into in
an antenuptial contract, and cannot be revoked at the
will of one party alone, as appears from the reason of
law, and the unanimous opinion of many authors.

SEC. 9.

CCXLVII. By an antenuptial contract, community
either in all or in some of the property may be ex-

---

[1] Bynkersh. *Q. J. Priv.* l. ii. c. 16, § 7.
[2] As Coren, *Consil.* ix. n. 44, & Voet. *ad Pand.* xxiii. 4, § 61. in med-

cluded; and this either expressly or even tacitly, as if it be agreed that the property of the parties should return to the side from which it came; or if the wife has stipulated that she should have her own property reserved to her: and to such a stipulation a reservation of the right of dowry and of legal mortgage may not only be expressly annexed, but is believed to be even tacitly understood.[3]

CCXLVIII. Besides the benefit of succession spoken of in the 236 and following *Theses*, the spouses may also in these antenuptial articles stipulate for themselves benefits of a different kind, as that one of them may have a particular thing solely for him or herself, or a particular sum, or an annual amount, or a portion of the dowry, even of one which has been promised to be paid after the death of the parent, for this should be paid to the widow or widower of the spouse who may have died before the parent.[4]

But a stipulation that the spouses may assist each other at pleasure does not confer on them any right more than they have by the common law.[5]

CCXLIX. The stipulation that the wife should have a share in the profits, but should not be liable in the losses, although disapproved of by *Grotius* and *Neostadt*. is neither repugnant to the reason of law,[6] nor to the favour shown to dotal contracts; nor does it even injure the creditors, since there can be no profit, unless the loss has been previously deducted.[7]

---

[3] Voet *ad Pand.* xxiii. 4. § 52; *Nederl. Adv.* d. iii. cons. 75, 76, & arg. *Placaat* of 4 Oct. 1540, art. 6 in fin. [See Th. 263].

[4] Voet ibid. § 23.

[5] Schrassert, *Consult & Adv.* d. ii. cons. 63.

[6] Inst. iii. 25 § 2 in med. [See Thes. 699.]   [7] Dig. xvii. 2. 30.

SEC. 10.

CCL. A stipulation giving the wife the election, upon the dissolution of the marriage, either to take a share in the profits, or to have her own property to herself, is not only clearly allowed by the Law of Holland, but also has nothing unjust or inequitable in it; and herein I agree with *Grotius* ;[1] though *Bynkershoek*[2] is of a different opinion. Such right of election accrues not only to the wife, but to her heirs also, whether this has been expressly stipulated or not; and may, even during the subsistence of the marriage, be exercised by the wife, if the husband should happen to be reduced to poverty.[3]

SEC. 11.

CCLI. Athough it is a correct rule that things omitted in an antenuptial contract should be taken to have been left to the disposition of the common law, yet there is nothing to prevent any doubts herein being determined by the customary rules of interpretation.[4]

CCLII. The community of profit and loss, which remains upon the exclusion of community of property, does not include an inheritance devolving either *ab intestato* or by testament, whether from a parent or relative, or from a stranger[5] (and the application of the rule of the Digest hereon is not impeded, but rather confirmed by the reason of our law) ; excepting where it has been expressly stipulated that *all kinds of profits*

---

[1] *Holl. Consult.* d. iii. st. 2. cons. 303.   [2] *Q. J. Priv.* 1. ii. c. 1.
[3] De Haas, *Nieuwe Holl. Cons.* cas. 38.
[4] Schrassert, *Obs. Pract.* 247, 252; Voet *ad Pand.* xxiii. 4. § 7, 71.
[5] Dig. xvii. 2, 9, 10, 11.

should be in common. And if we understand the doctrine laid down by *Grotius* in B. iii. ch. 21, § 10, in this sense, it will be found not repugnant to the present passage.

CCLIII. Under community of profits are also included life annuities and the profits derived from ships;[6] also the benefits of a usufruct,[7] but not such things as do not consist in fruits, such as lofty trees.

CCLIV. Under the head of profits are likewise included those things which have been purchased with money belonging either to the parties in common or exclusively to either the husband or the wife, even if there exist no community of profits between them; but in such manner, that the party to whom the money belonged becomes a creditor for the amount so spent.[8] It is otherwise, 1. If a thing purchased before the marriage has been delivered since the marriage; and 2. If some other arrangement has been made, *i.e.*, if the thing has been assigned at the instance of the husband to himself or to the wife; and this rule should hold especially in respect of apparel purchased for the use of either of the parties, contrary to the doctrine of *Voet.*[9]

CCLV. Where the community of property and of debts contracted before marriage has been excluded, though the community of profit and loss remains, the property of the wife cannot, during marriage, be taken in execution for such a debt, by the creditors of the husband.[10]

---

[6] Voet *ad Pand.* vii. 1 § 25; Coren. *Obs.* 7.   [7] Dig. xxiii. 3, 7, § 2.

[8] Schrassert, *Pract. Obs.* 68; Voet *ad Pand.* vii. 1, § 22, 24, and xxiii. 4, § 32, med.

[9] *Ad Pand.* xxiii. 4. § 34.

[10] Voet (*ad Pand.* xxiii. 4. § 50, vers. *uti et in quantum*, &c.) *dissentiente*.

Sec. 14.

CCLVI. No action can, from the reason of our laws, be maintained by either party, during the marriage, to compel a collation of any particular property which they had before the marriage promised each other in respect of the marriage ; but it is clear that the husband may maintain an action against the father of the wife, who has promised a dowry ; and this is the meaning of the maxim : *Met een Bruidegom mag men loven, maar met een Bruid moet men geven*—Love the Bridegroom, but give to the Bride. After the dissolution of the marriage, however, the married parties ought certainly to indemnify each other.

· Sec. 15.

CCLVII. Where the community of property only, and not of profit and loss, has been excluded, an accidental or casual loss occurring to the property of either of the parties is not common to both, but attaches to the owner of such property ; as rightly held by many authors since the time of *Grotius*.[1] The same rule applies to necessary expenses of an extraordinary nature.[2] Useful and luxurious expenses should be refunded to the extent to which the thing has been thereby improved.[3]

Sec. 16.

CCLVIII. The *Morgen-gave*, or Morning-gift, wont to be given on the day after the marriage as the reward

[1] Coren, *Consil.* 18 ; Voet *ad Pand.* xxiii. 4. § 49.
[2] Voet *ad Pand.* xxv. 1 § 2.   [3] Voet, ib. § 3, 4.

of chastity, although it ought from its nature to accrue
to the wife immediately, is according to our customs
acquired only after the marriage has been dissolved and
the creditors discharged.[4]

CCLIX. The *Douarie*, or Marriage-gift, promised as
a provision for widowhood, is correctly defined by *Bynkershoek*[5] as *a gift made by the first-dying spouse, and to
be paid on the day of his or her death to the survivor.*
It is less correctly held by the same learned author as a
debt; since, according to the intention of the Law of
Holland, it is simply a bounty or liberal gift, which is
not to be deducted till after the legitimate shares of the
children have been satisfied, but is to be reckoned in
the estate, and, therefore, if immoderate, diminished in
the same manner as an inofficious donation.[6]

CCLX. It is not lawful, therefore, so to charge a marriage gift upon property which after the death of one
spouse shall be in common between the survivor and
the heirs of the deceased, and the enjoyment or alienation whereof has been permitted to such survivor, as
that it should be deducted from the common estate
before a division takes place. And this I consider
unlawful even where the power of making a donation
has been expressly allowed ; since this should, as it
seems, be understood of a moderate gift, which is to
take effect *inter vivos.*

CCLXI. A marriage-gift promised by antenuptial
contract is not presumed to have been satisfied by a
legacy, even of an equal or larger amount left by testa-

---

[4] Arg. *Placaat* of the 4 Oct. 1540, art. 6 ; and see decision of the
Supreme Court, 27 July, 1612, in Neostad. *de Pact. Antenupt.* obs.
10, n. (b.)

[5] *Q. Jur. Priv.* l. ii. cap. 7.   [6] Cod. iii. 29. 5.

ment, unless the gift has at the same time been expressly·
revoked; on which point there is a decision of the
Supreme Court of Holland in *Rodenburg's* treatise *De
Jure Conjugum*.[1] Nor is it cancelled even by the
institution of the spouse as heir, if he or she has been
requested to restore the property of the first-dying to
his relatives. It would be otherwise, if after the death
of the survivor, the common estate is to be divided
between the relatives of both spouses.

Sec. 17.

CCLXII. The profits which have been promised to
a wife by antenuptial contract cannot be deducted out
of the property of the husband, whether a merchant or
otherwise, until after the creditors have been satisfied,
whether there has been community of profit and loss
between the parties, or not.[2]

CCLXIII. The right of dowry and legal mortgage,
which, upon exclusion of all community of property
and of profit and loss, the wife has stipulated for herself,
either expressly or tacitly (as by desiring that she
should have her own property reserved to her), since
it has been expressly adopted from the Roman Law,[3]
gives her a preferent right not only as against subsequent mortgage-creditors of the husband (as generally
laid down by commentators,[4] but also against those
who are prior in time, as frequently decided by the
Courts,[5] and also by the States of Holland in the cele-

[1] Tit. ii. cap. 4. § 6.
[2] *Placaat* 4 Oct. 1440, art. 6. *Rechtsgel. Obs.* part iii. obs. 38.
[3] *Plac.* ib. art. 6 in fin.   [4] Voet *ad Pand.* xxiii. 4. § 52.
[5] *Nederl. Adv.* d. ii. cons. 90 ; Van Leeuwen, *Comm.* b. iv. ch. 13, § 14.

brated rescript of the 15th of May, 1754,[6] in a case of the Treasury, upon a representation of the delegates of the States, of the 14th May, 1754.

CCLXIV. Whatever the spouses have promised to each other by antenuptial contract, they cannot revoke even by mutual consent by an act *inter vivos,* so far as such revocation might contain a donation, which is prohibited between husband and wife;[7] and even where such a revocation is quite consistent with law, *restitutio in integrum* may be obtained against it.[8] It has clearly, however, been received in practice that a wife may renounce the stipulation respecting dowry and legal mortgage in favour of the creditors of the husband.

CCLXV. A mutual promise made by antenuptial contract may be revoked by last will; but either of the parties may by a subsequent testamentary disposition, even without the knowledge of the other, revert to the stipulations in the antenuptial contract. This is likewise permitted, after the death of one of the parties, to the survivor; provided he or she has not in the meanwhile accepted any benefit under the will of the predeceased spouse.[9]

CHAPTER XIII.—SEC. 1.

CCLXVI. On the death of either of the spouses, the community of property may be continued between the survivor and the heirs of the deceased, either *ipso*

---

[6] See *Groot Plac. Boek*, d. viii. p. 613.

[7] Neostad. *de Pact. Antenupt.* obs. 4.

[8] Decis. of the Court, 31 Jul. 1609; *Decis. & Resol. van den Hove van Holl.* n. 199. [See also *'t Vervolg op de Holl. Cons.* 39, 130.—Tr.]

[9] D. Decis. And see Voet *ad Pand.* xxiii. 4. § 62.

jure (and this either for the benefit of,[1] or as a penalty against[2] the survivor), or at the desire of the parties concerned, declared either by testament or by agreement. So also there is nothing to prevent the community of profit and loss being continued.[3]

CCLXVII. Community may also be continued or introduced by the mutual testament of the spouses (who have instituted each other heir), as regards the property which is to be divided after the death of the survivor amongst the heirs of both the spouses:[4] and under such community (unless otherwise provided for), donations, legacies, and inheritances subsequently devolving on the survivor should also be reckoned.[5]

SEC. 2.

CCLXVIII. The old rule by which community of property was continued for the benefit of the surviving parent, between such surviving parent and the minor children,[6] has been abolished by a subsequent law in Zeeland,[7] and in Holland by most of the pupillary laws, which direct an inventory and assignment of the property to be made.[8] There is also a decision of the Supreme Court on this subject in the *Rechtsgeleerde Observatien*.[9]

CCLXIX. A continuation of the community may, however, in various places be permitted by the testa-

---

[1] See sec. 2.   [2] Sec. 3.   [3] Voet *ad Pand.* xxiv. 3. § 29.
[4] Voet *ad Pand.* xxxvi. 1. § 56.
[5] Bynkersh. *Q. J. Priv.* lib. iii. cap. 10.
[6] *Rechtsgel. Obs.* part iii. obs. 39.
[7] *Keur. van Zeeland.* cap. ii. art. 20, 27, 28 ; *Costum. van Middelb.* rubr. xiv. *van Success.* art. 2.
[8] Thes. 135, seq. ; and Thes. 142, seq.   [9] Part iii. obs. 40. p. 117.

ment of the first-dying parent, and with the consent of
the Orphan Chamber.[10] It may also, it seems, be done
by contract, whether by an antenuptial contract between
the parents themselves (as evident from the reason of
the law), or by that kind of contract which is entered
into with the consent of the relatives and guardians,
and with the approval of the Orphan Chamber.[11] In
this continued community, however, donations, legacies, and inheritances subsequently devolving on the
children will not be included.[12]

SEC. 3.

CCLXX. Almost all the commentators[13] misunder-
stand *Grotius*, as referring in this section to the continuation, at the survivor's pleasure, of the community
of property between himself and the minor children ;
whereas he rather means that such continuation has
been imposed as a penalty on a parent who fails to
make an inventory or to assign the property ; in order
that by the community thus improperly continued the
children might indeed participate in the profits, but not
be liable for the losses, which may afterwards arise.[14]

CCLXXI. This penalty has not, however, been
adopted everywhere in Holland and Zeeland ;[15] nor,

[10] Thes. 144.　　　　　　　[11] Ibid.
[12] See the laws cited in Thes. 140; and *Weeskeur. van Alkmaar*, &c.
tit. iv. art. 4.
[13] Groeneweg. not. 3. and Voet. § 28 & sqq. *ad Pand.* xxiv. 3;
Rechtsgel. Obs. part iii. obs. 40.
[14] See the Laws cited in Th. 142 in f. & *Weeskeur. van Vlissing.* art. 17.
[15] See *Weeskeur. van Rhynl.* art. 26 27 ; *Rotterd.* art. 14, 15, 16;
Gorinch. art. 33; *Grootebr.* art. 6; *Enkhuis.* tit. ii.; *Middelb.* art. 22,
24, 26, 27, 29, 66, sqq., 75, sqq. and *Ampl.* art. 8.

indeed, is *Grotius* correct in inferring a general law of Holland from several conflicting statutes.[1]

CCLXXII. The remarks of *Voet*[2] on the effect of this continued community of property as a penalty on the surviving parent are wholly foreign to the present subject and to the object of the above statutes: since a particular law introduced for the punishment of any individual cannot by any means be taken to constitute the general law of the land.[3]

CCLXXIII. His remarks[4] on the community (properly so called) continued by the will of the testator, or of those who have the right so to do, are more useful, and are equally applicable to the much-controverted question concerning the shares which, upon the survivor contracting a second marriage, and a fresh statutory community taking place between him and the second spouse, such survivor or *binubus*, the heirs of the pre-deceased spouse, and the second spouse are respectively entitled to out of such common estate.

CCLXXIV. And in order to explain and determine this question, on principles of law, we should look to the rule of the Digest, *Socius mei socii, socius meus non est*—the partner of my partner is not my partner.[5] Whence it follows—1. That here there are two societies or partnerships, one between the twice-married spouse and the heirs of the pre-deceased spouse ; the other between him and the second spouse : 2. That the second spouse is not a partner with the heirs of the predeceased spouse, nor conversely they with him : 3. That the

---

[1] Of which see *Rechtsgel. Obs.* part iii. obs. 40.
[2] *Ad Pand.* xxiv. 3. § 31, 32.
[3] Inst. iii. 26. arg. § 4.   [4] *Ad Pand.* ib. & § 33.
[5] Dig. xvii. 2. 20, 21, and 23. §. 1.

twice-married spouse on the other hand, is partner with both parties, *i.e.*, both the second spouse and the heirs of the predeceased spouse: 4. That the heirs of the predeceased spouse do not share in profit or loss with the second spouse, nor conversely the latter with them: 5. That, on the other hand, the twice-married spouse will share with each party, *i.e.*, take in common with them the profits as well as the losses, to be afterwards divided between himself and his other partner: 6. In order to determine what has been brought in collation into each society or partnership, regard should be had to the time when the second partnership was contracted; or, the shares of each partnership should be settled or allotted with reference to the time of the second marriage; and 7. From this allotment of shares is to be determined, at the termination of each partnership, what gain or loss has accrued to each, and in what manner such gain or loss is to be shared or divided.

CCLXXV. From what has been said, it follows—1. That it is not necessary, as maintained by *Van Wezel* and *Voet*,[6] to leave the whole matter to the uncertain decision of a judge (nor does the rule in Dig. xxxiii. 1. 13, § 1, furnish any argument in favour hereof, since this rule relates to a question not of law, but of fact). 2. That in dividing the common estate of the three partners at the termination of each partnership, the shares of the new partner and of the others will not *per se*, or from the nature of the thing, be equal, such as a third each; but will be equal or otherwise, according to the amount which the new partner had brought in, or the profit or

---

[6] Van Wezel, *de Connub. Bonor. Societ.* tr. ii. cap. 4, § 76. sqq. Voet *ad Pand.* xxiv. 3. J 32.

loss which has since accrued to each partnership. For example, suppose a twice-married spouse had, at the time of the second marriage, 600 florins in the common estate of himself and the heirs of the predeceased spouse, and the second spouse had 200 florins; the common estate of the twice-married spouse and the second spouse will then amount to 500 florins. Suppose no profit or loss to have since accrued to either partnership: then, at the time of the termination of both the partnerships, the second spouse will have 250 florins, the twice-married spouse 275 florins, and the heirs of the predeceased spouse 275 florins. Suppose, however, that an inheritance of 1,000 florins has devolved on the twice-married spouse, he will then bring 500 florins into his new partnership with the second spouse, who will then have for her half share of this gain or profit 250 florins, and the remaining 750 florins will be equally divided between the twice-married spouse and the heirs of the predeceased spouse. Lastly, suppose the twice-married spouse, in common with the heirs of the predeceased spouse, possessed 400 florins, and that the second spouse has brought to the twice-married spouse 200 florins, and that no profit or loss has since accrued to either partnership,—then, in like manner, the new common estate of the twice-married spouse and the second spouse will be 400 florins; whereof the second spouse shall have for herself 200 florins, and of the remaining 400, the twice-married spouse shall have 200 florins, and the heirs of the predeceased spouse 200 florins.

CCLXXVI. Provided, however, that if the shares of each society at the time the second marriage was contracted cannot be determined or settled either from books of accounts or from other credible instruments or vouchers, or even if nothing appears in respect of the profit or loss which may have since accrued, recourse should be had, according to the rule in the Digest,[1] to the decision of a judge. And such judge will, in the former case, after taking into consideration the condition of each spouse, *i.e.*, the predeceased, the twice-married, and the second spouse, define and determine, according to presumption of law, the share or estate of each of the parties to be either equal or otherwise ; or, even in the latter case, taking it for granted upon presumption of law that *no change of status has taken place*, will pronounce the common estate of all the parties to have remained in the same state since the time of entering into the second marriage.

Chapter XV.—Sec. 2.

CCLXXVII. Although the *testamentifactio,* or the right of making a will, is more extensive in Holland and Zeeland, than it was under the Roman Law, for it is allowed both to *filliifamiliæ* and to foreigners, and (since the entire abolition in Holland[2] and Zeeland[3] of the confiscation of property) even to persons condemned to death ; yet for the sake of public convenience, a law has been passed in Holland[4] (and adopted in Zeeland[5] and other places), which though very obscure, has yet been incorrectly understood by some authors as referring to the *testamentifactio,* active as

[1] Lib. xxxiii. tit. 1. 1. 13. § 1.
[2] *Resol. Hol, & W. Vriesl.* 1 May, 1732 [which see in Lybrecht's *Reden, Vertoog,* d. ii. *Bylagen,* p. 450.—Tr.]
[3] *Ord. Zeeland,* 16 Dec. 1735.
[4] *Plac. Holl.* 4 May, 1655.   [5] *Ord. Zeeland,* 12 Nov. 1655.

well as passive, of Catholics ;[1] but which *Bynkershoek*[2] and the Court of *Brabant*[3] have more correctly explained as referring only to the passive *testamentifactio* ;[4] with the exception of one clause of it, which relates to the active *testamentifactio,* and which is commented upon by *Bynkershoek* in Chap. II., and is the subject of our present consideration.

CCLXXVIII. It is provided by this clause, 1. That Catholic parents shall not under any title leave more to their Catholic children than to their Protestant children who are not otherwise undeserving ; 2. That those children who belong to the Catholic Church shall not in any manner dispose of by testament the property of the parents so left to them ; 3. That Catholics, whether priests or laymen, shall not through religious hatred leave anything to another Catholic, to the prejudice of their legitimate Protestant heirs. This part of the law, which is referable to *Art.* 21 of the Peace of Ghent, has been explained in a Resolution of the States of the 8th August, 1664, as including dispositions made through religious hatred to the prejudice of other legitimate heirs besides brothers.[5]

CCLXXIX. But although according to the real intention of this law, it does not take away, but only restricts, the *testamentifactio* of priests,[6] yet it seems to have been construed by the States[7] as only rendering it necessary that they should obtain a special privilege to dispose by testament, and should execute the testa-

---

[1] See *de Nieuwe Nederl. Jaarb. van* 1770, p. 940, sqq.
[2] *Q. Jur. Priv.* l. iii. c. 1 & 2.   [3] *Jaarb.* d. l. p. 973, sqq.
[4] Of which see under chapter xvi. § 3.—[Th. 284.]
[5] Lybrechts, *Reden. Vertoog over 't Notar. Ampt.* d. ii. Byl. p. 456.
[5] Bynkersh. d. l. p. 365, in fin. and sq.   [7] *Resol.* 13 May, 1734.

ment in the presence of two commis-ioners of the Court. But this has been altered by the Law of Holland of the 9th October, 1795, saving, however, the first, and as it would appear the third, but not the second, part of the Law of 1655.

CCLXXX. Those who are maintained in asylums for orphans or aged people, &c., cannot leave the property which they have brought with them to any other by will, not even property afterwards acquired by inheritance or bequest or donation, unless they have redeemed this right by a compromise. This privilege has been specially conceded to several institutions of this kind,[8] and is recognized by an interpretation of the States, of the 17th December, 1766.[9]

Sec. 5.

CCLXXXI. The will of a prodigal, which is just and equitable under the 39th Novel of *Leo*, is supposed to be valid in Holland also, as held by the Court on the 22nd November, 1616.[10*]

Sec. 7.

CCLXXXII. It may be inferred from a decision of the Court of the 27th November, 1543[11] (wherein, as in similar other decisions, a departure seems to have been made from a contrary custom, in favour of the equity

[8] See *Nederl. Jaarb.* 1750, p. 515, sq. in not.
[9] *Nieuwe Nederl. Jaarb.* 1766, p. 1217, sqq.; *Groot Plac. Boek*, d. ix. p. 217.
[10] *Decis. and Resol. van den Hove van Holl.* n. 116.
[*] [20 (?) November, 1616. See Lybrechts, *Red. Vert*, d. i. c. 19. p. 231.—Tr.]
[11] *Decis. en Resol.* n. 353.

of Civil Law), that spurious or illegitimate children
may by the Law of Holland make a will, though they
may not have obtained a special privilege to do so. At
Flushing, at least, this is a matter of positive law.[1]

SEC. 9.

CCLXXXIII. A surviving spouse who has made a
will jointly with a predeceased spouse as regards their
common property, and has been appointed heir to such
predeceased spouse, cannot make a different disposition
in respect of that portion of the common property
which ought to revert to the substitutes of the predeceased; but as regards that portion which would
devolve on his own heirs he may legally make a disposition;[2] unless both the spouses have by common
consent made a disposition of the common estate or of
the share of the survivor.[3]

CHAPTER XVI.—SEC. 3.

CCLXXXIV. The prohibition in the Placaat of
1665* against instituting Catholic priests and pious
foundations as heirs does not include paupers, or
orphan asylums established in the country.[4]

SEC. 4.

CCLXXXV. The Placaat of the 4th of October,

[1] *Costum. van Vlissing,* cap. xx. art. 1.
[2] Roseboom, *Costum. van Amsterd.* cap. xlii. art. 22, 23; and Boel
ad Loen. Decis. 187.
[3] Voet *ad Pand.* xxiii. 4, § 63; and xxviii. 3. § 11.
* [See Thes. 278.]
⁗ Bynkersh. *Q. Jur. Pr.* l. iii. c. l.; *Groot Plac. Boek.* d. vi. p. 355
sqq.

1540,[5] which has been recognised by various pupillary
laws passed by the States of Holland,[6] prohibits any,
even honorary, guardians being instituted as heirs by a
ward who may be competent to make a will, unless the
institution be made after the guardianship has terminated in respect of the guardians themselves, and the
accounts have been rendered: or unless the guardians
be the parents or such of the collateral relatives of the
ward as would succeed to him as legitimate heirs;
but even in the latter case, such collateral relatives
cannot be instituted to a larger amount than they
would be entitled to as successors *ab intestato*. The
children of a guardian (but not his wife, provided
the institution be not made in fraud of the law*),
as also the concubines of wards, are likewise prohibited.[7]

CCLXXXVI. Although the Placaat has confined
this prohibition against liberality to immovable property only, and various pupillary laws have simply
prohibited only the institution of heirs, and therefore
the acquisition under that title of movables also; yet
the reason of these laws, and the altered circumstances
in respect of pupillary estates, which now consist
almost entirely of public securities, render it necessary
that legacies of such movables also should be held as
coming within the prohibition.†

---

⁶ Art. 12.

⁶ As that of the Town of *Briel*, art. 78, 79.

* [H. de Groot, in *Holl. Consult.* d. iii. cons. 188, § 2.—Tr.]

⁷ Bynkersh. *Q. Jur. Priv.* 1. iii. e. 3.

† [See Van Leeuw. *Comm.* b. iii. c. 3. § 12; and Schorer's note on
this section of Grotius. *E. contra.* See *Holl. Consult.* d. iii. cons.
188; Groeneweg *de leg. abrog.* ad Cod. v. 38. 7; Voet *ad Pand.* xxviii.
5. 9.—Tr.]

SEC. 6.

CCLXXXVII. By the general Law of Holland, natural children, where there are legitimate children, can be instituted heirs by the father, only to the extent of a twelfth part.[1] At Leyden, however, they may legally be instituted to the extent of a fourth part;[2] and, if there be no legitimate children, to the whole estate, reserving a legitimate share to the parents.[3]

SEC. 7.

CCLXXXVIII. Under the law *hac edictali* (1. 6.), of the Code v. 9 (by which a second spouse is prohibited from taking a larger share than a child to whom the least share has been left), if an only son has been unjustly disinherited and the second spouse instituted sole heir by a testament, which is protected by the codicillary clause, such son would seem, from the favourable construction now put upon this clause, to be entitled to no more than a half of the property. If one of several children be disinherited, and the others instituted joint heirs with the second spouse, he will be entitled to his legitimate and Trebellianic portions, but must leave the remainder to the instituted heirs, the rule of the Code as regards the second spouse being, however, always observed.[4]

CHAPTER XVII.—SEC. 2.

CCLXXXIX. The law as to testaments and codicils

[1] See the decisions of 1684 and 1685, in *de Rechtsgel. Obs.* part i. obs. 36.

[2] *Ord. Leyd.* art. 150.   [3] Nov. lxxxix. c. 12. § 3. See Thes. 10.

[4] *Dissentientibus* Voet *ad Pand.* xx.ii. 2. § 131, and the Jurists in *'t Nieuwe Nederl. Adv.* d. i. cons. 3.

has not been thoroughly assimilated even by the law of the present day. For, in the *first* place, they differ as regards the number of witnesses, if executed according to the Roman custom; *secondly*, the institution of an heir is generally made by testament, not by codicil; and *thirdly*, codicils confirmed by a testament are valid, though written in a private instrument, without a notary and witnesses, but an heir cannot be instituted by such a private instrument.

CCXC. At the present day a testament wherein no heir has been instituted is valid; not so much on account of the favour shown to the codicillary clause, as on account of the practice and the reason of this rule of the Civil Law[5] having ceased.

Sec. 12.

CCXCI. There is nothing to prevent a legatee being a witness to a closed will or to one executed in the presence of seven witnesses; nor would even the institution of an heir in a testament executed before a notary and witnesses seem to be vitiated, if a legacy has been therein left to one of the witnesses.*

Sec. 13.

CCXCII. One who inserts anything in his own favour in a will, whether it be a closed will or one executed before a notary and witnesses, or even the joint will of a married couple, cannot take the thing so left.[6] This rule does not apply to antenuptial con-

---

[5] See Dig. L. 17. 7. [Th. 375.]
* [Pape. *Observ. ad Cons. Jurisc. Batav.* vol. i. cons. 103.—Tr.]
[6] Boel *ad Loen. Decis.* 137 ; Bynkersh. *Q. J. Priv.* l. iii. c. 8. [Lybrechts, *Reden. Vert.* d. i. p. 520.—Tr.]

tracts, nor to those cases which are excepted in the Civil Law, nor therefore to a case where the testator has specially approved of the bequest which a party has inserted in his own favour, as, for instance, by mentioning the name of the person to whom he has dictated the will ;[1] and this should, it seems, be maintained, in opposition to the opinion of *Bynkershoek*.[2]

SEC. 16.

CCXCIII. A will may be made according to the Roman custom,* in the presence of seven witnesses; as proved by the reason of the Law,[3] and implied in some Dutch Statutes,[4] and confirmed by the Statutes of Zeeland.[5] It does not appear whether the exception made in the Statutes of Leyden[6] is still followed in practice.

SEC. 18.

CCXCIV. A disinherison cannot properly be made by a will executed before a notary, unless two *schepenen* are present.[7]

SEC. 20.

CCXCV. Although notaries are prohibited from practising beyond the place where they have been

---

[1] Dig. xlviii. 10. 1. § 8 ; and 15. § 3.
[2] L. iii. c. 8. p. 428, and sq.
* [*i.e.* Orally ;—See V. d. Linden, *Inst.* p. 127.—Tr.]   [3] Thes. 17.
[4] Roseboom, *Costum. van Amsterd.* cap. xliv. art. 1, 2 ; *Costum. van Rhynland*, art. 88.
[5] *Costum. van Middelb.* rubr. xiii. art. 1.   [6] Art. 149.
[7] See the form of the Oath of a Notary, art. 4, in Lybrechts, *Reden. Vertoog.* t. i. p. 9.

admitted, yet a will *bonâ fide* executed before such a notary by a person ignorant of the law, does not seem to be invalid.[8]

SEC. 23.

CCXCVI. Wills made before a notary and two witnesses are in one respect similar to nuncupative wills, namely, that they will take effect, although the writing, though read and approved of by the testator, may not have been subscribed by him, or by the witnesses.[9] They have, however, other peculiarities, arising out of the nature of a written will.[10]

CCXCVII. A testator cannot prohibit the *grosse** or copy of the will being shown to his legitimate heirs after his death.   It was so decided by the Court on the 12th December, 1724, and approved of by the Supreme Court on the 18th September, 1725.[11]

SEC. 24.

CCXCVIII. Where two persons have made a joint will, whereby the first-dying appoints the survivor heir,

---

[8] *Decis. Supr. Cur.* 11 Jan. 1628 ; Coren, *Observ.* 37, and arg. Dig. i. 14. 3. [See *Rechtsgel. Obs.* part i. obs. 39, and Van Leeuwen's note on Peckius, *over het Bezetten,* c. xxiii. pag. 347 (ed. 1659, Dordrecht), and Van der Linden's *Supplem. ad Voetii Pand.* i. 14. § 7 (ed. 1793. Utrecht).—Tr.]

[9] Coren, *Obs.* 10. p. 27. init. ; and *Decis. Supr. Cur.* 28. Mar. 1744, in Lybrechts, *Reden Vertoog.* d. 1. p. 520.

[10] Bynkersh. *Q. Jur. Priv.* 1. 3. c. 5. p. 400. fin. and sqq.

[*] [See Lybrechts, *Red. Vert.* d. i. p. 298. The *grosse* is not the original, but only a copy or transcript made by the Notary, which derives its force from the *Minut.* The *Minut* is a Certificate or Declaration made by the Notary, in the presence of the witnesses, of what the testator, on the day of the date thereof, had willed and desired.—Tr.]

[11] See Lybrechts, d. 1. p. 529.

one of them may, during their joint lives, without the knowledge or consent of the other, recede therefrom by a new last will;[1] but the rule laid down by *Roseboom*[2] from the Statutes of *Antwerp*,[3]—that in this case he is prohibited from taking what the first-dying testator has left to him,—may be easily evaded by destroying or cancelling the latter will.

SEC. 29.

CCXCIX. A testament made *jure militari* is valid even after the lapse of a year from the termination of the expedition, provided the testator has not been discharged from service. This is evident from the Roman Law, and should prevail against the authority of *Grotius*, who does not correctly explain the text of the Inst. ii. 11. § 3.

SEC. 31.*

CCC. The privilege granted by the Code vi. 23, 31, to country-folks, of disposing of their property by a testament executed according to the Roman custom, does not seem to have ceased, at least in a case of necessity.[4]

SEC. 31.

CCCI. A testament made by the testator, whilst

---

[1] Boel *ad Loen. Decis.* 137.
[2] *Costum. van Amsterd.* cap. xlii. art. 23.
[3] Cap. xli. art. 50.
[*] [In Mr. Herbert's Translation of this section, for "*housekeepers*" read "*country-folks*," or "persons residing in the country."—Tr.]
[4] Voet *ad Pand.* xxviii. 1. § 13.

suffering from a pestilence, would appear to be privileged, and will be valid, if he dies of that disease.[5]

CCCII. Although a testament made *ad pias caussas* does not seem to be privileged by the Law of Holland, yet in the case of a legacy of this kind left by a codicil, the Supreme Court has shown some favour to cases of necessity.[6]

CHAPTER XVIII.—SEC. 5.

CCCIII. By a peculiar law of the City of *Zierikzee*, amongst those persons who ought necessarily to be instituted heirs, are included even the remoter legitimate heirs being citizens born and residing there, or who have come from elsewhere to reside there having taken up their domicile there six years previously; and to these a third at least of the inheritance ought to be reserved.[7]

SEC. 6.

CCCIV. The word *Children* (*Kinderen*), where the question relates to the intention of an ascendant, comprises all descendants, but where it concerns collaterals,

[5] See *Rechtsgel. Obs.* part. i. obs. 40, where also are quoted the decisions of the Court of the 2 July, 1649, and of the Supreme Court of the 21 December, 1651, to the former of which the date of the 25 July, 1649, and to the latter 21 December, 1652, are elsewhere assigned, viz., in the case of *Jan Gysbertsz, Cameryc* & *Dirk Jacobsz de Haer*, residing at *Woerden*, as heirs of the late *Haesjen Jansze*, plaintiffs in Appeal and Civil Request, against *Pieter Jansze*, also residing at *Woerden*.
[6] 31 July, 1625, in Coren, *Obs.* 31.
[7] *Costum. van Zierikzee*, cap. 13, in Smallegange, p. 521: *Ordd.* 4 June 1689 & 17 Mar. 1746, in Blondeel, *Versterf-recht*, p. 349, sqq.

refers only to children in the first degree; as decided by the Supreme Court.[1]

SEC. 8.

CCCV. The legitimate portion due to minor children may, by our law, be left to them, subject to the condition that the surviving parent need not pay them anything before majority, but may receive the fruits thereof for their maintenance.[2]

SEC. 9.

CCCVI. The passing over of a son already born, even by a father, does not render a testament *ipso jure* void; but if a posthumous child has been passed over, the testament, even if protected by the codicillary clause, will, by reason of the defect of will, become void by agnation, since the father is presumed not to have thought of him,[3] nor can such a will be sustained as a *fidei-commissum*.[4]

SEC. 10.

CCCVII. A son who has been passed over cannot maintain the *querela inofficiosi testamenti* otherwise than as one who has been unjustly disinherited; but if the codicillary clause has been added to the will, he is taken

[1] 31 July 1733, & 28 July 1736; Lybrechts, *Reden. Vertoog*, d. i. p. 305, 306.

[2] *Ordonn. op 't Collateraal, van* 17 May 1723, art. 5.

[3] Schulting. *ad Ulpian. Fragm.* t. xxii. § 18. not. 48; & *ad Paul. Sent.* l. iv. t. 5. not. 5.

[4] Dig. xxix. 7. 11, 12, 13. pr. & 19. [See also *Holl. Cons.* d. iv. cons. 21; p. 50; *Nederl. Advijsb.* d. iv. cons. 181.—Tr.]

to have been burthened with a universal *fidei-commissum* in favour of the instituted heir, reserving to him, however, not only his legitimate but also his Trebellianic portion.[5] Nor is a subsequent decision of the Court of the 4th November 1616 opposed hereto: since that decision, according to my MS. copy, relates not to a son, but to a father who had been passed over.[6]

SEC. 15.

CCCVIII. Since the *querela inofficiosi testamenti* is not maintainable where a parent, who cannot according to the *lex loci* succeed *ab intestato*, has been passed over, it follows from the reason of the law, that neither is he entitled to a legitimate share; and hence, a parent who by the new Aasdoms law succeeds *ab intestato* jointly with the brothers, is only entitled on account of his legitimate portion to a sixth, and not to a third part, even though the brothers have also been passed over by the testator. Here, however, it is different, according to the opinions of the lawyers, as well as the decisions of judges.[7]

SEC. 19.

CCCIX. A person who has been instituted sole heir to a part will succeed in proportion to that part, and the remaining part will belong to the heirs *ab intestato*; if appointed heir to a particular thing, he will be

---

[5] Neostad. *Dec. Cur.* 17.

[6] The text in the *Decis. & Resol. van den Hove*, § 329, should therefore be altered into *dat* PATER *preteritus*—the *father* who has been passed over, &c.

[7] Boel *ad Loen Decis.* 85, and in *Pref.* p. 15, sqq.

considered a legatee; as required by the reason of our law, which has superseded the rule of the Dig. L. 17. 7, and in the latter case follows the l. 13. of the Code vi. 24.

SEC. 20.

CCCX. Conditions in a last will which are in law or even naturally or actually impossible should be taken as not imposed. This is evident from the reason of the rule as received among the Romans, and from the rule laid down in *Thes.* 17.

SEC. 21.

CCCXI. A person instituted heir *from* a particular time does not become heir before such time, and the legitimate heir will in the meantime be the heir. Similarly, a person appointed heir *up to* a certain time ceases to be heir after such time; and the person whom the ·testator has substituted, either directly (as in the case of military substitution) or by way of *fidei commissum*, or, failing such substitute, the legitimate heir of the deceased will succeed to the inheritance.

CHAPTER XIX.—SEC. 9.

CCCXII. Although, in accordance with the reason of our law, pupillary substitution cannot be allowed amongst us,[1] yet there is nothing to prevent a *quasi*-pupillary substitution; as decided by the Superior Court on the 27th July, 1737.[2]

[1] Thes. 106.
[2] See Lybrechts *Reden. Vertoog.* d. i. p. 311.

CHAPTER XX.—SEC. 4.

CCCXIII. The rule of the Institute ii. 23. § 12, has been adopted amongst us, not only in respect of *Fidei-commissa*, but (in accordance with the intention of the Roman Law itself) in respect of legacies also;[3] and has been recognized by a decision of the Court of the year 1723.[4]

SEC. 6.

CCCXIV. The duty of one per cent. and a half per cent. which under the Resolution of the States of Holland of the 28th July, 1674, should be deducted as a realty-tax from a *fidei-commissum* of public securities, which are liable to such tax, has been tacitly abolished by the new law of the 16th June, 1795, by reducing the nominal interest of four per cent. to two and a half per cent.

SEC. 9.

CCCXV. The deduction of the Trebellianic portion cannot be prohibited, not only as regards children, but also as regards the grandchildren, who, upon the predecease of a child of the first degree, have been instituted heirs in their own right.[5]

SEC. 10.

CCCXVI. Although children burthened with a universal *fidei-commissum* may deduct their legitimate

---

[3] Grotius, *in Holl. Cons.* d. iii. st. 2. cons. 198.

[4] Lybrechts, ibid. d. i. p. 374. [See also *Nederl. Advijsb.* d. iii. cons. 246, 247, and d. ii. cons. 237.]

[5] Vinn. *Select. Quæst.* l. ii. c. 29; Boel *ad Loen. Decis.* cas. 85.

I

and Trebellianic portions, yet if there be five or more of them, they cannot take more than a half of the property.[1]

SEC. 11.

CCCXVII. The liberation of a thing from the bond of *fidei-commissum*, being as it were a dispensation from the Law, has properly been reserved to the States by the Law of Holland of the 23rd July, 1670; and since loss may frequently arise to those who are in expectation of the *fidei-commissum*, it has been most wisely provided by a Resolution of the States of Zeeland,[2] that immovable property should not be freed from the bond of *fidei-commissum*, unless after a full investigation into the matter, nor otherwise than for good reasons, which the testator had not foreseen; and (by a subsequent Resolution[3]) this dispensation should be granted not by a majority of votes, but by the common consent of all the States. Both these Resolutions were renewed by a Resolution of the 21st January, 1721. But by the former it was likewise enacted that the property should be sold (if there should at any time arise a necessity for selling it) by public auction; and that the proceeds thereof should be placed upon security in the Treasury of Zeeland, and should not be restored to any one without consulting the States.*

SEC. 12.

CCCXVIII. A *fidei-commissum* constituted *in rem*

[1] Vinn. d. l. and *Decis. & Resol. van den Hove van Holland*, n. 156 & 328 in fin.

[2] 26 November, 1639.   [3] 1 July 1683.

* [See Neostad. *Dec. Supr. Cur.* 74.—Tr.]

to the effect that the property should revert to the family, or should not be alienated out of the family, does not at *Amsterdam* prevent a contrary disposition, whether *inter vivos* or by testament; if constituted *in personam*, as that the heirs should not alienate the property beyond the family, it does prevent such alienation. The former, or *fidei-commissum in rem*, is said to contain a simple obligation, and does not admit relations beyond the family, unless it has been otherwise directed. The latter, which is directed against the person, and is a *fidei-commissum* properly so called, is termed a twofold obligation.[4]

CCCXIX. The Law of Holland concerning the registration of property prohibited from alienation by a *fidei-commissum*[5] has never been adopted in practice,[6] and the Court, in 1658, thought that it could not be revived without inconvenience.[7] At *Middelburg* a similar registration of immovable property subject to *fidei-commissum* is required by the law of the 6th August, 1597.[8]

Sec. 13.

CCCXX. The community of property, which is continued by desire of a deceased testator, differs from a *fidei-commissum* of the residue, wherein the rule in Nov. cviii. c. i., as regards the deduction of a fourth part of the testator's estate, should be observed; but it resembles the latter in this respect, that the portion

---

[4] *Handv. van Amsterd.* p. 552, sq.
[5] 30 July 1624.
[6] *Handv. van Amsterd.* p. 551.
[7] *Rechtsgel. Observ.* part i. obs. 42.   [8] Art. 7.

which the heirs of the deceased are entitled to cannot be diminished by donation or last will.[1]

CHAPTER XXI.—SEC. 4.

CCCXXI. Since the time of *Grotius* it appears to have been received in the practice of our Courts, that an heir may transmit an inheritance devolving on him (even though ignorant of it) to any successors, even strangers; nor does the analogy of our law seem to be opposed to this.[2]

· SEC. 6.

CCCXXII. Although a person who has been instituted universal heir cannot adiate in part by splitting the inheritance, yet one who has been instituted in part is not bound against his will to acknowledge the rest of the inheritance; for the right of accretion which obtained amongst the Romans from the necessity of their laws has, together with the rule of the Digest L. 17. 7. ceased to operate amongst us.

SEC. 7.

CCCXXIII. The executors of a testament, since they are as it were procurators appointed by the testator to manage his funeral, to recover what is due to him, to pay his legacies and debts, and to administer his property until a division thereof can be effected; and since therefore they manage the affairs of the heirs also, cannot debar the heirs from the inheritance unless the

---

[1] See Coren, *Obs.* ii. and another decision of the Supreme Court. 30 October 1642, in Van Leeuwen's *Comm.* B. iii. ch. 8. § 10.

[2] Boel *ad Loen. Decis.* cas. 56.

,testator has directed otherwise,[3] nor alienate the property without their consent. And hence it has not improperly been enacted at Middelburg that if all the heirs agree amongst themselves they may, after payment of what has been left to the executors in the testament, and on giving security to carry out the will of the deceased within a year, remove them from the office.[4]

SEC. 12.

CCCXXIV. In order to entitle an heir, after preparation of an inventory, to have the Falcidian portion reserved to him, he need not, it seems, exercise that formal benefit of inventory, which should at present be applied for and which is refused to the instituted heir, if the legitimate heir is willing to adiate unconditionally; but it is sufficient that an inventory has been made and publicly attested by a notary and witnesses.

CHAPTER XXII.—SEC. 16.

CCCXXV. If the thing bequeathed be subject to an annual rent-charge, which is redeemable, it is the duty of the heir to redeem it.[5] If it be not redeemable, the burthen of it attaches to the legatee. And regard seems to have been had to this rule in a decision of the Court reported by Neostadt.[6]

CHAPTER XXIII.—SEC. 5.

CCCXXVI. There is no reason why the right of

---

[3] Bynkersh. *Q. Jur. Priv.* 1. iii. c. i. p. 360, fin. & sq.
[4] *Costum. van Middelb.* rubr. xiii. art. 2.
[5] Grotius *in Holl. Cons.* d. iii. st. 2. cons. 190.
[6] *Cur. Decis.* 1 l. n. 2.

accretion, which arises from a conjunction of persons, and therefore from a probable inference as to the testator's intention, should not obtain even at the present day amongst co-heirs and co-legatees.[1] Amongst those, therefore, who are conjoined as regards the thing, or both as regards the thing and also by express words, there is no need of conjecture.[2] But conjecture may become necessary as regards persons conjoined by words only, since it may often appear doubtful whether mention was made of parts with the intention of severing or disjoining them, or merely for the purpose of defining them with greater precision.[3]

SEC. 20.

CCCXXVII. In respect of legacies *ad pias caussas* the deduction of the Falcidian portion does not regularly obtain, since it has not been adopted by any definitive usage or practice. And herein we follow the true intention of the Civil Law.[4]

CHAPTER XXIV.—SEC. 8.

CCCXXVIII. Although it has been 'held in our Courts that the *derogatory* clause by which a prior testament is protected, is cancelled by the *cassatory*, or at least the *general* clause in a subsequent testament,[5] yet it would seem that a subsequent testament in which the

---

[1] Voet *ad Pand.* xxx. 1. ult.
[2] Dig. xxx. 3. 25, § 1.
[3] See Coren, *Cons.* 24; and the sentence of the Supreme Court, 22 Dec. 1751, in Lybrechts, *Reden. Vertoog,* d. i. p. 304. [See Nederl. Advijs. d. x. cons. 4, 5, d. ii. cons. 4, 6, 8.—Tr.]
[4] In Nov. cxxxi. c. 12. See Thes. 23.
[5] Bynkersh. *Q. Jur. Priv.* l. iii. c. 6, 7; & l. ii. c. 16. § 6.

latter clause has not been inserted, should be upheld if there be no suspicion that the testator was induced by improper means to make the same.[6]

SEC. 9.

CCCXXIX. A prior testament wherein the derogatory clause has not been inserted, although it has not been revoked by a subsequent testament, is invalidated by such latter testament, unless the testator has expressly or tacitly willed otherwise. *Voet*[7] and others are of a different opinion, but without good reason.

SEC. 15.

CCCXXX. By the destruction of the *grosse** or copy of the testament, which is kept by the testator, the *minute* or original, which remains in the protocol of the notary, is not cancelled, unless it be proved that the testator had destroyed it with the view of dying intestate.[6]

SEC. 18.

CCCXXXI. It has been correctly decided by the Supreme Court[9] that the testament of a parent in favour of the children, though not expressly revoked in a subsequent solemn testament, is thereby annulled.

[6] See decision of the Court, 26 Sept. 1613, *Decis. en Resol. van den Hove van Holland*, n. 409.

[7] *Ad Pand.* xxviii. 3. § 8.

* [See definition, note, * p. 99, to Thes. 297.]

[8] Grotius in *de Holl. Cons.* d. iii. st. 2. cons. 156, [and d. iv. cons. 20.—Tr.]

[9] 18 May, 1629; see Coren, *Obs.* 29.

SEC. 21.

CCCXXXII. A disinherison made without a reason stated, does not by our present law, render the testament *ipso jure* void, but only lays it open to the *querela*.[1]

SEC. 22.

CCCXXXIII. A legacy clandestinely left to persons incapable of taking a legacy does not any longer pass to the Treasury, but, according to the analogy of the Law of Holland,[2] and also of Zeeland,[3] to the legitimate heirs.

SEC. 24.

CCCXXXIV. Those who have caused the death of the person to whom they would have succeeded as heirs or legatees cannot take that which has been left to them;[4] but their children are not prohibited from taking. In Zeeland, however, it is otherwise.[5]

SEC. 27.

CCCXXXV. The revocation of a legacy, made and signed by a testator on the margin of the *grosse* or copy, annuls such legacy; as decided by the Court in 1665;[6] but it does not annul it if not so signed; and the decision of the Supreme Court of the 25th March 1741,[7] should, it seems, be so understood.

---

[1] See Thes. 23.

[2] Bynkersh. *Q. Jur. Priv.* l. iii. c. 9. & see the Placaat of the 25 Feb. 1751.

[3] Arg. *Ord. Zeeland.* 1 Dec. 1786.   [4] Matth. *Paroem.* 6.

[5] Keur. van Zeeland, cap. 2. art. 26 ; Bynkersh. *Q. Jur. Priv.* l. iii. c. 9, in fin.   [6] *Holl. Cons.* d. v. cons. 45. p. 155·

[7] See Lybrechts, *Reden. Vertoog.* d. i. p. 298.

SEC. 28.

CCCXXXVL The words "*ten wederzyde,*"* (the effect of which has been carefully considered by the Jurists in *de Rechtsgeleerde Vragen*[8]) have reference to the sentences next preceding, wherein Grotius lays it down that a legacy would appear to have been tacitly annulled if the testator had made a donation of the thing left, or had alienated it without any necessity; but not if he had given it in pledge; for each of these cases becomes limited, or the presumption in each case drawn from these different acts of the testator fails, if there appear a contrary desire on his part.

CHAPTER XXV.—SEC. 3.

CCCXXXVII. By virtue of the reservatory clause, which operates as a confirmation of codicils, they may beyond a doubt be validly executed without witnesses.[9]

SEC. 4.

CCCXXXVIII. In codicils of this kind not only may legacies and particular *fidei-commissa* be constituted or annulled, but the name of an heir, or the amount of the hereditary shares, may also be declared;[10] and there is nothing to prevent even a universal *fidei-commissum* being thus left.

* [*Reciprocally*:—(Mr. Herbert's Translation.) Perhaps " *the one way or the other* " would, according to the present explanation, be a better rendering.]

[8] P. 101, sq.

[9] See Lybrechts, *Reden. Vert.* d. i. cap. 20. § 38. p. 323, sq.

[10] Bynkersh. Q. *Jur. Priv.* l. iii. c. 4, 5.

CHAPTER XXVI.—SEC. 12.

CCCXXXIX.—Although the rule is that the legitimate succession to movables should be regulated by the law of the domicile, yet the States of Zeeland, with the view of encouraging foreigners, have wisely enacted[1] that parents who come, together with their children, to take up their residence in Zeeland, may elect the statutory law either of their former domicile or of any other place, provided this be done in the presence of the magistrate, and a note or registry thereof be made in the public acts.

CCCXL. Since the succession to immovable property is regulated by the law of the place where it is situate, the debts of the deceased should not (according to the rule in Dig. xxviii. 5. 35 pr. & § 1.) be equally divided amongst heirs succeeding under different laws; but an account must be previously taken of the value of the particular shares of the estate, to which the different parties succeed under such different laws, and the debts should be divided proportionately amougst each class of heirs, and paid by each heir in the several classes, in proportion to his share. Nor does it seem that any distinction ought to be made between simple (chirograph) debts and those secured by pledge or special mortgage; for that class of heirs, who are obliged to pay the latter, will always have their remedy against the other class for proportionate indemnification. Those burthens, however, which are purely *real* and have been imposed on the immovable property itself, attach to the class of heirs who succeed to such

---

[1] *Ord. Zeeland,* 16 Dec. 1735.

immovable property. The Supreme Court seems, however, to have held otherwise.[2]

CCCXLI. A minor who has lost either of his parents is presumed to have retained, in respect of his succession, the last domicile of the deceased parent, unless his guardian has taken up another domicile for him, which, from the reason of law, he may do in the same manner as the surviving parent.[3]

CHAPTER XXVII.—SEC. 28.

CCCXLII. It appears clear that, by the Law of Zeeland, natural or spurious children may succeed *ab intestato* not only to their mother, but also to their maternal cognates.[4]

CCCXLIII. And, since the Law of Succession of 1599,[5] which adopts the Civil Law[6] *in subsidium*, the same rule seems to obtain in North Holland.[7]

CCCXLIV. And even in the southern part of Holland (excepting, however, South Holland, properly so called), the same rule may be adopted, from the equity of the Civil Law.[8]

CCCXLV. In Dordrecht, under a particular law,[9]

[2] See Coren, *Obs.* 21.

[3] Bynkersh. *Q. Jur. Priv.* l. i. c. 16.

[4] *Keur van Zeeland*, cap. ii. art. 23 ; *Costum. van Vlissing.* cap. xx. art. 2 ; *Costum. van Middelb.* rubr. xiv. art. 9, 10; junct. arg. Dig. xxxviii. 8. 2.

[5] Art. 14.

[6] Dig. xxxviii. 10. 4. § 2 ; xxxviii. 8. 2. 4.

[7] Blondeel, *Versterfrecht*, p. 215 & sqq.

[8] See Bynkershoek, *Q. Jur. Priv.* l. iii. c. 11, & the Ord. of 1483, in Van der Eyck, *Beschryving van Zuid-Holland*, p. 190, which does not appear to have been altered.

[9] *Costum.* art. 70, in Van de Wall, p. 1353.

and in South Holland,[1] adulterine and incestuous children also succeed to the mother.

CHAPTER XXVIII.—SEC. 3.

CCCXLVI. The rule of the ancient Aasdoms law, namely, that *the next in degree succeeds before all others.* was subject to two exceptions; the one, in respect of descendants,—who were preferred to ascendants; and the other in respect of ascendants,—who succeeded to the exclusion of collaterals.[2]

SEC. 6.

CCCXLVII. The ancient rule of succession under the Schependoms law, which still prevails in Zeeland, having been established with a view to the preservation of families, directs that, in default of descendants, the property should revert to that side from which it is presumed by law to have proceeded, namely, to the father. and mother if they be surviving, or to their children and representatives *ad infinitum;* then to the grandfather and grandmothers and their descendants; and after these, to the eight *stirpes* of great-grandfathers and great-grandmothers; and so on. But since the deceased was presumed not to have acquired anything from a surviving parent since the death of the other, neither such surviving parent nor his descendants could take anything. Further, when the property was thus divided by law amongst the *stirpes*, the right of accretion did not obtain amongst them.

---

[1] *Costum.* art. 11; ibid. p. 1356.
[2] *Costum. van Amsterd.* art. 2, 3; *Handrest.* p. 446.

SEC. 14.

CCCXLVIII. In North Holland, when children succeed to the first-dying parent, having community of property with the surviving parent, the whole of the dowry is brought into account in appraising the estate; and · afterwards, in dividing it with the survivor, the children collate a half part of it with him, as if devolving from the predeceased parent, and therefore to be reckoned in his half share; (and this rule should be maintained, in opposition to the opinion of *Voet*[3]); and after the death of the survivor, the children will then collate the other half with his brothers.[4] But in South Holland and in Zeeland the practice has been more in favour of the survivor, who is wholly excluded from the inheritance of the children, and the whole of the dowry is presumed to have devolved from the predeceased parent, and the whole of it is therefore to be collated with the surviving parent.[5] When the collation which, in the division of the common estate, has been made with such survivor, is different in one part of Holland from that which obtains in another part, it should be afterwards reclaimed in the proceeding or action for division of estate (*familiæ herciscundæ*) amongst the co-heirs of the predeceased parent; and therefore whatever the children who have received anything as dowry or otherwise have collated in this respect with the survivor himself, should be brought into account with them, to the extent to which it is liable to collation amongst the children.

---

[3] *Ad Pand.* xxxvii. 6. § 7.
[4] B. van Santen, *Generale Priviligien van Kennemerland*, p. 186 inf.
[5] See *Rechtsgel. Obs.* part ii. obs. 45, & *Supplem.* part iv. p. 243, sqq.

CCCXLIX. In this collation, which is to be made with the surviving parent, is included not only what has been given by the parents to the children on the occasion of their marriage, or in advancement of trade, or the like; but also simple donations made to the children ; this construction of the *art.* 29 of the Politi-cal Ordonnance of Holland, being rendered necessary by the whole analogy of our law.[1]

CCCL. Property which has not been valued, should either be brought into account at the time of the collation, or may be retained at the amount of its value at the time it was given. If the property had been valued, it may be retained at the amount at which it was so valued.[2]

Sec. 15.

CCCLI. Whether the Political Ordonnance of Holland* concerning the rules of succession *ab intestato*, has been adopted as law in the town of *Briel* and the territory of *Voorn*, may admit of a reasonable doubt, from the declaration of the Magistrates made in council on the 10th September, 1578,[3] and the 18th December, 1599;[4] nor does this controversy appear to have been determined by the Supreme Court in the case cited by Coren.[5]

CCCLII. The Colony of *Surinam* and the Island of *Curaçöa*, under certain Resolutions of the States

[1] See also *Keur. van Zeeland*, cap. ii. art. 22 ; *Costum. van Dord-*art. 62 (in Van de Wall, p. 1350); *van Zuid-Holland*, art. 10. (ibid. p. 1356).

[2] *Pol. Ord.* art. 29.

* [Of 1580; see B. ii. ch. 28. § 11.—Tr.]

[3] *Resol. van Holland*, 1578, p. 18.   [4] Ibid. 1599, p. 571.

[5] *Obs.* 1. p. 7.

General,[6] follow in respect of succession the rules of the Placaat of 1599. The other colonies in the *West Indies* are regulated by the Political Ordonnance of Holland, under a Resolution of the 13th October, 1629, and the 14th April, 1763. The *East Indian* colonies and the persons sojourning there, follow the Political Ordonnance, as declared by a Resolution of the 13th May, 1594, subject, however, to this modification, that the surviving parent, in case there be brothers or brothers' children on the side of the predeceased parent, succeeds to a half; but if there be none, then to the whole.[7] The same right has been conceded to the colony of *Berbice.*[8]

SEC. 25.

CCCLIII. After settling the succession of descendants of the father and mother, of brothers and sisters and their descendants, of the grandfather and grandmother, and of the uncles and their children, the Political Ordonnance regulates the rest of the succession by the three following rules : 1. That no ascendant should succeed, whose husband or wife has died;[9] 2. That the inheritance should always be divided into two shares according to the number of the two *stirpes*, paternal and maternal;[10] 3. That the right of representation as regards collaterals, should be limited to the grandchildren of brothers and the sons of uncles, and the rest admitted in right of degree;[11] excepting the descendants of brothers, who

---

[6] Surinam, 30 Aug. 1742; & Curaçoa, 17 Nov. 1752.
[7] *Resol.* 10 January 1661. [See Blondeel *Versterfr.* p. 631.—Tr.]
[8] *Resol.* 6 Dec. 1732, art. 30. [See Blondeel, *Versterfr.* p. 637.—Tr.]
[9] Art. 26.   [10] Art. 27.
[11] Art. 28.

exclude all other collaterals and parents of the second degree.[1]

CCCLIV. But from this precise rule of the Political Ordonnance the States themselves have departed in an Interpretation of the year 1594, and have it seems recalled into practice the ancient division of inheritances, under the Schependoms Law, into four, eight, or more *stirpes;* with this proviso, however, that in each *stirps* the right of representation ceases after the fourth degree, and a nearer excludes a remoter relative of the same *stirps.*[2]

CCCLV. It does not, however, follow from the above that the grandchildren of uncles, who do not possess the right of representation,[3] should be preferred to a remoter *stirps* of the same line, nearer in degree, as for instance, the son of a grand-uncle.

SEC. 31.

CCCLVI. Although the concluding words of *art.* 3 of the Placaat of 1599 concerning succession in North Holland expressly exclude half-brothers who are related on the side of the predeceased parent, where there is a surviving parent, and assign the inheritance to the latter alone (which rule has been followed by the Court,[4] in a decision of the 3rd November, 1608, and by *Grotius* in the text); yet the preceding words of the same article, as well as the reason of the law, with

---

[1] Art. 24 & 25.

[2] See also Neostad. *Decis. Supr. Cur.* 46; *Decis. en Resol. van den Hove van Holland,* n. 333, in fin.

[3] *Polit. Ord.* art. 28.

[4] *Decis. & Resol. van den Hove.* n. 175. [Van Leenwen's *Comm.* B. iii. ch. 14, § 4.]

equal clearness, admit them to a half of the inheritance. And this has been established as the more correct meaning of the law by various decisions of both the Courts,[5] since the time of *Grotius*. And the Supreme Court has cleverly detected the source of this error in the compilation of the law.[6]

SEC. 32.

CCCLVII. The grandchildren of full brothers and sisters, when they succeed by right of representation, if they be related to the deceased in a two-fold relationship, take two shares.[7]

CCCLVIII. When a half-brother and the children of full brothers succeed together, the latter have also the right of representation in respect of the half which they take out of the whole estate.[8]

SEC. 41.

CCCLIX. The meaning of *art.* 14 of the above mentioned Placaat of 1599 seems to be this,—that the Civil Law should not only be resorted to in the interpretation of the rules of succession laid down by that Law, so far as its principles will allow of it, but should also be called *in subsidium* for the purpose of determining other successions adopted out of the Roman Law, but not specified in this law of 1599.

CHAPTER XXIX.—SEC. 2.

CCCLX. If a parent has elected any particular

---

[5] See Boel. *ad Loen.* cas. 20.　　　[6] Coren, *Obs.* 29.
[7] Arg. art. 12. *Plac.* of 1599.
[8] Arg. art. 11, 12, 14; and see *Thes.* 9.

K

legitimate succession, on behalf of the children, and the children should die under the age of puberty, or after puberty, without leaving a testament, the inheritance passes as *ab intestato* to the heir, and those who have the power on attaining age of alienating or making a testament are not thereby deprived of the right of alienation or disposition *causâ mortis*. This election may be made either expressly or tacitly, as by directing that the property should revert to the side from which it proceeded.[1]

SEC. 4 AND 5.

CCCLXI. This election is frequently made not only by antenuptial contract,[2] but also by the testament of parents (but not of strangers), and also in divisory contracts made under the authority of the pupillary magistrate between a surviving parent and the relatives of the ward. It has been adopted in Zeeland in respect of testaments only ;[3] but at *Zierickzee* it is not permitted to the prejudice of a third party.[4]

CCCLXII. The election made in antenuptial or even in divisory contracts affects all the property of the children, whencesoever acquired : but an election made by testament extends only to those goods which devolve on the children from the parent testator.[5]

SEC. 6.

CCCLXIII. Any rule of legitimate succession may

---

[1] Neostad. *de Pact. Antenupt.* obs. 1 & 2 ; *Decis. & Resol. van den Hove*, n. 342. [2] Thes. 241.
[3] *Ord. Zeeland.* 16 Dec. 1735. [4] Of which see *Thes.* 303.
[5] Lybrechts (*Reden Vertoog. d.* ii. *Byl.* R. p. 481, seq.) dissents, but erroneously.

be adopted by such election; not only either of those now prevailing in Holland, but also that of the ancient *Aasdoms* or *Schependoms* law, or of the law of any other country. And such election may without doubt be validly made even in North Holland.

CHAPTER XXX.—SEC. 1.

CCCLXIV. It is evident from the Civil Law, and is tacitly implied in the Law of Holland,[6] that succession *ab intestato* is not to be restricted to the tenth degree of relationship; and the Supreme Court has, since the time of *Grotius,* so decided.[7]

SEC. 2.

CCCLXV. It would appear from *art.* 14 of the Placaat of 1599, that in North Holland, in default of all relatives, one spouse may succeed to the other under the edict *unde vir et uxor;* and it appears from the proceedings reported by *Loenius*[8] that the Treasury was not decided in respect of its rights herein. In South Holland,[9] as well as in Zeeland,[10] a different rule seems to have been adopted.

SEC. 3.

CCCLXVI. Although the Treasury, at least in South Holland, is entitled to the succession on default of relatives, yet the meaning and intention of the

[6] *Polit. Ordin.* art. 24.
[7] 14 March 1622; see Bort van '*t Holl. Leenrecht,* d. v. t. 3. c. 10. n. 8 and 9, p. 174.   [8] *Decis. cas.* 108.
[9] Neostad. *Decis. Supr. Cur.* 7.
[10] Bynkersh. *Q. Jur. Priv.* l. iii. c. 12.

Political Ordonnance excludes it even in case there be no relatives at all on one side : for the 28th *art..* on the default of collaterals having the right of representation, admits to the succession all other relatives, without distinction of *stirpes* ; and the 27th *art.*, adopting the division into two *stirpes*, allows the cognates of either *stirps* to come in.

CCCLXVII. In Zeeland the *Schependoms* law, by reason of dividing the inheritance into two, four, or more *stirpes*, admits the Treasury to the share of a *stirps* which is deficient.[1] But this law was at first overruled in practice[2] by equity ; and it has since, under a new law of the States,[3] entirely ceased to operate. The latter law, excluding the Treasury, directs that the next *stirps* should succeed by right of accretion in place of a deficient *stirps*.

CHAPTER XXXI.—SEC. 4.

CCCLXVIII. By the Law of Zeeland, one half the property of illegitimate children goes to the Treasury,[4] and the other half to the maternal relatives. In North Holland, all the property goes to the relatives of the maternal line.[5] And the same rule may, not without reason, be laid down as regards South Holland, since there also a spurious child is presumed to have acquired his property from the mother alone, and even in the succession of illegitimate children (to whom spurious children, as far as regards the mother, are analogous), the share of the deficient line accrues to the other line.[6]

[1] Grotius, *in de Holl. Cons.* d. 3. st. 2. cons. 197.
[2] *N. Nederl. Jaarb.* 1775, p. 1127, sqq.   [3] 1 Dec. 1786.
[4] Ibid.   [5] Law of 1599, art. 14, junct. art. 3, 6, 7, 9, 10.
[6] See *Thes.* 366.

CHAPTER XXXVI.—SEC. 2.

CCCLXIX. The reason of our law hardly allows of predial servitudes, which have been promised by con tract, being established by mere use and sufferance without a solemn cession in law; although *Grotius* is of a different opinion hereon.[7]

CHAPTER XXXVIII.—SEC. 8.

CCCLXX. Although the returns derived from ships are included under the term *profits*,[8] yet, since damages arising from the defective navigation of ships should be made good,[9] and as it is the daily practice among careful merchants to insure them against the dangers of the sea, the usufructuary ought, in the event of the ship being lost, to be answerable for neglecting this precaution.

CHAPTER XXXIX.—SEC. 3.

CCCLXXI. The security which, it appears, a usufructuary is amongst us bound to give, together with sureties, cannot be dispensed with by testament; unless the power of alienation has been conceded; in which case not the mere usufruct, but the property, subject to the burthen of restoring it, is considered to have been left.[10]

SEC. 5.

CCCLXXII. When a usufruct with the power of alienation has been left under the condition that the property should be restored after death, a *fidei-commis-*

---

[7] And see *Holl. Cons.* d. iii. st. 2. cons. 316.
[8] Dig. vii. 1. 12. § 1.   [9] Dig. vi. 1. 16. § 1 ; Dig. vii. 1. 65, pr
[10] Voet *ad Pand.* vii. 1. § 11.

sum of the residue would seem to be enjoined; and in this respect the inventory cannot be dispensed with.[1]

CCCLXXIII. Where the power of alienating in case of necessity has been granted to the usufructuary, so long as such necessity does not exist, there will only be a nude usufruct, and therefore the security cannot be dispensed with; and if after such security has been given, a portion of the property is alienated through necessity, the security will subsist in respect of the remainder.[2]

CCCLXXIV. If a surviving spouse has been instituted *heir* in usufruct of all the property, and a substitute appointed in express words to succeed after the death of such survivor, the survivor will be the universal heir; but the substitute (if words of *fideicommissum* have not been employed) will, after the death of the survivor, succeed in direct right to all the property which he had obtained from the deceased; or, if he had the power of alienation, to so much as remains of the estate.[3]

CCCLXXV. The same rule would apply, if in this case the testator had in express words *bequeathed* the usufruct of all the property, but had at the same time given the power of alienating. And even if the power of alienating had not been granted, the will would still by our law take effect, since a testament in which no heir has been instituted, is nevertheless valid at the present day;[4] and the words of a legacy or bequest may, in such an event, be favourably construed as the institution of an heir.

---

[1] Neostad. *Supr. Cur.* dec. 31.
[2] Coren. *Consil.* xv. n. 5, sqq.; Neostad. *Cur. Dec.* 20 in fin.
[3] See *Thes.* 311.   [4] Th. 290.

SEC. 16.

CCCLXXVI. The Supreme Court seems to have held that a usufruct is destroyed by a solemn cession of it to a stranger.[5]   *Voet*, however, is of a different opinion.[6]

SEC. 19.

CCCLXXVII. The Court has likewise decided that there might be a valid usufruct of apparel.[7]

SEC. 20.

CCCLXXVIII. A usufruct of moneys lent out on security is a proper, not a *quasi*, usufruct.[8]

CHAPTER XL.—SEC. 8.

CCCLXXIX. The law peculiar to some places, namely, that upon alienation of an *emphyteusis*, double *canon* or rent should be paid,[9] should not, according to *Groenewegen*[10] and others, be understood as giving the owner the election between recovering double rent and the right of *retractus*, but only as permitting the emphyteutee to alienate, on payment of double rent.

CCCLXXX. By the laws of Holland of the 31st October, 1620, and the 27th September, 1658, upon every alienation of an emphyteutic estate, the property

---

[5] *Decis. & Resol. van den Hove*, n. 74, junct. n. 100.

[6] *Ad Pand.* vii. 4. § 3.

[7] 14 May, 1612, *Decis. & Resol. van den Hove van Holl.* n. 358.

[8] Voet *dissentiente, ad Pand.* vii. 5, § 3.   [See Van der Linden's *Supplem. to Voet, ad Pand.* d. § 3.—Tr.]

[9] *Rechtsgel. Obs.* part i. obs. 54, & *Supplem.* part iv. p. 210.

[10] *Ad Cod.* iv. 66, § 3.

whereof belongs to the State, double rent should be paid;* and the remarks of *Voet* on this subject[1] should, therefore, be read with caution.

SEC. 9.

CCCLXXXI. Although the charges on the property, in a proper emphyteusis, attach to the emphyteutee, yet if the rent is nearly equal to the value of the fruits, the reason of the law requires that the duty of one and one half *per cent.* should fall on the owner.[2]

SEC. 10.

CCCLXXXII. In order to acquire a right of emphyteusis by an act *inter vivos*, a solemn cession in law seems to be necessary under the Placaat of 1529.

SEC. 19.

CCCLXXXIII. The right of the emphyteutee is extinguished by the non-payment of rent for the space of three years. In a Dutch emphyteusis, the direct *dominium* of which belongs to the State, other penalties than that of forfeiture have been imposed on such neglect, by a law passed since the publication of this work of Grotius.[3]

CCCLXXXIV. On the forfeiture of an emphyteusis, by non-payment of rent, not only the owner, but after his death his heir also, may claim the property.[4]

---

* [*Rechtsgel. Obs.* part i. obs. 54. Tr.]

[1] *Ad Pand.* vi. 3, § 31–35.

[2] *Nederl. Adv. Boek,* d. ii. cons. 222; & see Grotius, B. iii. ch. 18, § 4, in fin.

[3] *Plac. Holl.* 31. Oct. 1620.

[4] Voet (*ad Pand.* vi. 3. § 45), *dissentiente.*

SEC. 23.

CCCLXXXV. By the law of Holland of the 31st October, 1620, as modified by the laws of the 27th September, 1658, and the 16th June, 1703, all emphyteuses, the direct *dominium* of which belongs to the State, may be redeemed, if the rent does not exceed three florins, by the payment of thirty-two stivers for every stiver of the rent; if it does not exceed six florins, by payment of forty, and if it exceeds six florins, of forty-eight stivers for every stiver.

CHAPTER XLI.

CCCLXXXVI. Since proceedings have within our own time been taken in the Dutch Assemblies with regard to the abolition of feuds and feudal relations, and the Supreme Senate of the Dutch nation is as yet deliberating concerning it, the very prudent advice given by the Court of Holland in their letter to the Provisional Representatives, of the 8th December, 1765,[5] is worthy of commendation ; the 4, 6, 7, 8, 9, 10, 17, 18, 27, 29, & 32nd articles of which cannot be understood without a knowledge of the Feudal Law.

SEC. 2.

CCCLXXXVII. The *mala* or *recta feuda* of Zeeland differ from Dutch feuds : for they may be divided amongst the sons,[6] and in default of sons, may be

---

[5] *Missive van President en Raaden van den Hove van Holland en Zeeland, aan de provisioneele Representanten van het Volk van Holland ; houdende en gedetailleerd Plan en Concept-Publicatie, wegens de mortificatie van het Leenstelsel.*

[6] *Keur. van Zeeland,* cap. ii. art. 6, 7.

redeemed by the daughters, and even by agnates and cognates;[1] and, by the law of the 21st October, 1653, may be converted into hereditary feuds by payment of a certain price. But Dutch feuds are indivisible, excepting *good* or hereditary feuds, which have not a jurisdiction attached to them, and which, by the Law of the 4th December, 1660, may be divided by act *inter vivos*, with the consent of the Vicar of the Feudal Court, without a special privilege from the States.*

SEC. 5.

CCCLXXXVIII. A feud which has been purchased, but not as yet acquired by the purchaser by investiture, does not pass to the feudal successor, but to all the heirs, who will have to choose one from amongst themselves to be invested with the feud.[2]

SEC. 6.

CCCLXXXIX. In the difficult question, whether the succession to feuds should be regulated according to the laws of the place where the feud is situated, or according to the laws of the dominant Court to which the feud is subject[4]—if no provision has been made in this respect in the letters of investiture,—the more correct course is to follow the law of the dominant Court; since the feudal contract ought to be interpreted according

---

[1] Ibid. art. 8.

* [*Rechtsgl. Obs.* part i. obs. 55.—Tr.]

[2] Bort (*van de Roll. Leenr.* d. v. t. 3. c. 2. n. 19, sqq.) *dissentiente.*

[3] See Van de Wall, *Handv. & Privil. van Dordr.* p. 807, 808, in not.

to the law of the place where it has been executed.[4] And the arguments of *Voet*,[5] who is of a different opinion, do not prove the contrary; nor is the rule affected by the opinion of *Neostadt*[6] or of *Grotius*,[7] who adopt one rule of succession in respect of feuds on *Schependoms* territory, and another in respect of those on *Aasdoms* territory: and the reason is this,—that though there is one supreme feudal Court in Holland, which presides over both divisions of Holland, there cannot be one law in respect of the feudal succession, but the law ought to be different according to each territory.

SEC. 8.

CCCXC. If a feud has been purchased by a husband with the common property, it stands to reason that the whole of the price paid for it should at the time of the division be brought into the estate, and not, as some would have it, a half only. But where a division of allodial property is made, the husband should pay to the wife a half of the price out of his own property.[8] It can seldom happen, however, that any dispute should arise hereon except about words, since the matter, in effect, comes to the same thing.

CCCXCI. The price at which a feud has been purchased and the common estate thereby diminished, should be brought into collation: for the existing value of the feud, whether it is increased or diminished, is

[4] Dig. L. 17. 34, arg.   [5] *Digr. de Feud.* § 80.
[6] *De Feud. Holl. Orig. & Success.* c. v. § 46, sqq. & c. vi. § 28.
[7] B. ii. ch. 41. § 12, 24.
[8] Neostad. *Obs. Feud.* dec. ii. obs. 3; *Decis & Resol. van den Hove van Holl.* n. 348, 395.

profit or loss to the possessor only as the *dominus utilis :*[1] and it has also been so enacted in Zeeland.[2]

SEC. 9.

CCCXCII. If a vassal dies on *Schependoms* territory or in Zeeland, leaving a surviving parent and her children, but no relatives on the side of the predeceased parent, a new feud arises to the lord.

SEC. 24.

CCCXCIII. Since the rule in respect of succession to an ancient feud, which directs that a relative of the line to which the feud attaches should be preferred to others, is stricter than the other rule, which requires that the relative should be such as could succeed *ab intestato*, there appears to be no reason why in respect of *Schependoms* property a surviving parent may not, in default of brothers, succeed to a feud.

SEC. 40.

CCCXCIV. The investiture of a feud, or the act by which the direct lord grants the feud to any one, and receives him as vassal in *fidem et clientelam,* is necessary in order to transfer the right to the feud; but should not be confounded with the instrument of investiture. A renewed investiture to the successor of a vassal depends on the previous investiture, and does not transfer greater rights to him than he is entitled to upon the terms of the first investiture; and this is like-

---

[1] *Notab. Poinct.* art. 20. Neostad. *Obs. Feud.* dec. ii. obs. 3.
[2] *Keur. van Zeeland.* cap. ii. art. 16, in fin.
[3] Bort (d. v. t. 3. c. 7. n. 23. p. 163) *dissentiente.*

wise implied in the words "*saving our own rights and those of any third party*," which are generally inserted in the instrument.

CCCXCV. Homage (*Hominium*, which some incorrectly call *Homagium*) is an acknowledgment of the direct *dominium* made by the vassal, together with a promise of fidelity, ratified in most cases by oath. The vassal's obligation to render military service having however been abolished by our customs, this oath has been properly dispensed with by the law of the 18th January, 1736.

SEC. 51.

CCCXCVI. The jurisdiction of the Feudal Court extends to all disputes regarding feudal contracts, the right by which feuds are held, the duties imposed on a feud, the succession to a feud, and the loss or forfeiture thereof :[4] but not to a question whether or not any property is feudal ; which, inasmuch as the condition of the affirming and denying parties herein should be equal, and as in a doubtful case the property should be considered allodial, should be referred to the decision of the Ordinary Court : unless the defendant, in order to question the jurisdiction of the Feudal Court, denies by way of exception that the property is feudal ; in which case that question alone should be tried by the Feudal Court by way of a preliminary proceeding ; and the defendant cannot in the mean time be compelled to plead to the other conclusions ;[5] and, lastly, it rests with the plaintiff to prove that the property is feudal.[6]

[4] *Inst. Cur. Feud.* 7 April 1661.
[5] Neostad. *Obs. Feud.* dec. 4, obs. i.   [6] Ibid. dec. iii. obs. 3.

CHAPTER XLII.

CCCXCVII. Although in the acquisition of feuds, as of allodials, a distinction may be drawn between titles and modes of acquiring, yet care should be taken against supposing that any one can become a vassal without investiture.

SEC. 1.

CCCXCVIII. The grant of a feud (since it should not be confounded with investiture), when made by testament by way of legacy, may give the legatee an action *in rem ;* if, namely, the heir himself holds the primary feud, on which the property granted in sub-feud ought to depend. *Voet,* is however, is of a different opinion, but incorrectly.[1]

SEC. 2.

CCCXCIX. The privilege of disposing of feuds by testament generally includes also the right of substituting. In respect of this part of the formula, the words of the privilege, which had been erroneously corrupted, even as regards privileges previously granted, have been amended by the States by a public programma.[2] A substitution made by way of *fidei-commissum* in favour of the children, whom the party instituted might have, annexes the feud to the rest of the inheritance, and consequently all those who succeed to the rest of the inheritance succeed also to the

---

[1] *Ad Pand. Digr. de Feud.* § 30.
[2] 11 January, 1759 ; *Groot Plac. Boek,* d. viii. p. 654.

feud ; as decided by the Feudal Court on the 19th July, 1666.[3]

CCCC. Since the testamentary disposition of a feud, when made without having obtained leave to dispose by testament, is void in form, even the value of the feud so left is not payable.

SEC. 3.

CCCCI. There is a great difference between the acquisition of allodial property and of a feud by cession in law, both as regards the mode and the effect. The former is effected by a declaration of the lord made in the presence of a judge, and at once passes the *dominum* : the latter requires a waiver of the feud made by the lord in favour of the other, and does not pass the *dominium utile*, unless the purchaser or some other successor has been invested by the lord. If such waiver has not been made, the party alienating still remains the vassai.[4] By the most recent law, however,[5] the alienation of feuds *inter vivos* is valid when made in the presence of the ordinary judge, who is to notify the fact of the alienation to the Feudal Court.

SEC. 5.

CCCII. An annual rent cannot be charged on a feud, unless the purchaser is invested therewith as a feud by the lord. A feud may be charged with a mortgage, a dowry, or a usufruct, by the simple confirmation of the lord, without investiture.[6] In imposing an emphyteusis

[3] See Bort, p. 90, in fin.
[4] Neostad. *Obs. Feud.* dec. vi. obs. 3. p. 154.   [5] 7 May 1799.
[6] *Notab. Poinct.* art. 7 & 12.

on a feud, the reason of law requires that there should be an investiture.

Sec. 7.

CCCCIII. An ancient feud devolving on any one by succession *ab intestato* is not comprised in the rest of the inheritance, nor reckoned in the legitimate share left to a son; nor, on the other hand, is it reckoned in the estate, in estimating the legitimate shares of the other children.

CCCCIV. From this peculiarity of a feud, it follows that not only a relative, but even a son who is the successor to a feud and at the same time heir to the allodials, may acknowledge the feud and repudiate the rest of the inheritance; but a very equitable law of Holland[1] has done away with the inequitable results of a strict observance of this rule; and even in a case where the deceased had not been condemned for debt, permits feuds to be seized and sold *in subsidium*, for a debt of the deceased, which cannot be satisfied out of his allodial property. This law should, it seems, be understood as applicable to *recta feuda* also.

Sec. 8.

CCCCV. Both the *dominium directum* and the *dominium utile* of a feud may be acquired by the prescription of the third of a century, over the allodial propeity of another granted or accepted in feud. By the same prescription a vassal who has been wrongly invested with and has possessed a feud, may resist the rightful

[1] 21 March 1686.

feudal successor.[2] In Zeeland the prescription of twenty or of thirty years has also been adopted in respect of feuds.[3]

CHAPTER XLIII.

CCCCVI. A feud is either destroyed,[4] or lost,[5] and this either as respects the lord[6] or the vassal.[7]

SEC. 1.

CCCCVII. In default of relatives the surviving spouse does not succeed to a feud, not even in respect of Aasdoms property, for no alteration has been made in the law of 1599[8] as regards the succession to feuds.

CCCCVIII. A *feudum rectum*, in default of male issue of a son, does not devolve on a surviving uncle, although descended from the same grandfather and original vassal; but reverts to the lord; as declared in 1525, on the evidence of a great number of persons.[6]

SEC. 2.

CCCCIX. From the intention of the new law, as well as in equity, when a feud has been lost, or, being a hereditary feud, has been left open by defect of blood relatives, or has been forfeited for felony, the lord is bound *in subsidium* for a debt which the vassal may have contracted, so far as it can be satisfied out of the

---

[2] *Decis. Cur.* 31 July, 1643. & *Senat. Supr.* 20 Mar. 1655, in Bort, p. 103.

[3] See *Thes.* 209.   [4] Voet, *Digr. de Feud.* § 1, 2, 4, 5.

[5] Ibid. § 6, 7.   [6] Ibid. § 4, 5.   [7] Ibid. § 2, 6, 7.

[8] Art. 14.

[9] See Bort, d. v. c. 3. reg. 3. p. 133. & c. iv. n. 9. p. 135.

L

feudal property.[1] It is not clear, however, whether the same rule should obtain in respect of a *feudum rectum*.[2]

CCCCX. In either of these cases, viz., of an open inheritance or of forfeiture, the lord is bound to make compensation to the vassal or his heir for improvements made on the feudal property.

SEC. 5.

CCCCXI. A *feudum rectum* of Holland is prohibited, by a Resolution of the 25th June, 1619, from being converted into hereditary or allodial property. and by the same law hereditary feuds cannot be released from the feudal bond, except by the payment of a third part of the value. It has since[3] been enacted that those who hold fends from the States of Holland, to which a jurisdiction does not attach, may release them from the feudal *nexus* by the payment of a tenth part of their just value. This law does not, however, seem to affect *feuda recta ;* though the question has now been almost set at rest, for in the Letter of the Court already referred to,[4] no *feuda recta* are said to be any longer found in Holland. By the most recent law of Holland on the subject,[5] the feudal *nexus* may be dissolved even by those who have neglected to apply for investiture, by the payment of a twentieth part of the value.

SEC. 6.

CCCCXII. It is a common opinion (which the States

---

[1] So held 31 Jan. 1637 ; see Bort. d. vii. t. 2. c. 4. n. 26. p. 323, &. Dec. 1637; *Holl. Cons.* d. iii. st. 2. cons. 10, & inferred from arg. *Ord. Holl.* 21 Mar. 1686, of which see *Thes.* 404.

[2] See *Holl. Cons.* ibid.   [3] 12 Mar. 1722.

[4] (See Thes. 386) p 13. f. and sq.   [5] 4 October 1797.

of Holland seem to have approved of[6]) that neither the lord nor the vassal of an estate can acquire a discharge from the feudal *nexus* by prescription, even of the third of a century. This rule is, however, subject to certain limitations: 1. If a vassal has refused to pay homage to the lord by publicly contending that the property is not feudal; 2. If the lord has refused to keep his engagement to the vassal; 3. If the lord has failed to institute his action for forfeiture of the feud; 4. If the feud has been alienated as an allodial to a *bonâ fide* possessor. In these cases the prescription of the third of a century protects the possessor.

SEC. 7.

CCCCXIII. It stands to reason that a vassal may, even without the consent of the lord, release himself from the feudal *nexus* by a *refutatio* or waiver of the feud, especially since the rendering of military service has now ceased.

SEC. 8.

CCCCXIV. Since hereditary feuds may be alienated *inter vivos*, a guardian also may, under a decree from the magistrate, validly alienate the feud of a ward.

CHAPTER XLV.—SEC. 4.

CCCCXV. The tenths of fallow land do not belong to those who have the right of tithe, but rather to the State. Land which has been reclaimed from water, or had, by digging for turf, been submerged for a time, and in respect of which the possessors were originally

---

[6] *Placaat* of the 8 Dec. 1662.

liable to pay tithe, is not accounted as fallow land; as decided by the Supreme Court on the 17th July, 1792.

CHAPTER XLVI.—SEC. 9.

CCCCXVI. When the *jus superficiei*, or right to building on another man's property, has been acquired by purchase or other similar title, it cannot be taken away by the owner by the mere payment of the value, without the consent of the *superficiarius*. The reason of law does not permit it, nor is it allowed by the laws of Zeeland.[1]

CHAPTER XLVIII.—SEC. 13.

CCCCXVII. A person who has lent money for the purpose of building a new house or ship, does not, according to the more correct opinion, acquire a right of tacit mortgage; although it has been received in practice amongst us that the tacit mortgage allowed by the Civil Law to one who restores or renews a building, extends to the necessary repairs done to a building or a ship.*

SEC. 14.

CCCCXVIII. A person who has lent money for the funeral expenses or the last illness of a deceased person, possesses indeed a privilege even before mortgage creditors, but does not seem to have a tacit mortgage.†

---

[1] *Ord. Zeeland.* cap. ii. art. 15.

* [Van den Berg, *Nederl. Adv.* d. iii. cons. 281.—Tr.] •

† [See a decision, 21 May 1612, in Van Alphen, *Papeg.* d. i. p. 482, and in *de Decis. en Resol. v. d. Hove v. Holl.* n. 359, mourning clothes do not come under funeral expenses; Dec. & Resol. n. 181; Coren. *Observ.* 38, n. 40. 41; Van Alphen, *Papeg.* d. i. p. 485.—Tr.]

SEC. 15.

CCCCXIX. The Province of Holland has a tacit mortgage on the goods or property of those who are indebted in taxes, whether real or personal.[2] This right has also been granted to some who farm these taxes, such as bakers,[3] and others.[4] CCCCXX. A similar right belongs to the State over the property of its administrators or officers,[5] as well as over the property of those with whom it has entered into any contract, for we have adopted this legal mortgage also out of the Civil Law.[6] Nor is this affected by the Resolution of Holland of the 25th Februaiy, 1678, the object of which is widely different.

SEC. 16.

CCCCXXI. Wards, and others who are under guardianship or curateship, have a tacit mortgage over the property of their guardians or curators, even for debts due by the guardian himself previous to his guardianship :‡ and this right of mortgage passes to the heirs of the wards.§ By the law of *Dordrecht*[7] it has been

---

[2] *Resol. Holl.* 4 May 1746, 31 July 1749.

[3] 20 March 1680.   [4] 25 Aug. 1724, 12 April 1738.

[5] 19 July 1625. Placaat, 22 Jan. 1695, art. 36. fin. & 37. f.

[6] See *Waarschouw* of the 5 Feb. 1665, and *Thes.* 9. [The State has no tacit hypothec in respect of fines or penalties imposed in respect of criminal offences; Dig. xlix. 14, 67; but it has priority over other simple creditors in respect of the costs and expenses of a criminal prosecution; *Regtsg. Observ.* part ii. obs. 61, p. 145; *Holl Cons.* d. iii. cons. 163. See also Voet *ad Pand.* xx. 2, § 9.—Tr.]

‡ [Voet *ad Pand.* xx. 2. 16; *Holl. Cons.* d. i. cons. 18.—Tr.]

§ [See Voet *ad Pand.* xx. 2. 18, 19; and as to a parent-guardian, Vervolg der Holl. Cons. d. ii. cons. 21.—Tr.]

[7] 20 Dec. 1668.

specially provided that this right of mortgage should determine on the lapse of four years after the attainment of majority; which rule has been laid down there in respect also of other legal mortgages.[1]

CCCCXXII. The same right of tacit mortgage belongs to a ward over the property of a stepfather with whom the guardian-mother has contracted a second marriage,* and even over the property of a stepmother whom the guardian-father has married, as expressly laid down by various pupillary laws; which should, however, be understood to apply only to the case where community of property has been admitted into the second marriage: for in the absence of all community, the property of a stepmother should, according to the reason of law, be free from this burthen.

SEC. 17.

CCCCXXIII. The lessors of lands, in town as well as in the country, have a tacit mortgage over things brought and carried into such lands.[2]† In respect of lands in the country, the fruits growing thereon, and even those which have been carried into barns, are subject to the same right.[3] This right should be exercised,

---

[1] *Rechtsgel. Obs.* part. i. obs. 71.

* [Voet ad *Pand.* xx. 2. 11.—Tr.]

[2] *Rechtsgel. Obs.* part. i. obs. 72, & *Supplem.* part. iv. p. 214. sqq.; and see *Keur van Zeeland*, cap. ii. art. 35; *Costum van Middelb.* rubr. ix. art. 7, junct. rubr. v. art. 5; *Costum. van Vlissing*, cap. vii. art. 9; Ord. of *Haarlem* concerning Leases, of 1710, art. 13. sqq.; *Keur van Haarlem*, d. i. p. 211, where this right is fully and accurately treated of.

† [As to what things are included under the term "*invecta et illata*," see *Holl. Cons.* d. v. cons. 52, 53, and what not, Voet *ad Pand.* xx. 2, 5, and '*t Vervolg. der Holl. Cons.* cons. 65, p. 187.—Tr.]

[3] *Decis. en Resol. van der Hove*, n. 84.

or in order to preserve it the things should be put under arrest, before they are carried away from the land.‡ At some places it may be exercised even within a month after the removal.[4]

CCCCXXIV. Bleachers of linen have the right of detaining the linen for wages even previously due to them;[5] and also the right of preference, if they have delivered them, as they ought, to the curator of the insolvent's property, to be sold together with his other property.[6]

Sec. 18.

CCCCXXV. Cities, and, by reason of their similarity, country towns also, have a tacit mortgage over the property of those who collect taxes;[7] as also the Church over the property of its administrators.[8]

Sec. 21.

CCCCXXVI. A merchant should be preferred to the other creditors in respect of the price which his factor or agent has realised from his merchandise, and in respect of merchandise which the factor has purchased with the merchant's money, even in his own name,—so long as the same is to be found in the estate.[9]§

‡ [Groeneweg *de leg. abrog.* ad Dig. xx. 2. 9; Voet *ad Pand.* d. t. § 3.—Tr.]   [4] *Keur. van Leyden*, art. 135.

[5] *Placaat Holl.* 20 January 1614, & 9 May 1732.

[6] *Resol. Holl.* 3 April 1677.

[7] *Resol. Holl.* 19 July, 1625; *Deeis. Cur.* 1636, in Loen. cas. 69; *Resol. Holl.* 24 Feb. 1679; *Dects. en Resol. van den Hove van Holl.* n. 79.   [8] Ibid. n. 355·

[9] *Handv. van Amsterdam*, p. 539; Roseboom, cap. xxxvii. § 28, 29.

§ [See also Neostad. *Dec. Cur. Holl.* 45; Holl. Cons. d. i. u. 203; Bynkersh. *Q. J. Priv.* L iii. c. 15.—Tr.]

SEC. 23.

CCCCXXVII. A mortgage, whether general or special, and whether of movable or immovable property, is not valid, unless the duty of two and a half per cent. on the amount due was paid into the public Treasury on the same day on which the mortgage was effected;[1] *excepting*,—1. In respect of debts contracted in right of the Orphan Chamber; 2. Of tacit and legal mortgages; 3. Of contracts of bottomry; 4. Of a pledge of movable property which has been delivered to the creditor; and 5. Of mortgages for the price of immovable property called *Kustingen*, effected at the time of the sale.

CCCCXXVIII. Although by the general Law of Holland, a general mortgage of immovable property made in the presence of any judge of Holland, is valid everywhere, yet at Leyden an exception to this rule has been adopted in practice, in respect of a mortgage effected by a citizen of Leyden at any other place than in that town, and which does not affect immovable property situated there.[2]

SEC. 24.

CCCCXXIX. A general conventional mortgage of immovable property is extinguished, if the property mortgaged has been transferred to another for a valuable consideration (*titulo oneroso*). But it is otherwise in respect of a legal mortgage, which is left subject to

---

[1] *Waarschouw*, 5 February 1665. [Which see, Bœl *ad Loen. Decis.* cas. 17. p. 121.—Tr.]

[2] *Keur. van Leyd.* art. 139; which passage Bœl (*ad Loen. Decis.* cas. 17. p. 116.) incorrectly restricts to the case contemplated by the Law of the 26th Sept. 1656.

the rule of the Civil Law, a consequence of which, however, is that amongst us also, a *bonâ fide* possessor, if sued before the principal debtor or his sureties, is legally entitled to the *beneficium ordinis*.[3]

SEC. 27.

CCCCXXX. Securities (*obligatien*) may be pledged without the payment of the duty of two and a half per cent., provided they be delivered to the creditor.

SEC. 28.

CCCCXXXI. The Minute of the 5th February, 1665, of which we have already spoken,[4] has neither abrogated the rights of a mortgage executed publicly, as under the Code viii. 18. 11; nor introduced a new right of mortgage upon the mere payment of the duty of two and a half per cent.; but has only imposed a duty on the conventional mortgages already in use.

SEC. 29.

CCCCXXXII. Movable property which have been pledged either generally or specially without delivery, if alienated by the debtor, are discharged from the pledge: and this holds true also of securities, even where they have been mortgaged; but not as regards those instruments called *Kusting-Brieven*.[5]

SEC. 30.

CCCCXXXIII. A special mortgage of immovable property cannot be effected by convention, unless

[3] *Nov.* iv. c. 2.   [4] *Thes.* 427.
[5] *Nederl. Adv. B.* d. ii. cons. 161. [See infra, Th. 830.]

accompanied by payment of the two and a half per cent.
duty, and executed in the presence of the judge of the
place where the property is situate. It should also be
registered in the public acts; but is not rendered void
by the neglect to register it: though *Boel* is incorrectly
of a different opinion.[1]

SEC. 32.

CCCCXXXIV. In respect of a special mortgage of
immovable property, the *beneficium ordinis* does not
hold[2]*

SEC. 33.

CCCCXXXV. Property, whether movable or even
immovable, which has been mortgaged and delivered,
may, on the principles of the Civil Law as adopted by
us,[3] be retained as against the debtor himself, even for
a debt due on a note.[4]

SEC. 34.

CCCCXXXVI. A special mortgage of immovable
property is by the general Law of Holland preferred to
a prior general conventional mortgage.[5] It has also
been so enacted at Middelburg by the Law of the 2nd
August, 1597, which has been confirmed by the States
of Zeeland[6] (altering the 11th and 12th articles of *rubr.*

---

[1] Boel *ad Loen. decis.* cas. 17. p. 117.
[2] *Polit. Ord.* art. 36; and see *Costum. van Middelb.* rubr. viii. art. 14.
* [See Thes. 429. See also Neostad. *Decis. Supr. Cur.* 41.—Tr.]
[3] Thes. 18.   [4] Cod. viii. 27.
[5] *Polit. Ord.* art. 35.
[6] 6 Aug. 1597.

viii. of the Statute of Middelburg). The same rule seems also to have been adopted at Flushing.[7]

SEC. 36.

CCCCXXXVII. Since a tacit or legal mortgage has the same force as a special mortgage, it is preferred to a subsequent special mortgage, and from the reason of our law, even to a prior general conventional mortgage. On the other hand, it gives place to a prior special mortgage. There is, however, an exception to the former rule, in the case of the mortgage of movables which has been effected by delivery; and also in the case of that kind of mortgage of immovables termed *Kusting ;*[8] and to the latter rule, in case a legal mortgage is privileged, or has been confirmed, in respect of things brought and carried into a leasehold, by an arrest.†

SECS. 38, 39, AND 40.

CCCCXXXVIII. The peculiar right which has been confirmed to the Amsterdammers by the Charter of the 8th March, 1594, is two-fold : 1. That a mortgage of immovable property effected in the presence of any other judge in Holland should not affect property situated at Amsterdam ; 2. That a general mortgage effected at Amsterdam should be preferred to a subsequent special mortgage, except as regards those mortgages called *Kustingen.* And in order that this privilege might not be evaded by sales under a *voluntary decree,* it has been further provided by a Resolution of the

[7] *Costum. van Vlissing.* cap. xxii. art. 4 and 5.
[8] Of which see Th. 427, § 5.
† [See Thes. 423.]

States of the 30th January, 1608, that in such a case the seller should give security with proper sureties, to restore the price. Nor has this right been at all altered by the Minute of the 5th February, 1665, although this law provides that admissions of debt made in writing in the presence of the Schepenen (*Schepen Kennissen*) should no longer have the force of a mortgage, unless the duty of two and a half per cent. has been paid to the Treasury.

SEC. 41.

CCCCXXXIX. Although a creditor cannot without the authority of a judge sell property mortgaged to him, whether generally or specially, yet there is nothing to prevent his legally selling a pledge delivered to him, where it was originally stipulated that he might sell it.[1]

CCCCXL. It has been enacted in Zeeland[2] that a mortgage (namely, of immovables) should not be sold for the benefit of one of the creditors, unless the others to whom the same property has also been mortgaged have been cited.

SEC. 43.

CCCCXLI. It may reasonably be doubted whether a subsequent mortgagee can, amongst us, tender a debt to the prior mortgagee, even against his will, and thus step into his place and his rights.[3]

---

[1] Dig. xiii. 7. 5. [Rather, where there has been no stipulation to the contrary. Dig. xiii. 7. 4.—Tr.]

[2] *Ord. Zeeland.* 2 Feb. 1671.

[3] See Voet *ad Pand.* xx. 4. § 35. [Groenew. *de leg. abrog.* ad Cod. viii. 18. l. I.—Tr.]

SEC. 44.

 CCCCXLII. The bare knowledge of a creditor, who is not unaware that the property mortgaged to him would be sold, even publicly, is not to be taken as a tacit discharge of his mortgage.

CCCCXLIII. Where no payment of interest has been made, a third party in possession is secured by the prescription of thirty years, and the debtor or his heir by the prescription of forty years; but if interest has been paid, prescription does not run ;[4] though the Court has more than once decided otherwise.[5]

CONCLUDING CHAPTER.

OF THE RIGHT OF PREFERENCE AMONG CREDITORS.

CCCCXLIV. The question concerning the right of preference, on a meeting of creditors, is to be discussed, not before the judge of the place where the property is situate, but before the judge of the place where the debtor has made cession to the Court, or the inheritance has been adiated under benefit of inventory, or the property placed under the administration of curator. Neither can the Court of Holland, from the nature of the cause and the conflict of jurisdictions, entertain such a proceeding.[6]

CCCCXLV. A similar rule was laid down in the Convention between the provinces of *Holland* and *Utrecht* of the 31st October, 1687, the details whereof are given in a Resolution of Holland of the 25th September, 1687.

---

4 Neostad. *Cas. Decis.* viii. n. 2 ; *Decis. en Resol. van den Hove,* n. 160.
5 Neostad. ib. n. 3 ; *Decis. en Resol.* n. 186.
6 *Resol. Holl.* 10 July, 1677.

CCCCXLVI. The laws relating to the right of preference, or to the judges or commissioners of insolvent causes, so far as I have been able to discover, are as follows: Of *Monnickendam*, 1st March, 1653; of *Alkmaar*, 4th August, 1653; *Purmerend*, 8th November, 1655; *Leyden*, 2nd March, 1656; *Amsterdam*, 2nd April, 1659; and the latest, 30th January, 1777;[1] *Gouda*, 8th December, 1659; *Dordrecht*, 20th December, 1668; The *Hague*, 28th January, 1751;[2] *Rotterdam*, 2nd April, 1768;[3] and fuller than the rest, the Law of *Haarlem* of the 1st February, 1710;[4] which, having been compiled with all possible accuracy, might serve as an Ariadne-clue in the labyrinth of creditors.

CCCCXLVII. As regards the meeting of creditors and their rights of preference, this law is divided into four parts:

I. The *first* part lays down certain general rules; as

1. That special mortgages effected in the presence of a judge, should be preferred to prior general mortgages, resulting from convention, not from law.[5]

2. That, on the other hand, general mortgages of immovable property executed before a judge, and of movable property executed before a notary and witnesses, accompanied by the payment of the duty of two and a half per cent., should be preferred to debts on which that duty has not been paid, but as amongst themselves should take precedence according to time.[6]

CCCCXLVIII.—II. The *second* part of this Law

---

[1] *Handv. Tweede Vervolg*, p. 102, sqq.
[2] In *de Resol. van Holland*, 1751, p. 61.
[3] *N. Nederl. Jaarb.* 1768, p. 329, sqq.
[4] *Keur. van Haarl.* d. i. p. 128, sqq.
[5] Art. 5.   [6] Art. 6.

treats of the right of preference over particular property, especially movables, which obtains as against all creditors; and under this class are comprehended—

1. Owners, reclaiming their own property by virtue of their *dominium ;* and these are admitted even before the judicial expenses :[7] as, for instance, those who have sold property without taking security for the price,[8] or have deposited their property with another, or have lent or let it, or entrusted it to a factor or broker,[9*] or with whose money the property was purchased by the factor.

CCCCXLIX.—2. Those who have the right of retention, such as bleachers ;[10] and those who have received goods abroad on a bill of lading, and on the strength thereof have made themselves liable on bills of exchange or otherwise; and these are also preferred to creditors on bottomries subsequently contracted on the same goods.[11]

CCCCL.—3. Creditors to whom movables belonging to the debtor, and even chirographs of debts,[12] have been pledged and delivered : who are accordingly preferred as regards these, to all other creditors ;[13] and have also the right of retaining them on account of chirograph-debts, as already laid down ;[14] though not as against other creditors.

CCCCLI.—III. The *third* part of the law treats of the general right of preference in respect of the whole

---

[7] Art. 7, junct. art. 11; and see Roseboom, *Keur. van Amsterd.* cap. 37. art. 6.   [8] Thes. 203.   [9] Art. 8.

[9*] [Or Banker : see Voet *ad Pand.* xx. 4. § 13.]

[10] See Coren. *Obs. Rer. Jud.* 25.

[11] Expressly mentioned, art. 9 ; and Law of *Rotterd.* art. 29.

[12] Art. 30.   [13] Th. 430.

[14] Art. 10 : and see Law of *Rotterd.* art. 31.

mass of the property; and hereunder are comprehended—

1. The judicial expenses, incurred in respect of the
whole estate; and the expenses of execution;[1] the sala-
ries of the curators, and the fees of the advocates (subject, however, to a limitation, in the Law of *Haarlem*,[2]),
and also the expenses of the cession, even though all
the property of the debtor be subject to mortgage.[3]

CCCCLII.—2. Those who have lent money for the
funeral or last illness of the deceased.[4]

CCCCLIII.—3. The lessors of estates in town or
country, in respect of the things brought and carried
in, or of the fruits;[5] over which our law gives them a
right of mortgage,[6] not by virtue of the arrest, but of
the right of retention, which is confirmed by the arrest
(and this view is supported by the terms of the laws,
which require that the things so carried in should be
arrested on the land itself[7]). In many places, however,
this privilege is restricted to the rent due for the year
last elapsed and the current year; as for instance, in
South Holland,[8] and at *Amsterdam*,[9] and *Dordrecht*,[10]
Rotterdam,[11] and *Middelburg*;[12] and at *Flushing*,[13] where
there is a particular rule, that arrest should confer
preference.[14]

---

[1] Thes. 435.
[2] Art. 11; L. *Rotterd.* art. 25; Roseboom, *Keur. van Amsterd.* cap.
87, art. 7.
[3] *Nederl. Advijsb.* d. iv. cons. 6.
[4] Art. 12; Law of *Rotterd.* art. 26; Roseboom, cap. xxxvii. art. 8.
[5] Art. 13.   [6] *Decis. in Resol. van den Hove van Holl.* n. 82, 84.
[7] D. 1. *Costum. van Zuid-Holl.* art. 22; *Rhynland*, art. 99; Roseboom,
cap. xxxvii. art. 9; cap. li. art. 18, 19.   [8] D. 1.
[9] Law of 1659, art. 21. and the new law of 1777, art. 63.
[10] Law of 1668, art. 24.   [11] Art. 28.   [12] *Costum.* rubr. v. art. 5.
[13] Cap. xxii. art. 5.   [14] Cap. viii. art. 8.

CCCCLIV.—4. Domestic servants, for their wages for one year.[15]   The same rule has been laid down in the laws of *Dordrecht*[16] and the *Hague* ;[17] but at *Flushing* the right extends only to current wages.[18]   At *Leyden*, by the new law,[19] privilege has been given for half a year.   At *Rotterdam*, they have the privilege for a half year and the current half, only as amongst chirograph-creditors ; and the other servants have six weeks.[20]   As regards the law of *Amsterdam*, it has been laid down that domestic servants should have preference before other creditors in respect of all their wages, after the funeral expenses.[21]

CCCCLV.—5. This law of *Haarlem*[22] admits the Secretaries and Marshals of the City in respect of the price of movables sold by public auction and not yet paid for, and gives them preference over other creditors on all the movable property of the debtor.   But at *Leyden* the right of mortgage is given to an auctioneer over those goods only which were purchased from him, and are yet in the debtor's possession.[23]

CCCCLVI.—6. This law places debts and personal taxes due to the State or the City under the same rule as to preference ;[24] so that, as amongst themselves, they have preference according to time, but are not preferred to the price of immovable property sold to the debtor, nor to real taxes, nor to the expenses of repairs made within three years, nor to special mortgages ; and they are not any longer entitled to that privilege, which was allowed them under the general law of Holland.

---

[15] Art. 14.   [16] Art. 30.   [17] A. 1751.
[18] Cap. xxii. art. 5.   [19] 8 May 1659.   [20] Art. 36.
[21] *Vervolg. op de Holl. Cons.* d. i. cons. 10.   [22] Art. 15.
[23] *Keur. van Leyden*, art. 141.   [24] Art. 16.

M

Whence it follows, that these taxes are at *Haarlem* preferred not only to general conventional mortgages, but also to some of the legal mortgages, such as those which belong to a wife, children, and wards.[1]

CCCCLVII. In some parts of Holland, to which this right cannot be extended,[2] a distinction has been made, viz. :

a. Those taxes, which tend to the preservation of the immovable property on which they have been imposed, such as the tax for strengthening the dykes and for repairing public roads and canals, seem to have privilege among mortgage-creditors.[3]

CCCCLVIII.—*b.* But those real taxes which are imposed on the citizens in respect of possession, such as the house and estate-tax (*verpondingen*), of one and one half per cent., though they have been thought by many authors, and even by the Court of Holland, to have privilege among mortgage-creditors;[4] yet, according to the intention of the States of Holland, as declared by their law of the 3rd April, 1677, do not, in my opinion, possess this privilege; since they ought, as laid down by *Boel*[5] (many of whose arguments I do not, however, approve of), to give place to prior special mortgages.

CCCCLIX.—*c.* Personal taxes have, indeed, by the general law of Holland, the right of tacit mortgage, but do not at the same time have privilege over a mortgage; neither therefore does such privilege belong to the

---

[1] Art. 17, 18, 19. [2] Thes. 14.
[3] Neustad. *Decis. Cur.* 24, 35; *Decis. en Resol. van den Hove*, n. 172.
[4] *Decis. en Resol. van den Hove*, n. 172; Loen. *Decis.* cas. 17; Coren *Obs.* 17; Voet *ad Pand.* xx. 4. § 23.
[5] *Ad Loen. Decis.* ib. p. 180.

bakers who farm these taxes.[6] Nor is this opposed to
the decision of the Court[7] quoted by *Voet*;[8] for that
passage has been incorrectly reported, and according to
my MS. copy, which agrees with the one in the Public
Museum, should be read as follows : "*In the question of
preference on the goods of Gerrit Martensz, Cessionant,
it was on the 30th July,*1604, *decided that the tax on beer,
though farmed out, has right of preference over the goods
and lands of the estate from the date thereof,* by force ot
legal mortgage, *and should take rank* AFTER *the prior
special mortgage in favour of Job Bartiaansz: Also that
the legal mortgages should, as amongst themselves, have
preference according to their date:*—and in the *Leyden*
copy it runs as follows:—*26th July, &c.*—*take rank
before a later special mortgage.*" And it may be easily
shown that no doubt need be entertained, as maintained by Voet,[9] as to this question being now set at
rest.

CCCCLX.—7. In this Law of *Haarlem*,[10] married
women follow next, who, where community of property
has been excluded, may reclaim the property brought
by them into the marriage or acquired during the
marriage, unless these have perished by accident.[11]

CCCCLXI.—8. Children enjoy the same right in
respect of the property left to them by a predeceased
parent, and which remain in the possession of the
surviving parent.[12]

---

[6] Of which see *Thes.* 419.
[7] A. 1604, in *de Holl. Consult.* d. iii. App. p. 22 ; and see *Decis. en,
Resol. van den Hove,* n. 89.
[8] *Ad Pand.* xx. 2. § 8 ; and xx. 4. § 23.
[9] Voet, ib. dd. ll.   [10] Art. 17.   [11] Art. 21.
[12] Art. 18 ; and more fully laid down in art. 23, 24, 25, 26.

CCCCLXII.—9. In like manner, wards and others who are under guardianship or curatorship,—as regards that which is due to them in respect of the guardianship or curatorship.[1]

CCCCLXIII. And these three kinds of mortgage have, as amongst themselves, preference only according to time,[2] but no privilege. (This, however, is not the general Law of Holland, as is sufficiently evident from *Thes.* 263.)

CCCCLXIV. But by the law of the city of *Rotterdam* personal taxes due to the State, claiming them, have preference.[3]

CCCCLXV. In the law of *Haarlem*,[4] special mortgages posterior in time follow next; then general mortgages; and amongst the latter, regard is had to priority in time.[4]

CCCCLXVI.—IV. The *fourth* part of this law gives a special right of preference over all the immorable property; and herein have preference:

1. The judicial expenses,[6] and

2. The funeral expenses; so far as these and the judicial expenses cannot be satisfied out of the movables.[7]

3. Real taxes;[8] which are to be claimed within the time fixed by law;[9] which at *Dordrecht* is five years, to be computed back from the commencement of the current year.[10]

CCCCLXVII.—4. The repairs done to immovable property within the last three years.[11] The same period

[1] Art. 19.   [2] Art. 20.   [3] Art. 32, 33.
[4] Art. 32, see *Thes.* 437.   [5] Art. 6.
[6] Art. 27; see *Thes.* 451.   [7] Art. 27.   [8] Art. 27.
[9] Art. 28.   [10] Law of 1668, art. 27.   [11] Art. 29.

has been fixed by the Laws of *Alkmaar, Purmerend,* the *Hague,* and *Amsterdam.*[12]   At other places it is two years, as at *Monnickendam,*[13] and *Rotterdam.*[14]   The repairs ought, however, to be necessary repairs;[15] for the expenses of improvements take rank with chirograph-debts.[16]

CCCCLXVIII.—5. Rent imposed on windmills.[17]

6. Next follow emphyteutic rents, ground-rents, and perpetual or hereditary rents.[18]

CCCCLXIX.—7. Then come special mortgages, which, as amongst themselves, have privilege according to time.[19] Those mortgages, however, which are termed *Kustingen* are preferred to prior legal mortgages;[20] but they do not have this right after three years from the time when the last payment ought to have been made. The same period has been fixed by the Laws of *Alkmaar,*[21] and *Purmerend.*[22] By the Law of *Monnickendam*[23] the period is fixed at two years; but it appears that after the lapse of this period a right of general mortgage still remains.

CCCCLXX. In other places no provision has been made in this respect; and therefore this particular right of mortgage submits even after three years in respect of these debts, though a new chirograph may have been given for the interest thereon.[24]

CCCCLXXI. The interest, however, of these or other mortgage-debts, even though confirmed by a right of pledge, is no longer recoverable by virtue of the mort-

---

[12] Law of the 28th January 1752.   [13] Art. 3.
[14] Art. 7.   [15] Art. 37.   [16] Art. 38.   [17] Art. 30.
[18] Art. 31.   [19] Art. 32.   [20] Art. 32 ; see *Thes.* 437.
[21] Art. 3, 4.   [22] Art. 3, 4.   [23] Art. 2.
[24] *Decis. en Resol. van den Hove van Holl.* n. 201.

gage, after eighteen months, or two years, or, as enacted by several statutes, after three years.[1]

CCCCLXXII.—8. The above Law of *Haarlem*[2] still gives preference over personal debts to those who have after due notice by sommation and renovation* ween placed in possession, in execution of a judgment, and on the same day have paid the duty of two and a half per cent. At *Amsterdam* they have the same right.[3]

CCCCLXXIII. Amongst chirograph-creditors, those who have afterwards lent money to the same debtor on a fresh transaction are by no means preferred to those who may not have urged their claims at the meeting of creditors.[4]

BOOK III.

CHAPTER I.—SEC. 26.

CCCCLXXIV. The opinion entertained by *Voet* and *Groenewegen*,[5] viz.: that children who have attained the age of puberty may be made civilly liable on their own contracts, and be sued after they have attained majority or after the death of the parent, is wholly opposed to the analogy of our law.[6]

CCCCLXXV. We should not, however, too hastily conclude, with *Marckhart*,[7] that the *Senatusconsultum*

---

[1] See also the Law of *Haarlem*, art. 33.   [2] Art. 35.
* [See Van der Linden, *Inst.* p. 184.—Tr.]
[3] Roseboom, *Keur van Amsterd.* cap. xxxvii. art. 11, 12, 13, 23.
[4] *Vervolg. der Holl. Consult.* d. i. cons. 114.
[5] *Ad Pand.* xiv. 5. § 4.   [6] *Holl. Cons.* d. vi. st. 2. cons. 30.
[7] *Exercit.* 7.

Macedonianum has no force at the present day, merely because at present the *patria potestas* terminates on the attainment of majority. For it both affords a special defence in the case of a loan,* and also makes way for the equitable exceptions founded on that *S Ctum*, which may be adopted subject to the terms of our law.

SEC. 34.

CCCCLXXVI. Parents are not liable for the offences of their children, even though minors. By some laws, however, it is otherwlse provided in respect of lighter offences, resulting from presumed *lata culpa* on the part of the parent in the education of the children.†

CCCCLXXVII. Masters are not, as a rule, liable for the offences of their domestic or hired servants committed in the performance of their duty, if they have not been benefited thereby. They are liable, however, if the servants have been improperly employed in a work requiring skill.‡

SEC. 36.

CCCCLXXVIII. Obligations and actions may, like *dominium*, be acquired through an agent, without cession. This is evident from the analogy of our present law, as the Supreme Court seems to have correctly decided,⁵ influenced perhaps by the evidence

---

* [Holl. Cons. d. vi. st. 2. and pag. 392, 393.—Tr.]

† [See Van der Linden, *Supplem. ad Voetii Comm. ad Pand.* ix. 4, § 10.—Tr.]

‡ [Voet *ad Pand.* ix. 4. and 10.—Tr.]

⁵ A. 1624, in Coren, *Obs.* xxv. n. 24, sqq. besides others.

given on the subject by a great number of witnesses, on the 5th of October, 1619.[1]

SEC. 41.

CCCCLXXIX. Although a stipulation or agreement concerning succession to the property of a living person may be validly entered into in an antenuptial contract, as we have already laid down;[2] yet *Grotius*, following the reason of our law, which is in favour of free disposition by will, has not admitted the other successory pacts which are illegal under the Roman Law.[3]

SEC. 42.

CCCCLXXX. A stipulation permitting parate execution is not, according to Bynkershoek,[4] invalid.*

CCCCLXXXI. In like manner the stipulation of a penalty to secure the performance of an act is valid, being permitted also by the Civil Law;[5] provided it is not done in contravention of the rule in Cod. vii. 47,† or the legal rate of interest (where the agreement is one relating to interest) be not exceeded.[6]

[1] *Handv. van Amst.* p. 539. [2] Thes. 235, et sqq.
[3] See also Neostad, *Supr. Cur. Dec.* 112. Pape, however (*ad Cons. J. Ct. Bat.* vol. i. cons. 83), is of a different opinion.
[4] *Q. J. Priv.* l. ii. cap. 13.
* [But see Merula, *Man. van Proced.* l. iv. tit. 100. c. 1. § 10; and a decision of the Court of Holland, in *Dec. en Resol. v. d. Hove*, § 51; Van Alphen; Papeg. d. i. c. 32. pag. 507.—Tr.]
[5] Inst. iii. 15. § ult.
† [Viz.; that interest or damages should not exceed the amount of the principal.—Tr.]
[6] Dig. xix. 1. 13. § 26; *Decis. en Resol. van den Hove*, n. 51; Bynkersh. *Q. J. Priv.* l. ii. c. 14.

SEC. 43.

CCCCLXXXII. A reward promised for the purpose of bringing about a marriage does not seem to be
founded on an immoral cause or consideration.[7]

SEC. 46.

CCCCLXXXIII. As it has been the rule in the
practice of our courts, founded on the ordinary interpretation of the Civil Law, that in matters of strict
law, interest should begin to run from the time of *litis
contestatio ;*[8] so, under the same law, interest becomes
due upon delay on a *bona-fide* contract.[9] Voet[10] is of a
different opinion, following Groenewegen, who however, does not himself correctly understand the other
writers who had gone before him.

SEC. 52.

CCCCLXXXIV. A promise, which is not founded
on a just *causa debendi* or consideration, does not give
a right of action; although in other respects an action
is maintainable on a *nudum pactum.*‡

CHAPTER II.—SEC. 8.

CCCCLXXXV. Since the reason of the rule

---

[7] Bynkersh. ib. 1. ii. c. 6.

[8] *Decis. en Resol. van den Hove*, n. 250.

[9] Ibid. n. 91, 407 ; Neostad. *Supr. Cur. Decis.* 68. [See Van Leeuw.
Comm. b. iv. c. 7. § 8.—Tr.]

[12] *Ad Pand.* xxii. 1. § 11.

‡ [Huber. Hedend. Rechtsgel. l. i. § 1, 2 ; Grœeneweg. *de ll. abrog.*
ad Cod. ii. 13. 10 ; Coren, *Observ.* xiii. § 8. sqq. ; Voet *ad Pand.* ii. 14.
§ 9. See also Van Leeuw. *Comm.* b. iv. c. 4. § 1. and *Cens. For.* 1.
iv. c. 18. § 4.—Tr.]

regarding *patria potestas* is different amongst us from what it was amongst the Romans, there is nothing to affect the validity of a donation made by a father to a son whom he has *in potestate*, and accepted by the son if he has attained puberty, or, if below infancy, by some public person.[1]

SEC. 9.

CCCCLXXXVI. Although the proper and peculiar reason of the prohibition amongst us of donations between husband and wife does not hold where community of property has been excluded, yet our adoption of the Roman Law would even in this case prevent such acts of liberality between husband and wife; subject, however, to those exceptions* which are allowed by that law, so far as the analogy of our law does not reject them.

SEC. 11.

CCCCLXXXVII. By the Roman Law, according to the more correct opinion, a donation of all one's property is not indeed prohibited; but since the opposite opinion had long been considered more consonant with the Civil Law, it seems to have been adopted in practice by most persons, and also approved of in our Courts.[2]

---

[1] See Roseboom, *Keur. van Amsterd.* cap. 39. art. 7. [See Groenew. *de ll. abrog.* ad Inst. iii. 20. 4, 6, § 3; P. Voet *ad Inst.* iii. 20. § 6. n. 2 and ad Inst. xxxix. 5. n. 5; Van Leeuw. *Cens. For.* 1. iv. c. 12. § 8.—Tr.]

* [See Neostad. *de Pact. Anten.* obs. iv. in not. 3; Groenew. *de ll. abrog.* ad Dig. xxiv. 1 1. 31, § 8; l. 40; and *ad Dig.* xxxix. 5. l. 58 § ult. Holl. Cons. d. ii. cons. 118.—Tr.]

[2] *Holl. Cons.* d. i. cons. 169; Loen. *Decis.* cas. 123; Bynkershoek *Q. J. Priv.* 1. ii. c. 7. p. 260. See *Thes.* 21.

SEC. 13.

CCCCLXXXVIII. Where a donation has been made under the condition that the donor should receive aliment from the donee, if the condition is not fulfilled, an action is indeed maintainable *ob causam datorum*, the *causa* not having taken place ; but the *rei vindicatio utilis*, allowed in this respect by the Code viii. 55. 1, does not seem consistent with our customs.

SEC. 15.

CCCCLXXXIX. The rule of the Roman Law, as adopted by us,[3] requires that a donation exceeding 500 *aurei* in value should be registered ; provided, however, that a solemn cession of immovable property made in Court, or in the case of movables a declaration before a notary and witnesses, may be substituted in place of registration.

SEC. 18.

CCCCXC. Since it has been held by our Courts that a donation made by a childless person may be revoked on his getting children, the controversies which arise in respect of this right should be decided according to the words of the Code viii. 56. 8 ; and hence it would appear that this right of revocation belongs solely to the donor, and not to his children or heirs.*

SEC. 19.

CCCCXCI. If by an inofficious donation the chil-

---

³ Thes. 18.
* [Böker, *Rer. in Fris. jud.* c. 247.—Tr.]

dren have not been deprived of the whole of their legitimate portion, they ought to proceed by personal action for the deficiency.[1] If nothing has been left to them, the donation may be wholly rescinded by the *querela inofficiosi donationis,* unless made in favour of a son who is entitled to a filial portion.

SEC. 22.

CCCCXCII. Since a donation *mortis causa* is similar to a last will, it should be executed in the presen'·e either of five witnesses, or a notary and two witnesses.

SEC. 23.

CCCCXCIII. On the same principle, it follows that those who may make a testament may also make a donation *mortis causa.*

CHAPTER III.—SEC. 8.

CCCCXCIV. It is the common opinion of *Grotius* and the Dutch authors, supported by frequent decisions,[2] that co-debtors, who have engaged themselves each for the whole as principal debtors, are taken to have renounced the *beneficium divisionis,* which they are entitled to under Nov. xcii. cap. 1.

SEC. 17.

CCCCXCV. Inasmuch as the *Senatusconsultum Vellejanum* has been adopted by us from the Civil Law, it follows in reason that the same exceptions which are

Cod. iii. 28. 30, junct. Cod. iii. 29. 9, and Nov. 92.

[2] *Nederl. Advijsb.* d. iii. cons. 235.

made by that law, should also be allowed in our courts; amongst which is that of a woman who in her testament desires her heirs to pay what she owes in respect of suretyship.[3]

SEC. 18.

CCCCXCVI. It is a rule founded on reason, and confirmed by the authority of many authors,[*] that in order to render effectual the renunciation of the *SCtum Vellejanum,* which is permitted by our customs, it ought to be made by a public instrument, without which the engagement itself is void[4]; unless perhaps a different rule can be proved to have been adopted in Holland by custom.

SEC. 20.

CCCCXCVII. Even if it be good law that soldiers may at the present day become surety for appearance in court or for the satisfaction of a judgment, or in a case of hiring, yet it should, I think, be laid down that they cannot be thrust forward as such against the consent of the creditor.

SEC. 22.

CCCCXCVIII. A husband may amongst us (con-

[3] Dig. xxxi. 88. § 10; xxxii. 93. § 1; and see Sande, *Decis. Frisic.* l. iii. tit. 11. dec. 7.   [Holl. Cons. d. ii. cons. 317.—Tr.]

[*] [Sande, *Dec. Fris.* iii. 2. def. 2; Van Leeuw. *Comm.* b. iv. c. 4. § 2; *Bellum Jurid.* c. lxxviii. pag. 565, sqq.; Lybrechts, *Reden. Vert.* d. ii. 24. § 16. Groenewegen, who is of a different opinion (ad Cod. iv. 29. 23) appears to rely solely on a French jurist of the name of Bugnyon; and Voet, in expressing the same opinion, cites only Groenewegen. See Schrassert, *Obs. Pract.* iii. pag. 188.—Tr.]

[4] Cod. iv. 29. 23. § 2.

trary to the Rule in Roman Law) give sureties for payment of the wife's dowry; and this not only where it has been so stipulated in the antenuptial contract, but also in a case* where the husband *stante matrimonio* is in declining circumstances, and gives such security upon the order of a judge.[1]

SEC. 23.

CCCCXCIX. A surety who has engaged himself for a larger sum is by our law bound, without distinction, for the principal, and even for such larger sum, if the principal debtor has subsequently become indebted therein.†

D. A person who has bound himself as surety only for a certain time, is discharged when that time has elapsed; and one who has stood surety for a debt which is payable on a particular day, may, after giving notice to the creditor to be diligent, apply to be discharged.[2] A different rule seems, however, to have been adopted at *Amsterdam*;[3] and has been expressly admitted in respect of a surety in respect of eviction from immovable property sold and transferred.[4]

SEC. 25.

DI. It follows from the reason of our law that the

* [But see Voet *ad Pand.* xlvi. l. § 11.—Tr.]

[1] See the decision of the Supreme Court, 28th July 1675, in Van Leeuwen, *Cens. Forens.* part. i. lib. l. cap. 12. § 7; and Grotius B. i. ch. 5. § 24.

† [Van Leeuw. *Cens. For.* l. iv. c. 17. § 5; Voet ad Pand. xlvi. l. § 4.—Tr.]

[2] *Decis. en Resol. van den Hove*, n. 326. [See *infra*. Th. 836.]

[3] Roseboom, *Keur. van Amst.* cap. xlix. art. 12.

[4] Ibid. art. 19.

obligation of a surety may be contracted without any solemn form of words. The simple assertion, however, that any one is a substantial person is not amongst us held as an engagement of suretyship, though at *Antwerp* it is.[5]

SEC. 29.

DII. It is evident from the reason of the law that the benefits or privileges of sureties may be renounced not only specially, but also generally; whether the person, being acquainted with the law, has renounced them in express terms, or, being ignorant of the law, has in general terms declared that they were made known to him.[6]

DIII. Sureties who have bound themselves each for the whole, or each as principal debtor, are in some places taken as having renounced the *beneficia ordinis* and *divisionis*.[7]   At *Middelberg* it has been so enacted.[8]

DIV. Amongst those merchants who guarantee the solvency of another (*die staan del credere*), the privilege of sureties are supposed not to obtain.[9]

SEC. 30.

DV. A person who has engaged himself as surety for, and has paid on behalf of, an unwilling party, has

---

[5] Neostad. *Supr. Cur. Decis.* 5.

[6] Voet *ad Pand.* xlvi. 1. § 16 *dissentiente.*

[7] *Rechtsgel. Obs.* part. ii. obs. 66.

[8] *Costum van Middelb.* rubr. viii. art. 8, 10; to which the decision of the Court of 1610 has reference; which see in *de Decis. en Resol. van den Hove,* n. 325; where the words *als maar geen borge en is ge-steld,* should according to my MS. copy be altered into *als meer,* or rather according to the Leyden MS. be wholly expunged.

[9] Bynkersh. *Q. J. Priv.* l. iv. c. 13. p. 631.

no counter action against the debtor;[1] and the arguments of *Groenewegen*[2] and *Voet*[3] do not prove this rule of the Code to have passed into desuetude.

SEC. 31.

DVI. If cession of action has been made after some time to a surety who had paid in his own name, he may legally avail himself of it; but if he had paid in the name of the debtor, the cession would be unavailable, at least as against a co-surety or a third party holding a mortgage; as decided by the Court of Holland;[4] and *Grotius* has here correctly adopted this opinion, though *Groenewegen*, *Voet*,[5] and other jurists[6] are of a different opinion. The above decision has been adopted also at *Amsterdam*.[7]

SEC. 32.

DVII. The rule laid down in Holland by *Philip* II. in the Placaat of 1564,* viz., that a surety cannot be cited, unless the immovable property specially mortgaged (though alienated to and in possession of a third party), has previously been discussed, holds good by the law of Amsterdam, even where a *general* mortgage has been alienated to the third [party in possession;[8] and by the common law of Holland, it seems to hold

---

¹ Cod. ii. 19. ult.
² Groenew. *ad Cod.* ii. 19. ult.
³ Voet *ad Pand.* iii. 5. § 11. [Thes. 573.]
    Neostad. *Decis. Cur.* 12.   ⁵ *Ad Pand.* xlvi. 1. § 30, f.
⁶ See *'t Vervolg. der Holl. Cons.* d. i. cons. 52. [? 252.]
⁷ Roseboom, *Keur. van Amst.* cap. xlix. art. 8, 9.
* [See Lybrechts, *Reden. Vert.* d. ii. pag. 284.]
⁸ *Handv. van Amst.* p. 565, seq. Roseboom, *Keur. van Amsterd.* cap. xlix. art. 3, 4, 5, 14, 15, 16.

also where a general mortgage has passed by a lucrative title to such third party, or even where the movable goods of the debtor, which were mortgaged, are in the possession of another, not in his own right and by a just title, but on behalf of the owner.[9]

DVIII. The same rule has been adopted at *Middelburg*, where a surety has neither expressly nor tacitly renounced his privileges; and even where he has so renounced, it still obtains in respect of a special mortgage.[10]

Sec. 36.

DIX. That which parents have stipulated on behalf of their children, if it has not been promised with a view to the parents, seems to be acquired for the children.[11] The same rule should hold where the parents have promised any thing to the children.[12] The rule is different in the case of a promise made to the parent by the children who are *in potestate*, and therefore minors; unless perhaps the assent of the guardian appointed by the predeceased parent accompanies it.

Sec. 38.

DX. On a promise made to a third party, which such third party has accepted without authority, the party really interested would indeed acquire the right, provided he afterwards accepts the promise; or if such third party, who has assented without authority, be a public

---

[9] *Nederl. Advijsb.* d. i. cons. 31, where a decision of the Court of the 8 April 1661 is cited.

[10] *Costum. van Middelb.* rubr. viii. art. 9.

[11] See *Thes.* 104, and Roseboom, *Keur van Amst.* cap. xxxix. art. 9.

[12] See *Thes.* 485.

functionary, such as a notary : but beyond these cases
the party interested does not acquire any right (as
Grotius has correctly laid down), not from the subtlety
of the Civil Law, but from the very nature of the transaction, against which, in the absence of custom, the
authority of *Gronewegen, Voet*,[1] and others who dissent
herefrom, cannot prevail.

SEC. 39.

DXI. The security required from a legatee or a fidei-
commissary may, as well under our law as under the
Roman law, be legally dispensed with by testament.
And this is not affected by the two passages quoted by
Voet[2] out of *Neostadt*,[3] who therein treats only of
fructuary security.[4]

SEC. 41.

DXII. It properly follows from a correct interpretation of the Civil Law, that a person who has promised
to do an act may be condemned and compelled to perform the same ;* and it appears to have been so held by
the Supreme Court.[5]

SEC. 45.

DXIII. From the circumstance that verbal promises
do not any longer require the solemnity of a stipulation,†

---

[1] *Ad Pand.* xlv. 1. § 3.
[2] *Ad Pand.* xxxvi. 3. § ult.   [3] *Cur. Supr. Decis.* 3.
[4] See also Bynkersh. *Q. J. Priv.* l. iii. c. 10. 449. [See Thes. 3 l.]
* [As to the mode of enforcing, see Merula, *Manier van Proced.* b.
iv. tit. 29. c. 1 (ed. 1783, p. 397.)—Tr.]
[5] Neostad. *Supr. Cur. Decis.* 50. † [See Inst. iii. 15, pr. & § 1, 2.]

and that in entering into most contracts words are wont to be used, it cannot properly be concluded that almost all contracts are now verbal obligations.[6]

Sec. 48.

DXIV. Although it cannot be proved from the general laws, which are enumerated by *Gronewegen* in his notes on this section, and by the jurists in *de Rechts-geleerde Observatien*,[7] that all wagers are prohibited by the common law of Holland, yet it would appear from *Van Alphen*[8] and *Bynkershoek*[9] that causes are very rarely decided upon such wagers.

Sec. 54.

DXV. Verbal promises ought clearly, like the Roman stipulations, to be strictly construed ;[10] and the Court of Holland has so laid it down.[11]

Chapter IV.—Sec. 3.

DXVI. Though a compromise may be so entered into as to produce an alienation of the matter in dispute, yet a person who has been prohibited from alienating cannot, it seems, so compromise as to effect an alienation ; nor therefore can an heir, who is burthened with a conditional *fidei-commissum* do so without the consent of the fidei-commissary.[12]

---

[6] See *Thes.* 522. Voet (*ad Pand.* xlv. 1. § 1.) *dissentiente.*

[7] Part. ii. obs. 67.   [8] *Papeg.* d. 1. p. 302.

[9] *Q. J. Priv.* l. ii. c. 7. p. 251.   [10] Dig. xlv. 1. 99.

[11] *Decis. en Resol. van den Hove*, § 108; where the words *metten interessen* should, according to my MS. copy, be altered into *met een jaar interest.*

[12] Voet (*ad Pand.* ii. 15, § 8) *dissentiente.*

N 2

DXVII. Guardians may compromise on behalf of their wards, provided they do not thereby effect an alienation of the ward's property;[1] and this is not affected by the pupillary laws of particular places, cited by the jurists in *de Rechtsgeleerde Observatien ;*[2] for these do not constitute the general law of Holland;[3] and some of these laws, moreover, do not annul a compromise made by a guardian, but only render the guardian liable for any loss which may arise therefrom.[4]

SEC. 4.

DXVIII. A compromise made in respect of a matter already decided by the sentence of a judge, which cannot be appealed against, is not valid; being repugnant both to the reason of the civil law, and the very nature of the thing; nor has this been affected by the circumstance that the terms *pactiones* and *transactiones* are now almost convertible, as maintained by *Gronewegen ;*[5] nor is the l. 32 of the Code ii. 4, cited by *Voet*[6] opposed hereto.

DXIX. Since the Law in Dig. ii. 15. 6, has always been construed by the Court as referring to a compromise prohibited by law, it follows that amongst us also a compromise concerning things left by last will will not be valid, without previous inspection and examination of the terms of the will.[7] But except in

---

[1] See Dig. xlvii. 2. 54, § ult. & 56. § 4, & xxvi. 7. 46. § ult., and compare Thes. 17.

[2] Part. ii. obs. .0.   [3] Thes. 14.
[4] See *Weesk. van Leyden*, art. 53.   [5] Ad Cod. ii. 4. 32.
[5] *Ad Pand.* ii. 15. § 11.
[7] Thes. 23. in fin.

the case of dividing an inheritance with a ward,[8] there is no necessity to make an inventory previous to a compromise.

Sec. 5.

DXX. A compromise concerning offences, the prosecution whereof belongs to the public prosecutor cannot be *legally* made without the cognizance of the judge. This rule is adopted by the Placaat of the 19th May 1544,[9] the Criminal Ordonnance of the 5th July, 1570,[10] and 'the *Nader Ampliatie der Instructien van den Hove,* of the 24th March, 1644 ;[11] and the public utility and manifest equity of these laws sufficiently discountenance the contrary custom, or rather corrupt practice, whic⸱ the jurists in *de Rechtsgeleerde Observatien*[12] look upon with too great favour. The new law respecting the mode of precedure in criminal cases has[13] more correctly adopted the real intention of the ancient law, and permits compromises in respect of those crimes only to which a particular corporal punishment is not prescribed.[14]

CHAPTER V.—SEC. 1.

DXXI. *Literarum Obligatio,* which is here used by *Grotius* in a wider sense than under the Roman Law is any promise reduced into writing, to do something arising from any just cause or consideration, and even from any other nominate contract : and differs therefore essentially from the mere acknowledgment of a debt made in writing, to which no promise is annexed.

[8] Thes. 136, sqq.   [9] Art. 3.
[10] Art. 13.   [11] Art. 30.   [12] Part iv. obs. 40.
[13] Art. 161.   [14] Art. 160. junct. art. 50.

SEC. 2.

DXXII. Such a writing, however, when given in respect of a debt due upon some other just cause or contract, does not in a doubtful case act as a novation; nor ought it to be construed with strictness, but with reference to the nature of the former contract, although such contract may produce the same effects as those which in *secc.* 4, 5, 6, and 7, are specially ascribed to *literarum obligatio.*

SEC. 3.

DXXIII. *Grotius* has here correctly ascribed to a *literarum obligatio* given for money lent the same force under the Dutch Law as it had under the Roman Law, namely, that the action arising thereon is barred within two years by the exception *non numeratæ pecuniæ* pleaded by the debtor, unless the creditor can prove the receipt of the consideration by other evidence. Nor are the opposite opinions of *Loenius,*[1] *Vinnius,*[2] *Van Leeuwen,*[3] and of the jurists in their notes on *Merula,*[4] upon the decisions of the Court cited by *Gronewegen,*[5] and in the *Bellum Juridicum,*[6] applicable here; since they treat of provisional payment, whereas *Grotius* here speaks of condemnation on the principal case. Neither does the reason of the present law, which is appealed to by *Loenius*[7] and *Merenda*[8] in any manner militate against the taking of this exception; whilst on the other hand, the admissibility of it is favoured by the circum-

[1] *Decis. en Observ.* 119.　　　　[2] *Select Quæst.* L. i. c. 41. f.
[3] *Cens. Forens.* part. i. l. 4. c. 14. n. 6.
[4] *Man. van Proced.* l. iv. t. 40. cap. 14, p. 47. (ed. 1783.)
[5] *Ad.* h. l. and *ad. Cod.* iv. 30. 4.　　　　[6] *Cas.* 18.
[7] d. l.　　　　[8] *Contr. Jur.* l. xvi. cap. 44.

stance of the Supreme Court having in similar cases allowed the exception *non numeratæ dotis*,[9] and the replication *non solutæ pecuniæ*.[10]

DXXIV. The exception *non numeratæ pecuniæ* may be renounced in the same instrument by which the *literarum obligatio* is contracted. By this renunciation, however, the benefit of the exception is only considered to have been dispensed with in the same manner as if the two years had already elapsed, for by the present law this benefit is limited to that period; but in these cases the debtor is still permitted to prove the non-receipt of the consideration.

SEC. 6.

DXXV. When a note or chirograph has been made payable to the holder, any one who holds it may sue thereon; not only in those places where this is allowed by custom, as in South Holland,[11] *Dordrecht*,[12] and *Amsterdam*,[13] but elsewhere also; it being clearly allowed by the reason of our law.[14] Excepting, however, where the holder has obtained the instrument from the legal possessor by fraud, and the latter has given timely notice thereof to the debtor, or the debtor himself can prove *mala fides* on the part of the holder. If the holder himself is in possession of the instrument *bonâ fide* and by a just title, but the party from whom he derives his title had obtained it by theft, he is still entitled to

---

[9] Neostad. *de Pact. Anten.* obs, 11.
[10] Neostad. *Sup. Cur. Dec.* 4.
[11] Art. 38. See Van de Weld, *Handv. van Dordrecht*, p. 1362.
[12] Art. 39. p. 1344.
[13] *Handv.* p. 565. Roseboom, cap. xlvii. art. 5, 6; Loen. *Decis.* 98.
[14] Thes. 510, init. Bynkersh. *Q. J. Priv.* l. ii. cap. 11.

payment. If the instrument has been made payable to *Titius or the holder*, all that we have said would still apply, notwithstanding the statute of the 27th July, 1635, which relates only to the law of *Amsterdam*.[1] But if it had been made payable to Titius only, and he has afterwards indorsed it to the holder, the debtor may plead as against such holder payment or compensation made to Titius.[2] If made payable to Titius *or the lawful holder*, the holder ought to prove his own right, and if he be an ulterior holder, the right of all the prior holders.[3]

SEC. 7.

DXXVI. Provisional payment cannot be decreed on an instrument wherein the *causa debendi* or consideration has not been specified.[4] And this is not affected by the law of *Antwerp*,[5] nor by the decision of the Court reported by *Loenius*,[6] which was perhaps based thereon; for not only do the principles of the law and of public convenience incline the other way, but this very article of the statute of *Antwerp* seems afterwards to have been designedly omitted in the statute of *Amsterdam*, given by *Roseboom*,[7] who enumerates almost all the other articles of the law of *Antwerp*.

DXXVII. The practice of provisional payment having been introduced not from the Roman Law, but

[1] *Handv.* p. 567. Boel *ad Loen.* cas. 5.
[2] d. Stat. 27 July 1635.
[3] Bynkersh. d. 1. Roseboom. cap. xlvii. art. 8.
[4] Neostad. *Cur. Holl. Decis.* 58. *Holl. Consult.* d. i. cons. 303, f.
[5] *Stat. Antwerp*, cap. liii. art. 5.
[6] *Decis.* 5. p. 36, f. [7] Cap. 47.

on principles of equity and general convenience, in cases wherein a fuller investigation would require time, it may be decreed in all cases where the claim of the plaintiff is definite and liquid, by an interlocutory order of the judge; but it may, it seems, be validly opposed by equally liquid proof on the part of the defendant, not only in writing, but even by witnesses.[8]

Sec. 8.

DXXVIII. A debt is not proved, as against the other creditors, by an instrument, merely signed by the debtor, if not supported by other additional proof, or at least by an oath.

Chapter VI.—Sec. 9.

DXXIX. Since a ward is not himself civilly liable on contracts entered into without the guardian's assent, he may, where a bilateral contract has already been fulfilled, recover back a thing which he has parted with; but is not bound in respect of what he may have received, further than to the extent to which he has been benefited thereby. If, on the other hand, he desires to sue on a contract, which is indeed perfect but not yet fulfilled, he ought either to fulfil the entire contract, or wholly to recede from it.[9]

Sec. 11.

DXXX. The doctrine here laid down by Grotius, namely, that in real contracts a *locus pænitentiæ* is

[8] Van der Linden, *Form. van Proced.* d. i. b. 2. h. 6. § 13. p. 207.

[9] Dig. xix. 1. 13. § 29, junct. § 27, 28.

allowable previous to the delivery of the thing, should be understood only of a preparatory treaty, not of a definite and explicit promise, on which, though consisting of a *nudum pactum*, an action is maintainable.[1]

CHAPTER VII.—SEC. 9.

DXXXI. Since a depositary is liable in respect only of *lata culpa*, you cannot, as maintained by Grotius, require of him, although himself a very prudent person, the same amount of care or diligence as he is wont to use in his own concerns; nor can such a doctrine be supported by the l. 32 of the Dig. xvi. 3, which relates only to the common nature of man.[*]

SEC. 10.

DXXXII. A person who receives remuneration for the custody of a deposit, is not liable in respect of accidents, nor of *culpa levissima*, but only of *culpa levis*.[2]

SEC. 11.

DXXXIII. A depositary may retain the thing deposited, on account of necessary expenses;—according to the true meaning of the Civil Law, as well as under our own law, by which it is now settled that even a third party may, for the purpose of securing a debt due to him, arrest the deposit in the hands of the depositary.

[1] Roseboom, *Keur. van Amsterd.* cap. xlvii. art. 4.
[*] [See *Nederl. Advijsb.* d. i. cons. 305.]
[2] Dig. xix. 1. 1. § 8.

Sec. 12.

DXXXIV. A necessary sequestration† ought not, even at the present day, to be allowed without just cause, and this holds true in respect also of money paid (into Court); for Groenewegen[3] is wrong in concluding from the *Instructions of the Court* that this rule of the Civil Law has been abrogated by custom.[4]

DXXXV. If the money deposited in a public office cannot be recovered from the actuary, the magistrates who have conferred the office on him, and have not taken the security required by law, are from the reason of law bound to make good the deficiency.[5]

Chapter VIII.—Sec. 1.

DXXXVI. In order to a pledge properly so called being considered such by law, and also to exempt it from the payment of the duty of two and a half per cent., it ought to have been actually delivered.[6] Nor would the fictitious title of a *precarius* ‡ (by which a

---

† [Namely, a sequestration effected by order of Court, as distinguished from one effected by mutual consent. See *Holl. Cons.* d. iv. cons. 346, § 19; Damhouder, *Civ. Pract.* c. lxii. § 21; Matth. *de Auct.* i. 3. § 3.—Tr.]

³ Art. 36, 94; & *Ampl.* art. 11.

⁴ *Ad Cod.* iv. 4.

⁵ Voet (*ad Pand.* xix. I. § ult.) *dissentiente.* [See Neostad. Decis. Supr. Cur. 61.—Tr.]

⁶ *Waarsch.* 5th Feb. 1665. (See Boel. *in not. ad Loen.* cas. xvii. p. 127.—Tr.)

‡ [*Precarius.*—See Sandar's Justinian, iv. 15. § 4, note,—" By possessing *precario* is meant possessing by having extorted possession by prayer and entreaties. When the person from whom the possession had been extorted wished to do so, he could always resume it.—Tr.]

pledge which has not been properly delivered, may be retained by the debtor), be of any avail herein.[1]

SEC. 3.

DXXXVII. A pledge properly so called may be effected even in respect of immovable property, but not without a solemn cession in law, and the payment of the duty of two and a half per cent.

DXXXVIII. A person who desires to pledge or mortgage a debt due to him, the chirograph of which it is not the custom to deliver, and which is only regis-tered in the name of the creditor, ought, after the pledge has been contracted, to sell the debt to the creditor, under condition that it should be resold to him for the same price, on payment of the debt.

DXXXIX. It is clear that a contract of pledge as respects the property of a third person, is valid, even without the owner's consent; not, however, so as to create a right of pledge to the prejudice of the owner; unless the pledge has been effected in his own name by one whom the owner has authorized to pledge or alienate the thing on his behalf.[2]

SEC. 4.

DXL. If a creditor alleges that the pledge cannot be restored on account of accident, it is for him to prove the accident which has occurred,[3] and also that he has used proper diligence, if it be a case in which neglect may give a cause of action ; but, on the other hand, if

---

[1] Grot. in *de Holl. Cons.* d. iii. st. 2. cons. 174, n. 5.
[2] *Nederl. Advijsb.* d. ii. cons. 8.   [3] Ad Cod. iv. 23. ult.

the accident be of an extraordinary nature, and has been occasioned by extrinsic violence, he is *prima facie* presumed to have used proper diligence.

CHAPTER IX.—SEC. 6.

DXLI. *Groenewegen* and *Voet*[4] are not correct in stating that a *res commodata* may be arrested by the commodatory or borrower in his own hands for any other debt besides the expenses incurred in respect of it.

CHAPTER X.—SEC. 6.

DXLII. Inasmuch as loans of money on interest are wont to be made for the benefit as well of the creditor as of the debtor, the debtor may not, without the consent of the creditor, pay the principal before the time agreed upon, and thus discharge himself from his liability to pay interest.

SEC. 8.

DXLIII. The interest on an amount which is to be repaid within a certain time, continues to run upon default of payment; as decided by the Court,[5] contrary to the rule laid down in Cod. iv. 32. 7, and which had been adopted by the Court in a former decision.

SECS. 9 & 10.

DXLIV. As regards the question, whether interest is lawful or not, *Grotius* in his *Introduction*, which was written before his work on the *Rights of War and*

---

[4] *Ad Pand.* xiii. 6. § 10.　　　　[5] Loenius, *Decis.* cas. 29.

Peace, does not, as *Barbeirac* supposes,[1] express a different opinion to the one which he lays down in the latter work ;[2] nor is he even inconsistent with himself; for he there treats of the imperfect duty of a Christian abstaining through motives of charity and benevolence from receiving usurious gains without any loss to himself; whilst here he treats of the absolute right of a person who, as a compensation for the benefit which another derives from his money, stipulates for interest, and cannot therefore be deprived of it without loss to himself.

DXLV. As regards the legal rate of interest, there was formerly a difference of opinion in Holland. But the Court, on the 6th of May, 1610, decided that it would not allow a higher rate of interest than 6¼ per cent. in respect of a conventional mortgage, and 7 per cent. in respect of chirograph-debts.[3] Similarly the Supreme Court has held it lawful, where no mortgage has been given, to promise interest at seven or eight per cent.;[4] and where the rate has not been defined by express stipulation, it has allowed six per cent. as the ordinary rate.[5]

By the pupillary laws also, which were passed by the States, the rates of interest on the moneys of the wards were not uniform ; though never higher than 8⅓ per cent. At *Amsterdam,* on the passing of the laws concerning the public Bank, it was determined that a

[1] Not. Gall. ad. l. iii. c. 12. § 20. n. 9.
[2] L. lii. c. 12. § 20. n. 3.
[3] *Decis. en Resol. van den Hove,* n. 311 ; Loen. *Decis.* cas. 21.
[4] 31 July, 1621, Coren. *Obs.* 4.
[5] Neostad. *Decis. Supr. Cur.* 51. p. 199, init. And see *Holl. Consult.* d. iii. st. 2. cons. 79.

higher rate than four per cent. should not be permitted.[6] The Court also, since the rate of interest on public debts has been four per cent., has fixed the same rate in cases where no particular rate of interest has been promised ;[7] and rightly so.[8]

DXLVI. But now, since the public rate of interest has so risen that five per cent. has been promised for money voluntarily lent by citizens to the public treasury, and for which a mortgage is also granted ; and since there is no general Law of Holland or Rome prohibiting interest at six per cent., it would not seem to be illegal to stipulate for that rate, especially in respect of chirograph-debts.

DXLVII. The Placaat of *Charles V.* of 1540.[9] permitting merchants to stipulate the rate of twelve per cent., should only be understood in reference to bonds for a year or shorter period, and not for any longer time ; nor, since the resolution of the Court of the year 1590,[10] does it seem to have been any longer received in practice ; and they could not therefore legally stipulate for a higher rate of interest than six per cent.[11] This rate has, however, been since reduced by custom to five per cent.,[12] and even to four.[13] The two laws last cited seem, however, to relate to those cases only where interest accrues due on delay, and not

[6] *Willekeur v. Amst.* 24 Dec. 1682, art. 1, & of 27 Jan. 1684, art. 1. *Handv.* p. 681, sq.

[7] *Rechtsg. Observ.* part ii. obs. 71.

[8] Dig. xxii. 1. 37. arg. *Costum. van Rhynl.* art. 103.

[9] Art. 8.

[10] *Decis. en Resol. van den Hove,* n. 248.

[11] Cod. iv. 32. 2δ. § 1. arg. *Willekeur van Amsterd.* 28 Nov. 1609 ; *Handv. van Amsterd.* p. 540.

[12] 3 Oct. 1658, *Handv.* p. 541.   [13] 27 Jan. 1741, *Handv.* p. 520.

where it has been expressly promised by stipulation. Excepting however as to *Amsterdam*,—1. Where a sale and purchase has been effected without security being given for the price (*om comptant*); in which case eight per cent. may even now be claimed;[2] 2. Where the plaintiff in a case of insurance has wrongfully claimed and obtained provisional payment, and afterwards fails on the principal case; and, 3. Where the insurer having been condemned, does not immediately comply with the final sentence; in which two latter cases also eight per cent. may be claimed.[2]

DXLVIII. The prohibition against compound interest on private debts seems to extend to annual rents also; though *Groenewegen*[3] is of a different opinion.

DXLIX. The amount of unpaid interest may not exceed the principal; nor does it seem, therefore, that provisional payment of such can be decreed; although the Court has sometimes decided otherwise.[4]

CHAPTER XI.—SEC. 1.

DL. There is a great difference between a *Bottomry-bond* and a *Water-brief*, or *Byl-brief*, *i.e.*, an instrument by which the purchase of a vessel is acknowledged and the vessel itself specially mortgaged to the seller for the price, a clause of general mortgage being commonly added. This right of mortgage is not subject to the payment of the two and a half per cent. duty, and remains to the creditor, though not in possession of the

---

[1] *Willekeur. v. Amst.* 30 Jan. 1665, and 27 Jan. 1741. ibid. p. 520.

[2] *Ordonn. van Assur. en Avar. van Amsterd.* art. 47, 50.

[3] *Ad Cod.* iv. 32. 28.

[4] Merul. *Man. van Proced.* l. iv. t. 37. cap. 2. § 3. not. (e).

vessel, even after expiration of the period appointed for payment.[5]

DLI. The points of difference are these,—1. In a *Bottomry* the debt originates on a loan (*ex causa mutui*) ; in a *Byl-brief*, on a sale (*ex causa emptionis*) ; 2. In the former, on the loss of the vessel, the debt is at the risk of the creditor ; in the latter, if the vessel is lost, the personal obligation and the general mortgage still remain ; 3. By the former not only the vessel, but the merchandise also, may be mortgaged; by the latter, the vessel alone ; and, 4. In respect of the right of preference, a subsequent bottomry, as conducing to the preservation of the subject of the mortgage,[6] has priority over a prior mortgage by *Byl-brief*.[7]

DLII. Bottomry, properly speaking, is a contract, on which money is advanced upon the mortgage of a vessel, on the condition that if the thing mortgaged be lost, by accident during the voyage, the debtor should be free.

SEC. 2.

DLIII. A bottomry has, under our law, the following peculiarities :—1. That it is exempt from the payment of the two and a half per cent. duty ; 2. That it may be contracted by the master of the vessel ; 3. That it gives the creditor the privilege of mortgage in respect of a movable, which privilege accompanies it wherever it goes. But it possesses this particular privilege only where, looking to the origin of the trans-

---

[5] Barels, *Adv. over den Koophand.* d. i. cons. 75.
[6] Dig. xx. 4, 5, 6.
[7] Bynkersh. *Q. Jur. Priv.* l. iii. c. 16, p. 512.

action, the bottomry has been contracted in a foreign port.[1] It has, however, become the custom that a bottomry might be legally contracted in this country also, with the consent of the majority of the owners, and be constituted in respect even of merchandise, and should be exempt from payment of the two and a half per cent. duty; though a bottomry or merchandise contracted in this country ought not to enjoy this exemption.[2]

DLIV. A mortgage of vessels or merchandise, effected under the pretended name of bottomry, but wherein the creditor does not undertake the risks of the sea, does not extend the privileges of this contract to the acts performed thereunder.[3]

DLV. Since the object of the bottomry of a vessel is to procure the funds necessary for the voyage, a larger amount than is necessary cannot be lent on this contract; unless, perhaps, the rest of the money or the merchandise purchased therewith have been shipped in the vessel, and is therefore conveyed at the like risk of the creditor. And in this case, if the vessel arrives in safety, the amount stipulated even for this larger sum may be claimed, although such sum or the merchandise purchased therewith has perished: if, on the other hand, the ship itself is lost, the money also is lost,

---

[1] *Keur. van Amsterd.* 13 Aug. 1527; *Handv. van Amsterd.* p. 541. *Brief aan den H. Burgerm. van Amst.* 25 June, 1621; *Ibid.* p. 538. n. 21; *Waarsch.* 5 Feb., 1665. [Barels. *Advijs. over den Koophand.* d. i. cons. 72, pag. 387.—Tr.]

[2] *Ord. op den* 40. *penn. van* 1695, art. 36. *Ord. op den* 40. *penn. van de Schepen, van* 1699, art. 2. Bynkersh. *Q. J. Priv.* l. iii. c. 16. p. 515, sq.

[3] Bynkersh. *Q. J. Priv.* l. iii. c. 16. p. 515, sq. Barels, *Advies. over den Kooph.* d. i. cons. 71. p. 382.

though the residue of the money, or the merchandise therewith purchased, may have been saved.

DLVI. Bottomry and *Pecunia Trajectitia* differ in some respects, and are similar in others.

They differ from each other in the following respects: 1. In *pecunia trajectitia*, the money itself or the merchandise purchased therewith,[4] is conveyed at the risk of the creditor, but the money is not at once laid out at the place where it is lent;[5] but in bottomry the money is lent for the purpose of fitting out or repairing the vessel, or of purchasing provisions; and the merchandise which may be purchased therewith is not at the risk of the creditor; 2. *Pecunia trajectitia* is not at the risk of the creditor before the day on which it has been agreed that the vessel should set sail:[6] but in a bottomry all the risks of the sea, from the time the contract has been entered into, attach to the creditor; 3. In *pecunia trajectitia*, it is the money lent which is at the creditor's risk; in bottomry, it is not the money lent, but the vessel or mortgage bound for the amount, which is at his risk; 4. *Pecunia trajectitia* may subsist without a pledge or mortgage; but bottomry without a mortgage is a contradiction in terms.

DLVII. They are similar in the following respects: 1. That in both contracts the force of the obligation depends on the preservation of the object, the risk of which the creditor has undertaken: which in bottomry is the vessel or merchandise, and in *pecunia trajectitia* the amount lent or the goods purchased therewith;[7] and on their perishing, the entire obligation is cancelled

---

[4] Dig. xxii. 2. 1, in fin.   [5] Dig. xxii. 2. 1.
[6] Dig. xxii. 2. 3.   [7] Ibid l. 6.

including also any mortgage given *in subsidium ;*[1] 2. That the master, by altering the course of the vessel, takes the risk on himself ;[2] 3. That any rate of interest may be promised according to the measure of risk undertaken ; and 4. That the excessive rate of interest ceases on the risk ceasing.

DLVIII. Bottomry differs from *insurance ;* though in both contracts the risk attaches to a person other than the debtor: For, 1. There cannot be a bottomry unless the person who has undertaken the risk lends the money ; but an insurer does not lend any money, but on receiving a premium, undertakes to be responsible for the risk; 2. There cannot be a bottomry without a mortgage of the vessel or merchandise; but an insurance, where the premium has been paid, is not accompanied by any right of mortgage in favour of the insurer; 3. If the vessel has arrived in safety, though in a deteriorated condition, the entire amount lent on the bottomry, together with amount of the r sk, should be paid, according to the maxim *bodemery draagt geen avery,*—Bottomry bears no average; on the other hand, in insurance, allowance is made for loss by deterioration also.

DLIX. It has been questioned whether these three points of difference obtain in respect of a bottomry of merchandise also. It was decided at Amsterdam[3] that they do not; but that rather the opposite rule *bodemery op goederen draagt avery*—bottomry on goods bears average—should govern ; but it has since been

---

[1] Ibid.

[2] Cod. iv. 33. 3. *Holl. Cons. d.* iv. cons. 110.

[3] 18 March, 1705; *Advies. over den Kooph.* d. i. cons. 65 & Respons. 9 Nov. 1705; *Ibid.* cons. 67.

decided otherwise, and, as I think, correctly (looking to the nature of the transaction[4]), by the *Schepenen* of Amsterdam,[5] by the Court of Holland,[6] and by the Supreme Court.[7]

DLX. By the *risks of the sea,* which a bottomry creditor undertakes, are to be understood all risks whether occasioned by injury from wind and water, or by violence from enemies, or by the unskilfulness or negligence of the master (provided he does not deviate from his course).[8] Hence if a vessel has been captured by the enemy, but has afterwards been ransomed, the creditor nevertheless loses his right therein.[9] The same rule has been laid down in *de Nederlandsche Adviesboek* in respect of a bottomry of merchandise;[10] but an opposite opinion has been expressed by another jurist, who admits the creditor, after deduction of the amount paid as ransom.[11]

DLXI. In order to entitle the creditor to recover in full it is not sufficient that the keel of the vessel has been preserved; but it is necessary that the whole amount should be recoverable out of the vessel and its tackle and rigging ; otherwise the master is discharged by delivering up the vessel to the creditor, who will thus have as much as can be realized from the vessel ; according to the terms usually inserted in the contract —*Zo verre deze bodem zo veel te land brengt,*—so far as this bottom shall bring so much to shore.[12]

---

[4] Thes. 552.   [5] A. 1709.   [6] A. 1710.
[7] 27 Jun. 1711.—See Bynkersh. *Q. Jur. Pr.* l. iii. c. 16. p. 514.
[8] Verwer, *van Bodemery,* § 15. 17, & ad. § 24, p. 177.
[9] *Nederl. Adviesb.* d. 1. cons. 11.   [10] Cons. 52.
[11] A. 1707 : see *Advies. over den Kooph.* d. i. cons. 70.
[12] Verwer, p. 254.

DLXII. In case the vessel is lost, if anything can be realized from the tackle and rigging which may have drifted ashore, the whole of it goes to the creditor; for these also are wont to be expressly included in the mortgage, *op myn voorsz. schips-kiel en scheeps-gereedschap*— over my said ship and ship's tackle;[1] and even if not expressly so included, they tacitly follow the ship.[2]

DLXIII. The same rule is not applicable to the merchandise shipped on board, and not bound or included in the bottomry: for the cause just cited, *Zo verre deze bodem zo veel te land brengt*, is not to be extended farther than to the vessel and its tackle.

DLXIV. As regards the right of preference which attaches to a bottomry: 1. A bottomry is clearly on the same footing as a special mortgage of movables which have been delivered to the creditor;[3] 2. Since a bottomry is necessarily wont to be contracted for the purpose of preserving the property, it is preferred to a prior mortgage and to a *Byl-brief;* and a subsequent bottomry to a prior one;[4] unless several bottomries have been contracted within a short space of time at the same port, in which case they all have equal rights,[5] namely, when at the termination of the voyage, the creditors sue for their claims; since all of them have incurred the same risk during the same period. And the reason of this rule meets the doubts expressed on the subject by *Bynkershoek*.[6]

DLXV.—3. Debts subsequently contracted for the

---

[1] Verwer, p. 254. Bynkersh. *Q. J. Priv.* l. iii. c. 16. p. 509.
[2] Dig. xxi. 2. 44.
[3] See *Thes.* 450.   [4] Dig. xxi. 2, 5, 6.
[5] *Brief Amst.* 25th June, 1621. *Handv.* p. 538, n. 21.
[6] l. c. p. 513.

purpose of preserving a vessel already subject to a bottomry are preferred to the bottomry itself;[7] and, 4. The master of the vessel, after paying these debts, may sue for the same even without a cession.[8]

DLXVI.—5. It has been held,[9] that a *special* bottomry of particular goods should be preferred to a *general* bottomry of goods.

DLXVII.—6. If the consignee (or the party to whom the goods are to be delivered after conveyance) has on receipt of the bill of lading (or instrument whereby the master has acknowledged the shipment of the goods), and relying on this security, accepted bills of exchange or incurred other expenses, such as of insurance, he is preferred to the creditor of a bottomry subsequently contracted. This rule, which as *Verwer*[10] thinks, is contrary to the nature of bottomry, has been expressly laid down at *Amsterdam*[11] and *Rotterdam*.[12]

DLXVIII. Money lent on a bottomry of goods may be insured, provided it be stated in all the bills of lading, where it relates to a voyage to the East Indian Colonies or back to Holland, or otherwise in the bottomry itself, that the money has been received, adding the day and place, and the name of the persons : 1, by whom, and 2, to whom it was paid, and 3, for whose benefit it had been lent. It has been so provided at Amsterdam.[13]

[7] Dig. xx. 4. 6. § 1. Verwer, § 22, 23.

[8] Verwer, d. l. and p. 172.

[9] 8 Mar. 1706. *Advies. over den Kooph.* d. i. cons. 66.

[10] § 32.

[11] 30th Jan. 1682; *Handv.* 538, n. 22.

[12] Law of 1768, *van Executien en Præferentien*, art. 30.

[13] 26th Jan. 1693, art. 3; *Handv.* p. 660, and 10 Mar. 1744, art. 21 ; *ibid.* p. 665.

SEC. 3.

DLXIX. There appears to be no reason why the owner of vessels in foreign parts may not, as held by Bynkershoek,[1] contract a bottomry. It is frequently done in respect of goods.[2]

CHAPTER XII.—SEC. 6.

DLXX. As remuneration is not repugnant to the nature of *mandate* or 'commission,'[3] so by our customs remuneration may legally be recovered, not only where it has been promised, but even where it has not been promised, provided the act or service done be such as it is usual to give remuneration for.[4] Not so where there has been no promise, and the laws or customs are silent in respect of remuneration for any particular business; whence the somewhat more general doctrine of *Bynkershoek*[5] should, it seems, be taken with limitation.

SEC. 8.

DLXXI. A sudden and unexpected emergency wholly excuses a mandatory who either has not thoroughly fulfilled the mandate or has exceeded his limits.[6]

DLXXII. As on the contract of a mandatory the

---

[1] *Q. J. Priv.* l. ii. c. 16.

[2] Verwer, p. 255. n. 3, and p. 256. n. 4. *Advies. over den Kooph.* d. i. cons. 67 ; and see an instance in Bynkersh. p. 513.

[3] Dig. xvii. 1. 6.   [4] Dig. L. 17, 34, arg.

[5] *Q. J. Priv.* l. ii. c. 6. p. 247.

[6] Dig. xvii. 1. 30. See an instance in *de Advies. over den Kooph.* d. i. cons. 78. p. 405, sqq.

mandator may sue, even without cession of action,[7] so also may he himself be sued thereon in the direct action by one with whom the mandatory had contracted in his name.[8]

SEC. 10.

DLXXIII. A mandatory who has exceeded the limits of his mandate in respect of a purchase has no action for the excess, not even the action *negotiorum gestorum* ;[9] nor, if we follow the strict reason of the law, can he retain the thing for himself; which rule, however, should, perhaps, be tempered by equity,[10] if the thing be worth the price at which it was purchased, and could not be had at a lower price.

CHAPTER XIII.

DLXXIV. In that kind of *exchange* which is called local (*à locis*, from the two places to which it has reference) mercantile, or trajectitious, there generally are or are supposed to be four parties; first, the person who gives the value or money, and who is called the *remittent ;* secondly, the person who, upon receiving the value or a promise to pay it, gives the bill of exchange, and who is called the *drawer ;* thirdly, the person to whom the bill is addressed, and who is requested to make payment, who is called the *drawee ;* and, fourthly, he to whom the payment is to be made, and who is called the presentor, *payee* or *holder.* There may also be other parties, such as *indorsees* (*i.e.,* mandatories of

---

[7] Thes. 478.
[8] Coren, *Obs.* 28. n. 47, 48 ; Bynkersh. *Q. J. Priv.* 1. iii. c. 16. p. 508.
[9] Thes. 505.   [10] Voet. *ad Pand.* xvii. 1. § 4.

the holder duly appointed by him, to whom the payment may be made); *sureties* of the drawee; or third parties *accepting*, who, though the bill be not addressed to them, promise to pay it.

DLXXV. We should be careful to distinguish between exchange or the cambial transaction, and the cambial letters or bills of exchange, drawn in pursuance of it. The former is perfected by consent between the remittent and the drawer; the latter consists of a written mandate regarding the money to be paid to the holder at a time and place agreed upon; and which mandate becomes binding upon the acceptance of the drawee, and then produces that *literarum obligatio*, in its wider sense, of which we have spoken in *Thes.* 521.

DLXXVI. As to the nature of this transaction, and what kind of contract it most approximates to, there is much controversy. The opinion of *Dupuis* on the subject[1] seems to me to be the most correct; namely, that exchange (*i.e.*, the transaction which is entered into between the remittent and the drawer) is a certain species of sale and purchase, wherein the remittent, or party giving the value, stands in the place of the purchaser, who pays or promises to pay the price; and the drawer, who undertakes to draw the bill, stands in the place of the vendor.

DLXXVII. The object or purpose of this transaction may be twofold; for either the drawer, in order to be discharged from what he owes to the remittent, gives him the bill of exchange, by virtue of which the latter recovers the amount from some other person; in which case there

---

[1] *Tract. de l'art des Lettres de Change* (apud Savary, *Parfait Negociant*, tom. i. p. 431, sqq.) cap. 3, § 13, sqq. p. 434, sq.

is a *datio in solutum* or giving in payment, which stands in place of a purchase ;[2] or secondly, the remittent, requiring money at another place, bargains with the drawer for a bill of exchange, to be paid at such other place ; in which case there is a simple purchase and sale. This latter is called simple exchange (*zuivere wissel*) ; and the former mixed exchange (*gemengde of schuldwissel.*)[3]

DLXXVIII. The *merx* or the thing sold in such a transaction is not, properly speaking, the action or right of recovery which the drawer has against the drawee ; for he who sells a right of action is discharged, though, in consequence of the debtor's poverty, the action may have become worthless ;[4] whereas the drawer of a bill is not discharged unless the money has been paid. But the thing sold is the money itself, which is sold on the condition that it should be paid at the time and place stipulated in the bill of exchange. Nor is the l. l. of the Dig. xviii. l. opposed to this view ; for not only is money situated elsewhere saleable, but the value of mercantile funds also is subject to change, and even money itself, the value of which is fixed, rises or falls according to particular places.[5]

DLXXIX. From the nature of a sale many corollaries may be drawn in regard to exchange.

And, 1, indeed, neither party can without the consent of the other withdraw from such a consensual contract, even though the bill of exchange may not as yet have been drawn ; nor therefore can the remittent retract from

---

[2] Cod. viii. 45. 4.
[3] Phoonsen, *Wissel-styl*, cap. 35. p. 264, sqq.
[4] Dig. xviii. 4, 4, 5.
[5] Dig. xiii. 4, 3.

the bargain ;[1] but if there arise weighty suspicions and apprehensions of loss,—as, for example, if the purchaser at the outset of the contract entertains doubts of the indemnity,—he may demand personal security,[2] or claim restitution of the price or value already paid.[3]

DLXXX. Similarly, the drawer after he has received the value cannot withdraw from the contract, nor revoke the mandate for payment given to the drawee. If, however, the value has not been paid, he may legally retain the bill, where credit has not been given, until the value shall have been paid; or, even where credit has been given, if he afterwards has weighty reasons to apprehend loss, he may retain it until sufficient security has been given for the value.[4] And where the bill has already been delivered, and has been transmitted by the remittent, if indeed the latter continues to be the owner of it, the drawer may legally revoke his mandate; but if the *dominium* thereof has passed by endorsement to a third party for value paid, he cannot revoke it, since he ought to suffer the loss himself as the penalty of having given credit too rashly, rather than that the purchaser of the bill, who, without any fault of his own, has relied on the acknowledgment on the bill itself of the value having been received or taken in account, should be affected thereby.[5]

DLXXXI.—2. If the bill has been drawn payable on a particular day, the remittent (as purchaser) as well as his mandatory, the holder or indorsee, is bound to send it in due time to the place where it is to be paid,

---

[1] Dupuis, cap. v. § 8, 9. [2] Dig. xviii. 6, 18, § 1.
[3] Dig. xii. 4. ult.—Cod. viii. 45. 24. Dupuis, § 10.
[4] Inst. ii. 1. § 41 arg. Dig. v. 1. 41.
[5] See Dupuis, d. cap. v. § 23, & axiom. 4.

in order that it might be presented to the drawee for acceptance and payment. For since this kind of sale is usually made on the condition that the thing sold should be delivered on a particular day, the remittent who makes default in this respect is similar to a purchaser, who, having delayed to accept, takes the risk on himself.[6] It has, however, been especially enacted at Amsterdam that if the bill, though transmitted in due time, has, through any accident to the public courier, arrived too late, this default should not attach to the remittent.[7]

DLXXXII. If the bill be drawn payable at sight of so many days after sight, the rule above laid down does not hold ; and some delay, though not to an unreasonable extent, is allowed to the remittent. For the terms of the agreement between the parties should be observed.[8] And hence a traveller, who undertakes to convey a bill from the drawer to the party to whom it is addressed, is held to have had reasonable time allowed him for performing the journey he is about to undertake ;[9] but a merchant who has purchased such bill in the course of trade, ought to bear the risks of too great delay and the chance of the debtor subsequently making cession to the Court.[10] But many writers dissent herefrom.[11]

DLXXXIII.—3. The remittent, as purchaser, is bound to pay the price or value promised. At *Amsterdam* such payment is usually made the first or second

---

[6] See Dig. xlvi. 3. 39, pr.

[7] 31 Jan. 1764 ; see Reitz, *Grond-begins. van 't Wissel-regt.—door* Heineccius.—Middelb. 1774. p. 634, sqq. *Tweede Vervolg. van Handv. van Amsterd.* p. 81.

[8] Dig. L. 16. 137, § 2.   [9] Dig. xlv. 1. 137, § 2.

[10] Dupins, cap. vi. n. 20. sqq.

[11] See Reitz, ad *Heinecc.* cap. iv. § 24, not. 31, p. 179, sqq. *Advies. over den Kooph.* d, ii. cons. 2.

day after the delivery of the bill. and may even be recovered by parate execution.[1] If the value has not been paid, the drawer may claim back the bills, the *dominium* whereof he continues to retain, on account of the unpaid value ;[2] and if the remittent makes cession to the Court, he takes precedence before all the creditors.[3] We have already[4] stated the law as regards the case where a bill has been already transmitted by the remittent.

DLXXXIV.—4. The drawer, who has given a bill payable at a particular time and place, is similar to a vendor who has promised to deliver on a certain day, and ought to fulfil the condition of the contract.[5] He is bound to see that payment is made at the stipulated time and place.

DLXXXV.—5. Before the lapse of such period, however, he cannot be compelled to pay the amount, which the purchaser is entitled to, even though, the drawer not having accepted, the holder has made protest thereof. He ought, however (as is generally done in *bona fide* proceedings),[6] to give security to the holder or the remittent for the amount and expenses, if payment be not made in due time.[7]

DLXXXVI.—6. If the bill be not paid on the appointed day, the drawer is liable to the remittent, or to

---

[1] *Willekeur v. Amst.* 31 Jan. 1656; *Handv.* p. 543. n. 3. art. 2. Phoonsen, cap. viii. § 5. Roseboom, cap. L. art. 30. And see other laws in Reitz, *ad Heinecc.* cap. vi. § 3. not. 3.

[2] Inst ii. 1. § 41.

[3] Thes. 448. Heinecc. & Reitz, cap. vi. § 46. *Advies. over den Kooph.* d. ii. cons. 50. p. 195, sqq. & cons. 52. p. 208, sqq.

[4] Thes. 580.

[5] Cod. iv. 49. 4.   [6] Dig. v. i. 41.

[7] Dupuis, cap. vii. n. 7, and cap. x. u. 19. Phoonsen, cap. xiii. § 7. Heineccius & Rei'z, cap. vi. § 4. p. 306, sqq. Grotius, *infra*, cap. xlv. § 9.

the holder who has succeeded in his place, in the amount and expenses.[8]

DLXXXVII. Further: Many other obligations arise or may arise upon a bill of exchange; as,—

1. Where the remittent has authorized the holder, to whom he has transmitted the bill, to recover it if the mandate has been given only for his own benefit, and the mandatory is merely an agent to recover the bill, the remittent is bound to pay him the expenses which he has incurred, and a reward for his services (*provisie*).[9] But if the recovery has been authorized for the benefit of both the parties, and it has been agreed that the money should be paid to the holder as the creditor of the remittent, then, if the drawer has failed to pay, the remittent is bound to pay in addition to the holder, the re-exchange, *i.e.*, the value together with the expenses.[10]

DLXXXVIII.—2. The holder, as the mandatory of the remittent, is liable to him for neglect (*levissima culpa*) in presenting the bill to the drawer, and in recovering the amount from him; or, if a protest ought to have been made and has been forfeited, he is bound in the amount and expenses.[11] Moreover, if he be not a creditor of the remittent, but is to recover the amount for his benefit, he is bound to restore the amount he has received. If before the amount due on the bill has been paid, the holder makes cession to the Court,

---

[8] Dig. xix. 1. i. Dupuis, cap. xvi. n. 3, 19. Phoonsen, cap. xx. § 2. p. 158. Heinecc. & Reitz, cap. vi. § 4. p. 304, sqq.

[9] Dupuis, cap. viii. § 5, and cap. xv. n. l.

[10] Ibid. oap. viii. § 6. junct. cap. xv. n. 2., & sqq. Phoonsen, cap. xx. § 2.

[11] Heinec. cap. vi. § 8. Phoonsen, cap. xv. § 3.

the remittent may claim the bills as owner; and in this case he is preferred to all other creditors.[1]

DLXXXIX.—3. A drawer, who by a bill of exchange requires the drawee, not being his debtor, to pay a sum of money, is bound, in case he pays it, to restore the amount to him.

DXC.—4. If a drawee, after acceptance of the bill has not fulfilled the mandate so undertaken, he is liable to the drawer in the amount and expenses.[2] If he has not accepted, he is not, as a rule, liable, though he may be a debtor of the drawer's; for no one is bound to undertake a mandate.[3]

DXCI.—5. After acceptance of the bill, the drawee is liable to the remittent, as the purchaser of the right which the drawer had against him on the mandate so undertaken: he is also liable to a holder and indorsee, as the mandatories of the remittent.[4] It follows that an acceptance has the force of a promise,[5] or a *literarum obligatio.*[6]

DXCII.—6. All the prior indorsers are liable to the subsequent indorsees on the mandate, by which each has substituted the one next to him, for the recovery of the amount from the drawee, at the risk of each prior indorser,[7] so that the last indorsee may sue any one of the former indorsers whom he chooses. It is

---

[1] *Verzamel. van Casus-positien, Voorstellingen en declaratien betrekkelyk tot voorvallende omstandigheden in den Koophandel.* 1 e. Stuk, Amst. 1793. 8°. ibique cas. 13. p. 122, sqq.

[2] Reitz *ad Heinec.* cap. iv. § 38, not. 53.

[3] Ibid. cap. vi. § 5.

[4] Heinecc. cap. iii. § 17. junct. § 15, & cap. vi. § 5.

[5] Dupuis, cap. xvi. § 2.

[6] Thes. 425, in fin.

[7] Dig. xvii. 1. 22. § 2 & 45. § 7.

however, the custom for the next preceding indorser to be sued first.[8] There may also be a new obligation created, as on a sale, by which the indorser may become liable to his substitute, if the endorsement has been made for value received.[9]

DXCIII.—7. A drawer also, where the drawee has failed to pay, is liable to the indorsees; for the right acquired by the remittent upon the sale[10] is transferred by him by mandate to the payee, and by him to the indorsees: which obligation *Grotius* treats of in a subsequent chapter.[11]

DXCIV. Besides these obligations there are others which may arise in respect of a bill of exchange. Thus when the drawer has not accepted it, a third party may do so for the honor of the drawer, the remittent, or the indorsee, as we shall see hereafter. Moreover, although the drawee has accepted the bill, a third party also may by signing it render himself also liable;[12] which if done on the bill itself, is termed *L'Aval, or Avallum*;[13] and a party so subscribing becomes thereby liable *in solidum*, without the *beneficium ordinis* or *divisionis*,[14] and may be sued in the *cambial* action.* In both these respects such an obligation differs from that of a person who

---

[8] Reitz *ad Heinecc.* cap. iv. § 39, not. 58, p. 230, sq. Dupuis, cap. xvi. § 1, 7, 8, 19, &c p. 460, sq. Phoonsen, cap. ix. § 7. Savary, lib. iii. cap. 6. p. 89. *Advies. over den Kooph.* d. ii. cons. 17.

[9] See *Thes.* 586.

[10] Thes. 586.

[11] Chapter xlv. § 10.   [12] Ad § 3.

[13] Reitz *ad Heinecc.* cap. iii. § 26, not. 55. Savary, lib. iii. cap. 8. p. 109, vs. *L'Aval,* &c.

[14] Savary, d. l. vs. *Il est arrivé,* &c. p. 110. Heinecc. et Reitz, cap. vi. § 10. in not. p. 325, in f.

* [*Paraat. Wissel-regt.*:—See Van der Linden's *Instit.* p. 693.—Tr.]

P

by a separate instrument has simply engaged himself or intervened as surety for the drawee.[1]

DXCV. In addition to the acceptor, and even the drawer and remittent, being liable to the holder and his substitutes, the indorsees; and even all the prior indorsers to the subsequent indorsees; each *in solidum;* several parties may also become in other respects jointly liable *in solidum* on the cambial process; as where they have upon request accepted a bill, or where any party other than the drawee has bound himself *in avallo.*[2] So also from the wording of the bill itself there may be several joint-creditors *in solidum,* as where at the request of the remittent, who has himself promised to give a similar bill to another, the drawer has in the bill acknowledged to have received the value thereof, both from the remittent himself and from such other.[3]

SEC. 1.

DXCVI. *Exchange,* so far as it is transacted between the drawer and the drawee (which is all that Grotius here wishes to define), is a mandate regarding the payment of money to some one given by means of an instrument drawn up in due form, where it is also often usual and prudent to state that such instrument is a Bill *of Exchange;* which some authors require also as essential,[4] though others do not think it strictly necessary, provided the substantial requirements of a

[1] Heinecc. cap. iii. § 27, and cap. vi. § 10, 11.
[2] Heinecc. & Reitz. cap. iii. § 28, and in not. p. 134.   Phoonsen, cap. xxii. § 2.
[3] Voet *ad Pand.* xxii. 2, § 9. *Holl. Consult.* d. iii. st. 2. cons. 33.
[4] Heinecc. cap. iv. § 9.

bill are present, and the names of the drawer, drawee, and payee are mentioned, and the receipt of the value acknowledged. Other particulars which are generally observed herein may be found in the treatises of *Phoonsen*,[5] *Heineccius,* and *Reitz.*[6] It should also be stated in the bill whether it is the only bill, or the first, second, third, &c., which is requested to be paid, the others of the same tenor not being paid.[7] A condition may also be annexed to the payment, as, for instance, "provided the vessel arrives in safety;" as is done in those instruments called *Bottomry-bills.*[8]

DXCVII. In order to entitle a bill of exchange to the cambial process or *paraat wessel-regt,** it is necessary that the place where it was drawn and the place where it has to be paid should be different. At *Amsterdam* it is further required that one or other of the places should be beyond Holland;[9] but at *Rotterdam*[10] and at *Middelburg*[11] this is not necessary.

DXCVIII. The receipt of the value or consideration should be acknowledged in the bill;[12] but it does not matter in what manner it has been received; and the drawer may even take it upon himself (*de waarde in mij zelven*).[13]

DXCIX. It has been a question whether, upon a bill having been protested for non-payment by the drawee, the drawer, when sued by the holder or indorser or by the remittent himself, if he alleges the

---

[5] Cap. v. § 3, sqq.   [6] D. 1. § 2, sqq.
[7] Dd. ll. *Verzam. van Casus-position, &c. cas.* 2.
[8] Phoonsen, cap. 37.   * [Van der Linden's *Inst.* p. 693.]
[9] *Willekeur. van Amst.* 26 Jan. 1679 ; Handv. p. 546.
[10] *Keur. van Rotterd.* 24 Aug., 1720, art. 20. See Reitz *ad Heinecc.*
p. 633.   [11] Idem, p. 83.   [12] Heinecc. & Reitz, cap. iv. § 13, 14.
[13] Savary, l. iii. c. 4. p. 74. vs. *la troisième,* &c.

non-recept of the value, is entitled to the benefit *non numeratæ pecuniæ ?* The opinions of the lawyers and commentators, and the laws themselves, vary on the subject.[1]

DC. From the nature, however, of these transactions, and the reason of the Law of Holland, the following rules should, it seems to me, be observed hereon :

1. If the property in a bill of exchange belongs to an indorsee, who has given value to the remittent or payee, then the exception *non numeratæ pecuniæ* or of non-receipt of the value, cannot be pleaded against such indorsee by the drawer, who ought rather[2] to suffer the loss as a punishment consequent on having rashly given credit.[3]

DCI.—2. If the indorsement has been made without any mention of the value having been paid by the indorsee, then he, as the agent *in rem alienam* of the payee, may be met by the drawer with the same exception as the payee himself—not, indeed, the exception *non numeratæ pecuniæ* (which obtains only in respect of a loan, not of a sale), but the exception *contractûs non impleti,* or of the non-fulfilment of the contract, or the exception *doli* or of fraud, to be proved by the party pleading it.

DCII.—3. This exception, however, of the non-fulfilment of the contract will still be of less benefit to the party pleading it than the exception *non numeratæ*

---

[1] Uhl. Francf. *Wissel-Resp.* d. i. cas. 32, p. 157, sq.; d. ii. cas. 94. p. 158, 162, n. 9 ; junct. d. i. cas. 56. p. 438, sqq. Heinecc. & Reitz. cap. ij. l. § 10, & not, 22 ; and cap. iv. § 13, & *in subj. Diss.* cap. i. § 4, p. 474, and § 20. p. 506.

[2] Thes. 580, in fin.

[3] Dupuis. cap. v. n. 23. and axiom. 4 ; Uhl. Francf. *Wissel-resp.* ii. d. resp. 104.

pecuniæ[4] in preventing either provisional payment to the drawer or condemnation in cambial process.

DCIII.—4. As regards *Drooge Wissel*, or *Dry Exchange* (whereby, under the pretended name of exchange, a loan of money is promised to be repaid with interest at the same place and within a certain time[5]), if it be stated that the value has been received in ready money, there sems to be no reason why the exception *non numeratæ pecuniæ* should not hold good, at least in the principal case.[6] If it be stated simply that the value has been received, the exception *non impleti contractús* should, it seems, be permitted. And the same rule would, I think, apply to promissory notes, wherein, without any mention of exchange, money is promised to be paid, and the receipt of the value acknowledged.

In either case, however, it may be questioned whether it is not in accordance with the reason of the rule, which requires that the consideration should be expressed in the instrument,[7] to hold such a general acknowledgment of the consideration insufficient to justify a decree of provisional payment; excepting only in respect of bills of exchange, properly so called, where the place of payment is different from the place where they were drawn; and to which favour is properly shown on account of their utility to commerce.

DCIV. Bills of exchange are frequently made payable either to the payee or *his order*. But if no

---

[4] See *Thes.* 523, in med.

[5] Dupuis, cap. i. n. 5, Reitz *ad Heinecc.* cap. ii. § 20. p. 78, sqq. and p. 638, lit. D.

[6] See Phoonsen, cap. xxxix. n. 1, 3, 6, 7. Dupuis, d. l. Reitz *ad Heinecc.* cap. vi. § 30. p. 372, in not.   [7] Thes. 526

mention is made of the *order*, a simple indorsement
without a special cession, made by a written mandate
to recover, is by some authors held not to pass the right
of recovery.[1]   But others think differently.[2]

DCV. The time for payment may be stated in a bill
of exchange in three ways; either by the drawer himself fixing a particular day,[3] or by making it depend on
the presentment by the holder, payment being requested
either at sight or so many days after sight ;[4] or lastly,
by leaving it to be determined by custom, as *at usance*
or *at double usance*, &c.   The latter period varies much
in different places.[5]   At *Amsterdam* it is often a month,
or more or less, according to the distance of the place
whence the bill is sent.[6]   So also, custom has fixed the
time in respect of bills which are made payable on particular market days (*cambia feriarum*), as, for instance,
at the Easter market;[7] and which differ from the
cambia platearum, or local or mercantile bills, namely,
those of which we are properly now treating, and which
are usually transmitted and paid at other periods.

SEC. 2.

DCVI. Upon giving a bill of exchange, the drawer
generally writes what is called a letter of *advice* to the

[1] Phoonsen, cap. ix. § 6, in f. *Verzamel. van Casus-pos.* cas. 8. p. 88.
Advies. over den Kooph. d. ii. cons. 56. p. 220 sqq.

[2] Le Long, *Vervolg. van de Wissel-Styl*, &c. par. 20. p. 142. Heinecc.
& Keitz, cap. ii. § 8. & not. 13; Dupuis, cap. iv. n. 4, 9. p. 436, & cap.
xiii. п. 3, 4. p. 453.

[3] Dupuis, cap. iv. exempl. 8, & n. 28.   [4] Ibid. n. 25, sqq.

[5] Ibid. cap. iv. n. 29, sqq. Heinecc. & Reitz, cap. ii. § 13. p. 58, sqq.
& not. 29.

[6] Phoonsen, cap. xiv. § 10, sq.

[7] Heinecc. cap. ii. § 12, sqq. Phoonsen, cap. xxxiii. xxxiv.

drawee, in order that he may know what he ought to pay, and on whose account he ought to make such payment, and from whence he ought to recover the money so paid, in case he is not indebted to the drawer; and if the drawee has not received such advice, he may legally decline to accept the bill. If, however, he already knows on what account the bill has been given, it is usual to say in the bill " without further advice." [8] If the bill be drawn on commission, *i.e.*, for the benefit and at the risk (*voor rekening*) of a third party (whether such third party be the drawee himself or any other person), several particulars are to be inserted in the letter of advice, to be sent (where the matter concerns a third party) to such third party also.[9]

Sec. 3.

DCVII. If the drawer does not accept the bill, any one else may accept and pay it for honour, even where no protest has been made : but in the latter case the party who has paid it ought to obtain a cession of action from the holder, and he cannot obtain indemnity by cambial process, but only in the ordinary action.[10] On the other hand, where a protest has been made, the third party who has so accepted and paid the bill may obtain indemnity by the cambial process, even without cession.[11]

DCVIII. And this is what is termed acceptance *supra protest ;* and a bill may be so accepted not only by a third party, but even by the party holding it,

[8] Heinecc. & Reitz, cap. iv. § 16. p. 165, sqq. Dupuis, cap. iv. n. 5, 6.
[9] Phoonsen, cap. xxvi.
[10] Roseboom, *Keur. van Amster.* cap. L. art. 10.
[11] Ibid. art. 11.   And see Reitz *ad Heinecc.* cap. vi. § 9. not. 15.

whether as payee or indorsee, viz., by paying it himself;[1] and even by the drawee himself, if he be unwilling to accept it absolutely.[2] And he may even accept it alternatively, *i.e.*, either absolutely or *supra protest*, as where the bill has been drawn on him on account of a third party, from whom he does not hold any property, but expects to obtain from him the value of it before the day of payment; or where he has goods belonging to him, but has not yet received authority to pay the bill drawn on him.[3]

DCIX. The acceptance *supra protest* may be for the honour of the drawer, or the remittent, or of any of the indorsees.[4]

DCX. But when several parties offer at the same time to accept in this manner, he should be preferred who, 1, has received authority to accept from the party on whose account the bill had been drawn:[5] next, the party whom the drawer has so authorized;[6] 3. He to whom payment is to be made and who holds the bill, whether as payee or endorsee; as laid down by *Reitz;*[7] though *Phoonsen* more correctly maintains[8] that the drawee, if he be willing to accept in the alternative, *i.e.*, absolutely or *supra protest*, should be preferred;[9] 4. If the drawee declines to accept, except *supra protest* for the honour of the drawer, the payee who offers to accept on the same terms is to be preferred to him;[10] 5. A party who is willing to accept *supra*

[1] Dupuis, cap. ix. n. 6.   [2] Ibid. n. 5.   [3] Dupuis, ib. n. 13.
[4] Ibid. n. 5, 6, 7. p. 448. axiom 1.
[5] Ibid. u. 15. Heinecc. & Reitz, cap. iii. § 31, p. 141 & § 19, not. 38. p. 112. n. 1.
[6] Dupuis, d. 1. n. 16. & axiom 4.   [7] Reitz, d. p. 112. n. 2.
[8] Cap. xii. n. 9.   [9] Dupuis, d. 1. n. 17.
[10] Ibid. n. 18.

protest for the honour of the drawer should be preferred to one who is willing to accept for the honour of the remittent or of any of the indorsers.[11] And 6. One who offers to accept *supra protest* for the honour of a prior indorser should be preferred to one who offers to do so on behalf of a subsequent indorser.[12]

DCXI. An acceptor *supra protest* is bound to pay as on a promise, and may be sued in cambial process ;[13] but after he has paid the bill he has his remedy in like manner against the party for whose honour he had accepted, and against all those who were liable to the latter ;[14] but not against those to whom the latter was himself liable in turn.[15] Thus, a party who has accepted *supra protest* for the honour of the drawer may not sue the indorsers.[16]

DCXII. He who holds a bill of exchange, whether as payee or indorsee, is not bound to acquiesce in an acceptance *supra protest* given by a third party, unless under good security.[17] But where he acquiesces, if the acceptance *supra protest* has been given for the honour of the drawer, the latter cannot be compelled to give further security to the remittent. If the acceptance be for the honour of any of the indorsers, the drawer ought to give security to such acceptor or to the remittent.[18]

DCXIII. In the same manner as acceptance, so also may payment be made *supra protest*, upon the drawee

---

[11] Ibid. n. 19.　　　　　　　　[12] Ibid. n. 20.
[13] Roseboom, cap. L. art. 10. Heinecc. & Reitz, cap. vi. § 9. Phoonsen, cap. xii. n. 18.
[14] Dupuis, cap. ix. n. 10.　　　　[15] Dupuis, d. l. n. 11.
[16] See Evidence, Amsterd. 27 Feb. 1662; *Handv.* p. 544, n. 6; Reitz *ad Heinecc.* cap. vi. § 9, not. 16.　Phoonsen, cap. xviii. n. 11, 23.
[17] Phoonsen, cap. xii. n. 13.　　　　[18] Ibid. n. 15.

who has accepted failing to pay, provided protest of non-payment has been made.[1]

DCXIV. The drawee himself may also, without accepting a bill, pay it *supra protest* on account either of the indorser or of the drawer,[2] and on account of the latter, even where he has accepted absolutely.[3]

Sec. 4.

DCXV. A merchant is in general bound to accept a bill drawn by his agent,[4] provided it appears from the bill that he has drawn it in his character of agent.[5] In which case, if the drawee fails to pay, the agent, it seems, cannot by the Law of Holland be sued.[6]

Sec. 5.

DCXVI. From the nature of a mandate it follows that where a drawee has not yet acquiesced in it, he may absolutely decline to accept a bill drawn on him: and the laws so lay it down.[7] And this holds good even where the drawee is a debtor of the drawer's,[8] or may even have previously promised the drawer to accept it, in which case, however, he is liable on his promise (but in the ordinary process) for the amount and expenses.[9]

DCXVII. The drawee may also, on acceptance, fix a

---

[1] Phoonsen, cap. xviii. n. 1. Reitz *ad Heinecc.* cap. vi. § 9, in not. p. 323.

[2] Phoonsen, d. l. n. 2.   [3] Ibid. n. 3.

[4] *Stat. Antwerp.* cap. lv. art. 1.   [5] Phoonsen, cap. x. n. 5.

[6] See Heinecc. cap. iv. § 25. ibique Reitz, in not.

[7] *Stat. Antwerp.* d. l. Roseboom, cap. L. art. 1.

[8] Phoonsen, cap. x. n. 5.

[9] Phoonson, d. l. n. 6; *Advies. over den Kooph.* d. ii. cons. 46.

time, mode, or condition in respect of the payment, or the amount which he is going to pay; and these terms the holder may either reject, protesting the bill,[10] or accept, at his own risk.[11]

DCXVIII. The acceptance of a bill may be either by word of mouth, or by a writing, or by subscription on the bill itself.[12] But in order to prevent the holder making protest the acceptance should be by subscription on the bill, with the addition of the Christian name and surname of the acceptor and the date of acceptance, and, if the bill is accepted in the name of another person, the character or capacity of the subscribing party.[13] But in those bills in which a definite period has been fixed for payment, no date is necessary.[14]

DCXIX. An acceptance once given cannot legally be revoked,[15] unless there has been fraud.[16] If the acceptance has been written on the bill itself, but the bill be still in the hands of the acceptor, he may not, even in this case, erase it.[17]

Sec. 6.

DCXX. A short period of respite or grace is allowed

---

[10] Dupuis, cap. viii. n. 23.   Phoonsen, cap. x. n. 28, 29.

[11] Phoonsen, d. l. n. 29.   Reitz *ad Heinecc.* cap iv. § 27, not. 37.

[12] Phoonsen, cap. x. n. 8, 9, 10.

[13] See *Willekeur. v. Amsterd.* 31 July, 1660, *Handv. van Amsterd.* p. 543, art. 3; *Ord. v. Middelb.* 9 Sept. 1660, art. 3, in Reitz *ad Heinecc.* in *Append.* p. 620; and 24 Mar. 1736, art. 4; Ibid. p. 623; and also of *Rotterd.* 24 Aug. 1720, art. 2; Ibid. p. 628.

[14] Reitz *ad Heinecc.* cap. iv. § 26, not 34. p. 190.

[15] Phoonsen, cap. x. n. 27.   Dupuis, cap. x. n. 2, 3, & reg. 1.

[16] Ibid. n. 4, & reg. 2.

[17] Ibid. d. l. Reitz *ad Heinecc.* cap. iv. § 38. not. 54. But Dupuis (d. l. n. 6. 7.) *dissentiente.*

for the payment of bills of exchange, at least of those
which have been made payable on a particular day.
This period is different at different places. Amongst
us, it is six consecutive days.[1] At *Rotterdam*[2] and
Middelburg[3] the same period is allowed in respect of
bills payable at sight.

DCXXI. Where the value of the money required to
be paid by the bill has altered, then, if it has been
made payable in current money, the value of the money
at the time of payment should be had regard to ;[4] but
if made payable in a particular kind of money, that
value should be had regard to at which the money
stood at the time of the contract. The Placaat of
Holland on the 27th April, 1719, was enacted for the
purpose of preventing lo·ses arising from arbitrary
alterations in the value of foreign money.

DCXXII. By the Law of *Amsterdam* the acceptor
cannot require the bill to be delivered to him before
payment.[5]

DCXXIII. As regards the question, whether in paying a bill of exchange, a compensation or set-off can
take place; it is indeed, in the first place, quite clear
that the party who holds the bill, whether it be the remittent himself, or the payee or an indorser, ought to
permit the set-off of any definite or liquid debt due by
himself to the acceptor ;[6] but if such debt be due to the

---

[1] *Ord. v. Rotterd.* art. 8. Reitz *ad Heinecc.* cap. ii. § 14. not. 35.

[2] D. l. art. 11.

[3] *Ord. v. Middelb.* 24 March 1736, art. 3, 6, in Reitz, *in Append.*
p. 623.

[4] Reitz *ad Heinecc.* cap. vi. § 27, not. 38.

[5] *Willekeur. v. Amst.* 24 Jan. 1651, *Handv.* p. 542; & 26 Jan. 1679,
art. 7; Ibid. n. 10 p. 546; Roseboom, cap. L. art. 25, sqq.

[6] Heinecc. & Reitz, cap. vi. § 27, not. 39; & § 30, not. 44.

acceptor, not by such holder, but by one or other of the previous parties, whether it be the remittent or a prior indorsee, it seems equally clear that no set-off can be claimed;[7] for this reason, namely, that a subsequent indorsee derives the right which he has against the acceptor, not so much from the endorsement made by his indorser, as (where there has been a just endorsement) from the acceptance of the drawee himself, who has obliged himself principally and generally, as on a promise, to all those to whom the bill may have been transferred by a just title.[8] If, lastly, the drawee, being himself a creditor of the remittent, has not accepted simply, but has added the condition " in order to pay himself" (*om aan zig zelven te voldoen*), there seems hardly any doubt that not only the remittent, if he is himself the holder, but the payee also, and his indorsee, ought to permit a set-off of such debt.[9]

DCXXIV. Process of execution may be issued on a bill of exchange against the person and property of the acceptor, no less than of the drawer ; whereby he may be committed to civil custody, and his property placed under arrest.[10] To this rule, however an exception has latterly been allowed, and a different mode of procedure, consistently with the form of action, has been prescribed, where the bill is tainted with any apparent defect, or is met at once by a liquid exception.[11]

[7] Phoonsen, cap. xvi. § 27; Law of *Leipsic*, in Le Long, *Vervolg.*—*in Append.* p. 80.

[8] Phoousen. cap. x. n. 7.

[9] Dupuis, cap. viii. n. 2, sqq.

[10] See, ex. gr., *Willekeur. v Amsterd.* 2 Dec. 1664: *Handv.* p. 545. *Manier van Proced.* cap. vii. art. 19; Ibid. p. 615, & cap. ix. art. 59, sqq.

[11] *Keur. v. Amst.* 30 Jan. 1777, *Tweede Vervolg. der Handv.* p. 85.

SEC. 7.

DCXXV. Since from the nature of the contract of exchange, the drawer and the acceptor are liable to the payee each *in solidum*,—the former by virtue of the payee having as it were succeeded by purchase to the rights of the remittent; and the latter, as on a promise (in respect of which, however, the *beneficium ordinis* does not hold ;[1])—he may elect to sue which of them he pleases; as provided also by the laws of several places.[2] But by the law of *Antwerp*[3] and of *Amsterdam*,[4] this right is thus limited, viz.: if the acceptor has failed to pay, the payee should claim the amount first from the drawer ; and then, if the drawer also fails, and after a protest has been made to that effect, he may proceed against the acceptor. An exception has, however, been since[5] allowed to this rule, where the drawer has become insolvent, and proper proof therefore can be given. It could not, however, be the intention of the above laws that upon default of demanding payment from the drawer, the payee should lose his remedy against the acceptor,[6] but it would rather seem that he should lose the privilege of the summary proceeding, but by no means his ordinary action.

SEC. 8.

DCXXVI. The mandate inserted in a bill respecting

[1] Dupuis, cap. xvi. n. 1, sqq. & reg. 1. Neostad. *Supr. Cur. Dec.* 12.
[2] Reitz *ad Heinecc.* cap. iv. § 39. not. 57. p. 227 ; as *Ord. v. Middelburg* of 1736, art. 9 ; Reitz, ibid. p. 625.
[3] Cap. lv. art. 4.
[4] 2 Dec. 1664 ; see *Handv.* p. 545.
[5] *Willek. v. Amst.* 26 Jan. 1679, art. 3.
[6] Arg. a contrario d. *Stat. Antw.* art. 9.

the payment of the amount on a particular day should be strictly fulfilled, nor can the payment be made before such day, or forced upon the payee or indorsee against his consent; for it may be a matter of import- ance to him, or, even if he be willing, to the drawer himself, that the amount should not be paid earlier.[7]

SEC. 9.

DCXXVII. Under the expenses which should be paid by an acceptor, who has failed to pay the bill on the third day after the appointed time, are included also the expenses of protest incurred on the 4th, 5th, or 6th day of grace.[8]

SEC. 10.

DCXXVIII. Although many authors think that this passage of Grotius should be altered, and attach a not inept meaning to it when so altered;[9] yet there seems to me to be no necessity for any alteration. For here as well as in a subsequent passage,[10] he does not by the term *holder* mean that fourth party, whom in *Thes.* 574 we have termed the payee, holder, or presentor, or the party who represents him as indorsee; but the sender or remittent himself, who is described in the Statute of *Antwerp*[11] (which is here correctly interpreted) as " the party, who has paid the value of the amount mentioned in the bill, as the owner thereof." He, moreover, speaks

---

[7] Reitz *ad Heinecc.* cap. ii. § 5. not. 8. Dupuis, cap. xii.

[8] *Willekeur. v. Amsterdam*, 26 Jan. 1679, art. 9; *Handv.* p. 546. and *Rotterdam*, 24 Aug. 1720. art. 10, in Reitz, *in Append.* art. 8. 10. p. 630.

[9] See *Rechtsgel. Observ.* part. i. obs. 77, and in '*t Nabericht op de* 30. *Rechtsgel. Vrag.* p. 153, sqq.   [10] Chapter xlv. § 3.

[11] Cap. lv. art. 7.

of the acceptor, because he also is mentioned in the Statute as the party " to whom the bill comes (not *by whom it is held*—as incorrectly cited in the *Rechtsgeleerde Observatien*[1]), for payment," *i.e.*, whose duty it is to pay the bill. And hence the meaning both of the Statute and of this passage in Grotius, is this,—that the party who has paid value for the bill may, as the owner thereof, and whilst the matter remains in its integrity (*i.e.*, before the acceptor has paid the bill), revoke or procure the drawer to revoke the mandate given in the bill respecting the payment to be made to himself or to another; unless the party who is bound to pay the bill is not the mere mandatory of the drawer (for the drawer is designated in the Statute as the sender of the bill[2]), but has a right to the money which is to be paid. For it not unfrequently happens that a drawee may have such a right to the money; as where he has either been required by the bill to pay it to himself;[3] or, by virtue of an indorsement made by one who is indebted to him, he intends to pay it to himself; or lastly, having a right to set-off, he has *ab initio* accepted it under the condition that he might pay himself out of it.[4]

CHAPTER XIV.—SEC. 10.

DCXXIX. As in several cities of Holland, where it has been enacted that houses should not be pulled down,[5] as well in order to preserve the regularity and beauty of the town, as to prevent detriment to the revenue derived from the real tax called *Verpondinge;*

[1] D. 1.   [2] See also art. 4.   [3] Phoonsen, cap. xxxvi. § 18. sqq.
[4] Thes. 623. Dupuis, cap. viii. n. 2—10.
[5] *Keur. van Leyden*, art. 46; *Haarlem*, 7 Jan. 1785; *Vervolg der Keur*. d. i. p. 150, sqq.

so, also, a similar provision has been made by recent laws in respect of houses situated in the country, unless the consent of those who now hold the offices formerly discharged by the Delegates of the States has been obtained.[6]

DCXXX. *Res litigiosa*, or property in dispute in a suit, may now be alienated, saving the rights of the third party litigant, who, if he succeeds in the action, may recover the property which was in litigation from the new possessor by execution, without fresh proceedings.[7]

Sec. 13.

DCXXXI. Although money cannot regularly be bought or sold, yet there is an exception in respect of mercantile funds, which according to the usages of trade are wont to vary in value.[8]

DCXXXII. By the Canon Law, the sale of an annual rent-charge was permitted, where the rent was charged on land, but not where it attached to the person only.[9] But the custom of this country permits the sale both of personal and real rent-charges;[10] of the latter, however, only where the rent consists in money and does not exceed the legal rate of interest ; and not where it is to be paid in fruits, cattle, or species.[11]

[6] Law of Holland, 23 June 1797.
[7] See not. on Vromans, *de Foro Compet.* lib. iii..cap. 2. § 2, not. 7. p. 209.
[8] See evidence of the *Burgermeesters of Amsterdam*, 27 Jan. 1749. *Vervolg. der Handv.* p. 32.
[9] Boehmer, *Jur. Eccles. Protest.* lib. v. t. 19. § 47, sqq.
[10] Zypæus, *Not. Jur. Belg.* lib. iv. § *de reditibus*, n. 1. p. 140.
[11] Ord. of *Philip II.*, 5 Mar. 1571. art. 1, sqq.

Q

SEC. 14.

DCXXXIII. The creditor or purchaser cannot regularly claim the redemption of an annual rent-charge.[1] Amongst the exceptions, however, which are allowed herein, we cannot, it seems, properly include the case where the debtor is in default: though the Court of Holland is said to have so decided.[2] Clearly, a pact by which the vendor is bound to redeem the annual rent-charge on a particular day is not valid.[3]

SEC. 15.

DCXXXIV. The doctrine which *Grotius* here lays down, from the law of *Philip* II. of the 5th March, 1571, viz., that when it is not known for what price the annual rent had been purchased, it may be redeemed for sixteen times the value of one year's rent, has not been altered either by the law of Holland of the 11th August, 1655 (by which the rate of interest was reduced to four per cent.) or by the law of the 27th September, 1658 (which permits the debtors of the State to redeem their annual rents by payment of twenty-five times the yearly value): and therefore rent-charges constituted previous to the reduction of the rate of interest, may still be redeemed by payment of sixteen times the yearly rent. Those which have been since constituted are presumed to have been purchased according to the rate of legal interest allowed at the time, and must therefore be redeemed with twenty-five times the yearly rent.

---

[1] Matth. *Paroem. Jur. Belg.* par. 4.

[2] 20 Jan. 1662, in the case of *Arend Albertsz. Neef*, defendant in appeal, *vs. Simon Jansz Martensz*, of *Oostzanen*, plaintiff.

[3] *Keur. van Leiden*, art. 118. *Holl. Cons.* d. i. cons. 206.

SEC. 18.

DCXXXV. In this difficult passage, the meaning of *Grotius* seems to be, that where an annual rent-charge of a particular species of money, as, for instance, of *thalers*, has been established, it need not be paid or redeemed in the same species of money, nor the value thereof at the time of payment regulated by its value at the time of the contract; but that it may be paid either in the same species of money at its current value as fixed by law at the time of payment, or in any other kind of money of the same value; for it is the general presumption that in a contract of this kind the intrinsic value of the money was not had in contemplation, nor even the value which it possessed in trade at the time of the contract (which in those times often exceeded the legal value) but only the money as regarded its amount, in respect of which therefore the legal value at the time of payment is to be looked to. And, this, he says, is the true rule, although it may be stated in the contract itself, for instance, that a thaler should be estimated at thirty stivers; for this is added with the intention that the amount lent might not be estimated at the mercantile, but at the legal value, which the money possessed at the time of the contract. And he adds an exception, where in constituting the annual rent-charge, it has been expressly stipulated that the payment should be made in the same kind of money, estimated at the same value, as that mentioned in the contract, for here the terms of the agreement should be observed.[4]

---

[4] See an opinion of Grotius hereon, in *de Holl. Consult.* d. vi. st. 2. cons. 55; and decisions of the Court, 15 Mar. 1602, *Holl. Cons.* d. iv. cons. 49, f. & 20 October, 1608, *Decis. en Ressl. van den Hove*, n. 171.

Q 2

DCXXXVI. In former times, however, it was required by the Law of *Amsterdam*,[1] that annual rent-charges should be redeemed with the same kind of money, estimated at the same value as at the time the charge was established.[2] It was also so decided by the Court,[3] and even sanctioned by the Legislature,[4] as regards, namely, the principal amount, but not the annual rent. And it was so held by the Court, even more recently.[5] But the same Court has since then frequently decided, as testified by several jurists[6] (to whose opinions and decisions *Grotius* seems here to have had regard), that the principal amount may also be paid in money estimated at its present legal value. A similar decision, of the 14th October, 1624, is reported by *Loenius*;[7] and this seems also to have been the intention of the States General in their laws of the 13th February, 1619, and the 21st July, 1622,[8] and of the pupillary statute of *Leyden* of 1665[9] and of *Gouda*.[10] Nor is it affected by the decision of the Supreme Court of the 21st October, 1623, reported by *Coren*,[11] which relates to an excepted case, wherein there had been delay in payment.

SEC. 32.

DCXXXVII. A sale made under a *lex commissoria*

---

[1] 23 Dec. 1489; *Handv.* p. 540.

[2] See *Holl. Cons.* d. i. cons. 219, p. 360.

[3] 15 May, 1503; *Decis. en Resol. van den Hove.*, n. 339.

[4] Law of the 5 Mar. 1571, art 7.

[5] 4 Dec. 1584, in Neostad. *Decis. Supr. Cur.* 37; and several other decisions.

[6] A. 1611, 1614, in *de Holl. Consult.* d. i. cons. 219; d. ii. cons. 292; also cons. 125, 290, 291.

[7] *Decis.* 23.   [8] Art. 43.   [9] Art. 45.

[10] Art. 77.   [11] *Obs.* 16 & 23.

(or condition of forfeiture in case of non-payment within a certain time) is valid ; but not one wherein in case
of non-payment of the price within a certain time a
further amount, exceeding the legal rate of interest, is
promised as penalty.[12]

SEC. 32.

DCXXXVIII. Where land has been sold in the
lump, but with the number of *morgens* or acres specified,
although from the reason of law no action would lie for
the difference of extent, yet it has been decided in Holland that an action would lie if the difference exceeded
one acre.[13]   And *Grotius* has also expressed the same
opinion in the *de Hollandsche Consultatien ;*[14] from which
opinion he by no means departs in the present text, as
supposed by the jurists in *de Rechtsgeleerde Observatien ;*[15]
for the words " *een margen onder of boven* —a *morgen*
less or more,*" here signify what we usually term " more
or less than a *morgen* " (*plus minus een margen*) ; whereas
in the *Hollandsche Consultatien* he expressly says " a
whole morgen " (*een heel margen*).   Nor is this affected
by *art.* 95 of the *Costumen van Rhynland,* from which
a general law cannot be deduced,[16] nor by the decisions
of the Court reported in *de Decis. en Resol.* n. 408,
417, which seem to relate only to *Rhynland.*

[12] Dig. xix. 1. 13. § 26. *Decis. en Resol. van den Hove,* n. 51.
[13] So decided by the Court, on the 28 February, 1596, and by the
Supreme Court, 21 October, 1597 ; *Sententien van den Hogen en Prov.
Raad,* decis. 177 ; Neostad, *Decis. Cur. Holl.* 18 ; and again on the 31
July 1600 (according to my MS. copy), *Decis.* p. 77, and in a similar
case, 20 Nov. 1606, or 1608, *Decis. en Res. van den Hove,* n. 176.
[14] D. vi. st. 2. cons. 56.
[15] Part ii. obs. 75.
[16] Thes. 14.

SEC. 34.

DCXXXIX. The risks and benefits of a thing sold, after the completion of the contract, regularly attach even by the Law of Holland to the purchaser, and this not only as regards movable, but also immovable property; notwithstanding the contrary opinion of a lawyer whose opinion is quoted and rather hastily adopted by *Boel.*[1] There is, however, an exception mentioned by *Groenwegen*[2] and *Voet,*[3] and a similar exception adopted at *Amsterdam,* in respect of houses sold in execution and perishing before the first of May on which day they are to be ceded.[4]

CHAPTER XV.—SEC. 1.

DCXL. A purchaser, after he has committed default in the payment of the price, is bound to pay interest,[5] which from the reason of law may now at the highest be five per cent. ;[6] nor is it higher even at *Amsterdam* under the ancient statute of 1609, which so early as 1658 had already been abrogated by custom.[7]

SEC. 4.

DCXLI. One who has knowingly purchased the property of a third party (*rem alienam*), and has not taken care to secure himself as regards indemnification

---

[1] *Ad. Loen. Decis.* 34 p. 240, & sqq.

[2] Not. 82. ad h. l.   [3] *Ad Pand.* xviii. 6. § 6.

[4] Roseboom, *Keur. van Amsterdam,* cap. xxxiv. art. 31.

[5] As decided also by the Court, 5 Sept., 1613; *Decis. en Resol. van den Hove,* n. 407.

[6] Thes. 545, in fin. & 546.

[7] *Handv. van Amst.* p. 541.

for eviction, cannot according to the Civil Law,[8] as well as by the Law of Holland,[9] recover back even the price paid for it.

SEC. 7.

DCXLII. As regards a latent defect in the thing sold, it has been frequently held by the lawyers,[10] and was lately decided by the Court of Holland[11] (which decision has been confirmed in revision[12]) that the action for rescission of the sale and re-delivery of the thing,* or for recovery of the deficiency in value,† may be maintained thereon.

CHAPTER XVI.—SEC. 1.

DCXLIII. Besides the *legal retractus*, which is here spoken of, there is also the *conventional retractus*, arising from a stipulation annexed to a sale,[13] and which, at a meeting of creditors, is to be preferred even to a legal retractus.[14]

DCXLIV. The *family retractus*, which obtains amongst us, seems to be traceable not so much (as Bynkershoek supposes[15]) to the Feudal Law as to the

⁸ Cod. viii. 45. 27.

⁹ Thes. 17, 23; and see Van Leeuw. *Cens. For.* part. i. lib. iv. cap. 19 n. 14.

¹⁰ *Holl. Cons.* d. iii. st. 2. cons. 107. *Advies. over den Kooph.* d. ii. cons. 80.　　　　　　　　　　　　　　　　　　　¹¹ 29 Jul. 1796.

¹² 23 Dec. 1797, in the case of *Boode en Bert vs. Willem & Jan Willink*.

* [*Actio redhibitoria.*—See Dig. xxi. 1. 21. & Voet, ib.]

† [*Actio quanti minoris.*—See Voet *ad Pand.* ib. § 2.]

¹³ Dig xviii. i. 75; & xlv. 1. 122, § 3.

¹⁴ Coren, *Obs.* xxxii. n. 38, 39

¹⁵ *Q. Jur. Priv.* 1. iii. c. 13. p. 477.

ancient German Law ; as maintained by Van Spiegel ;[1]
and this view is supported by the Law of the Saxons,[2]
and the ancient *Chora Zelandiæ*,[3] and likewise by the
constant exercise of this right among the people of
Groningen and *Drenthe*, by whose laws a disposition of
ancestral property by antenuptial contract or testament
cannot legally be made without the consent of the
relations.[4]

SEC. 2.

DCXLV. The *jus retrahendi* arises immediately upon
the completion of a sale, from which, therefore, the contracting parties cannot withdraw, in fraud of him to
whom the right of reclaim or pre-emption belongs.[5]
A subsequent statute, however, altering the general
law,[6] permits it to be done *bonâ fide*, provided the withdrawal takes place before a judicial notice of the
exercise of such right has been given.

SEC. 3.

DCXLVI. Although in Holland legal *retractus* has
not been adopted by the general law, in respect of
allodial property,[7] yet in Zeeland the law is otherwise.[8]

[1] *Oorspr. en Hist. der Vaderl. Rechten*, cap. iv. § 15. p. 134.
[2] T. xvii. § 1, edit. Gaertner, Lips. 1730.
[3] A. 1256, art. 91.
[4] *Aanleid. tot de Gron. Rechtskenn*, l. iii. c. 3; *Landrecht van Drenthe*.
l. iii. art. 5, 52, junct. l. iii. art. 70, sqq.
[5] See *Costum. van Rhynl.* art. 21. *Costum. van Middelb.* rubr. xi.
art. 13.   [6] Thes. 14.
[7] Grot. *Holl. Consult.* d. iii. st. 2. cons. 148, n. 2 ; Bynkersh. *Q. J.
Priv.* l. iii. c. 13. p. 478.
[8] *Keur. van Zeeland*, cap. ii. art. 12. *Costum. van Middelb.* rubr. xi.
& rubr. viii. art. 18. *Costum. van Vlissing.* cap. xii. *Costum. van
Zisrikzee*, apud Smallegange, *Chron. van Zeel.* cap. ix. p. 520.

Sec. 5.

DCXLVII. It is quite clear that *retractus* (even as adopted in various parts of Holland) does not obtain in respect of public auctions held upon a judicial decree. Several authors, including *Bynkershoek*,[9] lay down the same rule in respect of other public sales.[10]   But this seems true in reference only to particular statutes,[11] and not universally.[12]

Sec. 7.

DCXLVIII. Family *retractus*, which accrues by right of cognation, may be exercised even by the son of the seller, whether upon attaining majority, or upon being placed, at the death of the father or mother, whose estate is sold by the surviving parent, under another guardian, though appointed over the person only. *Grotius* is of a different opinion[13] but his argument is now valid only as regards the statutes of Zeeland,[14] and not of other statutes, which simply admit the cognates, and do not name any of them specially.

DCXLIX. The rule laid down by *Voet* in his Commentary on the Pandects, *lib.* xviii. *tit.* 3, § 13, and by other commentators, viz.: that the right of family *retractus* is allowed only to those who, in addition to the right of consanguinity, have the right by law of

---

⁹ *Q. Jur. Priv.* l. iii. c. 14. p. 490, sqq.

¹⁰ *Rechtsgel. Observ.* part. iii. obs. 74.

¹¹ *Costum. van Rhynl.* art. 36 ; *Keur van Leiden*, art. 120, in fin.

¹² *Costum. van Vlissing.* cap. xii. art. 6; *Keur. van Zeel.* l. c ; *Keur van Putten*, xxiv. art. 1, 2, 4. Roseboom, *Keur van Amsterd.* cap. xxxv. art. 16, 17.

¹³ *Holl. Consult.* d. iii. st. 2. cons. 148. n. 6.

¹⁴ *Cap.* ii. art. 12.

succeeding *ab intestato,* seems hardly reconcilable with the words of the statutes; the right of consanguinity, and not of legitimate succession, being the principal qualification thereby required.

DCL. Although succession *ab intestato* has been extended, not only to the tenth, but even to farther degrees,[1] yet family *retractus* should, it seems, be restricted to the degrees mentioned in the statutes.

DCLI. The rule here laid down by *Grotius,* viz., that a cognate who has first offered (or instituted) the *retractus* should be preferred to any other, should, it seems, be restricted to cognates who are related in equal degrees.[2]

Sec. 8.

DCLII. In a family *retractus* a remoter cognate who owns the adjoining estate is, by reason of the twofold title, preferred to a nearer, as decided by the Court on the 9th of September, 1619.[3]

DCLIII. And those who are related in equal degrees are admitted equally; but the right of representation does not hold in such a case, as the statutes admit the nearest cognate only.[4]

DCLIV. If the nearest cognate has either expressly or tacitly renounced the *retractus,* the next is admitted. He is likewise taken to have tacitly renounced who has assisted in effecting the sale, or has stood security for

[1] Thes. 364.
[2] See *Rechtsgel. Observ.* part. i. obs. 80; and also '*t Vervolg. van de Holl. Consult.* cons. 42.   [3] *Decis. en Resol. van den Hove,* n. 143.
[4] See *Thes.* 649.

indemnification, or has subscribed to the deed of sale.[5]

DCLV. It clearly follows from the reason of law that the nearest cognate who has expressly declined the purchase of an estate offered to him has no longer the right of *retractus*. It is not necesary that he should be compelled to state his reasons as to the offer of sale made to him, except in those places where it has been so provided.[6]

SEC. 9.

DCLVI. Among those countries where family *retractus* has been adopted, there are some which, by a particular law,[7] allow it on the ground of vicinity or community of estates. Thus, in *Rhynland* those neighbours whose estates adjoin the property sold, separated only by a slight common fence (*gemengder veur ende aerde*), and especially partners or joint-owners, have a right of legal *retractus* ;[8] and the same rule obtains in the territory of *Ryswyk* and *Nieuwkoop*.[9] And at other places this right is allowed without distinction to all neighbours,[10] and also at *Middelburg*,[11] where the statutes admit joint-owners also.[12] At other places, again, as at *Flushing*,[13] it is allowed to partners or joint-owners only, and not to neighbours.

---

[5] Dig. xx. 1. 26. § 1. Dig. xx. 6. 8. § 15.   *Voet* is, however, of a different opinion,—*ad Pand.* xviii. 3. § 16.

[6] As in *de Keur. van Zeel.* cap. ii. art. 12 ; *Putten, Keur.* xxiv. art. 1.

[7] See Coren, *Obs. Rer. Jud.* xxxii. n. 62, sqq. p. 217.

[8] *Costum. van Rhynl.* art. 25.

[9] *Rechtsgel. Obs.* part. iii. obs. 75.

[10] Ibid. p. 199.   [11] *Costum.* rub. xi. art. 1 & 11.

[12] Bynkersh. *Q. J. Priv.* 1. ii. c. 16. n. 11.

[12] *Costum.* cap. xii. art. 1.

Sec. 10.

DCLVII. The time for instituting or exercising this right varies, but in most cases is one year. It is computed regularly, not from the day of sale, but from the day of delivery ; and where a solemn cession of the thing sold has been made, the time runs even against an ignorant party. Nor does any other relief seem to be allowed in most places against this prescription than that founded on minority ; and this is supported by the preamble of the new law of *Voorn*, passed in 1661.[1]

Sec. 11.

DCLVIII. In Holland and Zeeland it does not seem to be required that, pending a suit concerning *retractus*, the price itself and the other moneys payable herein, should be tendered in ready money.[2]

DCLIX. The person who exercises the right has in most places only to swear that he exercises it on his own behalf. At other places, however, it is necessary to add that the money wherewith he *retracts* is his own. That which is received as a loan is also taken as money, provided the retractor has, besides the estate claimed, sufficient property wherewith to pay. But this, if disputed, should not only be supported by his oath, but also proved by other evidence.[3]

DCLX. The person who exercises this right succeeds to the place and the rights of the purchaser, and hence

---

[1] *Keur. van Voorn*, p. 187. Bynkershoek (*Q. Jur. Priv.* l. iii. c. 14, p. 489), *dissentiente*.

[2] *Voet* too hastily expresses a different opinion,—*ad Pand*, xviii. 3. § 25, 26.

[3] *Rechtsgel. Obs.* part. 1. obs. 81.

he may claim property not yet ceded, by the *actio empti* ;[4] but if the property has already been ceded to the purchaser, he may claim that it be ceded to him anew by the seller, treating the former cession as defective.[5]

DCLXI. A *retractus* having once been instituted and decreed, if the retractor afterwards fails to comply with the conditions of the *retractus*, and the property thus remains in the possession of the purchaser, another who is posterior in order cannot claim the same from him.[6]

SEC. 13.

DCLXII. Upon the sale of an annual rent-charge, or of a debt secured by a special mortgage of land, it is the duty of the purchaser first to offer the *retractus* to the debtor, who is to make his option within eight days ; and if the purchaser fails to make this offer, the debtor may, in *Rhynland*, legally exercise the *jus retractus* within a year after he has become aware of it.[7] A similar rule has been enacted at *Amsterdam* ;[8] and at other places it has been extended even to personal debts.[9]

---

[4] *Costum. van Middelb.* rubr. xi. art. 7. in f.

[5] See further hereon, Voet. *ad Pand.* xviii. 3. § 27, 28.

[6] *Costum. van Rhynl.* art. 32. *Keur. van Nieuwkoop, van* 20 Sept. 1637, art. 24. p. 56.

[7] 28 Dec. 1559 ; apud Van Leeuwen, *over de Costum. van Rhynland*, art. 57. p. 223, sq.

[8] 12 Nov. 1475; *Handv.* p. 526.

[9] *Keur. van Leyden*, art. 121 ; *Gouda*, tit. *van Naasting*, art. 1-4. *Oudewater, van* 1605, art. 139-141 ; *Putten*, xxiv. art. 2 ; *Vlissing.* cap. xii. art. 8.

SEC. 14.

DCLXIII. Where such a right is not allowed by law, the party who owes a debt so sold, and which is not secured by a special mortgage, may, when summoned by the purchaser, always claim the right of the *Lex Anastasiana** even though he may not have been ignorant of the sale of the debt.[1] And in this sense may also be easily explained the customs of South Holland mentioned by *Van der Eick*,[2] of *Amsterdam*, by *Roseboom*,[3] and of the *Hague*, in the *Rechtsgeleerde Observatien*.[4]

DCLXIV. The *Lex Anastasiana* does not, however, apply—1. In a sale of an entire body of accounts;[5] and 2, in a sale of public Dutch securities.—as correctly laid down in the *Hollandsche Consultatien*,[6] and acknowledged and supported by valid reasons by the States of Holland in a consultation, issued to the States of *Groningen* on the 28th of December, 1759.[7]

CHAPTER XVII.—SEC. 1.

DCLXV. If the parties withdraw by mutual consent from a sale already consummated, a new sale takes place;[8] and therefore, where it relates to immovable property, the duty of two and a half per cent. should

---

* [*Ut nihil amplius accipiat. quam ipse vero contractu persolvit :* and see *Holl.* Cons. d. iii. cons. 34.]

[1] See Thes. 14, 17. Groenewegen (*ad. h.* § not. 18; and *ad. Cod.* iv. 35. 22, n. 4.) and Van Leeuwen (*Cens. Forens.* part. i. l. iv. c. 19, n. 25) are of a different opinion, but incorrectly.

[2] P. 410, art. 39. [3] Cap. xxxv. art. 22, junct. cap. xlvii. art. 9-11.

[4] Part iii. obs. 76, p. 201.

[5] *Holl. Cons.* d. iv. cons. 195, n. 3, 4.

[6] D. v. cons. 89, & d. vi. st. 2. cons. 2.

[7] *Nederl. Jaarb. van* 1760, p. 17-19. [8] Dig. ii. 14. 58.

be paid a second time ;[9] unless the withdrawal takes
place before the cession has been made, for the purpose of avoiding a suit with the purchaser, as decided
by the States.[10]

SEC. 3.

DCLXVI. A sale, founded on fraud on the part of
the vendor† may be rescinded or rather declared void
even without *restitutio in integrum*, in the ordinary
action founded on the contract itself.‡

CHAPTER XVIII.—SEC. 3.

DCLXVII. *Grotius* is correct in stating that a contract of *Emphyteusis* may be entered into without a
writing.[11]

SEC. 8.

DCLXVIII. Extraordinary burthens or charges imposed on immovable property subject to an emphyteusis would, it seems, attach, not to the direct lord,
but to the emphyteutee or tenant, who, by reason of
the perpetual right which he has in the property, stands
in a different position from that of a usufructuary, or
of a person charged with a *fidei-commissum*.

SEC. 10.

DCLXIX. Upon the forfeiture, by neglect, of an
emphyteusis, the tenant is not entitled to indemnifi-

[9] *Ordon. op den* 40. *penn.* 9 March 1744, art. 7.
[10] 5 Feb. 1768, *Groot. Plac. Boek,* d. ix. p. 1031.
† [Not of the *vendee.* See Noestad. *Dec. Supr. Cur.* 5.—Tr.]
‡ [See Nederl. Adv. Boek, d. iv. cons. 182, p. 531, sqq.—Tr.]
[11] Voet *ad Pand.* vi. 3 § 3.

cation from the direct lord, even in respect of those improvements, which he was not bound to make by the terms of the contract;[1] and the authority of the Civil Law hereon cannot be overruled by the arguments advanced against it by *Voet*.[2]

CHAPTER XIX.—SEC. 2.

DCLXX. The letting and hiring of property in town —(of country property we shall presently treat separately)—may be effected even without a writing, as may be inferred from those very laws concerning the stamp duty,[3] which are vainly cited by those* who maintain the opposite opinion.

DCLXXI. The lease of a house may therefore be continued even by tacit consent; and in this case it seems to have become the custom that whether the contract was originally in writing for a definite period, or not, the lease will continue after the termination of such contract, so long as the lessee continues to occupy.[4] This rule is, however, modified by some statutes, which annex the provision—unless the lessee has been ejected before the lapse of such definite period;[5] and the statutes of *Haarlem*[6] require that all doubt should be removed by a timely notice. As regards the practice

---

[1] Cod. iv. 66. 2.　　　　　　　　[2] *Ad. Pand.* vi. 3. § 52.

[3] A. 1677. art. 59 ; & A. 1744 & 1794, art. 71.

* [Groeneweg. in. not. ad. h. §; and Voet *ad Pand.* xix. 2. u. 10.— Tr.]

[4] Groeneweg. *ad. Cod.* iv. 65. 16. n. 6.

[5] Roseboom, *Keur. van Amsterd.* cap. li. art. 11. *Keur van Leiden*, art. 133 ; & see *Rechtsgel. Observ.* part. ii. obs. 78.

[6] Concerning Leases, 9 Sept. 1710 ; *Keur. van Haarlem*, d. i. p. 211.

in *Amsterdam* concerning the letting of warehouses, see Roseboom's *Keuren van Amsterdam*.[7]

SEC. 3.

DCLXXII. The common opinion of the commentators on Dutch Law, namely, that a lease of country property is not valid without a written instrument, cannot be supported either by the Placaat of the 22nd of January, 1515, nor by *art.* 31 of the Political Ordonnance, declared by the laws of the 26th September, 1658, and the 24th February, 1696. The rule laid down by these laws is that farmers cannot, under the pretext of a continued or renewed lease, remain on the land against the consent of the landlord ; but ought, at the end of the period fixed by the contract, immediately to quit the estate held in lease, unless they can prove by a writing that the lease has been prolonged. But in the absence of such a writing, they should, nevertheless, after having quitted the estate, be allowed a hearing in court— *i.e.*, they may show that the lease had been prolonged verbally or without a writing. This is manifest from the words of the laws above quoted, and may be easily proved from the law relating to the public stamp duty,[8] and is also confirmed and supported by decisions of the Court,[9] which has admitted other proofs in such cases.

The same rule should, it seems, be followed under the Law of Zeeland.[10]

[7] D. 1. art. 33, sqq.   [8] Art. 61.
[9] In *de Sententien van den H. en Prov. Raad.* Dec. 27. And see Groeneweg. *ad Cod.* iv. 65. 24. n. 5.
[10] *Ord. Zeel.* 26 Jan. 1664, art. 1 ; and *Ord. van 't Zegel*, 21 Sept. 1756, art. 40.

R

SEC. 9.

DCLXXIII. A lease of lands *in longum tempus*, even for more than ten years, may legally be effected by private agreement, notwithstanding the decision of the Court of the 8th April, 1609,[1] from which the Court has since departed.[2] If, however, the lease has been contracted for twenty-five years or more, it is not only subject to the payment of the duty of two and a half per cent., but a solemn session in law is also necessary.[3]

SEC. 10.

DCLXXIV. Although by the general law as adopted either wholly or with modifications by particular statutes, it is permitted to a lessee to sublet land leased to him,[4] yet by the Law of Holland of the 16th September, 1658,[5] an exception has been made in respect of country lands, which cannot be sublet without the consent in writing of the landlord.

SEC. 11.

DCLXXV. Whether a landlord may, according to the law of the Code iv. 65. 3., in a case of necessity, eject the lessee from a house let to him, appears to me clearly to admit of much doubt; it being hardly con-

---

[1] *Decis. en Resol. van den Hove,* n. 331.

[2] Van Leeuwen, Comm. b. iv. ch. 21, § 9.

[3] *Plac. op den* 40 *penn.* A. 1744, art. 9. junct. art. 19.

[4] *Costum. van Rhynland,* art. 98 ; *Middelb.* rubr. ix. art. 5; *Vlissing.* cap. vii. art. 8; *Amsterd.* Roseboom, cap. li. art. 1-5; *Haarlem,* A. 1710. art. 5; *Keuren van Haarlem,* d. i. p. 211.

[5] *Pol. Ord.* 26 Sept. 1658, renewed by Ord. of the 24 Febr. 1696, art. 9.

sistent with the spirit of our laws, by which a lease is
of greater force than a sale. And it has hence, not
without reason, been specially prohibited at *Amsterdam*[6]
and *Haarlem*.[7]

DCLXXVI. If the lessee, or even the lessor, has
made cession to the Court, the lease expires after a
short delay, at the customary time for removal; which
varies in different places.[8]

SEC. 12.

DCLXXVII. By some statutes it is permitted to a
lessee to adapt a house let to him, for a shop or work-
shop, according to his trade; provided the house be
not thereby deteriorated, and at the end of the term
he restore it at his own expense to its original state.[9]

DCLXXVIII. The lessee of property cannot discharge himself against the lessor's consent, by paying
a sum of money as compensation, in place of occupation
of the property. This is evident from the reason of
our law, and it has therefore been properly so provided
by the statutes of *Haarlem*.[10]

SEC. 13.

DCLXXIX. By the recent laws of various places,
domestic servants may be dismissed from service, with-

---

[6] Roseboom, cap. li. art. 9.   [7] D. Cost. A. 1710. art. 3.

[8] *Ord. Amsterd.* 17 Jan. 1777, art. 63; & 8 April 1751. *Keur van
Leiden,* art. 122; *Keur van Haarlem,* A. 1710, art. 2; *Keur van
Rotterd. van* 5 Nov. 1768.

[9] Roseboom, d. cap. li. art. 15, 16; *Keur van Haarl.* art. 11, 12,
Costum. van Middelb. rubr. ix. art. 10, 11, 12.

[10] A. 1710, art. 3.

out receiving any compensation, even before the termination of the period of hiring.[1]

SEC. 14.

DCLXXX. A lessee cannot convert pasture into arable land; though in the first years of a long lease he may do so.[2]

CHAPTER XX.—SEC. 14.

DCLXXXI. If a ship conveying merchandise has been wrecked before it entered port, the whole freight for the merchandise which has been saved should be paid, without any deduction for salvage. It was so decided by the Commissioners of *Amsterdam*,[3] and by the Court[4] and the Supreme Court.[5] This rule is not, however, approved of by the Jurists in the *Adviesboek*,[6] nor does it seem to have pleased the merchants of that period;[7] though it is clearly consistent with the reason of our law, and has also been adopted in the practice of our Courts; saving to the owner of the merchandise the right of recovering contribution of the salvage, by way of gross average.

[1] Placaat of the Court, 29 Nov. 1679, art. 10. *Ord. Amsterd.* 31 Jan. 1758, art. 8; *Haarlem*, 19 Dec. 1693, art. 5; *Leyden*, 8 March 1703, art. 12.

" *Rechtsgel. Observ.* part iii. obs. 77. Voet *ad Pand.* xix. 2. § 29.

[3] 21 Feb. 1686.

[4] 29 April 1698, *Advies over den Kooph.* d. i. p. 194. sqq.

[5] 16 Feb. 1707; Bynkersh. *Q. J. Priv.* l. iv. c. 24. p. 722.

[6] D. l. cons. 39. p. 179, sqq.

[2] D. l. p. 206. Verwer *in not.* ad art. 3. *Plac. van Philip* ii. p. 95, sqq.

SEC. 15.

DCLXXXII. The right of retention or of tacit mortgage, which the master of a vessel possesses for the freight due to him, may be exercised in respect also of merchandise delivered for conveyance not by the owner only, but also (for instance) by a factor or other agent.[8]

SEC. 16.

DCLXXXIII. Besides this right of retention, the master may also, in default of the owner paying the freight, retain for himself so much of the goods (estimated at their actual value) as will pay the amount due to him for freight. It is so laid down in the Laws of *Wisbuy*,[9] which, though not approved of on this point by the later law, have nevertheless not been altered.

SEC. 17.

DCLXXXIV. Whether merchants may, under the laws now in force, relinquish and cede to the master, besides the goods packed in cases, any other goods also, on account of freight, seems to be a doubtful question ; but is answered in the negative by *Verwer*[10] and the jurists in *de Adviesen over den Koophandel*.[11]

Similarly, it is not settled whether a master, who in a case of urgent necessity has sold the goods, may discharge himself by ceding the ship to the merchants. By the Law of *Rotterdam*,[12] however, this right is

---

[8] *Advies over den Kooph.* d. i. cons. 9.   [9] Art. 37.

[10] In not. ad. *Plac. Philip* tit. *van Schipp. & Koopl.* art. 9.

[11] Id. i. cons. 8.   [12] A. 1721, art. 159.

expressly given to the master; but not so by the law of *Dordrecht*,[1] though it is in a great measure copied from the law of *Rotterdam*.

SEC. 18.

DCLXXXV. The recent laws of *Amsterdam*,[2] *Middelburg*,[3] *Rotterdam*,[4] and *Dordrecht*,[5] have made careful provision regarding the contract of hiring and service between the master and crew of a vessel, and the manner in which the crew may be compelled to perform their engagements.

SEC. 21.

DCLXXXVI. The just grounds on which a sailor might formerly claim to be discharged from service,—viz.: where he had acquired a vessel of his own, or had married,—are expressly disallowed by the laws of *Rotterdam*[6] and *Dordrecht*;[7] and by the laws of these two places[8] and of *Amsterdam*[9] and *Middelburg*,[10] it is left to the discretion of the Commissioners of Maritime Causes to determine what are just grounds.

SEC. 23.

DCLXXXVII. By the law of *Amsterdam*[11] and of *Middelburg*,[12] a sailor desiring without just cause to be discharged before the commencement of the voyage, is mulcted of half his wages: at *Rotterdam*[13] and *Dordrecht*[14] he is compelled to perform fully the engagement undertaken by him.

---

[1] A. 1775. [2] A. 1643. art. 25-30.
[3] A. 1693, art. 17-21, 27-30. [4] A. 1721, art. 174-177, 186-191.
[5] 29 Sept. 1772, art. 1, 6, 7, 9, 12-16. [6] Art. 179. [7] Art. 2.
[8] *Rotterd.* art. 178, 181; *Dordr.* art. 4. [9] Art. 30. [10] Art. 24.
[11] Art. 30. [12] Art. 24. [13] Art. 182. [14] Art. 5.

SEC. 25—30.

DCLXXXVIII. What is here stated as to conveying the *venture* or private merchandise of sailors free of freight, was at first limited by laws passed by the States General, and has since been wholly abrogated by custom.[15]

SEC. 35.

DCLXXXIX. Verbal injuries committed by a sailor, whether to the master of the vessel or to the other sailors, are under the new laws punishable by a fine of six florins: real injuries of a more serious nature are to be notified by the master upon the return of the vessel to the Public Prosecutor, and are punishable by the judge according to law.[16]

SEC. 37.

DCXC. A sailor who merely conceals his ignorance, is by the new law punished by forfeiture of his wages, and compelled to make good any loss that may arise; but if he has fraudulently represented himself as a skilful seaman, he is corporally punished.[17]

SEC. 38.

DCXCI. A sailor who, after the voyage has commenced, quits the vessel without the leave of the master, or fails to return at the appointed time, is liable to a

[15] Verwer, ad *Plac. Philip.* tit. *van Schipl.* art. 15; *Rechtsgel. Obs.* part. i. obs. 85.
[16] *L. Amsterd.* art. 37, 38; *Middelb.* art. 39, 40; *Rotterd.* art. 239–243; *Dordr.* art. 63–67.
[17] *L. Rotterd.* art. 194, 195; *Dordr.* art. 20; *Middelb.* art. 26.

fine of six florins.[1] The fine in a case of desertion or drunkenness is higher, besides the liability to make good any loss which may have accrued.[2]

DCXCII. By the law of *Dordrecht* the punishment of qualified theft is prescribed against a sailor who steals any part of the goods, or the rigging of the vessel ;[3] and all those who may have been in the vessel are compellable to give evidence on oath on the matter.[4]

SEC. 39.

DCXCIII. It is a peculiarity in the hiring of sailors, that in case the destination of the voyage in respect of which they have let their services is altered, the master may nevertheless retain them in service, even against their consent, at a reasonable increase of wages. This is very carefully set forth in the new laws of *Amsterdam*,[5] *Middelburg*,[6] and *Rotterdam*.[7]

SEC. 42.

DCXCIV. If the vessel is wholly lost by shipwreck, the sailors lose their wages ; if the rigging or merchandise be saved, they are entitled to their wages so far as it can be realised out of the rigging, or of the freight due to the master in respect of the goods so saved.[8] If they have themselves been instrumental in saving them, they are entitled also to salvage.[9]

[1] *L. Amsterd.* art. 32; *Middelb.* art. 34.
[2] *L. Middelb.* art. 33, 34; *Rotterd.* art. 188–192; *Dordr.* art. 17.
[3] *L. Dordr.* art. 59.   [4] Art. 60.   [5] Art. 34, 35, 36.
[6] Art. 36–38.   [7] Art. 202, 204, 206, 210.   [8] Th. 681.
[9] *L. Amsterd.* art. 45; *Middleb.* art. 45, in fin.; *Rotterd.* art. 219. Sec **Verwer** *in not. ad* art. 12. *Plac. Philip.* n. ii. p. 112, sqq.

SEC. 44.

DCXCV. If a sailor dies a natural death or in the performance of his duty, whether ·on the outward or homeward voyage of the vessel, his heirs are, under the new law of *Rotterdam*,[10] entitled to the whole of his wages.

SEC. 46.

DCXCVI. By the law of *Dordrecht*[11] the master and sailors of a vessel are prohibited from shipping illicit goods without the knowledge of the owners, under penalty of corporal punishment and of making good any loss arising therefrom.

SEC. 48.

DCXCVII. Agreeably to the rule stated in this section, it has also been laid down in *de Adviesen over den Koophandel*[12] that the owners of a vessel are not liable to the master beyond the share they have in the vessel.

CHAPTER XXI.—SEC. 1.

DCXCVIII. Every community of profits does not constitute or produce the effects of a partnership.[13]

SEC. 5.

DCXCIX. A partnership which has been contracted on the condition that the profits should be in common,

---

[10] Art. 248.

[11] Art. 61, 62. [12] D. i. cons. 6.

[13] As correctly laid down in *de Advies. over den Koophand.* d. ii. cons. 65, p. 263, sqq.

but that one party alone should bear the losses, does not seem to be illegal, and this not only for the reason stated by *Voet*,[1] but chiefly because the insurance of risks is permitted by our laws and customs; and this is the consideration on which *Grotius* has proceeded in an opinion given by him in *de Hollandsche Consultatien*.[2]

SEC. 7.

DCC. In the action *pro socio** it is not necessary under our Law that there should be a cession or delivery of the property acquired by one partner since entering into the contract, but it is brought into the accounts of the partnership, and is *ipso jure* shared in common.[3]

DCCI. By *slight blame (levis culpa)*, for which a partner is liable, is to be understood such neglect as he would not be guilty of in respect of his own affairs.[4]

DCCII. As regards the right which third parties have against several partners, it is indeed clear that the contracts of one of them whom the others employ to manage the business as their agent bind such others also;[5] but the doctrine of *Voet*,[6] that by the law of the present day the latter may (as in the case of ship-owners) discharge themselves by ceding their share in the partnership to the creditors, seems wholly opposed to the reason of law.

DCCIII. Whether partners are liable, each *in solidum*, on the contracts of one or more of them who are in the

---

[1] *Ad Pand.* xvii. 2. § 8.   [2] D. iii. st. 2. cons. 303. p. 541.
* [See defin. Van der Linden, *Inst.* p. 578.]
[3] Coren, *Obs.* xxv. n. 50, p. 91.
[4] *Advies over den Kooph.* d. ii. cons. 63, p. 249, sqq.
[5] Voet. *ad Pand.* xvii. 2. § 13.   [6] Ib. § 13, in f., and § 15.

place of agents for the others or for each other, in that they allow him or them or each other to contract in the name of the firm, has been the subject of opposite opinions among the lawyers. In the *Hollandsche Consultatien*[7] it is answered in the affirmative, upon the authority of the Statute of *Antwerp*.[8] But others have maintained the negative;[9] and this seems also to have been the opinion of *Grotius*.[10] The former opinion has, however, been since adopted by the custom of *Amsterdam*, as testified by an eminent jurist[11] and a great number of merchants.[12] And several advocates and proctors practising in the Courts of *Amsterdam* have testified in Court to the same effect;[13] and the merchant *Verwer*[14] and several learned advocates of recent times,[15] as well as a number of merchants,[16] have given their adherence to the same opinion.

DCCIV. Where, however, a partnership has been entered into between two persons, one of whom contributes the money, and the other his services, on the condition that the latter alone should manage the business, and that the profits should indeed be shared in common, but that the former should not be liable for

---

[7] D. i. cons. 151, p. 255, in f.; cons. 283, and cons. 303, p. 488, in f.; d. ii. cons. 235, in f. p. 463.   [8] Cap. 52. art. 1.

[9] De Pape *in Obs.* ad vol. i. cons. 283, p. 283.

[10] *Holl. Consul.* d. iii. st. 2. cons. 143. n. 5.

[11] 23 Jun. 1708, in *de Advies. over den Kooph.* d. ii. cons. 61.

[12] 16 Feb. 1707; Ibid. cons. 60.

[13] 29 Jan. 1710; *Handv. van Amsterd.* p. 507, 508.

[14] *Zeerecht*, Edit. 1711, p. 171. in fin. & edit. 1730, p. 188.

[15] In an opinion—29 June, 1790; which see in *de Verzamel. van casus-positien, &c. betrekkelijk tot den Kooph.* Amst. 1793. cas. 18.

[16] 30 Jun. 1790, ibid. p. 164, seq. See Dupuis, *L'Arts des Lettres de Change,* apud Savary, t. i. p. 470.

the losses beyond the amount contributed by him; in such a case a different rule is to be observed, and the former partner will not be liable for debts beyond the amount which he has brought into the partnership. Such partnerships, like those in France called *Societes en commandite*, may, from the reason of our law, be entered into amongst us.[1] Lest, however, the persons who contract with the working partner should rely on the credit of the other partner to their own prejudice, it would seem to be required amongst us, where the terms of the partnership have not been made public, that the money partner should not hold himself out publicly as a partner, nor be designated as such in the name of the firm used by the other.

SEC. 8.

DCCV. If a partner who has not yet brought into the partnership what he was bound to contribute makes cession of his property, his creditors or the curator or assignee of his estate have no rights as against the partnership so long as the other partner has not received what he was entitled to. It is so laid down in the *Hollandsche Consultatien;*[2] and the jurists have recently given the same opinion,[3] which has also been confirmed by several merchants.[4]

SEC. 10.

DCCVI. Besides several other points of difference

---

[1] Savary, *Parf. Negoc.* part. ii. lib. i. cap. 1. p. 189, sqq. & cap. 2. p. 207, sqq.

[2] D. iii. cons. 6–9.   [3] 19 Dec. 1754.

[4] *Vervolg. der Holl. Consult.* d. ii. cons. 98.

which exist between a universal partnership and the statutory community of property between husband and wife, the following should be chiefly noted: 1. That in a partnership profit and loss are shared in *geometrical* proportion,[5] but in the statutory community in *arithmetical* proportion; 2. That one partner cannot, *without the other's consent*, make a disposition of the common property ;[6] whilst a husband may do so by virtue of his marital authority, *without the wife's consent ;* and, 3. That one partner is liable to the other for *blame* or *neglect ;* whilst a husband is not responsible to his wife.[7]

Chapter XXII.—Sec. 2.

DCCVII. The pact called *Admiraalschap,* or Sailing-Company, which it was formerly necessary to enter into, and may even now be legally entered into,[8] between merchant vessels for mutual defence against enemies and pirates, is not improperly classed under partnership, since the laws themselves introduce a community in respect of the losses arising from such mutual defence, and define the form of the agreement.

Sec. 5.

DCCVIII. The profits realized out of a vessel taken from the enemy or from pirates, do not go in common to all the ships associated in the Sailing-Company, but belong only to those which have assisted in capturing it.[9]

---

[5] Grotius, *supra* § 5.   [6] Dig. x. 3. 28.
[7] *Holl. Consult.* d. i. cons. 47. n. 5 ;—d. iii. st. 2. cons. 182. n. 3, 9—11.
[8] Ordonnance of *Rotterdam,* concerning Shipping, of 1721, art. 252, sqq.
[9] *Nederl. Adv.* d. ii. cons. 200 ; Bynkersh. *Q. J. Pub.* l. i. c. 18. p. 136.

CHAPTER XXIII.—SEC. 2.

DCCIX. In a partnership contracted between.several owners of one vessel, or the owners of several vessels, the following peculiarities are observed :—1. That some of the owners, who have the majority of shares in the vessel, may sell the whole in community of profit and loss;[1] 2. That in case of a disagreement between the owners, the majority may let the vessel ; and when it has been so let, they may, in case the others are un-willing after notice to contribute their share of the money necessary for rigging or arming the vessel, raise the amount on a contract of bottomry ; or, if advanced by themselves, recover it out of the share which the others have in the vessel.[2]

SEC. 3.

DCCX. If one of the owners is also master, and owes either solely, or jointly with other consentient part-owners, a half share in the vessel, he may under-take a voyage for such hire as may seem reasonable in the estimation of just arbitrators;[3] which, however, by the Laws of *Rotterdam* and *Dordrecht* last cited, is only allowed where the master, either solely or together with the consentient part-owners, has the majority of shares in the vessel.[4]

CHAPTER XXIV.

DCCXI. Besides the laws concerning *Insurance*

[1] *Ord. Rotterd.* 1721, art. 171; *Dordr.* 1775, art. 166.
[2] *Ord. Rotterd.* art. 172; *Dordr.* art. 167.
[3] *Wisbuische Zee-rechten,* art. 65–67.
[4] *Ord. Rotterd.* art. 173; *Dordr.* art. 168.

enumerated by Bynkershoek,[5] the following deserve notice:—1. The *Amplification* of the *Law of Middelburg*, of the 4th February, 1719;[6] 2. The new *Law of Amsterdam* of the 10th March, 1744,[7] and the *emendations* and *interpretations* thereof, of the 27th April, 1745,[8] the 30th January, 1756,[9] and the 31st January 1775.[10] 3. The *Law of Dordrecht* entitled "*Instructie voor Schepenen van't Watergerecht, en Ordonnantie op het stuk van Assurantie en avarye mitsgaders van Zeezaken, en de manier van Procedeeren omtrent dezelve,*" passed on the 29th June, and promulgated on the 13th July, 1775.

SEC. 1.

DCCXII. *Insurance* is a contract nominate, consensual and of good faith, whereby, in consideration of a certain price or *premium*, the losses which may arise from unforeseen danger to the property of another are undertaken to be made good. This price or *premium* (which, considering the nature of the contract, does not depend altogether on custom) may, it seems, consist of other things besides money, and is fixed by the consent of both parties in proportion to the extent of the risk undertaken, so that no question can arise thereon as to enormous injury (*læsio enormis*).[11] By *loss* is understood not only the destruction but also the deterioration of the thing;[12] and *unforeseen* danger is that of which

[5] *Q. J. Priv.* l. iv. c. l. p. 519, sq.
[6] *Groot Pl.* d. v. p. 1287.
[7] *Handv.* p. 662, sqq.
[8] *Handv.* p. 1666.
[8] *Tweede Vervolg der Handv.* p. 89, sqq.
[10] Ibid. p. 91, sqq.
[11] Byukersh. *Q. J. Priv.* l. iv. c. 5. p. 564.
[12] New *Ord. Amsterd.* art. 35; *Rotterd.* art. 70.

both the contracting parties are ignorant; for if either of them is aware that a loss has already occurred, the contract is *ipso jure* void.[1]

SEC. 2.

DCCXIII. This contract, having received from custom and law the definite form and force of an obligation, ought to be considered a nominate contract, depending on *consent* alone, and therefore binding even though the premium may not have been paid: as decided by the Court on the 24th of November, 1639; though the words of the Law of *Amsterdam* of the 5th December, 1620, seem to require the contrary. This law appears, however, to have been abrogated by custom, as testified by *Roseboom*[2] and *Boel*;[3] and this is likewise rendered certain by the new Law of *Amsterdam* of 1744,[4] and the more recent Law of 1775, altering the 60th article; and by the general Law of Holland of the 13th November, 1773, which allows this contract to be entered into verbally, provided it be reduced into writing under seal within fourteen days.[5]

SEC. 3.

DCCXIV. Insurance-brokers are at all places prohibited from entering into this contract in their own name. A similar prohibition has been enacted at *Rotterdam* respecting the Commissioners of Insurance

[1] Bynkersh. *Q. J. Priv.* l. iv. c. 26. n. 6.

[2] *Costum. van Amsterd.* cap. xxx. ad. art. 36. p. 145.

[3] *Ad. Loen Decis.* cas. 93. And see Bynkersh. *Q. J. Priv.* l. iv. c. 2. p. 535, sqq.

[4] Art. 37.   [6] *Groot Pl. B.* d. ix. p. 1341.

Causes and their Secretaries.[6] It seems to be otherwise at *Middelburg*.[7] and, probably, at *Amsterdam*[8] and *Dordrecht*.[9]

DCCXV. A person who has no mandate or authority to effect an insurance may, nevertheless, legally take the precaution of having an insurance effected on behalf of another;[10] but one who from the commencement has managed any business as his own, and not as a partner (being, for instance, the joint-owner with another of a vessel or goods), and has taken care to insure on his own behalf for a larger amount than he was interested for, cannot afterwards assign such an insurance *pro parte* to his partner.[11] It is so laid down in the *Neder-landsche Adviesboek*, and by *Bynkershoek*; but this doctrine does not quite support the rule in *de Adviesen over den Koophandel*,[12] viz.: that a partner, who has no mandate, and has not expressly named his partner, cannot even *ab initio* act so as to effect an insurance by way of *negotiorum gestio* on behalf of the partner.

SEC. 4.

DCCXVI. Although originally Insurances related chiefly to things exposed to the dangers of navigation and transport ; yet they have since been extended to buildings also and other goods, which are liable to destruction by fire ;[13] and indeed to everything wherein

---

[6] New *Ord. Rotterd.* art. 82. [7] *Ampl.* 1719, art. 4.
[8] Arg. New *Ord.* art. 39, in fin. [9] *Ord.* art. 80.
[10] *Nederl. Adv.* d. iii. cons. 17 ; Bynkershoek, *Q. J. Priv.* l. iv. c. l. p. 524.
[11] *Nederl. Advies.* d. ii. cons. 120; Bynkersh. d. l. p. 523.
[12] D. i. cons. 26, 27.
[13] New *Ord. Amsterd.* art. 18 ; and the latest Ord. of 1775.

S

any one has an interest, provided it be accurately defined in the contract.[1]

DCCXVII. Insurances against the dangers of the sea may be effected in respect of the following :

1. Vessels.[2] It is required, however, that the vessel should have arrived at the place where the danger begins ;[3] and if the vessel be of the kind called "*vuuren blaas*"* it should be so stated.[4] There is nothing to prevent the insurance of an old ship.[5]

2. All kinds of merchandise ;—even such as are liable to be easily spoilt.[7]

3. The expenses of loading the vessel; and the premiums of insurance already paid or yet to be paid.[7]

4. The freight payable for the conveyance of goods,[8] in respect of which the new Law of *Amsterdam* has provided more fully,[9] altering the former law ;[10] for even the rigging of a vessel may now be legally insured.[11] The rule at *Middelburg* is the same.[12]

5. Merchandise belonging to the crew.[13] But at *Amsterdam* and *Middelburg* it is otherwise.[14]

---

[1] *Handv. Tweede Vervolg*, p. 91 sq.

[2] New *Ord. Amstrd.* art. 7 ; New *Ord. Rotterd.* art. 25 ; *Ord. Dordr.* art. 29 ; *Middelb.* art. 4 ; and *Ampl.* art. 3.

[3] New *Ord. Amsterd.* art. 13, in f.

* [These would appear to be vessels built of the *vuur-hout*, a species of pine.—Tr.]

[4] Ib. art. 8.   [5] Bynkersh. *Q. J. Priv.* 1. iv. c. 6. p. 567

[6] New *Ord. Rotterd.* art. 25 ; *Dordr.* art. 29.

[7] New *Ord. Rotterd.* art. 25 ; *Dordr.* art. 29 ; *Amsterd.* art. 2. and New Ord. art. 22 ; *Middelb.* art. 3 ; and *Ampl.* art. 2.

[8] New *Ord. Rotterd.* art. 26 ; *Dordr.* art 30.

[9] New *Ord. Amsterd.* art. 15.   [10] Old *Ord. Amst.* art. 10.

[11] New *Ord. Amst.* art. 7.   [12] Arg. *Ampl.* art. 2, 3.

[13] New *Ord. Rotterd.* art. 26 ; *Dordr.* art 30.

[14] Old *Ord. Amst.* art. 11, and New, art. 13 ; *Middelb.* art. 6.

6. Money lent on the bottomry of vessels or merchandise,[15] in respect of which the new Law of *Amsterdam* has made most careful provision.[16]   It is required, however, that an insurance of this kind made in favour of the bottomry-creditor should be expressly so stated in the policy of insurance.[17]   And according to the custom which has since obtained, not only the money itself which has been lent, but also the goods therewith purchased and shipped on board, are at the risk of the insurers.[18]   But goods which are bound, to their full value, on a bottomry, cannot be insured in favour of the bottomry-debtor.[19]

7. The amount paid as ransom for those who have been taken prisoners by the Turks.[20]

8. Everything connected with commerce, navigation, the importing and exporting of goods, and with travelling.[21]   Under which may also be classed the risk apprehended from the poverty of the first insurer, provided notice thereof be given to him, and the right of action which lies against him be assigned to the second insurer;[22] for it is not lawful to derive gains from an insurance made in one's own favour.[23]

---

[15] New. *Ord. Rotterd.* art. 26; *Dordr.* art. 30.

[16] Art. 19, 20, 21, and *Ampl.* d. art. 21; A. 1756; *Handv. Tweede Vervolg*, p. 89.

[17] D. art. 21; *Ampl.* ;—which settles the doubts entertained hereon by Bynkershoek, *Q. J. Priv.* l. iv. c. 26. n. 7, in f.

[18] Bynkersh. ibid. l. iv. c. 16, p. 658. sqq.

[19] New *Ord. Amst.* art. 21, and *Ampl.* A. 1756.

[20] New *Ord. Rotterd.* art. 26; *Dordr.* art. 30; New *Ord. Amsterd.* art. 14;—which settle the doubts of Bynkershoek hereon, *Q. J. Priv.* l. iv c. 1. p. 526, sqq.

[21] New *Ord. Rotterd.* art. 26. f.; *Dordr.* art. 30.

[22] New *Ord. Amst.* art. 25; and the interpretation thereof, A. 1756.

[23] Arg. *Ord. Middelb.* art. 31, 32.

9. Provisions kept in a vessel for daily consumption may also 'by the laws of *Middelburg*[1] and *Amsterdam*,[2] be insured against the risks of the sea ; but not by the laws of *Rotterdam*[3] and *Dordrecht*.[4]

10. At *Amsterdam*[6] an insurance may be effected on the expectation or anticipation of the profits to arise from any undertaking, estimated at a particular value. But at *Rotterdam* this is prohibited.[6] It has, however, been decided by the Supreme Court,[7] that if such an insurance has been effected there, with a renunciation of the law, it would be valid elsewhere.

DCCXVIII. Gunpowder and bombs are no longer prohibited from being insured, provided they be specially mentioned.[8] Property of the enemy cannot be insured, even where the insurer is aware of it.[9]

DCCXIX. At *Amsterdam*,[10] *Dordrecht*,[11] and *Middelburg*,[12] a ship, with all its appurtenances, may be legally insured for the full value. At *Rotterdam* it may be insured to the extent of seven-eighths ; and the remaining one-eighth cannot be insured.[13] This law of *Rotterdam*, as well as that of *Middelburg*, has set at rest the arguments of *Bynkershoek* hereon.[14]

DCCXX. By the laws of *Middelburg*,[15] *Rotterdam*,[16]

---

[1] New *Ord. Middelb.* art. 3.   [2] New *Ord. Amst.* art. 7.

[3] New *Ord. Rott.* art. 27.   [4] *Ord. Dordr.* art. 31.

[5] New *Ord. Amst.* art. 17.   [6] New *Ord. Rott.* art. 28, 29.

[7] Bynkersh. *Q. J. Priv.* l. iv. c. 5. p. 557. sqq.

[8] *Ord. Middelb. Ampl.* art. 3 ; New *Ord. Amsterd.* art. 10 ; New *Ord. Rotterd.* art. 41 ; *Dordr.* art. 43.

[9] Bynkersh. *Q. J. Publ.* l. i. c. 21.

[10] New *Ord. Amst.* art. 7.   [11] *Ord. Dordr.* art. 34.

[12] Arg. *Ampl.* art. 2, 3.   [13] New *Ord. Rott.* art. 31.

[14] *Q. J. Priv.* l. iv. c. 6. p. 569.   [15] *Ampl.* art. 2.

[16] New *Ord. Rott.* art. 25 ; junct. aet. 31.

and *Amsterdam*,[17] merchandise may also be now insured for the full value (though under the former law it was otherwise[18]). But in respect of some kinds of merchandise, which are liable to be easily spoilt, if they have been insured under the general term *merchandise*, no losses which do not exceed ten per cent., or if expressly specified, three per cent., are made good.[19] A similar exemption from making good losses below three per cent. is allowed by the new law of *Rotterdam*,[20] and by the law of *Dordrecht*.[21]

DCCXXI. Goods which are liable to deterioration may, by the laws of *Rotterdam*[22] and *Dordrecht*,[23] be legally insured, not only where they have been specifically enumerated, as formerly, but also generally under the terms " perishable and imperishable goods ; " and, by the law of *Amsterdam*,[24] even simply under the general term *merchandise*. This may probably be done also at *Rotterdam*[25] and *Dordrecht*.[26]

SEC. 5.

DCCXXII. If the thing insured had already perished and it was possible that the party assured could have become aware of it before the contract was entered into the insurance so effected is *ipso jure* void ; unless (as

---

[17] New *Ord. Amst.* art. 22.
[18] Bynkersh. *Q. J. Priv.* 1. iv. c. 4. p. 550, and c. 13. p. 626.
[19] New *Ord. Amst.* art. 34, declared by the Law of 1756.
[20] Art. 44.   [21] Art. 46.
[22] New *Ord. Rott.* art. 25.   [23] *Ord. Dordr.* art. 29.
[24] d. *Ord. Amst.* art. 34, (supplying from art. 17 of the Old Ordonn.)
[25] Compare New *Ord. Rott.* art. 41, with art. 3 of the Old Ordonnance.
[26] Compare *Ord. Dordr.* art. 29, with art. 43.

expressly provided by the new law of *Amsterdam*;[1] from which the rule laid down by *Bynkershoek*[2] is to be restricted) the assured party himself, as well as the person who effected the insurance on his behalf, declare on oath that they were not aware of the loss. In other places he is not even allowed to take the oath, unless the insurance has been effected against all risks, or at all events.[3]

DCCXXIII. If, however, it be an insurance *at all events*,* an oath of ignorance should not, it seems, be tendered by the party assured, but is only to be taken if the insurers desire it.[4] *Bynkershoek* thinks otherwise, and refers to a decision of the Supreme Court;[5] which decision, however, is not sufficiently borne out by the old laws of *Middelburg, Amsterdam,* and *Rotterdam.*[6]

DCCXXIV. In such a case the insurer himself is also admitted to prove the knowledge on the part of the insured. By the term *knowledge* is understood not only positive but also probable knowledge; but not such as is founded on mere rumour.[7] If knowledge has been proved, the party assured is punished not only by the loss of his action, and by condemnation in double the premium of insurance, but also on a public accusation for criminal falsehood.[8]

DCCXXV. A vessel and merchandise cannot be insured after the voyage has commenced, unless the time

---

[1] New *Ord. Amst.* art. 12.   [2] *Q. J. Priv.* l. iv. c. 7. p. 575.
[3] New *Ord. Rotterd.* art. 35, 36; 37; *Dordr.* art. 38, 39.
* [Insurance upon good or bad news.—V. d. Linden, *Inst.* 651.]
[4] New *Ord. Rotterd.* art. 37. *Dordr.* art. 40.
[5] *Q. J. Priv.* l. iv. c. 11. p. 615.
[6] Old *Ord. Midd.* art. 23; *Amst.* art. 21; *Rott.* art. 9.
[7] Bynkersh. *Q. J. Priv.* l. iv. c. 16. p. 653.
[8] New *Ord. Rotterd.* art. 39, 40; *Dordr.* art. 42.

at which the vessel set sail be mentioned in the policy, or the party assured has declared in writing that he was not aware of the time.[9] By the law of *Amsterdam*,[10] if he has declared himself to be ignorant of the departure of the vessel, mention should also, it is said, be made of the day on which the instructions to effect the insurance were despatched, and of the latest intelligence received concerning the vessel and the merchandise.

DCCXXVI. If, where the vessel has already set sail, the time of its departure has not been mentioned in the policy, according to the laws cited in the preceding *Thesis*, but the insurer himself is proved to have been aware of it through other sources, the contract will not be thereby vitiated, since the insurer has not been misled in any manner;—as decided by the Supreme Court on the 7th of February, 1739.[11]

DCCXXVII. The clause—that the contract should remain valid, although the vessel might have set sail earlier than was mentioned—where both parties have acted in good faith, has sustained the contract before the Supreme Court.[12] It was not, however, approved of at *Amsterdam*,[13] and by the recent law has been declared to be of no force.[14]

SEC. 6.

DCCXXVIII. The duties of an Insurance-broker,

---

[9] New *Ord. Rotterd.* art. 32—34; *Dordr.* art. 35—37. Bynkersh.
Q. J. Priv. l. iv. c. 12. p. 616—618.

[10] New *Ord. Amst.* art. 3. and the latest of 1775, art. 3.

[11] Bynkersh. *Q. J. Priv.* l. iv. c. 17. p. 663.

[12] 15 Jan. 1740; Bynkersh. *Q. J. Priv.* l. iv. c. 12. p. 665—669.

[13] New *Ord. Amst.* art. 3.   [14] Latest *Ord. Amst.* art. 3.

and the fees payable to him, are defined by the laws of *Middelburg, Amsterdam, Rotterdam,* and *Dordrecht.*

DCCXXIX. It is clear that an insurance may be contracted *ab initio* by mere consent, without writing;[2] but it should be reduced to writing and duly stamped within fourteen days;[3] and therefore there is no *locus pœnitentiæ* in the meantime.[4]

DCCXXX. All such stipulations or conditions as are not prohibited by law may be annexed to an insurance (even one in respect of which the laws themselves have prescribed particular forms), and should be strictly performed. If, however, they have not been fulfilled, the insurer will not be thereby discharged, unless such non-fulfilment has occasioned loss. This rule may, I think, be deduced from the excellent decision of the Supreme Court of the 8th of September, 1728.[5]

DCCXXXI. Conditions inserted in the policy itself should be taken as repeated in a supplement or appendix subsequently added to it, unless it has been agreed otherwise;—as decided by the Supreme Court.[6]

DCCXXXII. Conditions which are expressly prohibited by the laws of insurance, if inserted in such a contract, either vitiate the entire contract, as under the law of *Rotterdam,*[7] or at least are invalid in themselves,

---

[1] *Ord. Midd.* art. 9, 10; *Amst.* art. 3, & New *Ord.* art. 38, 39; *Rott.* art. 21, & New *Ord.* art. 76—79; *Dordr.* art. 76—79, 81.

[2] *Ord. Rotterd.* art. 20; Latest *Ord. Amsterd.* art. 60, 61. Bynkersb. *Q. J. Priv.* 1. iv. c. 26. n. 1.

[3] *Publ. Holland.* 13 Nov. 1773. Supra, *Thes.* 713.

[4] *Advies. over den Kooph.* d. i. cons. 12. p. 58, sqq.

[5] Bynkersh. *Q. J. Priv.* 1. iv. c. 14. p. 635—637.

[6] Ibid. 1. iv. c. 11. p. 606—608.

[7] New *Ord. Rott.* art. 71-75.

and cannot be confirmed by a renunciation of the prohibitory law.[8]

DCCXXXIII. Although the name of the vessel
should also be mentioned in the policy of insurance,
yet a description seems to be sufficient; as in a case
mentioned by *Bynkershoek*.[9]   Nor would even a change
in the name, made *bona fide*, affect the contract, provided the identity of the vessel remains certain, as decided by the Supreme Court.[10]

DCCXXXIV. If it be stated in the insurance that
the risk was to commence, not from the place where
the goods were shipped, but from some other place,
but the vessel, meeting a favourable breeze, has passed
by such latter place, the insurance is still valid.[11]

DCCXXXV. By the term *circumjacent* places,
which is usually employed in a policy of insurance, are
understood the neighbouring places, rivers, ports, and
harbours, although they may not have been expressly
named;[12] but not places at a great distance.[13]

DCCXXXVI. If the insurance has been effected
up to some port, river, or harbour expressly named,
but the contracting parties have made no mention of a
neighbouring town to which the goods have been consigned, in such a case the place so named should be
taken as the limit of the risk.   There is a particular
case hereon, mentioned by *Bynkershoek*.[14]

---

[8] Bynkersh. *Q. J. Priv.* l. iv. c. 6. p. 570, sqq.
[9] Ibid. l. iv. c. 12. p. 618, sqq.
[10] 20 Feb. 1722; Bynkersh. *Q. J. Priv.* l. iv. c. 11, p. 610—612.
[11] Bynkersh. *Q. J. Priv.* l. iv. c. 1. p. 521, sq.
[12] New *Ord.* art. 4 ; Bynkersh. ib. l. iv. c. 6. p. 571, sq.
[13] Bynkersh. d. l. c. 10. p. 601—603.   See also p. 598—600.
[14] Ibid. c. 15. p. 645—650.

DCCXXXVII. If the insurance was effected up to a particular place, and the loss occurred before the vessel had arrived there, the insurer is liable, though the vessel may afterwards have sailed past such place, bound perhaps to some other place.[1]

DCCXXXVIII. Upon a loss occurring, the value of the goods insured, as stated in the instrument, is to be proved not only by the oath of the party assured, but also by other evidence.[2]

DCCXXXIX. The damage arising from the loss of the goods is estimated at the price at which they were purchased, adding thereto the expenses incurred on them up to the time of their shipment; but in case the goods were only spoilt, but have reached the place to which they were consigned, the damage is computed at the price at which they would have sold there, if they had arrived in good condition. The freight and other expenses are not taken into account herein, but these may be separately insured; and where this has been done, the loss is taken to have occurred as much in this respect as in respect of the goods themselves, and is to be made good in the same proportion.[3] Where freight is not payable for the goods which may perish, an insurance of such freight becomes void.[4]

DCCXL. If goods which have been insured at the same time arrive partly sound, partly spoilt, then, in computing the loss, not only the spoilt goods, but the sound portion also, are taken into account; and the loss

---

[1] As decided by the Supreme Court, 27 June 1720; Bynkershoek, d. l. iv. c. 10. p. 603—605.

[2] Bynkersh. *Q. J. Priv.* l. iv. c. 17. p. 663—665.

[3] New *Ord. Amsterd.* art. 35, declared by the Ordonn. of 1756.

[4] - Ibid.

is reckoned at so much per cent., as all the goods taken together are reduced in value,—the profit, namely, of the sound portion being set off against the loss of the spoilt portion.[5]

DCCXLI. If a vessel which has been insured arrives in safety, but damaged either by tempest in mid seas, or by ice in the *Greenland* fisheries, the insurer is not liable for such damage.[6]

SEC. 7.

DCCXLII. Under the term *risks of the sea* are comprehended all losses resulting from the violence of the waves, the winds and tempest, but not from the unskilfulness of the master or the pilot.[7]

DCCXLIII. A person who has given an insurance against violence from the enemy, adding a condition in the policy itself, that the vessel and the goods seized might be redeemed up to a certain amount, ought to make good both the price which has been paid as ransom, and the damage which may have occurred to the vessel and goods since their redemption.[8]

DCCXLIV. Under the term *enemies* in the formula of an insurance, pirates also are included. Friendly nations are not included. Where, however, their friendship is doubtful, express mention of them is also now required.[9]

DCCXLV. The owner of a vessel cannot insure

---

[5] *Verzam. van Casus-posit.* cas. 5. p. 43. sqq.

[6] *Advies. over den Kooph.* d. i. cons. 25.

[7] *Advies over den Knooph.* ibid. d. i. cons. 13.

[8] New *Ord. Amst.* art. 16.

[9] See also New *Ord. Rotterd.* art. 42; *Dordr.* 44.

against the fraud or deceit of the master;[1] but he may against the fraud of a substitute appointed without the owner's knowledge.[2] The owners of the merchandise may, however, legally insure against the fraud and deceit as well of the master as of a substitute.[3]

DCCXLVI. An insurance may also be legally effected in favour even of the owner, against the faults of the master, whether of omission or commission.[4] The desertion, however, of a vessel which has stranded and cannot be recovered without greater expense, is not to be considered even as fault on the part of the master; as decided by the Supreme Court.[5]

SEC. 8.

DCCXLVII. The risks of insurance of a vessel, as appeared to *Bynkershoek* in his own times,[6] attached to the insurer from the day on which it was agreed that the vessel should set sail; but it has since been expressly enacted at *Amsterdam*,[7] and has perhaps become the custom in other places also, where the laws are silent on the subject,—in analogy to a similar provision respecting insured goods,—that the risk should commence from the day on which the goods begin to be shipped on board. But there is no doubt that any other time may be fixed by the contract.[8]

---

[1] Bynkersh. *Q. J. Priv.* l. iv. c. 4. p. 553, sqq.
[2] New *Ord. Rotterd.* art. 43; *Dordr.* art. 45.
[3] N. *Ord. Rotterd.* art. 42; *Dordr.* art. 44, and other laws.
[4] Bynkersh. *Q. J. Priv.* l. iv. c. 4. p. 556.
[5] 16 June 1728; See Bynkersh. ibid. l. iv. c. 14. p. 634, sq.
[6] Bynkersh. ib. l. iv. c. 2, p. 529, sqq.
[7] New *Ord. Amst.* art. 5. in fin.
[8] Arg. Dig. l. 17. 34; N. *Ord. Rotterd.* art. 48; *Dordr.* art. 50.

DCCXLVIII. The risk terminates when the vessel having arrived in port has discharged her cargo; provided this be done within twenty-one days, according to the Law of *Amsterdam*,[9] or according to the laws of *Rotterdam*[10] and *Dordrecht*,[11] within fourteen days; which seems also to be the rule under the law of *Middelburg*.[12] DCCXLIX. The exceptions to this rule are—1. Where as soon as the vessel has arrived in port the owners of the vessel have, upon a contract entered into with the owners of the goods, despatched the vessel, laden as it was, on another voyage, and have certified this arrangement by effecting, for instance, a fresh insurance, the risks under the former insurance having now terminated;[13] 2. Where the vessel has been insured for a particular period;[14] and 3. Where the insurance has been effected simply as from port to port, and no terms have been inserted in the contract relative to the time of unloading the vessel.[15]

SEC. 11.

DCCL. If where the vessel has been insured, the master by his own act, though without the knowledge of the party assured, alters the course of the vessel, the insurer is thereby discharged.[16] But upon an insurance

---

[9] New *Ord Amst.* art. 5. in f.   [10] *Ord. Dordr.* art. 49, 51.

[11] New *Ord Rott.* art. 49.

[12] Arg. *Ord. Midd.* art. 11, in f.

[13] *Advies. over den Kooph.* d. i. cons. 24.

[14] Bynkersh. *Q. J. Priv.* l. iv. c. 3. p. 539.

[15] See Placaat of King *Philip* of 1563, t. vii. art. 13, which would, in this case, appear to be still observed. Bynkersh. *Q. J. Priv.* l. iv. c. 2. p. 529, & c. 15. p. 647, f. sqq.

[16] *Advies over den Kooph.* d. i. cons. 21. p. 123—125; New *Ord. Amst.* art. 6, in fin. See also Dig. xiv. l. 1. § 5.

of goods, if the course has been altered by the act of the master without the consent of the party assured. the insurer is not thereby discharged ;[1] unless the goods insured belong to the owner of the vessel himself.[2] The master, however, by whose act the voyage was altered, remains always liable, and therefore the right of action which lies against him should be assigned to the insurer who is not discharged.[3]

DCCLI. What we have stated as to the insurer of a vessel, or of goods belonging to the owner, being discharged by the act of the master, even if the alteration of the course was made without the knowledge of the party assured—is applicable, at *Amsterdam* (from the general wording of the new law), even to a case of fault on the part of the master. But as regards other places the same rule can hardly be adopted ; but on the contrary, the insurer would, it seems, be discharged only in case the course was altered in fraud by the master.[4]

DCCLII. If the course of the voyage is alleged to have been altered at the desire of the party assured, and thereupon a question arises, whether the insurer has been discharged or not, the burthen of proof lies on the insurer ;[5] and in practice, the oath of the party assured is also admissible herein.[6] The mere intention or purpose to alter the course, not carried into execution, does not discharge the insurer.[7]

---

[1] New *Ord. Amst.* ibid.   [2] Ib. art. 6, in f.
[3] New *Ord. Rotterd.* art. 52; *Dordr.* art. 54.
[4] Bynkersh. *Q. J. Priv.* l. iv. c. 8. p. 586.
[5] Ibid. l. iv. c. 7. p. 582: c. 8. p. 585.
[6] Ibid. c. 16. p. 657. See also c. 5. p. 562, sqq.
[7] Ibid l. iv. c. 3. p. 545; & c. 5. p. 562, sqq.

DCCLIII. The course is taken to have been altered, not only if the vessel proceeds in an entirely different direction, but also if sailing indeed directly towards the port in respect of which the insurance was effected, it has passed it by, with the goods on board of her, bound perhaps to some other port with the rest of the goods.[8] Also, if before it has arrived at the destined port, it has touched at other ports[9] (as decided also by the Supreme Court),[10] unless it has been agreed that it might touch at other ports also,[11] or might sail *any where*.[12] But an alteration of the course through necessity does not affect the parties.[13]

SEC. 12.

DCCLIV. If a vessel in which insured goods are conveyed, be detained by a foreign people, or has been rendered wholly unfit for the voyage by some serious injury, the goods may be conveyed in another vessel, at the risk of the insurer, to the place to which they were consigned; if the injury be of a less serious nature, the party assured ought to allow a short time for the repair of the vessel.[14]

DCCLV. Where a vessel which has been insured has been rendered totally unfit for navigation by some serious injury, but without fraud on the part of the

---

[8] *Verzamel. van Casus-posit.* cas. 12.
[9] Bynkersh. *Q. J. Priv.* 1. iv. c. 16. p. 655.
[10] 7 May 1735; ibid. p. 65⁻.   [11] Ibid. c. 4. p. 554, sq.
[12] Ibid. c. 5. p. 564, sqq. c. 7. p. 581.
[13] Ibid. c. 9. p. 591, sqq. & p. 596.
[14] *Ord. Amst.* art. 8; New Ord. art. 26; *Middelb.* art. 15; *Rotterd.* art. 13; and New Ord. art. 53, 54; *Dordr.* art. 55.

master, it may be at once relinquished to the insurer.[1]
If the injury is not quite so serious, and is capable of
being repaired at a small cost, the duty of repairing the
vessel is incumbent on the owner or the master, and
should be strictly performed by him, as is generally
provided for in the policy of insurance.[2] If the vessel
is detained under an arrest, a period of six months or a
year should elapse before it can be relinquished to the
insurer, who ought in the meantime to give pledges or
personal security for the loss.[3]

SEC. 13.

DCCLVI. If the vessel has been taken by the enemy
or by pirates, the party assured may at once assign the
same or the goods insured therein, to the insurer, and
is not bound to wait for an opportunity of ransoming
them, or recovering them by legal proceedings, though
he ought in the meantime to render assistance for this
purpose.[4]

DCCLVII. The losses which an insurer has undertaken to make good ought, in most places, to be made
good within three months; but at *Rotterdam*[5] and
Dordrecht[6] within a month. The entire loss should be
made good ; excepting in the case in *art.* 33 of the
New Law of *Amsterdam.*

---

[1] *Ord. Rotterd.* art. 12: & New Ord. art. 62; *Dordr.* art. 64.

[2] *Tweede Vervolg. der Handv. van Amst.* p. 92.

[3] New *Ord. Amst.* art. 26; New *Ord. Rotterd.* art. 65, 66; *Dordr.*
art. 67, 68.

[4] *Nederl. Adviesb.* d. iii. cons. 248; *Advies. over den Kooph.* d. i.
cons. 14. p. 70, f. 71, f.; & cons. 16. p. 88, and cons. 23. p. 130.

[5] New *Ord. Rott.* art. 68.   [6] *Ord. Dordr.* art. 70.

SEC. 14.

DCCLVIII. The party assured ought to communicate to the insurer all information he may have received of any loss either already sustained or apprehended, in respect of the goods insured: and at *Amsterdam* this is required to be done through the secretary or marshal of the Chamber of Insurance.[7]

SEC. 15.

DCCLIX. The insurer is not liable for any internal defect in the goods insured, not arising from any fault on the part of the master or crew, and without external violence.[8] The same rule has been laid down by the Law of *Amsterdam*[9] in respect of an internal defect in the vessel.[10]

DCCLX. The insurer is not bound to make good any loss, which, viz., at *Middelburg*,[11] does not exceed one per cent., and at *Rotterdam*[12] and *Dordrecht*,[13] three per cent. At *Amsterdam*, where the former laws[14] required the same rate as obtains at *Middelburg*, but the new law is silent on the subject, the latter rate would seem to be the one adopted by usage and custom, even where it has not been expressly provided for by agreement.

Losses exceeding one or three per cent. (respectively) should, it seems, at all these places, be made good

---

[7] As carefully provided for in the New *Ord. Amst.* art. 36; and the latest Ordonnance of 1756, art. 36.

[8] New *Ord Amst.* art. 32; N. *Ord. Rotterd.* art. 45; *Dordr.* art. 47.

[9] New *Ord. Amst.* ib.   [10] See *Verzam. van Casus-posit.* cas. 19.

[11] *Ord. Middelb.* art. 18.   [12] New *Ord. Rotterd.* art. 44.

[13] *Ord. Dordr.* art. 46.   [14] Old *Ord. Amst.* art. 26.

T

without any deduction : as also expressly required by
the form of an *Amsterdam Insurance*,[1] in the words
" *en dat zonder korting* "—*and that without deductions.*

There, however, it is generally the custom, in estimating and paying such losses, to deduct two per cent.
whenever the loss exceeds fifty per cent., and the matter
is settled by compromise, without recourse to legal
proceedings.

SEC. 16.

DCCLXI. If the goods insured have not been sent,
or a smaller quantity only has been sent, or lastly if the
goods sent have been insured for a larger sum than
they were worth, the premium of insurance may be recovered back, deducting half per cent.: but if the goods
have already been shipped in boats or lighters to be
conveyed to the vessel, a deduction of one per cent. is
allowed.[2] So, if besides the goods destined for foreign
parts, other goods also which the vessel should convey
on her return home (*de retouren*) have been insured in
one and the same policy, but no such goods have been
so conveyed home, then the premium paid in respect of
the latter may be recovered back.[3] The same right of
repetition or recovery exists (subject to a deduction
of one per cent.) in respect of the vessel also, if after
having been insured, it does not proceed on the voyage,[4]
or even, if being bound for various ports, it has touched
only at some, and is yet on its voyage ; provided, however, the premium in this case has been fixed as from
port to port or in respect of each port ; for if one entire

[1] *Handv. Tweede Verv.* p. 93.   [2] New *Ord. Amst.* art. 23.
[3] *Advies. over den Kooph.* d. i. cons. 19. p. 112, sqq.
[4] New *Ord. Amst.* art. 93.

and undivided amount has been fixed in respect of the
whole voyage, the entire amount may be retained.[5]
DCCLXII. At *Rotterdam* this restitution of the
premium paid for goods not sent is not claimable, if
the name of the vessel or of the master has not been
mentioned in the instrument; unless it has been otherwise stipulated in this respect in the contract of insurance.[6] The same rule has been laid down at *Dordrecht*.[7]

Sec. 17.

DCCLXIII. Several insurers who have signed the
same policy, though at different times, are held equally
liable to make good the loss, and also to refund the premium, if circumstances render it necessary;[8] regard
being had, namely, to the amount for which each has
bound himself.[9] And, considering the reason of the
rule, it is equally applicable to those who have signed
different policies; whence also the ancient laws do not
make any distinction between one and several policies.[10]
But if an insurance effected by several policies can be
proved to exceed the value of the thing insured, there
is, under the new laws, an exception made to this rule,
viz. : that those who have signed the prior policy remain
liable for the whole amount of their insurance, whilst
the others are discharged from making good the loss
only to the extent of the excess, and are bound in their

---

[5] As held on the 28 Oct. 1790; *Verzam. van Casus-posit.* cas. 20.
[6] New *Ord. Rotterd.* art. 56—58.   [7] *Ord. Dordr.* art. 58—60.
[8] New *Ord. Amst.* art. 24; N. *Ord. Rotterd.* art. 59 ; *Dordr.* art. 61.
[9] *Ord. Rotterd.* art. 19, in f. ; & New *Ord.* art. 70 ; *Dordr.* art. 72.
[10] Placaat of King *Philip* of 1570, art. 13 ; *Ord. Amsterd.* art. 23
Middelb. art. 25 ; & *Rotterd.* art. 19.

respective turns to refund the premium.[1] Not very dissimilar to this is the provision in the Placaat of King *Philip* of 1563,[2] viz. : that if the same goods have been twice *bonâ fide* insured, at different places, and hence by different policies, that policy alone should remain valid which is prior in time, and the latter become void to the extent at least to which the former had left nothing which might still be insured.

DCCLXIV. It being the object of this law to place all the insurers upon an equal footing from the moment of their entering into the contract of insurance,[3] and therefore to render each insurer liable only in proportion to the sum for which he had engaged himself, it follows that several insurers are not joint debtors, and that therefore, upon the insolvency of one, his liability does not fall upon the others, but should be borne by the assured party himself; and hence (supposing such a case to arise) it would be lawful to contract a new insurance against all risks, in the form appointed by the new law of *Amsterdam*.[4] So also, it follows from the same principle, that a party assured may always release any of the insurers he chooses (whether they have signed previous to or after the others), even without the consent of the rest; for the remaining insurers after the discharge of the others, do not thereby become liable for more than they were originally bound for; and only the remainder of the risk already insured will remain. So if an insurance has been effected either above the value, or has even been effected twice over, the matter will still, as regards those who have not been

---

[1] New *Ord. Amst.* art. 24. [2] Tit. vii. art. 15.
[3] Th. 763.   [4] New *Ord. Amst.* art. 25, amplified in 1756.

discharged, remain as if the others had not been dis-charged; since their liability, being limited[5] or cancelled[6] by the law itself, cannot be augmented or revived by the discharge of the others, made without their know-ledge or consent.[7] But as regards the assured party himself, the dissolution of the contract remains bind-ing, and he has no longer a right of action against those whom he had discharged, their risks having been trans-ferred to himself.[8] On these principles ought the tes-timony or opinion of the merchants of *Amsterdam*, given on the 21st October, 1599,[9] to be understood, or rather amended.

All other matters in connection with both these questions are fully treated of by *Bynkershoek*, in his *Quæstiones Juris Privati*.[10]

DCCLXV. This community of rights among several insurers does not, however, prevent those who may have signed the same policy at different times, fixing differ-ent rates of premium.

SEC. 18.

DCCLXVI. The premium of insurance, whatever its amount may be, should at Amsterdam, by the new law, be paid down at once at the time the policy is signed. But if credit be given by the insurer to the broker, he only can afterwards be sued, unless he hap-

---

[5] New *Ord. Rotterd.* art. 70; New *Ord. Amst.* art. 24.
[6] Placaat of King *Philip* of 1563, t. vii. art. 15.
[7] Dig. 1. 17. 155; Dig. xii. 2. 10.
[8] See Dig. i. 7. 25; Cod. ii. 3. 4; Dig. xxi. 1. 14. § 9.
[9] See *Handv. van Amst.* p. 541, in fin. & sq.
[10] L. iv. c. 2. p. 531, sqq.

pens to become insolvent, and the party assured cannot prove that he has already paid the premium to the broker.[1] It can only be claimed in a personal action, and no lien or right of pledge is allowed by the law to the insurer, as security for the premium, either on the thing insured or on the other property of the debtor.[2] A broker, however, who has paid the premium to an insurer, has by the law of Amsterdam,[3] a right of retention over the policy of insurance.

SEC. 19.

DCCLXVII. The rate of interest on premiums not paid by a broker (since the ancient law of *Amsterdam* of 1610 cannot, from the intention of the new law, be any longer adopted in practice) seems at present to be the ordinary rate. But as regards an insurer, if he has, after due inquiry into the amount of the loss, been condemned in a definite sum, he ought to pay eight per cent. thereon ;[4] and he is liable for this interest, if claimed, even though having been absolved in the first instance, he has been condemned in appeal. *Bynkershoek*[5] is of a different opinion; but his arguments, unless I am mistaken, may be easily answered.

SEC. 21.

DCCLXVIII. The cognizance of insurance matters belongs to the Judges or Commissioners appointed for

[1] New *Ord. Amst.* art. 37.
[2] *Holl. Cons.* d. i. cons. 282 ; Bynkersh. *Q. J. Priv.* l. iv. c. 2. p. 538.
[3] New *Ord. Amst.* art. 39.
[4] New *Ord. Amst.* art. 50.
[5] *Q. J. Priv.* l. iv. c. 3. p. 547, sq. and c. 4. p. 550.

these causes ;[6] and, on appeal, to the *Schepenen* ;[7] and not, in the first instance, to the Court, even upon the privilege of minors or of widows, or upon prorogation of jurisdiction.[8]   On account, however, of the peculiar nature of a cause, the parties whereof reside at different places, the States have sometimes approved of the Court exercising jurisdiction herein, rejecting the complaints of the magistrates of *Amsterdam;* to whom, however, as also to the citizens of other places, where there are judges appointed for these causes, it was at the same time permitted, in the contract itself, to prorogue the jurisdiction of their own tribunal even in these causes ;[9] a form of such contract being given for that purpose.[10]   At *Rotterdam,* those insurances only which relate to commerce and navigation are referred for decision to the commissioners ;[11] and at *Dordrecht* the same rule has been adopted.[12]

DCCLXIX. Inasmuch as the action against an insurer is prescribed by the lapse of eighteen months, or of three-years, under penalty of being barred (*op pœne van verstek*),[13] it stands to reason that *restitutio in integrum* against such prescription may not be granted to a major.   At *Rotterdam,* however,[14] and at *Dordrecht,*[15] it

---

[6] New *Ord. Amst.* art. 43, 44. [See Van der Linden's *Institutes* 665].
[7] Art. 49.
[8] *Nad. Ampl. der Instr. van den Hove, van* 1664, art. 8.
[9] *Resol. Holl.* 12 July 1736, *Groot Plac. Boek,* d. 7. p. 933 ; *Handv. van Amst.* p. 662.
[10] Ibid. p. 668, sqq. n. 1—5, *en Tweede Verv.* p. 92, sqq. n. 1—5.
[11] New *Ord. Rotterd.* art. 1, 23, 24.   [12] *Ord. Dordr.* art..5, 6.
[13] New *Ord. Amst.* art. 30 ; New *Ord. Rotterd.* art. 69 ; *Dordr.* art. 71. *Advies. over den Kooph.* d. i. cons. 21. n. 1.   Bynkersh. *Q. J. Priv.* l. iv. c. 12. p. 621.
[14] New *Ord. Rott.* art. 69.   [15] *Ord. Dordr.* art. 71.

, is permitted on just cause being shown ; but it should not, it seems, be too readily granted.[1]

CHAPTER XXVI.— SEC. 6.

DCCLXX. It has not only been enacted by particular laws, but should also, it seems, be considered a rule of the general law, that besides the guardians from whom the wards have failed to recover by the *actio tutelæ* what was due to them, the pupillary magistrates* also may be sued *in subsidium*, where through fraud or neglect they either have failed to take security, or have in any other manner caused loss to the wards : and the decision of the Court of the 23rd of March, 1646, and of the Supreme Court of the 30th of May, 1653, proceed on this principle.[2]

CHAPTER XXVII.—SEC. 1.

DCCLXXI. Upon the principles of the Civil Law as adopted amongst us,[3] as well as from the affinity of *Negotiorum Gestio* to Mandate, it seems quite evident that amongst us also the acts of a *negotiorum gestor* should regularly be considered gratuitous.[4]

[1] Bynkersh. d. l. cap. 14. p. 639, sq.
* [*Wees-Meesters.*]
[2] *Rechtsgel. Observ.* part. iii. obs. 80. Van Leeuwen, in not. *ad Peck.* *Van 't hand opleggen* (*de Arrest.*) d. xliv. n. 8. [Voet (*ad Pand.* xxvii. 8. § 5.) and Groenewegen (*de ll. abrog.* ad Inst. i. 24. § ult.) restrict the remedy against magistrates to cases of fraudulent neglect only. See a consultation of Grotius, in *Holl. Cons.* d. iii. st. 2. cons. 302.—Tr.]
[3] Thes. 17 & 18.
[4] Thes. 570.—Bynkershoek (*Q. J. Publ.* l. i. c. 5, p. 42), *dissentiente.*

CHAPTER XXVIII.—SEC. 4.

DCCLXXII. Although from the reason of the law one partner cannot, without the other's consent, dispose of property held in common :[5] yet it has been received as a rule in certain places that the party who has the smaller share in a building held in common, ought to follow the wishes of him who owns the larger share, whether the latter desires to occupy it himself at a rent fixed by a judge, or to let it to a third party ; provided, however, the owner of the smaller share should always be preferred to a stranger.[6] If they be part-owners in equal shares, it should either be determined by drawing of lots which of them is to occupy, or, what is more equitable (as enacted at *Leyden*), the occupation of the property should be allowed for a term of five years to the party who offers most.[7]

SEC. 5.

DCCLXXIII. The meaning of this somewhat obscure passage may be clearly understood from the Latin version in the *Rechtsgeleerde Observatien*.[8] It relates to the division of the use or occupation, not of the land itself.

SEC. 6.

DCCLXXIV. The custom in *Rhynland* and other places, that a party who has the smaller share in land

---

[5] Dig. x. 3, 28. It has also been so enacted in South Holland. See *Costum. van Zuid. H.* art. 31, in Van de Wall, *Handv. van Dordr.* p. 1360.

[6] *Rechtsgel. Obs.* part. iii. obs. 81.   [7] *Keur. van Leid.* art. 123.

[8] Part. i. obs. 90 ; and *Supplement*, p. 226.

may call for a division, but not the one who has the larger share,[1] is founded, it seems, on this not unjust principle, that after the shares of each part-owner have been settled and allotted, in digging the ditch equally through the land, more is to be taken from the part-owner who has the smaller share than from him who has the greater ; which can by no means be done without his consent. Whence also this right is limited to the case where the larger shareholder is willing that the ditch should be wholly on his share of the land.

SEC. 8.

DCCLXXV. A thing which does not allow of being divided, such as a house,—after it has been offered for competition amongst the part-owners,—passes to him who owns the larger share, at the price which the other part-owner has offered for it, unless he prefers to relinquish it for the same price to the smaller shareholder.[2] If the shares of the part-owners are equal, the thing simply passes to him who offers most.[3] At some places also, the judges may interpose in fixing the price.[4]

DCCLXXVI. One partner or part-owner cannot regularly compel the other to a public sale of the property held in common between them, not even if he be a ward :[5] except in the case of vessels ; which the majority of owners may dispose of by public sale; as testified by a large number of the merchants of *Amster-*

---

[1] *Rechtsgel. Obs.* part. iii. obs. 82.
[2] *Keur. van Leiden*, art. 123, in f.   [3] Ibid. See Cod. iii. 37. l.
[4] See *Rechtsgel. Observ.* part. iii. obs. 84.
[5] *Holl. Cons.* d. iv. cons. 254.

dam,[6] and frequently decided by both the Courts.[7] The same rule has been laid down by the laws of *Rotterdam* and *Dordrecht*.[8] At *Amsterdam*, if the vessels be such as trade to *Norway*, *Sweden*, and the *Baltic Sea*, even a minority of the owners, who jointly own a fourth part of the vessel, may compel the majority to sell it, provided, however, they previously offer their shares in the vessel to the others, at a valuation to be fixed by arbitrators appointed by a judge.[9]

SEC. 9.

DCCLXXVII. A part-owner, who has the smaller share in a house, may also, without the other's consent, cause it to be repaired; but it is not permitted to any of them to alter the form of the building, except with the consent of all.[10]

SEC. 13.

DCCLXXVIII. The reason of our law would hardly seem to permit that by the pact by which hereditary debts are divided amongst coheirs, or even by desire of the testator, a creditor of the estate may acquire the right of suing. or be compelled against his own consent to sue, any particular coheir for the entire debt.[11]

[6] Ibid. d. vi. st. 2. cons. 51. p. 432.   [7] Ibid. cons. 50. p. 429.
[8] Thes. 709.   [9] *Ord. Amsterd.* 31 Jan. 1687; *Handv.* p. 1493.
[10] *Ord. Middelb.* 19 Dec. 1617, art. 12; *Groot Plac.* d. iv. p. 1069; *Vlissing.* 12 Mar. 1628, art. 7; *Haarlem*, 7 Sept. 1708, art. 11; *Keur. van Haarl.* d. i. p. 204.
[11] Groenewegen, however (*ad Dig.* xxxi. 69. § 2.), and Voet (*ad Dig.* x. 2. § 27) *dissentientibus*.

CHAPTER XXIX.—SEC. 6.

DCCLXXIX. If a voyage has been delayed by the act of the merchant, the sailors should be paid, not a fourth part of the sum allowed for demurrage, under the term *lay-days*, but only their just wages for the time during which the voyage has been so delayed.[1]

DCCLXXX. *Average,* which is accurately treated of in the new law of *Rotterdam,*[2] is there defined as " the loss arising from any voluntary act done with the view of preserving the vessel and goods, or of averting greater and probable damage." Such loss is to be made good by contribution from the vessel and goods; and is termed *gross* average ;[3]

DCCLXXXI. And differs from what is termed *common* or *ordinary* average, which is to be made good by contribution from the goods alone.[4] But as to this, it has now almost become the custom that when a vessel is to be laden with goods on account of several merchants (*stuk-goederen*), the master in the bill of lading stipulates for a certain percentage on the freight, such as ten per cent. (which is the ordinary rate), on account of such loss: but if the whole vessel has been chartered by one merchant, and there has been no express agreement in this respect in the charter-party, then two thirds of the average attach to the merchant, and one third to the master.[5] Under this kind of average

---

[1] See Placaat of King *Philip,* tit. *van Schippers en Koopluiden,* art. 4; ibique Verwer. *in not.* p. 70.

[2] Concerning Shipping—1721, art. 83, & sqq. (which preceded the Law of Dordrecht of 1775. art. 82, sqq.)   [3] Thes. 785, infra.

[4] Weitsen. *van Avaryen,* § 7. junct. Verwer, ib. *in notis.*

[5] Verwer, *Toegift van grond-regelen,* pag. 116—121, and in *Append.* n. 15. p. 272, sq.

are included the ordinary port-duties, the regular charges of the pilot, and the payments made to boats or lighters ordinarily employed, where there has been no accident, for the purpose of discharging the vessel;[6] but not, at the present day, that which is mentioned by *Weitsen* in *sec.* 5. of his *Treatise on Average.*[7]

SEC. 9.

DCCLXXXII. Losses arising from a sailor having been wounded or maimed in the performance of his ordinary duties in a vessel are borne by the master or owner of the vessel;[8] if in the defence of the vessel, it is included under gross average;[9] as also if in an engagement arising from the refusal of a salute;[10] whence the rule laid down by *Bynkershoek*[11] cannot, at least on this point, be received.

SEC. 10.

DCCLXXXIII. If a vessel which has been chartered during time of war for a voyage puts in to some port in fear of the enemy, who has not, however, given it chase, and remains there, waiting perhaps for a convoy, the expenses of such delay cannot be reckoned as gross average, as decided by the Supreme Court on the 19th January, 1722.[12] It is otherwise, if the intelli-

---

[6] Verwer, dd. ll.; Weitzen, *van Avaryen,* § 3, 6, 7.

[7] Verwer, ib. *in notis,* p. 222.

[8] And see New *Ord. Rotterd.* art. 99; *Dordr.* art. 98; *Middelb.* art. 48.

[9] D. *Ord. Rotterd.* art. 97.   [10] Ib. art. 98; *Dordr.* art. 97

[11] *Q. J. Priv.* l. iv. c. 24. p. 724.

[12] Bynkersh. *Q. J. Priv.* l. iv. c. 25. p. 734, sqq.

gence of the war arrived during the voyage, or the vessel, having received directions to sail under the protection of a convoy, has not met it, and has therefore delayed the voyage.

DCCLXXXIV. Under furniture of a vessel, which when cut away or thrown overboard in a case of danger is reckoned as average, is also included a boat such as may be conveniently placed in the vessel. Goods deposited in the boat, if thrown overboard, are not accounted as average.[1]

DCCLXXXV. In order that losses voluntarily incurred might be reckoned as average, it is required that the master should hold counsel with the merchant or his factor, if present, or if they dissent, then with the crew;—the opinion of the majority of whom should be acted upon.[2] The Law of *Rotterdam*,[3] however, requires the advice, not of all the crew, but chiefly of the master and the principal sailors. If the master has neglected to take such counsel, he is personally liable for the loss.

SEC. 12.

DCCLXXXVI. If a vessel, whilst remaining in a port to avoid danger, has discharged some of the goods, or during any other imminent danger, has lost them either in defending itself or by throwing them over-

---

[1] *Ord. Rotterd.* art. 90; *Dordr.* art. 89.

[2] Plac. K. *Philip.* tit. *van Schipbreeking*, art. 4, 10; Verwer, *Toegift van Grondregelen*, p. 114; Bynkersh. *Q. J. Priv.* l. iv. c. 24. p. 719; *Ord. Rotterd.* art. 96. junct. art. 144, 145.

[3] *Ord. Rotterd.* ibid.

[4] Ibid. art. 96. And see *Ord. Dordr.* art. 95. junct. 141, 142.

board, or giving them as ransom to enemies or pirates, &c., but has shortly afterwards perished in the same danger, no contribution can be demanded by way of average, but every one retains to himself whatever belongs to him out of goods saved.[5] On the other hand, if the vessel having escaped such peril, has since perished in a subsequent disaster, and from such latter disaster a part of the goods of some value has been saved, the owners of these goods should contribute towards the losses, which arose from the prior danger, but not towards the loss of the vessel, or of the goods which perished with it.[6] But the freight of the goods saved should in either case be paid, without deducting salvage, as decided by the Supreme Court on the 16th February, 1707 ;[7] but the expenses incurred in saving them, and consequently the salvage, should be paid by way of average, the freight also being subject to contribution herein.[8]

DCCLXXXVII. In estimating the value of goods which have been thrown overboard, or even of goods which have been saved, a distinction has been adopted in custom, contrary to the Placaat of King *Philip*, which *Grotius* has here followed ; viz. : between losses occurring before and after half the voyage had been accomplished ; in the former case they are estimated at the price at which they were purchased ; in the latter at the price at which they might have sold.[9] *Bynkers-*

---

[5] Bynkersh. *Q. J. Priv.* l. iv. c. 24. p. 721, sqq.   *Ord. Rotterd.* art. 101.   [6] *Ord. Rotterd.* art. 103–105.
[7] Bynkersh. d. l. p. 722. (Supra, *Thes.* 681.)
[8] *Ord. Rotterd.* art. 104.   So also under the Law of Dordrecht, *Ord.* art. 100–104.
[9] Bynkersh. *Q. J. Priv.* l. iv. c. 21. p. 698.

hoek,[1] however, less correctly, states that this distinction does not apply to goods which have been saved.[2]

DCCLXXXVIII. In computing the value, with reference to which contribution is to be made, it was formerly left to the option of the owners of the goods whether they would have the master contribute the value of the vessel, or the entire freight of all the goods.[3] But by the laws of *Rotterdam*[4] and *Dordrecht,*[5] this option is no longer permitted; and either the value of the ship or of the freight, whichever is greater, should be contributed.

SEC. 13.

DCCLXXXIX. Money which has been saved is also subject to contribution towards average. Formerly it contributed in proportion to its intrinsic value;[6] but at present, from the intention of the Law of *Rotterdam,*[7] according to its external or current value. But contribution for the money thrown overboard is only to be made, provided timely notice was given to the master before it was thrown overboard, that (for instance) such money was in a certain package, though he may have been previously ignorant thereof; but if such intimation has not been given, the money thrown overboard is not to be made good.[8] The ancient custom at *Amsterdam*—

---

[1] P. 699.

[2] See the forms of citation in *Amsterdam,* Verwer *in not.* ad art. 6. Plac. K. *Philip.* tit. *van Schipbreeking,* p. 106, 107, & Ord. *Rotterd.* art. 117; & *Dordr.* art. 116.

[3] Bynkersh. *Q. J. Priv.* 1. iv. c. 24. p. 725, in f.

[4] *Ord. Rotterd.* art. 114.　　　　　[5] *Ord. Dordr.* art. 113.

[6] Plac. K. *Philip.* tit. iv. art. 7.　　　　[7] *Ord. Rott.* art. 110, 111.

[8] Ibid.; and *Ord. Dordr.* art. 110, which lays it down more explicitly.

that a half only of the money and of gold and silver which have been saved should be subject to contribution, and also that contribution towards money and gold and silver which have been lost should be made only to the extent of a half—is said to be still observed.[9]

Sec. 14.

DCCXC. Things thrown overboard, cut away, or spoilt, not voluntarily with a view to avoiding any danger, but from some other necessity ; as well as losses arising from neglect or fraud ; are not accounted as average.[10]

DCCXCI. Things thrown out of a vessel which has been overladen are not reckoned as average; but as regards such losses, not only the master, but the owners of the vessel also are liable, in proportion to the share which each of them has in the vessel ; the goods also of the merchant, at whose request the vessel may have been so overladen, being bound in tacit mortgage for such loss, and liable to be detained in the vessel.[11] If the loss has happened to the goods of such merchant himself, and the master had warned him of the danger, he alone suffers the loss, and will have no redress against the master.[12]

DCCXCII. Goods which have been deposited in an improper place, as for instance on the deck, and have been thrown overboard in a case of danger, do not

[9] *Wisbuische Zee-regt.* art. 38. § 3 ; whereon see Verwer, p. 25, and Id. on Plac. K. *Philip*, tit. iv. art. 7. p. 107. And the rule laid down by Bynkershoek (*Q. J. Priv.* L iv. c. 24 p. 726, sq.) should be amplified from these laws.

[10] *Ord. Rotterd.* art. 106, 107; *Dordr.* art. 105, 106.

[11] *Ord. Rotterd.* art. 127.   [12] Ibid. art. 108 ; *Ord. Dordr.* art. 107.

constitute average, and the loss arising therefrom is to be made good by the master at once.[1] At *Amsterdam* there is a special exception in respect of vessels return-ing from the *Baltic* Sea, and having goods placed be-tween the orlop deck and the gallows (*tusschen den Overloop en de Koebrug*),[2] and which does not seem to have been altered by any subsequent laws relating to Insurance or Average.[3]

SEC. 16.

DCCXCIII. The master of a vessel which has suf-fered average has not only a right of retention over the goods saved which are subject to contribution,[4] but also a right of pledge thereon.[5] This right belongs also to the owner of goods thrown overboard, over the goods saved, and over the vessel itself;[6] and the con-tribution may even be recovered by a personal action, at least by the action under our shipping-laws.[7] And in this sense should the laws of *Amsterdam* on the subject[8] be understood.

DCCXCIV. Those who are liable to make contri-bution are discharged by relinquishing the vessel or the goods saved, as also expressly provided by the laws of *Rotterdam*[9] and *Dordrecht*.[10]

---

[1] See also *Ord. Rott.* art. 91; *Dordr.* art. 90.
[2] Law of *Amst.* 14 Jan. 1607, art. 3; *Handv.* p. 657.
[3] Verwer. *ad Plac. K. Philip*, art. 8. p. 108, in not.
[4] Voet, *ad Pand.* xiv. 2. § 11.
[5] As laid down by the Jurists in *de Advies. over den Kooph.* d. i. cons. 45. p. 237.
[6] As settled by the *Ord. Rotterd.* art. 118; & *Dordr.* art. 117.
[7] Bynkersh. *Q. J. Priv.* l. iv. c. 24. p. 727, sqq.
[8] Ord. of 1744. art. 53, 54; of 1756, art. 54; & of 1775, art. 53,54.
[9] *Ord. Rott.* art. 119.
[10] *Ord. Dordr.* art. 118.

DCCXCV. The period of prescription by which these actions for contribution are limited[11] should, it seems, depend upon the general rules concerning prescription, and not, as *Voet* thinks,[12] on the laws relating to the prescription of eighteen months and three years adopted in respect of insurances.[13] For the law of *Rotterdam*, throughout that portion of it which relates to average,[14] and also the law of *Dordrecht*,[15] make no provision concerning the prescription of these actions; whilst, on the other hand, in treating of insurances, both these laws[16] expressly lay down three shorter terms of prescription in respect of actions against insurers. And it is quite clear that *art.* 30 of the law of *Amsterdam* of 1744, when taken in connection with the preceding and following articles, should be understood in the same sense.

CHAPTER XXX.—SEC. 6.

DCCXCVI. Although, on the more correct rule of the Civil Law, the *condictio indebiti*, or action to reclaim, is not maintainable for a sum paid under a mistake of law,—and it cannot be proved that a contrary rule has been adopted in the practice of the Courts,—yet the reason of the Law of Holland, which is supposed to excuse ignorance of the law even in a judge,[17] and in general affords equitable relief by means of *restitutio in integrum* in cases barred by the rigour of law,[18] seems to

[11] Thes. 793. [12] *Ad. Pand.* xiv. 2. § 11, in fin.

[13] Thes. 769.

[14] *Ord. Rott.* art. 83–119. [15] *Ord. Dordr.* art. 82–118.

[16] *Ord. Rotterd.* art. 69 ; *Dordr.* art. 72.

[17] Groeneweg. *ad Inst.* iv. 5. pr. § 1.

[18] Voet *ad Pand.* iv. 6. § 9, sqq.

U 2

require that a *condictio indebiti* should be allowed even
in the case of a mistake of law.[1]

SEC. 10.

DCCXCVII. A person who, though absolved by a
wrong sentence, has paid a debt which was justly due,
cannot, by our Law, any more than by the Roman Law,[2]
reclaim it.[3]

CHAPTER XXXI.—SECS. 8 AND 9.

DCCXCVIII. Since the reason why the Civil Law
allows a *locus pænitentiæ* in innominate contracts is,
that an action does not lie on a nude pact,[4] and since
amongst us this reason does not apply,[5] our law does
not seem to admit of this *pænitentia.*

CHAPTER XXXIII.—SEC. 9.

DCCXCIX. The killing of an adulterer discovered
in the act, by a father or a husband, is to be excused
on the ground of justifiable anger.[6] And this rule is
not affected by the circumstance that at the present
day adultery is not capitally punished ; on which insufficient ground *Groenewegen* argues in favour of the
contrary opinion.[7]

---

[1] *Holl. Consult.* d. iv. cons. 9. p. 24, sq.
[2] Dig. xii. 6. § 28.   [3] Groenewegen (*ad Dig.* xii. 6. 28) *dissentiente.*
[4] Dig. xix. 4. 1. § 2, vers. *alioquin,* &c. junct. Dig. ii. 14. 7. pr. § 2, 4.
[5] Thes. 484.
[6] Dig. xlviii. 5. 24, arg.; *Holl. Cons.* d. i. cons. 331; Van Leeuwen,
Comm. B. iv. ch. 37. § 8.   [7] Ad. Cod. ix. 9. 4. n. 2, sqq.

DCCC. *Grotius* is also correct in stating here that the ravisher of a virgin, if apprehended in the act, may be killed with impunity by the father,[7] although on this point also *Groenewegen*, as well as *Brouwer*,[8] expresses a different opinion.

CHAPTER XXXV.—SEO. 8.

DCCCI. The practice which prevails amongst us, that where a virgin who has been violated sues for dowry or marriage, she may, after tendering on oath to the effect that she was verily violated, and that she has never lain with any other man, call upon the ravisher to deny by the purgatory oath that he had lain with her;—this practive, as regards the claim for dowry, seems to hold even as against a man who is already married; provided it be supported by weighty presumptions.[9] The Statutes of *Flushing*[10] agree in almost every respect with the Dutch Law.

CHAPTER XXXVI.—SEC. 2.

DCCCII. Many of the more stringent laws of Holland concerning defamation, as also the recent Placaat of the 7th March, 1754, seem to have reference to injuries against public persons, or to those acts by which civil discords are recalled to memory; and hence the punishment of slander against private individuals on other matters is not fixed, but discretionary.

[7] Arg. *Polit. Ord.* art. 18; and *Plac. Holl.* 25 Feb. 1751.
[8] *De Jur. Connub.* l. ii. c. 23. n. 30.
[9] See Boehmer. *ad Carpzov. Pract. Crim.* quæst. 68. obs. 7
[10] Cap. xx. art. 4.

DCCCIII. The rule of the Roman Law, as deducible from the more correct interpretation of the 18th law of the Dig. xlvii. 10., viz., that the truth of a libel or accusation excuses the offender from the punishment for verbal injury, has not only been adopted by the Law of Zeeland,[1] and in certain parts of Holland,[2] but should, it seems, from the reason of our law, be received everywhere; unless an uninterrupted custom to the contrary can be proved at any place.[3]

CHAPTER XXXVII.—SEC. 7.

DCCCIV. In order to understand the rule laid down by *Grotius* in *secc.* 7 and 8, and in *Chap.* xxxviii. *sec.* 15 *& seqq.*, it should be observed that under loss, fraud, or blame, are included not only the cases mentioned in these sections, where a regular delict is committed, but also the cases treated of in *Chap.* xxxviii., for in these cases also there may be fraud or blame, although this is not insisted upon by *Grotius* in the latter chapter; because they often occur accidentally; for which reason also a certain obligation *quasi ex delicto* has been introduced by our laws.[4]

DCCCV. He who has no buoy floating over his anchor is presumed to be guilty of fault; but so, that if the fault is not proved by his adversary, he is admitted to take the purgatory oath ; being nevertheless bound to make good a half of the loss.[5]

---

[1] *Nieuw. Ampl. Pol. Ord.* 24 January 1673, art. 11.

[2] *Handv. van Kennemerl.* Edit. van Santen, 1652, p. 185; *Costum. van Rhynl.* art. 14. See hereon Van Leeuwen, p. 162. Kemp, *Beschry-ving van Gorinchem*, p. 371, art. 86.   [3] Thes. 18.

[4] Shipping-laws of *Rotterdam*, art. 255, 256, 259–262.

[5] Ibid. art. 263, 264; *Dordr.* art. 180, 181.

DCCCVI. As regards losses arising in this and other cases from the fraud or fault of the master, the author of the damage is indeed in the first place liable for the whole, but the owners of the vessel may also be sued in proportion to the share which each has in the vessel; they having their counter-action against the master (though *Bynkershoek*[6] is of a different opinion). For the owners of the vessel which injured the other ought to be responsible for those acts of the master which concern the navigation of the vessel; or should be held liable on the ground that they are liable also for losses accidentally caused by the vessel. And not only has it been so decided by the Supreme Court,[7] but it has been enacted by the Laws of *Rotterdam*[8] and *Dordrecht*;[9] where it is also provided that the owners may discharge themselves by ceding their shares in the vessel. They are not, however, each liable *in solidum*, or beyond what they owe in respect of the loss in proportion to their shares.[10]

SEC. 8.

DCCCVII. If, when a vessel which is at anchor has run aground, the master of another vessel which lies close to it weighs anchor for the purpose of avoiding damage, and removes his vessel, and in so doing suffers loss, such loss should be made good to him.[11] If when requested by the master of the vessel which is aground, to weigh anchor and remove his vessel, he

[6] *Q. J. Priv.* l. iv. c. 23.   [7] 23 Dec. 1733, Ibid. p. 716.
[8] Art. 256, 268; which Bynkershoek had not seen.   [9] Art. 185.
[10] Coren, *Obs.* 40; Bynkersh. l. iv. c. 20. p. 688. f. seq.
[11] *L. Rotterd.* art. 265, in f.; *Dordr.* art. 182, in f.

refuses to do so, or does not allow the other to do it himself, and in consequence thereof the latter suffers damage, he is liable thereon, and liable indeed for the whole loss.[1] But this, though certainly true as regards the master, is not applicable to the owners, since they are not in such a case liable to a greater extent than stated in the preceding *thesis*, and are discharged by ceding their shares in the vessel.[2]

SEC. 9.

DCCCVIII. The old rule that a judge who adjudicates improperly is bound to make good the loss,[3] seems to have passed into desuetude since the adoption of the Civil Law in the decision of disputes;[4] unless either fraud or clearly inexcusable blame can be shown.[5]

CHAPTER XXXVIII.—SEC. 2.

DCCCIX. A person through whose fault a fire broke out in his own house, if it extended further, was formerly, under a statute of *Amsterdam*,[6] liable for the injury arising to the neighbouring houses; but it may be reasonably questioned whether this rule still holds under the present law.

---

[1] Bynkersh. *Q. J. Priv.* l. iv. c. 22. p. 703.

[2] *L. Rotterd.* art. 268, junct. art. 265, 266, *Dordr.* art. 185, junct. art. 182, 183.

[3] *Rechtsgel. Observ.* part iv. obs. 46. See Van de Wall, *Handv. van Dordr.* p. 121, 143, sqq. *in not.*; De Timmerman, *ad Consuet. Mediob.* rubr. vi. art. 4.

[4] Groenew. ad Inst. iv. 5. pr.

[5] As in the case in *'t Nieuw Nederl. Adv.* d. i. cons. 46, p. 505, sqq.

[6] 9 Nov. 1541; *Handv.* p. 859.

SEC. 5.

DCCCX. *Grotius* is not in error here, as supposed by the jurists in the *Rechtsgeleerde Observatien*,[7] but merely narrates the then practice under the Edict concerning things placed or suspended in a dangerous position; and allows the action under that Edict to such persons only as have been injured by the thing falling.

SEC. 9.

DCCCXI. Skippers, innkeepers, and stablekeepers are no longer liable in double the amount for the delicts of their servants, but only for the actual amount of damage.[8] But such servants only are to be understood as any one voluntarily keeps in his service, not those to whom any employment, such as a public office, has been given by public authority.[9]

SEC. 16.

DCCCXII. The provision under the shipping-laws, that losses arising from the accidental collision of ships, should be borne in half-shares by each party—this, as regards any damage sustained by the vessels themselves, which have run foul of each other, most jurists agree in thinking applies not only to ships but also to river vessels. But the provisions, contained either in the laws themselves, or adopted from an interpretation of them, viz. :—1. That this should also include damage

[7] Part i. obs. 98.
[8] Voet *ad Pand.* iv. 9, § ult.   See a case in *de Holl. Cons.* d. i. cons. 182.
[9] *Vervolg. der Holl. Cons.* d. i. cons. 119.

sustained by the goods conveyed in such vessels;[1] and
2. That a half of the damage, whether sustained by the
vessel or the goods, should be made good by each party
by way of gross average, by contribution from the
vessel and the goods;—whether these provisions are applicable to river vessels also, and to the goods conveyed
in them, seems to be a matter of much controversy.
Several authors, and chiefly *Bynkershoek*,[2] maintain the
affirmative. But the opposite opinion seems, and not
without reason, to have been adopted in the practice of
the Courts, and has also been approved of by the
Court of Holland.[3]

DCCCXIII. By damage arising from the collision
of vessels, is understood that which is sustained not
only by the vessels themselves, but also by the goods
contained therein, as maintained by *Bynkershoek*,[4] and
decided by the Supreme Court.[5] And the same rule
would hold even where one of the vessels had no cargo.[6]
This subject is also expressly defined by the Laws of
Rotterdam[7] and *Dordrecht*;[8] where it has also been
enacted that the vessel and the goods should be held
bound or liable for the damage, and that the latter may
therefore be detained by the master; and hence the
observations of *Neostadt*,[9] quoted by *Bynkershoek* in
chap. xxi. p. 696, are no longer applicable in practice.

DCCCXIV. Not only should the damage arising
directly from the collision be made good, as maintained

---

[1] Th. sq.   [2] *Q. J. Priv.* l. iv. c, 19, 20.
[3] 31 July 1665.—See Verwer, *Zee-rechten*, p. 128, sq. in not. § 13,
14; & *Advysen, Certifikaten, &c.*, post 3am. edit. d. operis; Amst.; 1739.
[4] *Q. J. Priv.* L iv. c. 18. p. 675, sqq.   [5] D. l.
[6] Coren. *Obs.* 41; whereon see Bynkersh. d. l. c. 21.
[7] Art. 225.   [8] Art. 172.   [9] Decis. Supr. Cur. 49.

by *Groenewegen*,[10] but also that which is proved to have afterwards resulted from such collision, as correctly laid down by *Bynkershoek*.[11]

DCCCXV. The damage should be made good by both the vessels in half-shares, in arithmetical proportion as enacted in express terms by the Placaat of *Charles* V.[12] And on this principle is the Placaat of King *Philip, tit.* 5 *art.* 1, to be understood; the second and third articles of which also furnish a valid argument in favour of this rule. The Laws of *Rotterdam*[13] and *Dordrecht*[14] also admit the same proportion; and the Supreme Court has likewise so decided.[15] *Bynkershoek*, however, has endeavoured to maintain by several arguments that the geometrical proportion ought to be followed herein.[16]*

DCCCXVI. If the damage arising from the collision is attributable to the fault of both parties, then the loss is not in common, as formerly held by the Supreme Court;[17] but each party bears his own loss.[18] This is supported also by the Laws of *Rotterdam*[19] and *Dordrecht*.[20]

SEC. 17.

DCCCXVII. If one of two vessels which are lying

---

[10] Not. 18. ad. h. l.

[11] *Q. J. Priv.* 1. iv. c. 22. p. 708; the Jurists in *de Advies. over den Kooph.* (d. i. cons. 28.) are, however, of a different opinion.

[12] Art. 46.   [13] Art. 255.   [14] Art. 172.

[15] Neostad. *Supr. Cur. Decis.* 48, 49.   Coren, *Obs.* 40, 41.

[16] *Q. J. Priv.* 1. iv. c. 20. p. 68, sqq.

* [See also Van der Linden, *Inst.* p. 641.]

[17] Neostad. *Supr. Cur. Dec.* 49.

[18] Bynkersh. *Q. J. Priv.* 1. iv. c. 22. p. 705, sqq.

[19] Art. 262   [20] Art. 179.

at anchor or are moored, begins to drift, from the violence of the wind or the sea, and from no fault of the master, and either causes damage to the other lying alongside, or suffers damage itself, it must make good one half the damage of such other vessel and bear all its own damage ;[1] and this, although the other vessel may not have released its cable, unless this might have been done without incurring any risk, when the master of the drifting vessel requested it.[2] It has also been so enacted at *Rotterdam*[3] and *Dordrecht*.[4] The adjacent vessel is also not liable for any damage it may have occasioned to the drifting vessel in endeavouring to avoid a collision.[5]

DCCCXVIII. In the port of the *Texel*, it is said to be the usage, that if, during a storm, several vessels begin to drift, and run against each other, they may, during the danger, cut each other's cables, without becoming liable to make good the damage.[6] If there be no immediate danger, and the drifting vessel is at anchor, another vessel towards which it is drifting, has no right to cut its cable, without necessity.[7]

DCCCXIX. In case a drifting vessel runs foul of the cable of a vessel alongside, without any fault on the part of the crew, and the crew of the former vessel cut away such cable, and the latter having lost its anchor is wrecked,—no express rule applicable hereto has been laid down in the shipping laws.[8] But it may

---

[1] Bynkersh. *Q. J. Priv.* L iv. c. 21. p. 701.

[2] Ibid. c. 22. p. 704.   [3] *L. Rotterd.* art. 257, 258

[4] *L. Dordr.* art. 174, 175.   [5] Dd. ll.

[6] *Advies. over den Kooph.* d. i. cons. 31.

[7] Ibid. cons. 32 & 33, in quæst. 2.

[8] Ibid. cons. 29, 30.

be collected from the Placaats of King *Philip*[9] and the Emperor *Charles*,[10] and the Laws of *Rotterdam*[11] and *Dordrecht*,[12] that the drifting vessel is liable not for a half only of the loss, but for the whole; since its crew, without the consent of the master of the other vessel, did that which he himself was not bound to do.[13]

DCCCXX. If two vessels lying at anchor, and without breaking their cables, injure each other by striking and rubbing against each other, the loss of the one is not, as many suppose, set off against the loss of the other, but, from the reason of our law, is common to both, as correctly laid down by Bynkershoek.[14]

Sec. 18.

DCCCXXI. If a vessel under sail runs foul of another which is lying at anchor, it has no remedy as regards its own loss, but should make good the losses of the other to the extent of a half; unless the former has been in fault, in which case, and if the master of the other vessel can prove it, it is liable for the whole loss; but if he cannot, he ought to establish his own innocence from blame by the oath of himself and his crew.[15] If the vessel which was at anchor could, without itself incurring any risk, have avoided the damage, then all claim for damages ceases.[16]

---

[9] Art. 2.   [10] Art. 47.   [11] Art. 257.   [12] Art. 174.
[13] *L. Rotterd.* art. 258; *Dordr.* art. 175. Thes. 817.
[14] *Q. J. Priv.* l. iv. c. 18. p. 673, seq.
[15] *L. Rotterd.* art. 259–261.
[16] Ibid. art. 262; and see *L. Dordr.* art. 176–179; by which statutes the concluding part of the former Placaat of King *Philip* (tit. 5. art. 3.) seems to have been partly abrogated.

CHAPTER XXXIX.—SEC. 13.

DCCCXXII. Although the payment of a debt should be made to the true creditor, yet an exception is allowed in favour of the administrators of the *East India* Company; viz., that they are discharged by payment of the salary of a deceased mariner or soldier to those persons who have proved themselves by the testimony of two witnesses to be the heirs of the deceased;[1] and it has been decreed by the States General,[2] that they should acquire a discharge by paying or delivering even an inheritance in this manner, provided, upon the appearance of the true heir, they cede to him their action against the party to whom the goods have been delivered and his sureties.

SEC. 14.

DCCCXXIII. A debt due to a ward may indeed regularly be paid to his guardian; but, where the Orphan-Chamber has not been excluded, a debt which is secured by a note or other instrument should be paid to the pupillary magistrates themselves, not to their actuary or to a dative guardian.[3]

CHAPTER XL.—SEC. 2.

DCCCXXIV. In order that the deposit and consignation in court of money tendered to a creditor, who has refused to receive it, might operate as a release of the debtor, it is indeed necessary that the tender should

---

[1] Voet *ad Pand.* xlvi. 3. § 5, in f.   [2] *Resol. Holl.* 22 Jun. 1751.
[3] *Weeskeur. van Leyden*, art. 51, aliisque.

have been made in the presence of witnesses, but it is not necessary, as maintained by *Van Leeuwen,*[4] to cite the creditor.

SEC. 6.

DCCCXXV. Compensation may be correctly pleaded both against a creditor who is insolvent,[5] and against one who has obtained letters of Respite,[6] and much more so, against one to whom a *Surcheance* (or postponement of payment for a certain time*) has been granted.

DCCCXXVI. Where an insurance has been effected by one person on behalf of another—the name of the owner of the thing insured being expressly mentioned —compensation of a debt due by himself (the agent) cannot be pleaded against him by the insurer, when sued upon the insurance to make good any loss.[7] If the name of the owner has not been mentioned, compensation may be pleaded.[8]

SEC. 7.

DCCCXXVII. Compensation may be pleaded even after sentence, against the execution, as decided by the Court ;[9] although the Supreme Court had previously decided otherwise.[10]

---

[4] *Cens. Forens.* part. i, l. iv. c. 35. u. 1, 2.
[5] *Holl. Cons.* d. iii. st. 2. cons. 75.
[6] Voet *ad Pand.* xvi. 2. § 9. [Van der Linden, *Inst.* 464.]
* [Van der Linden, *Inst.* 380.]   [7] *Holl. Cons.* d. iii. cons. 80.
[8] *Advies over den Kooph.* d. i. cons. 17.
[9] *Decis. en Resol. van den Hove,* u. 272.   [10] Neostad. *Dec.* 95,

CHAPTER XLI.—SEC. 9.

DCCCXXVIII. Although *Acceptilation** does not any longer require amongst us the words of interrogation and promise, and by the *pactum de non petendo* or agreement of non-claim, an obligation is, from the reason of our law, *ipso jure* released; yet according to the intention of *Grotius*, there seems to remain this difference between the two acts, viz., that the former is a present and absolute remission of the debt, simply effected, which releases a co-promisee also, and affects a co-stipulator; whilst the latter is a promise *in futuro* not to claim a debt, involving a future act on the part of the creditor in abstaining from claiming the debt from the party with whom he stipulates, or from his heir; which therefore neither benefits a co-debtor, nor, on the other hand (since it consists only of the act of the creditor who so promises), affects a co-creditor.[1] Whence also the former cannot be effected under a condition or for a certain time only; whilst the latter may.

DCCCXXIX. An agreement between an insolvent debtor and the majority of his chirograph creditors did not, amongst the Romans, excepting in one case,[2] bind the remaining minority of the creditors; and this rule was both approved of by the Emperor *Charles* V. in his Placaat of 1544,[3] and seems to have been had in regard by the States in their Resolution of the 26th July, 1596.[4] It has since, however, been the rule, under various par-

* [Release by donation; see Text, § 5, supra.]
[1] Dig. ii. 14. 27.
[2] Dig. ii. 14. 7. § 17, 19; & ll. sqq.
[3] Art. 35.
[4] *Resol. van Holl. van* 1596, p. 307, f. sqq.

ticular Laws of Holland, that the minor part of the creditors ought to follow the majority, if three fourths of the creditors who are entitled to two thirds of the debts, or two thirds of the creditors who are entitled to three fourths of the debt, consent to the agreement; provided this agreement has been entered into by public authority, and the other provisions against fraud and collusion have been complied with. It has been so enacted at *Leyden*[5] and *Haarlem.*[6] The law of *Amsterdam*[7] was also formerly the same; but by the new law[8] it has been provided that whilst the property of the insolvent is merely in public custody, two or more creditors, to whom a twentieth part of the debt is owing, or even one to whom at least a sixth part is owing, may oppose an agreement entered into with the other creditors being confirmed by public authority, and thus prevent the property being immediately released from custody or sequestration.[9] But if the debtor, in consequence of such opposition, or even on a suspicion of fraud, is declared insolvent, then, after the creditors have received whatever could be realized out of the property, a debtor who has become impoverished by mere change of fortune, and has not acted fraudulently, is discharged from all liability, and *restituted*, provided one half of the creditors to whom a half of the debt is due consent to such restitution.[10] The law of *Dordrecht*[11]

---

[5] *Keur. van Leyden*, art. 204. n. 14, & 2 March 1665, 26 Decr. 1672, 27 March 1699, & 26 Sept. 1768.

[6] 10 Aug. 1709; *Keur. van Haarlem*, tom. i. p. 127, sqq.

[7] *Ord. Amst.* 13 Sept. 1659, *Handv. van Amst.* p. 687; 29 Jan. 1729, ibid. p. 690.

[8] 30 Jan. 1777; *Handv. Tweede Vervolg.* p. 104, sqq.

[9] Art. 13—17, d. l.   [10] Art. 42. d. l.

[11] 20 Decr. 1668, art. 11—14; *Groot Plac. B.* d. iv. p. 468, sq.

x

does not much differ from the laws we have referred to in respect of other parts of Holland.

DCCCXXX. Those creditors who have taken sureties, or the mortgage of immovables, or a pledge of movables duly delivered, or (as appears to me quite clear, though *Voet*[1] is of a different opinion) even those who hold a pledge of movables, the possession of which remains with the debtor, but whereon the duty of two and a half per cent. has been duly paid,—are left in the enjoyment of their rights.[2]

DCCCXXXI. Similar rules have been laid down in Zeeland by the general law of the 11th December, 1649, and the new law of the 27th June, 1776.[3]

DCCCXXXII. In the case in Dig. ii. 14. 7. § 19, where, even under the Roman law, in inducing an heir to adiate the inheritance of an insolvent debtor, the minor part of the creditors were obliged to follow the majority, such majority was estimated according to the amount of the debts, without reference to their number;[4] and the same rule should be followed under the present law also, except only at those places where, as regards agreements with creditors, the same rule has been expressly laid down in respect of an heir as in respect of a living insolvent debtor (as at *Amsterdam, Dordrecht, Leyden* and *Haarlem*); which does not, however, seem to have been done in Zeeland.[5]

---

[1] *Ad Pand.* ii. 14. § ult.

[2] Dig. ii. 14. 10. pr.; *Ord. Amst.* 1659, art. 9. and 1777, art. 19; *Dordr.* art. 14; Leid. A. 1672. [See the case of *Tatham* v. *Andree*, from Ceylon, decided by the Privy Council; 12 Weekly Rep. 22.—Tr.]

[3] Art. 10-16.   [4] Dig. ii. 14. 8.   [5] L. cit.

Chapter XLII.—Sec. 2.

DCCCXXXIII. The dissolution of a contract, effected not by way of gift, but by mutual consent, appears to have a wider effect than, and is different from, the mode in which consensual obligations are annulled by contrary consent,[6] for it will apply to any kind of contract, and may always be effected by the restoration of the thing given or the withdrawal of the cause or consideration of the contract.

Sec. 4.

DCCCXXXIV. By the term *Leesting*—Satisfaction —*Grotius* does not here mean *any* kind of satisfaction which may consist even in giving a pledge or mortgage (the obligation yet remaining in force),[7] nor even an acceptilation ; but only a giving in payment.

Chapter XLIII.—Sec. 4.

DCCCXXXV. Novation, amongst us also, as amongst the Romans,[8] is not held to have taken place, unless there appears to have been an intention to effect a novation; as decided by the Court on the 11th of November, 1609.[9]

DCCCXXXVI. A prorogation or postponement of the day of payment is not a novation, and therefore does not discharge a surety.[10] It is otherwise as regards

---

[6] Inst. iii. 24. § 4. [7] Inst. ii. l. § 41. [8] Cod. viii. 42. ult.

[9] *Decis. en Resol. van den Hove*, n. 201. And see *Thes.* 522; *Utr. Cons.* d. i. cons. 113 ; *Bell. Jurid.* cas. 30.

[10] Vinn. *Sil. Quæst.* l. ii. c. 42. *Nederl. Adv.* d. iv. cons. 247. [See also V. d. Linden, *Gewijsden*, p. 263 ; Leyd. 1803.—Tr.]

the prorogation of an obligation contracted for a particular time.[1]

CHAPTER XLIV.—SEC. 5.

DCCCXXXVII. An assignation, although accepted by the debtor of the assignor, does not operate as payment, nor have the effect of a novation or delegation from the consenting creditor having acceded to it,[2] unless it is proved to have been accepted by him as a transfer in payment or a sale of the right of action.[3]

CHAPTER XLV.—SEC. 1.

DCCCXXXVIII. Although in an assignation it is in most cases the debtor of the assignor who is requested to make payment, yet there is nothing to hinder payment being requested not of the debtor, but of the assignor who is about to have credit given him.[4]

DCCCXXXIX. From the definition of a bill of exchange given by Grotius in B. iii. *chap.* 13. *sec.* l. and the present definition of an assignation, *Lybrechts*[5] seems incorrectly to conclude that in bills of exchange there should be a *charge* or *command*, and in assignations a *request;* a distinction which could not occur to Grotius, who was not ignorant of the rule in Dig. xvii. l. 1. § 2.

[1] See *Thes.* 500. To which may be referred the case in *Bell. Jurid.* cas. 74.

[2] Neostad. *Decr. Cur. Holl.* 38 ; Schrassert, *Obs. Pract.* 420.

[3] Conf. *Stat. Antwerp,* cap. lxiv. art. 1 & 2.

[4] Conf. Heinecc. *Elem. Jur. Camb.* cap. iii. § 20.

[5] *Reden. Vert. over 't Not. ampt.* part. ii. cap. 39, § 3, junct. cap. 38. init.

DCCCXL. Neither can the other distinction be upheld, viz., that in a bill of exchange there are or are supposed to be four parties, whilst in an assignation there are only three,[6] for this does not always apply; nor can payment be requested of a debtor the less by a bill of exchange than by an assignation, because there happens to be only three parties to the bill.

DCCCXLI. The principal distinction is that in exchange a two-fold transaction is effected[7]—viz., a sale and purchase between the remittent and the drawer[8] (for which reason in a bill of exchange the receipt of the value should be expressly acknowledged);[9] and a mandate to pay money, between the drawer and the drawee :[10] whilst, on the other hand, in an assignation, there is only a simple mandate to pay money to the assignee.[11]

DCCCXLII. There frequently occurs also another distinction, viz.: that in bills of exchange it is customary, or under some laws is required, that mention should be made of the exchange; which at *Amsterdam*, in respect of bills drawn in Holland and payable in that city (even though as regards proceedings thereon,[12] they are not entitled to the summary process),[13] seems to produce rights different in other points, between such bills and a simple assignation.

DCCCXLIII. There is no real exchange, unless the bill has been drawn at one place and is to be paid at another ;[14] which in an assignation is not necessary.

---

⁶ Reitz *ad Heinecc.* cap. iii. § 21.
⁷ Th. 575.   ⁸ Th. 576.   ⁹ Th. 598.   ¹⁰ Th. 596.
¹¹ Savary. *Parfait. Negot.* tom. ii. par. 47. p. 184.
¹² *Willekeur. v. Amst.* 26 January 1679, art. 8.
¹³ Th. 597.   ¹⁴ Th. 597.

So, in the former a time is fixed for payment;[1] but not always so in an assignation.

DCCCXLIV. These transactions differ also in their effects. For bills of exchange cannot regularly be revoked;[2] but an assignation may; unless there has been a sale for value paid.

DCCCXLV. On a bill of exchange, when accepted, the summary cambial proceedings may be maintained; on an assignation, when accepted, only the ordinary action as for money promised.

DCCCXLVI. Similarly, upon non-payment of a bill of exchange, the drawer also may be sued in the cambial process; but where payment of an assignation has not been made, the assignor is not so liable.

DCCCXLVII. In case a bill of exchange has not been paid on the day appointed, a solemn protest should be made by the holder; but in the case of an assignation, this is not required; though the assignor should be informed of such non-payment. If no day has been appointed in the assignation, the recovery thereof may be deferred. At Amsterdam, however, in respect of cheques or receipts given on bankers (*Quitantien op Cassiers*), it is the rule, that if negotiated by the creditor himself they should be recovered within ten days, if delivered by a third party, within three days, or credit is held to have been given to the banker by the party holding them.[3]

DCCCXLVIII. A party to whom an assignation without the appointment of a day of payment, has been made, ought to take care not to delay too long the

---

[1] Th. 584, 605.   [2] Th. 579, sq.

[3] L. 20 Jan. 1776. *Tweede Verv. der Handv.* p. 83.

recovery of the payment assigned to him; for otherwise, he would, from the nature of a mandate, be under
a still greater liability to make good the loss than the
holder of a bill of exchange wherein no particular day
of payment has been fixed.[4]

DCCCXLIX. The assignate, or party whose debt
is assigned, can by no means be compelled to accept
the assignation, although the time for payment of the
debt which he is requested to pay may not only have
arrived, but have even elapsed.

DCCCL. Although an assignation may be indorsed,
in the same manner as a bill of exchange, yet there
is this distinction between the two, viz., that in an
assignation, a subsequent indorsee, in case of non-payment, has his remedy only against the last indorser, not,
as in a bill, against *any* prior indorser.[5]

DCCCLI. The other distinction, mentioned by
Reitz,[6] can hardly be said to exist at present, viz.: that
assignations may be taken in arrest or execution, whilst
bills cannot, for even at *Amsterdam*,[7] bills which have
been protested are only prohibited from being detained
in arrest, in the first instance, in the hands of a notary;[8] and there is no other prohibition in the Statutes
of Holland passed on this subject; though at the same
time it would not be unadvisable so to circumscribe the
right of arrest, that whilst the bills remain unpreju-

---

[4] Th. 582.
[5] Th. 592. Verwer, *van Bodemer.* in not. p. m. 188. Reitz. *ad*
Heinec. cap. iii. § 21, not. 42 ; n. 10. p. 120, and p. 125. not. 48. in f.
[6] *Ad Heinecc.* d. p. 120. u. 11, and p. 128.
[7] *Willek. v. Amst.* 24 Jan. 1651, confirmed 31 Jan. 1656 ; Phoonsen,
in app. p. 9. *Handv.* p. 542, 543.
[8] See hereon Phoonsen, cap. xix. n. 11. in not.

diced, the money payable thereon might be kept under arrest. Nor, it seems, ought there to be any distinction whether they are payable at a public bank, or at the private residence; although money in a bank, or the right of disposing of it, cannot be put under arrest.[1]

SEC. 2.

DCCCLII. Assignations and Bills of Exchange are similar also in this respect, viz.: that they have not *per se* the effect of a delegation, and that the drawer or assignor is not discharged except by payment.[2]

SEC. 3.

DCCCLIII. The holder of a bill, whether he be the remittent or the payee, or an indorsee, or any other to whom it has been delivered, ought, if no particular time for payment has been fixed, and if payment *ex gr.* depends upon its presentation, to present it in due time to the drawee for acceptance. The time, however, within which it should be presented has not been fixed by our laws.[3] In bills wherein a particular day has been fixed for payment, this presentation for acceptance is indeed advisable, but not necessary,[4] and the opinion in *de Adviesen over den Koophandel, d.* ii. *cons.* 24, seems to apply to such bills.[5]

[1] *Willek. v. Amst.* 31 Dec. 1670. See hereon Reitz, d. 1. nol. 53. in f. p. 130.

[2] Roseboom, *Costum. van Amst.* cap. 1. art. 3; Dupuis, cap. xi, p. m. 451.   [3] Phoonsen, cap. x. n. 21, 22.

[4] Dupuis, cap. vi. n. 4, 5; Savary, tom. i. lib. 3. c. 5. p. 75; Reitz *ad Heinecc.* cap. iv. § 26. p. 187.

[5] And see *Verzam. van Casus-posit.* cas. 15. p. 132, sqq.

DCCCLIV. If the bill has not been accepted, a protest should be made in that behalf within three days, not only in the case of bills wherein no particular day has been fixed for payment, but also of those wherein a day has been fixed; for the laws make no distinction herein.[6] But whether, in this case, a fresh protest of the subsequent non-payment should also be made seems to depend on the particular circumstances of each case.[7]

SEC. 4.

DCCCLV. If, after the bill has been accepted, it is not paid on the day it falls due, a protest of such non-payment may be made, not indeed on the same day (the whole of which is allowed to the debtor),[8] but on the following day.[9] It has, however, almost become a custom, and is indeed more advisable, not to make the protest before the fourth day of grace, in order that the holder might not lose the expenses incurred on the bill;[10] or, if payment happens to be tendered before such time, he might incur losses in other respects. Clearly, a protest made on the very day is of no use;[11] unless the acceptor had previously become insolvent.[12]

[6] Roseboom, *Cost. van Amst.* cap. 1. art. 4.
[7] Phoonsen, tot. cap. xiii, and particularly n. 4 & 8; Dupuis, cap. vii. n. 7. Infra, *Thes.* 861, 862. See *Advies. over den Kooph.* d. ii. cons. 33.   [8] Inst. iii. 15. § 2.
[9] *Keur. v. Amst.* 6 Febr. 1663; *Handv.* p. 544; *Keur. van Rotterd.* 24 Aug. 1720, art. 8, in Reitz. *ad Heinecc.* in Append. p. 630; & *Ord. Middelb.* 24 Mar. 1736, art. 7; ibid. p. 624.   [10] Th. 627.
[11] *Advies. over den Kooph.* d. ii. cons. 44; Dupuis, cap. vii. n. 3, & reg. i. p. 445.
[12] *Advies.* ib. cons. 38. p. 143, sq.; cons. 43. p. 166; cons. 44. p. 171, & cons. 45. p. 176, sqq.

DCCCLVI. The time within which a protest should be made is defined by the most recent law,—a distinction being made between bills drawn here and payable in a foreign country, and those drawn in a foreign country and payable here,—as follows, viz., that as regards the former, the protest should be made according to the law of the place where the bill is payable;[1] but as regards the latter, within six consecutive days after that on which payment was due.[2] If, however, the bill is payable at a bank, and it happens to be closed during the six days, the protest should be made at the most within three days after the opening of the bank;[3] and this rule has been extended to those bills also, which where the bank had reopened before the lapse of the entire period of six days, might still have been paid on the fifth or sixth day.[4]

Sec. 5.

DCCCLVII. If the protest be not made within the above time, the holder loses his remedy against the drawer and the indorsers. This has also been specially provided at *Amsterdam*.[5] Such a protest is also necessary in respect of bills drawn by the drawer on himself

---

[1] See hereon more fully, Dupuis, cap. xiv. n. 14, sqq.

[2] See *Willek. v. Amst.* 31 July 1660, art. 1, 2; *Handv.* p. 543; *Rotterd.* art. 7, 8; *Middelb.* art. 2, 3.

[3] *D. Willek. Amst.* A. 1660, art. 2; *Publ. Amst.* 6 Feb. 1663; art. 2, 3; Handv. p. 544, and *Willekeur.* 26 Jan. 1679, art. 4; Ibid. p. 545.

[4] *Willekeur. v. Amst.* 31 Jan. 1764, in fin. *Tweede Vervolg. van Handv.* p. 81. [Reitz. *ad Heinecc.* p. 249 & 636.]

[5] *Keur.* 29 Mar. 1661; *Handv.* p. 543. n. 5.

and then indorsed, if the holder desires to have his remedy against the indorsers also.[6] DCCCLVIII. This protest for non-payment is not necessary as regards the drawer, if he is clearly not interested therein, as where he has drawn on a party who is not indebted to him, or at least the drawee has no money in his hands on the appointed day wherewith to pay the bill.[7] But if the drawee was indebted to the drawer, and the holder has not protested within the proper time, even where one day has been allowed to elapse by mistake, it has been correctly laid down that the drawer is discharged, although perhaps he cannot be proved to have sustained any loss in consequence of the tardy protest.[8]

Sec. 6.

DCCCLIX. If the acceptor refuses to pay, or conceals himself, or is publicly accounted as insolvent, the protest should, as well by the former as by the most recent law,[9] be made within three days.[10]

Sec. 7.

DCCCLX. Although the holder cannot during the period of grace enter into any agreement with the

---

[6] Phoonsen, cap. xvii. n. 13; *Verzam. van Casus-posit* cas. 9. p. 92, sqq.

[7] *Holl. Cons.* d. iii. st. 1. cons. 59; d. vi. cons. 37; Phoonsen, cap. xvii. n. 12. in not; Savary, l. iii. c. 6. p. 94. 95; & cap. 10. p. 124.

[8] *Advies. over den Kooph.* d. ii. cons. 11; others, however (ibid. cons. 9, 10), dissenting.

[9] Since the law of *Amsterdam* of 1660, art. 2.

[10] On the evidence given 17 Mar. 1663; *Hand. van Amst.* p. 544.

acceptor, as to granting time or remitting a part of the debt;[1] yet he is not prohibited from accepting a part of the debt, and afterwards protesting for non-payment of the remainder :[2] but he cannot, even after the period of grace, enter into any stipulation or accede to any agreement between third parties, unless he renounces his right against all the parties concerned—the drawer, the remittent, and the prior indorsees ;—and in the agreement itself reserves to every one his own rights.[3]

SEO. 8.

DCCCLXI. The protest for non-acceptance or non-payment of a bill, should in the first instance be sent to the party from whom the holder received the bill, or directly to the drawer, notice, however, being at the same time given to the former.[4] But whether the bill itself should be sent together with the protest, or whether it is safer to transmit it to some other friend— these are questions which cannot be disposed of in a single definition. If, however, the protest be for non-acceptance, it may be more advisable, and sometimes also necessary, not to transmit the bill itself; so that when the day for payment arrives, it may be presented a second time, and, on default of payment, a fresh pro-

---

[1] *Stat. Antw.* cap. lv. art. 10; Roseboom, cap. 1. art. 7; Savary, 1, iii. c. 6. p. 80.

[2] Phoonsen, cap. xvii. n. 19, 20; *Advies. over den Kooph.* d. ii. cons. 35.

[3] Dupuis. cap. xvi. reg. 4, 5. p. m. 475.

[4] *Stat. Antwerp.* cap. lv. art. 11; Roseboom, cap. 1. art. 8; Phoonsen. cap. xix. n. 3, 4, 5.

test may be made: which should be decided upon according to the circumstances of each case.[5]

SEC. 9.

DCCCLXII. If a bill has been protested for non-acceptance, the remittent may legally demand from the drawer, or the holder from the remittent or drawer, or lastly even the subsequent indorsees from the prior indorsers, personal or other security for the payment of the sum mentioned in the bill, together with the amount of the exchange and re-exchange, if the bill should afterwards happen to be returned protested for non-payment.[6] In the Statute of *Antwerp* last quoted,[6] a second case is given, where security may similarly be demanded, viz., when, after acceptance, payment is not made on the appointed day, and the days of grace have not yet elapsed. For where the days of grace have elapsed, if protest has been duly made, the holder may at once claim indemnity in full right; or, if no protest has been made, he is without any remedy against the indorsers and the drawer.[7]

SEC. 10.

DCCCLXIII. Upon acceptance of the bill, the drawee becomes liable to all the parties concerned,—to the drawer,[8] the remittent, the holder, and the indorsees ;[9] and may be sued in the summary action in

---

[5] See supra, *Thes.* 854 ; & Phoonsen, ib.—and see Savary, l. iii. cap. 6. p. 81.

[6] *Stat. Antwerp.* cap. lv. art. 2 ; Savary, l. iii. c. 6. p. 81 ; Phoonsen, cap. xxxi. § 7, sq.

[7] Supra, *Thes.* 857 : and see *Thes.* 579, 585.

[8] Th. 590   [9] Tb. 591.

exchange.[1] From the nature of the transaction, however, he has himself no counter-action against the indorsers.[2]

DCCCLXIV. Upon the person who has accepted the bill failing to pay, the remittent, as well as the holder or indorsees, after protest duly made, have their remedy against the drawer. But the drawer, if he had drawn the bill upon the mandate of a third party, will have such third party liable to him on the *actio mandati contraria*. And hence the jurists and the merchants have both given it as their opinion,[3] that the drawer, the drawee who has accepted, and the mandant, are liable to each other *in solidum*.

DCCCLXV. A subsequent indorsee, also, who holds the bill, may sue the prior indorsers; nor is it necessary that he should first proceed against the drawer, or, where the bill has already been accepted, and protest of the non-payment thereof duly made as against the acceptor, that he should make another protest as against the drawer.[4] He may sue any one of several indorsers whom he chooses.[5]

DCCCLXVI. If, however, a person has upon the mandate of another merchant bought a bill already drawn which he *bonâ fide* and after diligent inquiry believed to be a good bill, and has had it endorsed to himself for value paid, but has himself indorsed it to his mandant, and he to another; he may indeed be sued upon it by that other,[6] but not by the mandant, for whom he had

---

[1] Th. 624.
[2] See the evidence given at *Amsterdam*, 27 Feb. 1662: *Handv.* p. 544.
[3] 29 July 1788; *Verzam. van Casus-posit.* cas. 6.
[4] *Willek. v. Amst.* 31 January 1764.   [5] Th. 592.
[6] Dupuis, cap. xvi. n. 11.

directly acquired the property in the bill; as held by
the jurists on the 26th August, 1788; and confirmed
by several merchants on the 29th August, 1788.[7]
Others, however,[8] restrict this rule, but, as appears to
me, incorrectly,[9] to the case where the party has received any salary or remuneration for the business.

DCCCLXVII. A drawer, who after receiving value
has fraudulently drawn bills on one whom he knew
could nowhere be found, or would not pay the bill, is
liable not only for the principal amount and the amount
of the exchange and re-exchange, and all other
damages, but is also liable in a further amount for the
use of another's money. And hence it has been generally
enacted at *Amsterdam*[10] that the drawer, if the bill has
not been accepted or paid, should pay to the remitter
three per cent. on the principal.[11] The same rule has
also been laid down at *Middelburg.*[12] At *Rotterdam*
interest at the rate of four per cent. should be paid.[13]

DCCCLXVIII. If the bill has travelled through
several places, and the holder desires to recover the re-
exchange from the drawer, he ought regularly to draw
a bill of re-exchange on the place at which the former
bill was drawn:[14] unless there is no exchange between
the place where the payment ought to have been made,
and the one where the bill was drawn.[15]

---

[7] *Verzam. van Casus-posit.* cas. 7.

[8] *Advies. over den Kooph.* d. ii. cons. 41.   [9] Consult Th. 570.

[10] *Willek. v. Amst.* 26 Jan. 1679, art. 2.

[11] *Handv.* p. 545.

[12] *Ord. Middelb.* 24 March 1736, art. 8; see Reitz. in *Append. p.*
625.

[13] *Keur. Rotterd.* 24 Aug. 1724, art. 16; Ibid. p. 632.

[14] Savary, l. iii. c. 11. p. 133, sqq.

[15] Dupuis, cap. xv. n. 16, sqq. p. 459, sqq.

DCCCLXIX. As regards the re-exchange and other losses, both the drawer, and the drawee who has accepted, are indeed each liable to the holder *in solidum*; but the drawer himself can sue the drawee for such loss, or plead it by way of exception against him, only in case the drawee was indebted to him at the time of accepting the bill, or at least previous to the day of payment, or, if the bill has not been accepted, had previously (whether indebted to the drawer or not) given his consent to the bill being drawn on him.[1] Excepting in these cases, he must bear the loss himself.[2]

SEC. 11.

DCCCLXX. Since the acceptor, the drawer, the indorsers, and the remittent are all liable to the holder, each *in solidum*, without benefit of division or excussion,[3] he may, in case they all become insolvent, institute his action against any one of them he chooses; and indeed, as against the party whom he first sues, for the whole amount; but as against the others, only for such amount as he has failed to recover from the goods of the former; for that which he has recovered from him, *ipso jure* diminishes his claim against the others; and he ought in respect of such portion to cede his action to the assignee of his estate; and so forth.[4] He cannot, however, consent to any agreement for remitting any part of the debt to the party whom he first sues, without the consent of the others, from whom he cannot afterwards recover the residue without a cession of action.[5]

[1] Savary, l. iii. c. 11. p. 133. [2] And see *Thes.* 616.
[3] Dupuis, cap. xvi. n. 1, sqq.
[4] Ibid. n. 20, sqq. p. 462, sqq. Phoonsen, cap. xli. § 45, sqq.
[5] Dupuis, ib. p. 470, 472.

Conclusion of the Subject.

DCCCLXXI. *Janus Bondt*, in his dissertation *de periculo damni ex falso in literis cambialibus commisso*,[6] has accurately treated of the liabilities arising from the forgery or falsification of bills of exchange ; and from the following precise and simple principles, viz. : 1 That no one can be made liable on a contract without his own consent ;[7] 2. That no one can acquire a right from his own wrong ;[8] 3. That no one can transfer to another that which he does not legally possess ;[9] 4. That he who contracts with another ought to be careful in whom he confides ;[10]—from these principles he draws the following general rule,—*that a loss arising from forgery in a bill of exchange, where the party who has committed the forgery cannot be found, falls on him who has contracted with that party and derives his title from him.*

DCCCLXXII. This rule applies, whether the forgery has been committed in the bill itself, or in the endorsements ; and whether in the name of the persons who have subscribed to the bill, or in the sum payable thereon ; and whether before or after acceptance ; and even, if in consequence of the sum having been falsified, the acceptor has paid a larger sum, the drawer, as mandator, is not bound to repay more than he has drawn for ; though *Reitz*[11] is of a different, but clearly incorrect, opinion.

DCCCLXXIII. If a false endorsement has been

---

[6] Lugd. Bat. 1788.

[7] See Dig. 1. 17. 34.

[8] Dig. xlvii. 2. 12, § 1 ; Cod. ix. 22. 18.

[9] Dig. 1. 17. 54.

[10] Dig. 1. 17. 19 ; Cod. vi. 2. 2

[11] *Ad Heinecc.* cap. vii. part. 2. § 11. p. 433, sq.

Y

made by a person who has stolen the bill, it is indeed clear that the holder, from whom it was stolen, may by right of his ownership claim it from the thief himself, or from the indorsees who derive their title from him;[1] but if it has been already paid to the falsifier or his indorsees, there is a doubt whether the holder may claim it equally from the drawee? For the affirmative, there is the circumstance—that by the mere act of payment the rightful owner cannot be deprived of his *dominium* or ownership; and that the drawee is bound to know to whom he makes payment.[2] For the negative see the authorites cited below.[3]

CHAPTER XLVI.—SEC. 2.

DCCCLXXIV. Although this doctrine of *Grotius*, viz. : that prescription extinguishes a personal action, not by force of the exception taken, but *ipso jure*,—seems to be in accordance with the express words of certain ancient statutes ;[4] yet it is not free from difficulties; for if an action for the principal debt is barred *ipso jure* by the lapse of thirty years, how can the hypothecary action against the same debtor remain for a period of forty years ?—which, however, Grotius himself has laid down in B. ii. ch. 48, § 44, and is supported by 1. 2 of the Code viii. 31.[5]

---

[1] See *de Advies. over den Kooph.* d. ii. cons. 39.

[2] Dupuis, cap. xiii. § 13, & reg. 2.

[3] Verwer. in not. *ad Tract. de Bodemeria,* § 31. p. 195, sq., and Dig. xvii. 2. 52. § 3. junct. Dig. l. 17. 128. pr.

[4] *Bechtsgel. Obs.* part. ii. obs. 97 ; *Costum. van Rhynland,* art. 102.

[5] And see Aver.an. *Int. Jur.* l. ii. c. 12.

SEC. 5.

DCCCLXXV. In respect of annual rents, it is not the mere prescription of thirty years which releases the debtor; but as many prescriptions are necessary as there are annual payments;[6] and it has also been so decided by the Court.[7] But if the estate, from which the annual rent is to be paid is in the possession of a third party, to whom the creditor has given no notice of this incumbrance, such third party is protected by the 30-years prescription (as decided by the Court on the 5th of June, 1609);[8] or, at least, by the prescription of the third of a century, as declared by the Court in 1629.[9]

SEC. 7.

DCCCLXXVI. Whether the prescription of two years introduced by the Placaat of the 4th of October, 1540,[10] and approved of in the *Instructions of the Supreme Court* of 1582,[11] as regards the fees of Advocates and similar other debts, not due on a writing, is still received in practice, has been a subject of controversy. Two of the judges, in *de Decisien en Resolutien van den Hove*,[12] and other jurists[13] maintain the negative; and in Merula's *Civil Practice* it is cited also as the opinion

---

[6] Cod. vii. 39. 7, § ult. vs. *in his etiam promiss.*; Bynkershoek, *Q. J. Priv.* l. ii. c. 15.

[7] 10 May, 1613; *Decis. en Resol. van den Hove*, n. 399; & 28 Jan. 1637; Loenius, *Decis.* 76.

[8] *Decis. en Resol. van den Hove*, n. 186.

[9] See Loen. *Decis.* 45, p. 293.   [10] Art. 16.   [11] Art. 165.

[12] N. 433, § 2.

[13] See Not. ad Merula, *Man. van Proced.* l. iv. t. 108. cap. 2. § 1, 2.

of the Court.[1] *Coren*[2] on the other hand, maintains the affirmative. And in this conflict of opinions, the proof of a custom contrary to the law, may, I think, be justly thrown on the party alleging it.

CHAPTER XLVIII.—SEC. 1.

DCCCLXXVII. Although in transactions which are *ipso jure* void, such for instance, as have been contracted in fraud or fear, it is usual for the sake of greater security to apply for *restitutio in integrum*,[3] yet this is not a matter of necessity; and upon proof of *læsio*, the defendant should be absolved, even without relief.[4]

DCCCLXXVIII. Where relief has been applied for, but has not as yet been granted by the judge who has taken cognizance thereof, this does not amongst us as under the Canon Law,[5] suspend the contract or transaction, and therefore does not even prevent a sentence of provisional payment.[6]

DCCCLXXIX. It would hardly seem to be permitted either by our customs, or by the analogy of the Dutch Law, that relief should be granted on the ground of minority, to a widow under twenty-five years of age, who has been injured (*læsa*) in a contract; and herein we agree with *Rodenburg, Groenewegen*, and *Voet*.[7]

---

[1] 23 May, 1681.　　[2] *Consil.* 16, 29.　　[3] Voet *ad Pand.* iv. 1, § 13.
[4] Groeneweg. *ad Cod.* ii. 41. § 5, sqq.　See *Thes.* 666.
[5] X. *de in int. rest.* c. 6.
[6] Neostad. *Supr. Cur. Dec.* dec. 73; Voet *ad Pand.* iv. 1. § 25.
[7] *Ad Pand.* iv. 4. § 9. See *Thes.* 506, in f.

SEC. 10.

[See note* below.]

SEC. 11.

DCCCLXXX. The rule laid down by *Groenewegen*,[8] and *Voet*,[9] viz.: that relief is not to be granted to a girl under twenty-five years of age against a promise of excessive dowry or marriage-gift,—does not seem to be sufficiently supported by the arguments advanced by them.

SEC. 13.

DCCCLXXXI. *Grotius* here quite correctly, and in accordance with the reason of law, lays down that the right to relief on the ground of fraud or fear is not prescribed by the lapse of four years, but is perpetual, *i.e.*, endures for thirty years; and this opinion is supported by the law of the Digest[10] and Code.[11] We need not, therefore, notice here the doubts of other authors on the subject.†

CHAPTER L.—SEC. 1.

DCCCLXXXII. The practice as regards the tender of the suppletory oath in Court by one party to the

[* Read the text of Grotius, in Mr. Herbert's Translation, as follows: "This is not to be understood of contracts which minors enter into without their guardians (for these are null); but of those which they enter into *with* their guardians, or are contracted by the guardians alone."—Tr.]

[8] *Ad Cod.* ii. 34. & *Cod.* ii. 30. 1.   [9] *Ad Pand.* iv. 4. § 18, 19.

[10] Dig. iv. 3. 28.   [11] Cod. ii. 20. 4.

[† Viz. Groeneweg. *de ll. abrog.* ad Cod. ii. 53.7; Cod. ii. 21.8; Voet *ad Pand.* iv. 3. § 20; and iv. 2. § 18.—Tr.]

other, not only prevailed amongst us in former times,[1] but is still allowed by our customs.[2] This oath may be tendered even in respect of minor offences, as in a case of injury, or of damage arising from injury;[3] but not in respect of graver offences.[4]

CHAPTER LI.—SEC. 2.

DCCCLXXXIII. That the benefit of *Cessio bonorum* had already come into use amongst us towards the end of the 15th century, appears from a report of certain disputes between the magistrates of *Leyden*, respecting its having been too readily granted to the Count of Holland.[5]

DCCCLXXXIV. Since the benefit of *Cessio bonorum* does not discharge a debtor, so also it does not prevent the condemnation of a debtor who had been previously summoned, execution being, however, suspended, until the judge shall have decided upon the application for the benefit; as decided by the Supreme Court on the 27th July, 1776. It does not even suspend the effect of an arrest already obtained, as decided by the same Court on the 14th November, 1776; although, after cession has been applied for, an arrest cannot, pending the application, be imposed on the

---

[1] *Rechtsgel. Obs.* part ii. obs. 99; *Keur. van Leiden.* van 1583, art. 128, & edit. 1658, art. 190.

[2] See not. ad Merula, *Man. van Proc.* l. iv. t. 71. cap. i. § 3. p. 213. [edit. 1783.]

[3] Voet *ad Pand.* xii. 2. § 10.

[4] Ibid. § 27; *Rechtsgel. Obs.* part. ii. obs. 99. and *Supplem.* part iv. p. 257.

[5] See Privil. 30 July 1501; in Mieris, *Handv. van Leyden*, p. 193.

debtor; as decided by the Court on the 11th July, 1791.[6]

SEC. 3.

DCCCLXXXV. If the benefit of Cession is applied for by a person who is detained under arrest by the Court, the Court cannot itself take cognizance of the application, as long since held by the Court itself;[7] but whether detained by the Court, or by any other judge it is the judge of the domicile who should take cognizance of it; as decreed by a Resolution of the States of the 23rd September, 1688.[8]

SEC. 4.

DCCCLXXXVI. If a foreigner is detained in arrest, or has been condemned by the sentence of a judge, in Holland, the benefit of *Cessio bonorum* should not be granted to him, unless the same indulgence is granted to Dutch citizens in his own country; as held by the Court of Holland on the 21st March, 1640,[7] and by the Supreme Court.[9]

SEC. 5.

DCCCLXXXVII. Guardians are not entitled to the benefit of cession as regards a debt due by them in respect of their guardianship; as expressly laid down

---

[6] See van der Linden, *Form van Proced.* b. ii. h. 31. § 3, p. 396, sqq.
[7] Voet *ad Pand.* xlii. 3. § 6.
[8] *Rechtsgel. Obs.* part. iii. obs. 100. [See Gr. Plac. Boek, d. iv. pag. 463.] And see Decision of the Supr. Court, 15 April, 1723, in Bynkershoek, *Q. J. Priv.* l. i. c. 3. p. 38.
[9] Loen. *Decis.* 94.
[10] See Groeneweg. *ad Cod.* vii. 71. 4, § 3.

in various pupillary laws,[1] which *Voet*[2] does not seem to have seen.

DCCCLXXXVIII. A person who owes a fine or pecuniary penalty, in respect of a delict, based on fraud even where corporal punishment in case of the delinquent's inability to pay the fine has not been put in the alternative with the pecuniary punishment, is not discharged from custody, by the benefit of *Cessio bonorum ;* as decided by the Court on the 3rd December, 1637,[3] and by the Supreme Court on the 21st March, 1738.[4] As regards delicts arising from neglect (*culpa*), a different rule should be observed ;[5] notwithstanding the doctrine of *Bynkershoek,*[6] that there can hardly be a delict unaccompanied by fraud ; for there really are such, and Grotius himself has enumerated several.[7]

SEC. 7.

DCCCLXXXIX. The benefit of *Cessio bonorum* even in those places where the cedent in former times suffered a certain amount of ignominy, does not, as *Groenewegen* and others[8] have supposed, discharge him from the remainder of his debts. The contrary appears from a Charter granted on the complaint of the inhabitants of Leyden.[9]

---

[1] *Keur. van Enkhuisen, Alkmaar, Monnickendam, Purmerend, de Zype,* t. vi. art. 4 ; *Briel.* art. 89 ; *Gorinchem,* art. 31.
[2] *Ad Pand.* xlii. 3. § 5, in fin.   [3] Loen. *Decis.* 81.
[4] Bynkersh. *Q. J. Priv.* l. ii. c. 12.
[5] Dig. xvii. 2. 63. § 7.   [6] Ibid. p. 307.
[7] B. iii. ch. xxxiii. § 5, 6 ; ch. xxxvii. § 2, 6, 7, 8 ; ch. xxxviii. § 16, 17, 18.
[8] *Ad Dig.* xlii. 3. 6. See also Boel *ad Loen. Decis.* 94. p. 589, sqq.
[9] Mieris, cited Th. 883.

SEC. 8.

DCCCXC. In order to obtain letters of *Respite* or *Induction*, it is required that the debtor should give good personal[10] or other security, to the satisfaction of his creditors, for the payment of all his debts. The *cautio juratoria*, or security of his oath, is not sufficient.[11]

DCCCXCI. In respect of letters of respite, the consent of the majority of the creditors is also necessary; though the Placaat of 1544[12] makes no mention of this requisite (which circumstance is relied upon by the jurists in the *Rechtsgeleerde Observatien*,[13] in arguing against the rule laid down by *Grotius*). For it was not the Emperor *Charles* who first introduced this benefit out of the Roman Law, nor did he dispense with this requisite, which under the law of the Code, vii. 71. 8. is necessary; but he rather has expressly approved of it in *art.* 35, which can by no means be understood as referring to letters of induction, of which no mention whatever is made in the Placaat, or in the *Instructions of the Court*, and which were perhaps as yet unknown at that time. Nor does the opinion of *Voet*[14] and others affect the subject, supported as they are by no new argument, and which cannot therefore overrule the authority of *Grotius*, and the manifest utility and equity of the law of the Code above cited.

DCCCXCII. The application for letters of *induction* is usually made to the Court, as the common

---

[10] Code i. 19. 4; *Placaat van 1544*, art. 32, 33, 34.

[11] *Bell. Jur.* cas. 39. p. 259 ; & cas. 53. p. 415.

[12] Art. 32.   [13] Part. iv. obs. 50·

[14] *Ad Pand.* xlii. 3. § 20.

superior tribunal; and all the creditors are cited by the Court, to answer before the judge of the debtor's domicile, concerning the grounds on which the delay is applied for, or suffer themselves to be *induced* to allow this indulgence. If the majority of the creditors consent to it, the judge, by virtue of his office, decrees the confirmation of the mandate.[1]

DCCCXCIII. These letters differ from the induction which some judges have the right of granting, to persuade a creditor to grant a debtor, who has already been summoned, time for payment; and it is to this kind of induction that the decrees of the Court in *de Decisien en Resolutien van den Hove*, n. 48 & 346[2] as well as the case reported in *Loenius' Decisions, cas.* 18, have reference.

DCCCXCIV. The benefit of safe-conduct (*seureté du corps*) has also been adopted by us. This may be obtained from the States by debtors who are in concealment or residing in a foreign country, under apprehension of arrest, and who believe that they are able to effect an equitable arrangement with their creditors. It is not, however, granted, except with the consent of the majority of the creditors; nor as against a sentence of the Supreme Court, or any other sentence which has passed into a *res judicata*.[3] If to the application there are added letters commendatory from the magistrates of a Dutch State, then after the principal creditors have been heard by the Commissioners appointed for

---

[1] See Van der Linden, *Form van Proced.* B. ii. h. 33.

[2] There is a fuller report of the latter decision in *'t Groot Plac.* B. d. i. p. 1454.

[3] *Resol.* 19 Oct. 1605; *Decis. en Resol. van den Hove,* n. 23; *Groot Plac.* B. d. viii. p. 69.

the causes of improverished debtors, a previous application for the advice of the Court is not necessary.[4]

DCCCXCV. The fourth benefit (but one not a little opposed to equity and the principles of law) is the benefit granted by the supreme power, called *Surcheance van Betaling*, or suspension of payment, by which, without any consent of creditors, and without any security, personal or real (which in former times was properly required by the States[5]), a delay of one year is granted to the debtor,—all actions, arrests, and executions, whereby the creditors may recover their dues, being in the mean time suspended. The States, however, to prevent too great an abuse of this remedy, have directed various precautions to be observed herein.[6]

CHAPTER LII.—SEC. 2.

DCCCXCVI. *Grotius* has elsewhere,[7] as well as in the present treatise, laid down that a compromise may be rescinded on the ground of enormous wrong (*enormis læsio*); and the Supreme Court is also said to have so decided;[8] though the date of the decision is not known.[9] But such a doctrine can hardly be received, consistently with the reason of law, unless the practice of the Court

---

[4] *Resol. Holl.* 9 Dec. 1763; *Groot Plac. B.* d. ix. p. 19. Van der Linden, *Form van Proced.* B. iv. h. 7. § 6.

[5] 26 July, 1596; *Resol. van Holl. van* 1596, p. 308.

[6] *Resol. Holl.* 26 Feb. 1784; and 15 Nov. 1793; *Groot Plac. B.* d. ix. p. 558, 564. And see Van der Linden, *Form van Proced.* B. iv. h. 7, § 7, 8.

[7] In *de Holl. cons.* d. iii. st. 2. cons. 304. n. 1, 2.

[8] See Bronchorst, ἐναρτιοφ. cent. ii. assert. 58, in f.

[9] *Rechtsgel. Obs.* part. i. obs. 100.

has overruled the latter.[1] This, however, is clear, that the Supreme Court has refused to rescind a compromise which had been confirmed by a voluntary condemnation.[2]

DCCCXCVII. If in an assignment of property made by a surviving parent to the children, the parent or the creditors have been prejudiced, they are relieved by *restitutio in integrum.*[3]

DCCCXCVIII. What *Grotius* has here laid down, viz., that the remedy under the Code iv. 44. 2, is applicable to all transactions, should not, according to *Voet,*[4] be extended to matters of strict law, in respect of which this remedy cannot hold ; but should be understood, as *Grotius* himself has elsewhere laid down,[5] of permutatory contracts.

DCCCXCIX. This remedy under the Code iv. 44. 2, does not hold as against public sales held under the order of a magistrate, as, for instance, in execution of a judgment; as decided by the Supreme Court.[6] In other sales, which have been voluntarily effected, some authors think it should be allowed ;[7] but this, though in accordance with the Civil Law, appears to me to be hardly reconcilable with our customs.[8]

SEC. 4.

DCCCC. Though relief on the ground of minority

---

[1] Voet *ad Pand.* ii. 15. § ult. & xviii. 5. § 14. in f.
[2] 13 September, 1623; Coren, *Obs.* 14.
[3] *Decis. en Resol. van den Hove. van Holl.* n. 106.
[4] *Ad Pand.* xviii. 5. § 14.
[5] *De Jur. B. & Plac.* l. ii. c. 12, § 11. n. 1.
[6] Neostad. *Supr. Cur. Decis.* 75, 128.
[7] See Voet *ad Pand.* xviii. 5. § 16.
[8] See van Leeuwen, *Cens. For.* part i. l. iv. c. 44. n. 3.

is prescribed in four years, yet it may be easily proved from the Roman Law, supported by the analogy of our own law, that a minor as well as a major may be relieved on the ground of enormous wrong, at any time within thirty years.[9]

SEC. 5.

DCCCCI. According to the more correct rule of the Roman Law, the remedy under the Code iv. 44. 2, is by action on the contract itself; but it has become the practice in our Courts to take advantage of it by way of *restitutio in integrum.*[10]

---

[9] See *Thes.* 881.   [10] Groeneweg. *ad Cod.* iv. 44. 2.

INDEX.

A.

ABDUCTION

distinguished from Rape, *Thes*, 71.

defined, 72.

consequences of, *ib.*

community does not take place on, 218.

ABSENTEES

property devolving on, 167.

ACCEPTANCE

of a bill of exchange, force of, 590.

how given, 618.

not revocable, 619.

liability of drawee upon, 863.

on behalf of another, 510.

for honour, 594.

in *aval*, *ib.*

supra protest, defined, 607.

———— by whom, 608.

———— for whom, 609.

———— several parties offering, 610.

———— liability of acceptor, 611.

———— of the other parties, *ib.*

———— holder not bound to acquiesce in, 612.

ACCEPTILATION

distinction between and *Pactum de non petendo*, 828.

ACCEPTOR

supra protest, rights and liability of, 611.

cannot revoke acceptance, 619.

cannot require the bill to be delivered before payment, 622.

supra protest, cannot sue with cession of action, 607.

———— when entitled to the summary process, *ib.*

ACCIDENT

to a deposit, 532.

———— pledge, 540.

ACCOUNTS

of guardians, 120, 157.

books of, left by a surviving parent, 147.

ACCRETION, 322.

among co-heirs and co-legatees, 326.

succession by, in Zeeland, 367.

ACTIO PAULIANA

to rescind fraudulent alienations, 200.

ACTION

on espousals, 57, 58.

———— ———— when debarred, 85.

for indemnity, by wife against husband, 98.

in rem, considered as an immovable, 179.

in personam, considered as a movable, *ib.*

by possessor against owner, 212.

by lessee against owner, 213.

for collation, not maintainable during marriage, 256.

may be acquired through an agent, 478.

on a donation, to compel performance of a condition, 488.

cession of, to a surety, when effectual, 506.

———— seller when discharged, 578.

pro socio, 700.

conditio indebiti, 796, 797.

prescription of, 206, 874.

ACTS

validity of, when not executed according to *lex loci*, 41.

ADIATION

does not pass an inheritance *ipso jure*, 182.

ADIATION (continued)
rights of creditors to compel, 832.

ADMINISTRATION
of property granted to wife, during husband's insanity, 101.

ADOPTION
of children, 102.

ADULTERER
homicide of, when excused, 799. 800.

ADULTERY
ground for divorce and forfeiture of rights, 88.

ADVENTITIOUS PROPERTY
of minor children, 105.

ADVICE
letter of, 606.

ADVOCATE
fees of, entitled to preference, 451.

AGENT
property of, when and to what extent bound in tacit mortgage to principal, 426.
liability of, on a bill drawn by him on the principal, 615.

AGREEMENT
not comprehended under movables or immovables, 178.
between insolvent and his creditors, 829.
—— does not affect creditors holding security, 830, 831.

ALIENATION
by husband of the wife's property, 97, 98.
in fraud of creditors, before cession, 199.
—— may be rescinded, when and how, 200.
of movables and securities, by simple delivery, 201.
of ships and annual rents, ib.
of immovable property, 202.
by testator, of property already bequeathed, 336.
of usufruct, 372, 373.
of emphyteusis, 379, 380.
of a matter in dispute, by compromise, 516.

ALLODIAL PROPERTY
if purchased by husband with common money, 390.
difference between acquisition of, and of feuds, 401.

ALLUVION
augmentation by, not subject to a fidei-commissum, 211.

ANALOGY
of laws, 20.

ANNUAL RENTS
purchased for a ward, have certain peculiarities, 154.
how charged on a feud, 154.
charged on a legacy, 325.

ANNUITY, see Annual Rents.

ANNUS LUCTUS, see Year of Mourning.

ANTENUPTIAL CONTRACT, see Contracts, Antenuptial.

APPAREL
usufruct of, 377.

APPEAL
against judgment of the Court, on the opposition of banns, 80.
against decision of the ordinary judge, 81.
against decrees in prodigal cases, 164, 165.

ARREST
not affected by comity, 36.
for establishing jurisdiction, 175.
of deposit in the hands of the depositary, 533.

ARROGATION
of children, 102.

ASSENT
on behalf of a third party, 510.

ASSIGNATION
effect of, 837.
mode of effecting, 838, 839.
distinction between and exchange, 841-851.
when revocable, 844.
action on, 845, 846.
assignor should be informed of non-payment, 847.
without appointment of day of payment, 848.
debtor cannot be compelled to accept, 849.

ASSIGNATION (*continued*)
may be endorsed, and rights against indorsers, 850.
may be taken in arrest, 851.
does not operate as a delegation, 852.

ASSIGNMENT
upon dissolution of community, 142.
instrument of, to be kept in custody of Orphan Chamber, 147.
to children, on death of parent, 270.
by a surviving parent to the children, relief against, 897.

ASYLUMS
persons maintained in, 280.
—— may take under a will, 284.

AUCTION
goods sold by, 184.

AUCTIONEERS
right of mortgage and preference, 455.

AVAL
acceptance in, 594.

AVERAGE
defined, 780.
gross and *common*, 780, 781.
gross, salvage recoverable by way of, 681.
losses arising from disablement of sailor, 782.
—— incurred in apprehension of the enemy, 783.
loss of boat, or goods deposited therein, 784.
losses, when reckoned as average, 785.
—— how apportioned, 786.
value of goods how estimated, 787, 788.
money, 789.
losses, when not accounted as, 790, 791.
goods deposited in an improper place, 792.
right of retention and mortgage for, and contribution how recovered, 793.
discharge from, by relinquishing the vessel and goods, 794.

AVERAGE (*continued*)
prescription of action for contribution, 795.

B.

BANK
money deposited in, may not be arrested, 857.

BANNS, see *Proclamation*, *Espousals*.

BENEFICIUM·ORDINIS
of bona-fide possessor of a legal mortgage, 429.
does not hold in special mortgage of immovables, 434.

BENEFICIUM non numeratæ pecuniæ
when pleadable by drawer against holder, payee, or indorsee, 592, 600.
obtains only in cases of loan, 601.

BENEFIT OF INVENTORY, see *Inventory*.

BEQUEST
to children by a stranger, how administered, 103.

BERBICE
rule of succession ab intestato in, 352.

BIGAMY
punishment of, 62.
law of· Zeeland respecting, 63.
children born in, when legitimate, 64, 65.

BILL OF EXCHANGE
drawer may retain or revoke, when, 580.
payable on a particular day, ought to be sent in due time for presentment, 581.
payable after sight, should be presented when, 582.
delay in presentment, when excused, 581, 582.
substantial requirements of, 596.
summary proceedings on, 594, 595, 597.
several debtors or creditors *in solidum* on, 595.

Z

BILL OF EXCHANGE (*continued*)
conditions may be annexed to, 596.
receipt of value should be acknowledged, 598.
when transferable, 604.
time of payment, how stated, 605.
acceptance, *supra protest*, see *Acceptance*.
payment *supra protest*, see *Payment*.
drawee, when bound to accept, 615.
———— may decline to accept, when, 616.
acceptance of, how given, 617.
payment of, where value of money has altered, 621.
acceptor cannot require delivery of bill, before payment, 622.
set-off, when allowed in payment of, 623.
mode of procedure, and execution on, 624.
proceedings on, 625.
payable on a particular day, should be strictly paid, 626.
distinction between, and *Assignation*, 841–852.
cannot be revoked, 844.
does not operate *per se* as a delegation, 852.
time of presentment, 853.
protest of, see *Protest*.
liability of drawer, where he has drawn on a fictitious person, 867.
re-exchange, how recovered, 868.
————————when recoverable and from whom, 869.
liability of, and order of proceeding against, the several parties, 870.
forgery or falsification of, 871–873.
holder may receive a part and protest for the remainder, 860.
liability of acceptor upon acceptance, 863.

BILL OF EXCHANGE (*continued*)
if drawn on the mandate of a third party, 864.
liability of drawer on non-payment, 864.
———— indorsers, 865.
if purchased on the mandate of another, 866.

BILL OF LADING
consignee who has made himself liable on, preferred to a subsequent bottomry, 449, 567.

BLEACHERS
right of preference and retention for wages, 424.

BONDS
classed as movables, 181.

BOOKS OF ACCOUNT
left by a surviving parent, remain with the guardian, 147.

BOTTOMRY
difference between, and *Byl-bond*, 550, 551.
defined, 552.
peculiar rights of, 553.
not subject to 2½ per cent. duty, 427.
wherein creditor undertakes no risk, 554.
amount lent on, 555.
difference and similarity between, and *Pecunia trajectitia*, 556, 557.
differs from insurance, 558, 559.
risks of, defined, 560.
rights of creditor, 561, 562.
of vessel does not include the cargo, 563.
preference of, 564, 567.
of goods, money lent on may be insured, 568.
may be contracted by owner of a vessel in foreign parts, 569.
debt contracted on the strength of bills of lading abroad, preferred to, 449.

BOTTOMRY BILLS
conditions annexed to, 596.

BRIEL
rule of succession *ab intestato*, 351.

BROKERS
  insurance-brokers, prohibited
  from contracting in their
  own name, 714.
BUILDINGS
  right of erecting on another's
  land, 416.
BYL-BOND
  defined, 550.
  ·difference between, and bottomry, 551.

C.

CAMBIAL PROCESS
  when maintainable, 597.
  acceptor *supra protest*, when
  entitled to, 607.
CAMBIUM, see *Exchange*.
CANON LAW, see LAWS, *Canon*.
CAPTURE
  of enemy's ship, by private
  vessel, 191.
  of vessel by the enemy, 192.
CASSATORY CLAUSE, see
  Clause.
CENSUS
  fines referable to immovables,
  180.
CESSIO BONORUM
  alienation before and after,
  199.
  insolvent purchasing property
  shortly before, 204.
  preference and concurrence
  of creditors, see *Preference*.
  expenses of, entitled to preference, 451.
  lease expires upon, 696.
  antiquity of, 883.
  effect of, 884, 889.
  cognizance of, to whom it belongs, 885.
  when granted to a foreigner,
  886.
  not granted to guardian as
  respects a debt due on the
  guardianship, 887.
  debts founded on delict, how
  far affected by, 888.
  by a father who had promised
  a dowry, good ground for
  dissolution of espousals, 60.

CHARTER, see *Privilege*.
CHEQUES
  on bankers, 847.
CHILDREN
  unborn, when considered as
  already born, 45.
  born in bigamy, 64, 65.
  marriage of, erroneously supposed to have obtained
  puberty, 66.
  adoption and arrogation of,
  102.
  inheritance bequeathed to, by
  strangers, how adminis-
  tered, 103.
  property acquired by, 104.
  adventitious property of, 105,
  emancipation of, 107.
  marrying or attaining age or
  higher rank, are freed from
  the paternal power, 108.
  upon deportation of father,
  pass to the power of mother
  or guardian, 109.
  may be discharged from
  tutelage before majority,
  110.
  under age, not admitted as
  guardians, 112.
  property devolving on, by
  whom administered, 140,
  141.
  property assigned to, by whom
  administered, 143.
  division and assignment of
  property, 142.
  notes and movables belonging
  to, in common with another,
  how disposed of, 148.
  property belonging to several,
  how disposed of, 149.
  by whom educated, 150, 151.
  ———— maintained, and till
  when, 152.
  money of, how invested, 151,
  155.
  minors may obtain *Venia
  Ætatis*, at what age, 161.
  Legitimate, defined, 169.
  born after dissolution of marriage, 170.
  legitimation of, by marriage,
  171.

z 2

CHILDREN (*continued*)
legitimation of by rescript, 172.
prescription does not run against minors, 210.
marriage of minors, without consent, does not introduce community, 218.
bound to collate property received as dowry or otherwise, 223.
birth of, does not cancel antenuptial contract, 236.
cannot be deprived of their legitimate share, by antenuptial contract, *ib.*
legitimate portion of, preferred to *doarium*, 259.
continued community between surviving parent and, 266—276.
rights of, in a continued community, 269, 270.
division of property between parent, second spouse, and, 274—276.
illegitimate, may make a will, 282.
———— succession to, 368.
of a guardian cannot be instituted heirs by the ward. 285.
natural, may be instituted as heirs, and to what extent, 287.
———— succession of, by the law of Zeeland, 342.
————————— by the law of North Holland, 343.
————————— by the law of Southern part of Holland, 344.
disinherison of, 288.
———————— how effected, 294.
comprise all descendants, when and when not, 304.
legitimate portion of, may be left under condition, 305.
passing over of, how far invalidates a testament, 306.
may maintain *querela inoff. testam.* when, 307.
domicile of, 314.

CHILDREN (*continued*)
cannot be prohibited from deducting the Trebellianic portion, 315.
cannot take more than a half of the property on account of the Trebellianic and legitimate portion, 316.
adulterine or incestuous, succession of, by the law of Dordrecht, 345.
collation between surviving parent and, 349, 350.
succession of, see *Succession.*
may receive a donation from the father, 485.
rights of preference in respect of property left by predeceased parent, 462.
parent not liable for offences of, excepting—476.
promises made to parent, on behalf of, 509.
———— to children by the parent, *ib.*

CHIROGRAPHS (Notes of Hand)
cannot be alienated, when, 97.
in blank or payable to bearer, 98.
of debts due to a ward, 147.
belonging to a ward in common with another, 148.
payable to holder or lawful holder, 525.

CHURCH
tacit mortgage of, over the property of her administrators, 425.

CITIZENS, 26.

CITY
tacit mortgage of, over the property of its tax-collectors, 425.

CLAUSE
Cassatory and *Derogatory*, how far effective or necessary, 328, 329.
Reservatory, force of, 337.
Codicillary, force, 288, 307.

CODICIL
and Testament, distinction between, 289.

CODICIL (*continued*)
  private, heir cannot be insti-
    tuted by, 289.
  may be executed without
    witnesses, by virtue of
    reservatory clause, 337.
CODICILLARY CLAUSE
  affects the passing over of a
    son, how far, 307.
  disinherison, how far affected
    by, 288.
COHABITATION
  cancels conditions in espou-
    sals, when, 47.
  consent of parents to the
    espousals, previous to, 50.
  accompanying bigamy, 62, 63.
CO-HEIRS
  a creditor cannot sue, or be
    compelled to sue, a particu-
    lar co-heir, 778.
COLLATION
  of property received in dowry
    &c., 223.
  no action maintainable during
    marriage for, 256.
  between surviving parent and
    heirs, donations included in,
    349.
  value of property, how deter-
    mined, 350.
  of the price paid for feuds,
    390, 391.
  of allodial property, 390.
COLONIES
  East and *West Indian*, rule
    of succession *ab intestato* in,
    352.
COMITY, 36.
  recognises the *status* of a
    person, 42.
COMMISSION, see *Mandate*.
COMMISSIONERS
  of matrimonial causes, 76, 78,
    79, 80.
COMMODATUM
  arrest of, by the Commoda-
    tory, 541.
COMMUNITY
  exclusion of, does not prevent
    the husband alienating the
    wife's property, 92.
  ———— in profit and loss, 93.

COMMUNITY (*continued*)
  of property and profits, 99.
  of property between surviving
    parent and children, 142, 144.
  by marriage, alienation under
    title of, 202.
  takes place *ipso jure* on mar-
    riage, 216, 218.
  affects future as well as
    present property, *ib.*
  origin of, 217.
  does not obtain, when, 218.
  cannot be excluded after
    marriage, 231.
  introduced by antenuptial
    contract, 232.
  rules respecting, 233.
  may be excluded by antenup-
    tial contract, 247.
  of profit and loss, does not
    include inheritances, 252.
  ———————— what things
    included in, 253, 254.
  exclusion of, protects wife's
    property against creditors
    of the husband, 255.
  ———— includes acciden-
    tal losses and necessary
    expenses, 257.
  ———— includes useful
    and luxurious expenses, to
    what extent, *ib.*
  on marriage, does not include
    feuds, 220.
  ———— includes money
    realised by sale of feud, *ib.*
  ———— does not include
    fidei-commissa and Trebel-
    lianic share, 221.
  ————————includes debts con-
    tracted before marriage, 222.
  may be excluded how, 227.
  continued, as penalty against a
    surviving parent, 270.
  exclusion of, legal mortgage,
    when, 247, 263.
  may be continued after pa-
    rent's death, 266, 276.
  continued, differs from a *fidei-
    commissum*, 320.
  right of joint-owners to let or
    occupy the common pro-
    perty, 772.

COMPENSATION, see *Set-off.*

COMPOSITION
with creditors, 829.
———————— does not affect those who hold security, 830.

COMPROMISE
alienation by, 516.
guardians may enter into, 517.
of a matter already decided by sentence, 518.
inventory, when necessary in, 519.
of crimes and offences, 520.
rescission of, 896.

CONCUBINE
cannot be instituted heir by a ward, 285, 286.

CONDICTIO INDEBITI
defined, Grot. *Introd.* B. iii. ch. 30, § 4.
not maintainable for money paid by a married woman on her own contract, 96.

CONDITIONS
in Espousals, see *Espousals.*
in antenuptial contracts, 97. 99, 234—250.
———————— publication of, not necessary, 99.
annexed to dowry, 245.
impossible, should be taken as not imposed, 310.
of forfeiture in sales, 637.

CONFISCATION
of property, 94.

CONFUSION, see *Merger.*

CONSENT
of parents, confirms a marriage, retrospectively, 75.
does not discharge the children from the penalties of the Placaat of 1540, *ib.*
of guardians to proclamation of espousals, 125.
of relatives and guardians to marriage, *ib.*

CONSIDERATION
immoral, reward promised for bringing about a marriage not founded on, 482.
just, necessary to maintain an action, 484.

CONSIDERATION (*continued*)
in a written obligation, 521.
receipt of, should be acknowledged in a bill of exchange, 598.
good, debt due on, not affected by a new written obligation, 522.
necessary for a decree of provisional payment, 526.
want of, see *Beneficium non numeratæ pecuniæ.*

CONSIGNATION
of money into court when it operates as a release, 824.

CONSIGNEE
incurring liabilities on bills of lading received abroad, preferred to a subsequent bottomry, 449, 567.

CONTRACTS
antenuptial, of majors, 13.
———————— conditions in, see *Conditions.*
executed according to *lex loci contractus,* 39.
antenuptial, defined, 228.
———————— who may enter into, and whose consent necessary, *ib.*
———————— may be entered into without writing, 229.
———————— when effectual, as against creditors, *ib.*
———————— inventory annexed to, 230.
———————— in absence of, community takes place, 231.
———————— community introduced by, 232.
———————— rules respecting, 232.
———————— subjects of, 233.
———————— most usual stipulation in, 234.
———————— succession may be defined by, 235.
———————— testamentary disposition by, *ib.*
———————— stipulations in, concerning succession, 236—240, 248—250.

CONTRACTS (*continued*)
antenuptial, how far revocable, 239, 241, 246.
———— concerning the succession of the children, 241—243.
———— community may be excluded by, 247.
———— things omitted in 251.
———— profits due to the wife under, 262.
———— right of dowry and legal mortgage upon, 263.
————cannot be revoked *inter vivos*, 264.
———— mutual promise made by, may be revoked by will, 265.
———— election of succession by, 362.
divisory election of succession by, 361.
of a ward, entered into without the guardian's consent, 529.
locus pænitentiæ, 530.
dissolution of, by contrary consent, 833.
of *emphyteusis* need not be in writing, 667.
founded on fraud or fear, how avoided, 877.
rescission of, under Cod. iv. 44, 2., 898, 899, 901.
See further *Acts*.
CONTRIBUTION
in average, 782.
———— how recovered, and right of retention and mortgage for, 793.
And see *Average*.
COURT
Feudal, jurisdiction of, 396.
CREDIT
things supplied on, for domestic use, 99.
CREDITORS
rights of, against common estate, 145.
prescription against, *ib*.
alienation in fraud of, 199.
payment to one, by insolvent, 200.

CREDITORS (*continued*)
when affected by antenuptial contract, 229.
preferred to widow, when, 253.
preference of, 447—473.
placed in possession, preference of, 472.
on chirographs, preference of, 473.
cannot sue, or be compelled to sue a particular co-heir, 778.
composition with, 829.
in adiation of inheritance, minority bound to follow majority, 832.
holding security not affected by a composition, 830, 831.
CRIMES
commission of, ground for divorce, 88.
fine or confiscation of property for, of husband, does not affect wife's estate, 94.
compromise of, 520.
CROWN, see *State*.
CULPA
levis, partner liable for, 701.
CURACOA
rule of succession *ab intestato* in, 351.
CURATORS
over persons incapable of managing their own property, 164.
over prodigals, how and by whom appointed, 165.
married woman may be appointed, over husband, 168.
CURATORSHIP
termination of, 166.
CUSTOMS
ancient, have the force of law, 5.
special, 8.

D.

DAMAGE
to vessels, who are liable for and to what extent, 805—807.

DAMAGE (*continued*)
from placing things in a dangerous position, 810.
from collision of vessels, 812—814.
————— by whom made good. 812, 815—821.

DEBTS
contracted during marriage, 99, 225, 226.
————before marriage, 222, 224, 232.
division of, upon dissolution of marriage, 223.
arising, *ex delicto*, 225.
of a deceased person, how divided amongst heirs, succeeding under different laws, 340.
due on a good consideration, not affected by a new written obligation, 522.
not proved as against third parties by an instrument merely signed by the debtor, 528.
personal, upon sale of, debtor may claim the *jus Legis Anastasianæ*, 663.
————when not, 664.
due to ward, should be paid to whom, 822.
consignation of, when it operates as a discharge, 824.
not due in writing, prescription of, 876.

DEBTORS
when taken to have renounced the *beneficium divisionis*, 494.
may not repay money lent on interest before the time agreed upon, 542.
may claim the *jus leg. Anast.* when, and when not, 663, 664.

DECISIONS
have the force of law, when, 3.

DECREE
of the Court of Magistrates respecting alienation of minor's property, 129, 133.
————————— requisites of, 131, 132.

DEFAMATION
punishment for, 802.
justification of, 803.

DEFECT
in things sold, gives an action for rescission of sale, 642.
in things insured, 759.

DEL CREDERE COMMISSION
merchants selling on, not entitled to the privileges of sureties, 504.

DELICT
accidental, or founded on fraud or blame, 804.
of servants, when and how far masters liable for, 811.
debts founded on, how far affected by *cessio bonorum*, 888.

DELIVERY
alienation of movables by, 201.
and sale do not pass the property, unless—, 208.

DEPORTATION
of a father, 109.

DEPOSIT
if sold without owner's consent, 183.
may be arrested by a third person in the hands of the depositary, 533.

DEPOSITARY
how far liable for neglect, 531.
not liable for accidents, &c., 532.
may retain the deposit for expenses, 533.

DEROGATORY CLAUSE, see *Clause.*

DISCHARGE
from guardianship, 161.

DISCOVERER
of uninhabited lands, 190.

DISINHERISON
of a son by a testament which is protected by the codicillary clause, 288.
how effected, 294.
does not render a will *ipso jure* void, 332.

DISPUTES
between parents and children respecting marriage, 80.

————and suitors, 81.

DISSOLUTION
of marriage, division of property and debts on, 223—225.
of contract by contrary consent, 833.

DIVISION
of common property between surviving parent and children, 142.
of property belonging to several wards, 149.
of inheritance—alienation on, 202.
of debts amongst heirs succeeding under different laws, 340.
no distinction made between simple and mortgage debts, ib.
things which do not admit of, 775.
of property between a second spouse, the binubus, and the children of the former marriage, 274—276.

DIVORCE
on what grounds, 88, 89.

DOARIUM, see *Marriage-gift.*

DOMICILE, 30, § 1.
of a minor who has lost either parent, how determined, 341.
change of, cannot be prohibited by antenuptial contract, 228.

DONATION
by husband, how far binding on the wife, 93.
causa mortis, wife may make without knowledge of husband, 100.
giving to a surviving parent is included in a continued community, 267.
———— children, when not included, 269.
by surviving parent, out of a continued community, 320.

DONATION (*continued*)
by a testator of the property bequeathed, annuls the property, unless—, 336.
included in the collation between the surviving parent and heirs, 849.
by a father to his minor son, valid, 485.
between husband and wife prohibited; subject to exception, 486.
of all one's property, invalid, 487.
under condition that donor should be maintained by donee, 488.
exceeding 500 *aurei*, how affected, 489.
made by a childless person, revocable on the birth of children, 490.
right of revoking belongs to the donor alone, ib.
inofficious, rescission of, 491.
mortis causâ, how affected, 492.
———— who may make, 493.

DOWRY
due, even after separation, to the innocent party, 90.
alienation under title of, 202.
collation of, 223.
by parent, 244, 246.
by stranger, 245, 246.
reservation of, upon antenuptial contract, 247.
to be paid to the surviving spouse, 248.
husband may sue the wife's father for, 256.
right of, when preferred to mortgage, 263.
———— wife may renounce in favour of the husband's creditors, 264.
how charged on a feud, 402.
payment of, husband may give sureties for, 498.
action for, against a ravisher, 801.

DRAWEE
of a bill of exchange, 574.
—— not being the debtor of drawer, is entitled to repayment, 589.
liable to drawer in damages, when, 590.
——— payee, holder or indorsee, 591.
if not advised, may decline to accept, 606.
may accept *supra protest*, or even alternatively, 607.
may pay *supra protest*, without accepting, 614.
when bound to accept, 615.
may decline to accept, 616.
may be sued on his promise to accept, *ib.*
may fix time, mode, or condition of payment, 617.
may pay a bill, though countermanded, when, 628.
liability of, on acceptance, 863, 870.

DRAWER
of a bill of exchange, 574.
—— not discharged until payment, 578.
may retain the bill or demand security, when, 580.
may revoke the bill, when, *ib.*
may claim back the bill, when, 583.
entitled to preference, when, *ib.*
bound to see payment made, 584.
cannot be compelled to pay a bill protested before the time, 585.
bound to give security, when, *ib.*
liable to the payee or holder in damages, when and to what extent, 586.
——drawee, not being his debtor, 589.
right of, against drawee for damages, 590.
liable to indorsees, when, 593.
may take the value on himself, 598.

DRAWER (*continued*)
when bound to give security upon an acceptance *supra protest*, 612.
may be called upon for security when, 862.
liability of, on non-payment, 864, 867, 870.

DUTY
on transfer of ships, &c., 202.
immovable property, 202.
payable on withdrawal from a sale, 665.

DWARS NAGT, 175.

E.

EDUCATION
of minor children, 150, 151.
parent how far responsible in respect of neglect in, 476.

ELECTION
of succession, see *Succession*.
given to wife, by antenuptial contract, accrues to her heirs, 250.

ELOPEMENT, see *Abduction*.

EMANCIPATION
of children, see *Venia Ætatis*.

EMPHYTEUSIS
alienation of, permitted on payment of double rent, 379.
belonging to the State, alienation of, 380.
burthens on, by whom payable, 381.
right of, how acquired *inter vivos*, 382.
how extinguished, 383.
upon forfeiture of, property reverts to owner and his heirs, 384.
the *dominium* whereof belongs to the State, redeemable, 385.
how charged on a feud, 402.
contract of, may be entered into without writing, 667.
extraordinary charges on attach to the tenant, 668.
upon forfeiture of, tenant not entitled to indemnification, 669.

ENDORSEMENT
of instrument not payable to holder, 525.
of bill not payable to order does not pass the right of recovery, 604.

ENEMY
ship of, if captured by private vessel, 191.
if vessel captured by, 192.
rights of bottomry creditors, when vessel has been captured by, 560.
in the formula of an insurance, includes pirates also, 744.

EQUITY
when resorted to, 24.

ESPOUSALS, 25, 47.
conditions of, cancelled by cohabitation, 47.
————————immoral or impossible, 48.
de presenti and de futuro, 49.
may be rescinded by mutual consent, ib.
clandestine, 50.
public, 51.
of minors, 52, 53.
cannot be contracted by parents on behalf of their minor children, 52.
may be contracted by males above 25, and females above 20,—52.
of a minor female above 20,— 55, 56.
of a widow who is under age, 56.
action on, 57.
of two, which is preferred, 58.
remedy upon, against a married party, 58.
punishment against a person contracting two espousals, 59.
may be dissolved by either party on just grounds, 60.
relief against, 61.
of a married person, 62, 63.
proclamation of, consent of parents necessary to, 76.
————————— between persons above 25 and 20,—78.

ESPOUSALS (continued)
proclamation of, opposition to, 79—81.
————————— should be made, where, 83.
————————— debars a prior sponsus unless really ignorant, 85.
of wards, in some places not permitted without consent of guardians, but— 125.

ESTATE
common, if not solvent, 144.
———— redemption of by surviving parent, 145.
————widow's right of abandoning, 226.
———— profits promised to wife out of, 262.

EXCEPTION
non numeratæ pecuniæ, prescription of, 206.
————————— against a written obligation, 523, 524.
See further Beneficium non num. pecuniæ.
under Senatusconsultum Vellejanum, 495, 496.
of non fulfilment of contract, or of fraud when pleadable by a drawer, 601, 603.
————————will not prevent provisional payment, 602.

EXCHANGE
defined, 596.
contract of, parties to, 574.
distinction between and bills of exchange, 575.
nature and peculiarities of, 576—578.
neither party may withdraw from, but—, 579, 580.
simple and mixed, 577.
dry, defined, 602.
————want of consideration pleadable in, ib.

EXCUSE
of guardian, when, and to whom submitted, 124.
————————— by whom decided, ib.

EXECUTION
    process of, on a Bill of Ex-
        change, 624.
    houses sold in, and perishing
        before the day of cession,
        639.
EXECUTORS
    need not allege excuse, 105.
    bound to produce will and
        inventory, when, 140.
    cannot debar the heirs from
        the inheritance, or alienate
        property without their con-
        sent, 323.
    may at *Middelburg* be dis-
        missed, when, *ib.*
EXILE
    of a father, 109.
EXPENSES
    useful, lessee cannot deduct,
        214.
    necessary, useful and *luxurious*,
        where community has been
        excluded, 257.
    judicial, preference of, 451,
        466.
    funeral, preference of, 466.
    depositary may retain deposit
        for, 533.
    payable by acceptor on non-
        payment of bill, 627.
EXTENT
    difference of in land sold in
        the lump, how far compen-
        sated for, 638.
EXUÆ
    jus, abolished, 174.

F.

FALCIDIAN Portion, see *Portion*.
FALLOW LAND
    tenths of, belong to the State,
        415.
    land reclaimed from water
        not accounted as, 416.
FAMILA
    consent of, to antenuptial
        contracts, 13.
FATHER
    administers property be-
        queathed to children by a
        stranger, 103.

FATHER (*continued*)
    not entitled to property ac-
        quired by children in ser-
        vice, 104.
    entitled to property acquired
        by their industry, *ib.*
    has no usufruct in adventi-
        tious property of children,
        105.
    may claim that children should
        be maintained from adven-
        titious property, *ib.*
    if appointed guardian by
        Orphan Chamber, loses the
        office upon a second mar-
        riage, 121.
    ———— but may be re-
        appointed, when, *ib.*
    of wife, husband may sue for
        dowry, 256.
FEAR
    relief on the ground of, when
        prescribed, 881.
FEES
    prescription of, 876.
FEUDS (*Fiefs*)
    do not come into community,
        but—, 220.
    Letter of the Court of Hol-
        land concerning, 386.
    direct of Zeeland, differ from
        Dutch fends, 387.
    succession to, 388, 389, 393,
        403, 404, 407, 408.
    if purchased by husband with
        the common money, 390,
        391.
    upon death of vassal, leaving
        children or paternal rela-
        tives, 392.
    investiture of, 394.
    homage, 395.
    jurisdiction over, 396.
    acquisition of, 397.
    grant of, by testament, 398.
    privilege of disposing of, 399.
    substitution by way of *fidei-
        commissum*, 399.
    disposition of, by testament,
        400.
    differerence between acquisition
        of, and of allodial property,
        401.

FEUDS (continued)
charges on, how effected, 402.
ancient, succession to, 403.
may be mortgaged, when, 404.
may be acquired by prescription, 405.
destruction or loss of, 406.
bound in subsidium for debts of vassal, when, 409.
lord, bound to make compensation for improvements, 410.
direct, cannot be converted into hereditary or allodial, 411.
how released, ib.
cannot be dissolved by prescription, 412.
———— excepting, ib.
waiver of, 413.
guardian may alienate, 414.
FIDEI-COMMISSARY
security required from, may be dispensed with by testament, 511.
may tender oath to the heir, 313.
FIDEI-COMMISSUM
not affected by legitimation of natural children, 172.
augmentations by alluvion not subject to, 211.
not included in a community, 221.
may be imposed by antenuptial contract, 242.
children burthened with may deduct their legitimate and Trebellianic portion, ib.
on property left to a stranger to the exclusion of a child, 307.
rule of Inst. ii. 23, § 12,—313.
of public securities, not subject to the realty-tax, 314.
dissolution of, law of Zeeland concerning, 317.
in rem and in personam, at Amsterdam, 318.
registration of, not necessary, 319.
difference between, and continued community, 320.

FILIUSFAMILIAS
when relieved against contracts entered into with the father's consent, 61.
FIRE
extending from house to house, 809.
FISHING
right of, 188.
FOREIGNERS
defined, 172.
succession to, 174.
condition of, in judicial proceedings, 175.
naturalized, 177.
residing temporarily in the country, 30, § 1.
cessio bonorum, when granted to, 886.
FORGERY
in a bill of exchange, 871—873.
FRAUD
sale founded on, how rescinded, 666.
delict founded on, 804.
in a judge, 808.
relief on the ground of, when prescribed, 881.
FRAUDULENT ALIENATIONS, see Alienations.
FREIGHT
for merchandise, payable upon wreck of the vessel, 681.
master's right of retaining goods for, 682.
———— of appropriating the goods on account of, 683.
right of owner to relinquish the goods for, 684.
on private merchandise of the sailors, 688.
insurance of, 717, 739.
when subject to contribution to average, 786.
FRUITS
tacit mortgage of a lessor over, and how exercised, 423.
FUNDS
mercantile, are transferable, 631.
FUNERAL
money lent for, 418.

G.

GIFTS
  made to children by their
    sponsors, 104. see *Marriage-
    gift.*
  on marriage, see *Marriage-
    gift.*
GOLD
  sold to a goldsmith, 184.
GOLDSMITH
  gold or silver sold to, 184.
GRACE
  days of, 620.
  —— holder may not enter
    into any agreement with
    acceptor during, 860.
GRANDCHILDREN.
  cannot be prohibited from
    deducting the Trebellianic
    portion, 315.
GRANDMOTHER
  may be appointed guardian,
    114.
GRAND PARENT
  not included under the term
    parent, 77.
GUARDIAN
  marriage of, with the ward,
    74.
  consent of, not neccessary to
    proclamation of espousals,
    77.
  mother or grandmother may
    be appointed, unless under
    25 years, 114.
  persons not admitted to act
    as, 115.
  testamentary, in some places
    should be confirmed by the
    magistrates, 116.
  where Orphan Chamber has
    been excluded, *ib.*
  legitimate, not recognised by
    law of Holland, 117.
  nearest relatives should be
    appointed as, *ib.*
  over persons who already have
    a guardian, 118.
  appointed by a predeceased
    father and the surviving
    mother, *ib.*
  permitted to appoint a substi-
    tute, 119.

GUARDIAN (*continued*)
  uncertain persons may be ap-
    pointed, *ib.*
  security to be given by *uncer-
    tain,* *ib.*
  testamentary, if appointed sim-
    ply, or with exclusion of
    Orphan Chamber, 120.
  —————— law of Zecland
    hereon, *ib.*
  when bound to render ac-
    counts to Orphan Chamber,
    120.
  father appointed as, by
    Orphan Chamber, lays down
    the office on second mar-
    riage, 121.
  —————— but may be re-
    appointed when, *ib.*
  from the father's side should
    be associated with the
    mother, 122.
  nominating a proper person
    equivalent to claiming the
    guardianship, 123.
  desirous of being excused,
    124.
  excuse of, by whom decided
    ib.
  when bound to explain reason
    of dissent to the ward's
    marriage, 125.
  power of, over marriage of
    ward, *ib.*
  power of alienating ward's
    property, 129.
  alienation by, requisites of
    130—132.
  acts of, binding on the ward,
    133.
  security to be given by, 134.
  should call for inventory, 135,
    136.
  inventory when dispensed
    with, 138, 144.
  when bound to make an in-
    ventory, 140, 141, 146.
  division of common property
    between parents and, 145.
  may invest the ward's money
    in lands, 153.
  is bound to take good security,
    155.

GUARDIAN (*continued*)
remuneration of, 156.
accounts of, 157.
suspected, may be removed,
162.
over persons incapable of
managing their own pro-
perty, 164.
or their children cannot be
instituted as heirs, by ward;
unless—, 285, 286.
wife of, may be instituted
heir, *ib*.
may select the minor's domicile, 341.
property of, bound in tacit
mortgage to the ward,
421.
may compromise, 517.
on default of, magistrates
may be sued *in subsidium*,
770.
when entitled to payment of
the ward's debts, 823.
not entitled to *cessio bonorum*
as regards debts due to
ward, 887.

GUARDIANSHIP
of property bequeathed to
children by a stranger,
103.
persons under 25 years cannot
undertake, 112.
soldiers excused from, 113.
mother or grandmother, when
admitted to, 114.
termination of, 110, 160.
father lays down office of,
when, 121.
of father, 122.
of mother, *ib*.
surviving parent who does
not claim the, subject to
punishment, 123.
nominating a proper person,
equivalent to claiming, *ib*.
one who acts *bonâ fide*, not
liable to the responsibilities
of, *ib*.
continuation of, by a decree,
160.
discharge from by *Venia
Ætatis*, 161.

H.

HEIRS
of a ward, when entitled to
his property, 159.
division of property between
parent, second spouse, and,
274—276.
guardians or their children
cannot be instituted as, unless—, 285, 286.
natural children may be instituted, and to what extent,
287.
institution of, generally made
by testament, 289.
cannot be instituted by private codicil, *ib*.
institution of, not necessary
in a testament, 290.
————— not vitiated by
a legacy to one of the witnesses, 291.
disinherison of, how effected,
293.
if instituted to the exclusion
of children, 307.
sole, succession of, 309.
instituted from or up to a
particular time, 311.
cannot be prohibited from
deducting the Trebellianic
portion, 315.
legitimate, cannot deduct more
than half of the property,
ib.
portion of, in a continued
community, cannot be dis-
posed of by the surviving
parent, *ib*.
may transmit inheritance to
successors, 321.
universal, cannot adiate in
part, 322.
to a part, not bound to acknowledge the rest, *ib*.
executors cannot alienate
without consent of, 323.
may, at *Middelburg*, dismiss
the executors, when, *ib*.
when bound to redeem an
annuity charged on pro-
perty bequeathed, 325.

HEIRS (*continued*)
right of accretion amongst, '326.
persons causing the death of the testator, 327.
————— children of, *ib.*
succeeding under different laws, 340.
collation between surviving parent and, 349, 350.
ab intestato, succession of, in *Briel* and *Voorn*, 351.
in the colonies 352.
under the *Political Ordonnance* of 1580 and *Placaat* of 1599, 353—359.

HOLDER
of a note payable to holder may sue thereon, unless—, 525.
of a note payable to *lawful* holder, *ib.*
of a bill of exchange, 574.
————— when entitled to sue the drawer for damages, 586.
————— when entitled to his expenses and re-exchange, 587.
————— liable to payee for neglect, 588.
————— may accept *supra protest*, 607.
————— not bound to acquiesce in an acceptance *supra protest* unless—, 612.
————— accepting terms fixed by the drawee, does so at his own risk, 617.

HOMAGE, 395.

HOMICIDE
of an adulterer discovered in the act, 799, 800.

HOUSES
in a city or country-town may not be pulled down, 629.
sold in execution, perishing before the day of cession, 639.
money lent to build, 418.

HUNTING
right of, 185, 187.

HUSBAND
authority of, 13, 91.
may alienate wife's property, even where community has been excluded, 92.
contracts of, how far binding on the wife, 93.
cannot alienate immovable property and notes of the wife when, 97.
may alienate movable property, notes in blank or payable to bearer, 98.
consent or knowledge of, not necessary to wife's testament or donation *causa mortis*, 100.
authority of, not destroyed by insanity, 101.
property of wife, when liable for debts of, 235.
may sue the wife's father for dowry, 256.
may give sureties for payment of dowry, 498.

I.

INCAPACITY
arising after majority, 164, 165.

INCORPOREAL, see *Property, Incorporeal.*

INDORSEE
may proceed against drawer, when, 593.

INDORSEMENT
of assignations, 850.
See *Bill of Exchange, Assignation.*

INDORSER
prior, liable to subsequent indorsee, 592.
may be called upon to give security, 862.
liability of, 865, 870.
————— if the bill has been purchased on the mandate of another, 866.

INDUCTION
letters of requisites previous to obtaining, 890.
————— how applied for, 891.

INDUCTION (continued)
to persuade a creditor to grant time, 893.

INFAMY
punishment of, 59, 63.

INFIRMITY
persons incapable of managing their own property through, 164.
See Prodigal.

INHERITANCE
bequeathed by a stranger, how administered, 103.
does not pass ipso jure to the heir, 182.
alienation upon division of, 202.
not comprehended under profits, 252.
devolving on a surviving parent included in a continued community, 267.
————— children, when not included, 269.
transmission of, 321.
a universal heir cannot adiate in part, 322.
inventory when necessary, 519.
adiation of, see Adiation.

INJURIES
verbal and real, caused by sailors, 689.

INSANE PERSON
property of, under control of Orphan Chamber, 167.
wife of, cannot be appointed curator, ib.

INSANITY
of parent, how it affects the marriage of the children, 79.
of husband, during marriage, 101.

INSOLVENCY
preference and concurrence in, see Peference and Cessio Bonorum.

INSOLVENT
fraudulent purchase by, 204.
set-off may be pleaded against, 825.
composition with creditors, 829

INSOLVENT (continued)
————— does not affect creditors holding security, 830, 831.

INSURANCE
of vessels, usufructuary liable for neglecting to effect, 370.
differs from Bottomry 558, 559.
laws concerning, 711.
defined, 712.
premium of, ib.
binding, even if premium not paid, 713.
brokers prohibited from contracting in their own name, 714.
————— duties of, 728.
may be effected by a person, without authority to do so, when, 715.
by joint-owner or partner, ib.
of buildings and goods, 716.
against the dangers of the sea, 717, 718.
void, if the thing insured has already perished, 722.
at all events, 723, 724.
deduction in respect of perishable goods, 720.
after commencement of voyage, 725—727.
how effected, 729.
conditions annexed to, 730, 731.
how far affected by non-performance of the conditions, 730.
conditions prohibited by law, 732.
name and description of vessel, 733.
risk, commencement of, 734, 747.
————— limit of, 736, 737.
————— termination of, 748, 749.
————— defined, 742.
circumjacent places defined, 735.
value of goods, how proved, 738.
————— how estimated, 739, 740.

2 A

INSURANCE (*continued*)·
against violence from the enemy, with power of redemption, 743.
if vessel arrives safe, though damaged, 741.
enemies in the formula include also pirates, 744.
against fraud of the master or his substitute, 745.
against faults of the master, 746.
how affected by deviation from the course, 750, 751.
burthen of proof as to deviation, 752.
what is considered a deviation, 753.
how affected by detention of the vessel, 754, 755.
if the vessel has been disabled, 755.
———— taken by the enemy, 756.
when losses should be made good, 757.
party assured bound to inform the insurer of losses. 758.
internal defects in the thing insured, 759.
amount of the loss to be made good, 760.
return of premium, 761, 762.
liability of several insurers, 763—765.
premium, when payable and how recoverable, 766.
———— rate of interest on, 767.
cognizance of insurance causes, 768.
prescription of action, 769.
set off against agent, 825.

INSURER
not bound where the vessel arrives safe, though damaged, 741.
risks begin to attach to, when, 747.

INTEREST
payment of, interrupts prescription, 443.

INTEREST (*continued*)
of mortgage debts, preference of, 471.
in matters of strict law, 483.
on default, *ib.*
money lent on, cannot be repaid before the time agreed on, 542.
on amount payable within a certain time, 543.
legal rates of, 545, 546, 547.
compound, 548.
cannot exceed the principal, 549.

INTERPRETATIONS
of the law, 3.
extensive and *restrictive*, 9.

INVENTORY
upon the death of either parent, 135.
guardian may call for, when, 136.
cannot be dispensed with by the first-dying parent, 137.
may be dispensed with, when, 138.
omissions in, 139.
of property devolving on the children, 140.
objects of, 142.
on death of the surviving parent, 146.
how made, *ib.*
of goods brought in marriage, 230.
community continued, in failure of, 270.
benefit of, 324.
of property left in usufruct, 372.
when necessary in a compromise, 519.

INVESTITURE
of a feud, 394, 397.

ISLANDS
uninhabited, pass to the discoverer, 190.

J.

JOINT-OWNERS
right of, to occupy or let the joint property, 772.

JOINT-OWNERS (*continued*)
of things which are not divisible, 775.
one part-owner cannot compel a public sale of the property, 776.
rights of, as regards repairs and alterations, 777.

JUDGE
not bound to observe foreign statutes, 33, 34.
when liable for money deposited in a public office, 535.
when liable for mal-adjudication, 808.

JUDICIAL ACTS
executed according to *lex loci judicii*, 40.

JURISDICTION
ordinary, persons exempt from, 30, § 1.
of judge adjudicating on acts done beyond his, 31, 32.
over questions of preference, 444, 445.

JUS SUPERFICIEI
cannot be taken away without consent of *superficiarius*, 416.

JUSTIFICATION
of slander, 803.

K.

KUSTING BRIEF
defined, 179.
action on, considered as an immovable, *ib.*
not subject to the 2½ per cent. duty, 427.
not affected by alienation of the property, 432.
preferred to tacit mortgage, 437.
———— prior legal mortgages, and how far restricted, 463, 470.

L.

LANDS
uninhabited pass to the discoverer, 190.

LANDS (*continued*)
reclaimed from water not accounted as fallow land, 415.
right of building on, see *Jus Superficiei*.

LAST WILLS, see *Wills*.

LAW
general, should be promulgated, 1.
———— cannot be made up of particular laws, 14.
Roman, received *in subsidum*, 6.
———— rules concerning adoption of, 7—24.
———— equity of, has superseded ancient laws, 16.
———— which depend on peculiar constitution of the Roman State, 20.
of neighbouring States, rules concerning reference to, 7—24.
Canon, 25.
who bound by, 26.
conflict of, 27 and *seqq.*
strictness of, 32.
as between parties to a suit, 40.
division of debts amongst heirs succeeding under different, 341.
ignorance of, 796.

LEASE
may be effected without writing, 670, 672.
of a house may be continued by tacit consent, 671.
of lands, in *longum tempus*, may be effected by private agreement, 673.
for 25 years or more, how effected, *ib.*
may be sub-let, 674.
goes before a sale, 675.
may, by the Civil Law, be revoked in a case of necessity, *ib.*
expires upon *cessio bonorum*, 676.
cannot be cancelled without lessor's consent, 677.

LEGACY
not comprehended under movables or immovables, 178.
left to a surviving parent included under continued community, 267.
———— a child, when not included, 269.
does not annul a marriage-gift, unless so provided, 261.
rule of *Inst.* ii. 23. § 12. applicable to, 313.
ad pias causas, deduction of Falcidian portion, 327.
clandestinely left to persons incapable of taking, 333.
persons who have caused the testator's death, cannot take, 334.
———— children of may, *ib.*
revocation of, on the margin of the *gros*, 335.
how far affected by donation, alienation, or mortgage of the thing left, 336.
of a feud, 398.

LEGATEE
may be witness to a testament, 291.
cannot take anything inserted by himself, unless—, 292.
may tender the oath to the heir, 313.
when bound to undertake annuity charged on legacy, 325.
right of accretion amongst co-legatees, 326.
legacy left to one incapable of taking, 333.
who has caused the death of the testator, 334.
———— children of, *ib.*
security required from, may be dispensed with, 511.

LEGITIMATE AGE, see *Majority.*

LEGITIMATE CHILDREN defined, 169.
See *Children.*

LEGITIMATE PORTION, see *Portion.*

LEGITIMATION
by marriage, 169, 171.
by rescript, 172.
———— does not affect third parties, *ib.*

LENDER
rights of preference of, 448.

LESSEE
selling the property let, 183.
rights of, who has built on the land with lessor's consent, 213.
cannot deduct *useful* expenses, 214.
may sublet, 674.
by some laws permitted to adapt a house to his trade, 676.
cannot discharge himself from the lease, without the lessor's consent, 677.
cannot convert pasture into arable land, 680.

LESSOR
not bound to restore value of trees planted on leasehold, 215.
tacit mortgage of, over fruits, and things brought and carried in, 423, 453.
———— how exercised, *ib.*
rights of preference of, 448.
may by the Civil Law, eject the lessee in a case of necessity, 675.

LEX ANASTASIANA
privilege under, holds in respect of the sale of personal debts, 663.
does not obtain, when, 664.

LEX COMMISSORIA, see *Condition of Forfeiture.*

LEX HAC EDICTALI, 69, 237, 288.

LEYDEN
law of, respecting espousals, 59.

LIBEL
See *Defamation.*

LITERÆ CAMBIALES, see *Bills of Exchange.*

LITERARUM OBLIGATIO, see *Obligation, Written.*

LOCUS PÆNITENTIÆ
in real contracts, 530.
in respect of innominate contracts, 798.

LOSS
accidental, where community of property has been excluded, 257.
See *Insurance, Bottomry.*

LUCRUM NUPTIALE
forfeiture of, by adultery, 88.

M.

MAGISTRATES
not bound to observe foreign laws, 33.
authority of, as regards espousals, 51.
may be sued by ward, when, 770.
——————— on default of actuary, when, 535.

MAINTENANCE
of minor children, on whom chargeable, 152, 305.

MAJORITY
attainment of, determines the paternal power, 108.
discharges the ward from tutelage, 110.
by marriage, does not qualify a person to act as guardian, 112.

MAJORS, see *Children.*

MANDATE
if property sold without, 183.
remuneration when recoverable for services, 570.
non-fulfilment of, when excused, 571.
mandator may sue and be sued upon, 572.

MANDATOR, see *Mandate.*

MANDATORY
who has exceeded his limits cannot sue for the excess, nor retain the thing, unless ——, 573.

MARKET
public, things sold in, 184.

MARRIAGE
second, contracted by a person already married, 64.
of a child erroneously supposed to have attained puberty, 66.
second, punishments against, 69.
of a guardian or his child with the ward, 74.
between Protestants and Roman Catholics, 73.
of minors, without parent's consent, 75.
——————— parents may oppose even after publication of banns, 78.
disputes concerning, 80, 81.
of children whose parent is of unsound mind, 82.
celebration of, 83, 87.
dissolution of, 88, 89, 274—276.
debts contracted during, 99, 225, 226.
of child determines paternal power, 108.
does not qualify a person under 25 years to act as guardian, 112.
of wards, without consent, 125.
second, of surviving parent, 142.
——————— proclamations of, not permitted, until assignment to children, 142, 144.
children conceived before, 169.
——————— born after dissolution of, 170.
legitimation by, 171.
registration of, *ib.*
merger of estates on, 216.
community of property, 217, 218.
clandestine, 218.
debts contracted before, 222, 224.
no action for collation maintainable during, 256.
action for indemnity maintainable, upon dissolution of, *ib.*

MARRIAGE (*continued*)
reward promised for bringing
about, 482.
See further *Community, Dissolution.*
MARRIAGE-GIFT
defined, 259.
when due, and may be diminished, if immoderate, *ib.*
cannot be charged on common estate, when, 260.
when cancelled by legacy, 261.
———————— institution as heir, *ib.*
MARRIED PERSONS
contracting new espousals, how punished, 62, 63.
when liable for debts contracted before marriage, 232.
cannot sue each other during marriage for collation, 256.
cannot revoke antenuptial contract, 264.
may revert to it, after revocation, when, 265.
community continued after death of one, between the survivor and the children, 266, 267.
division of property between, and the heirs of a former marriage, 274-276.
mutual testament of, how far revocable by the survivor, 283.
———————— by either, 298.
may succeed to each other in North Holland, 365.
cannot make donation to one another, excepting—, 486.
MARRIED WOMEN
right of mortgage and preference of, 460.
MASTER
how far liable for the offences of servant, 477.
right of, to discharge himself by ceding the vessel, 684.
cannot ship illicit goods without owner's consent, 695.

MATERIALS
value of, when recoverable by lessee, 213.
MATRIMONIAL CAUSES, 25.
MERCHANDISE
insurance of, 707, 717, 718.
perishable, may be insured, 721.
———————— deductions allowed in insurance of, 720.
See further *Insurance.*
MERGER
of estates, on marriage, 216.
MINORITY
relief on the ground of, when prescribed, 206.
MINORS
cannot contract espousals without the parent's or guardian's consent, 50, 52, 55.
relief against espousals of, 53, 55, 56.
marriage of, without parent's consent, 75.
banns of marriage between, 76, 125.
marriage of, where parent is of unsound mind, 82.
———————— consent of relatives or guardians to, 125.
cannot appear in court without guardians, 127.
contracts of, 128.
movable property of, may be alienated, when, 129.
immovable property of, how alienated, 130-132.
may obtain relief against acts of the guardian, 133.
MONEY
lent out on security, usufruct of, 378.
lent for the purpose of building a house or ship, 417.
———————— funeral expenses and last illness, 418.
deposited in a public office, 535.
lent on interest, cannot be repaid before the time agreed upon, 542.
alteration in the value of, 621.
subject to contribution in average, 789.

"*MORE OR LESS*"
difference of extent in land sold in the lump, when compensated for, 638.

MORGEN GAVE
defined, 258.
when due, *ib.*

MORTGAGE
not comprehended under movables or immovables, 178.
by *Kusting-brief*, see *Kusting-brief.*
legal, need not be formally ceded, 202.
—— of lessee against lessor for value of materials, 213.
—— of wife, upon antenuptial contract, 247, 263.
—— —— may be renounced in favour of the husband's creditors, 264.
—— possessor of, entitled to the *Beneficium ordinis*, 429.
—— preferred to subsequent special mortgage, and to prior general mortgage, when, 437.
—— of tax-farmers, 419.
—— of the ward over the property of his guardian, 421.
—————— of stepfather, 422.
—— of lessors over things brought into the land, 423.
—— of cities and towns, 425.
—— of principal over the property of his agent, 426.
—— for money lent to build a house or ship, 417.
—————— for funeral expenses and last illness, 418
—— of the State, 419, 420.
—— of the master for freight, 682.
—————— for losses arising from overloading a vessel, 791.
—————— for average, 793.
general, affected before a judge, valid, 428.
—— how extinguished, 429.
—— rights of, 465.

MORTGAGE (*continued*)
conventional, duty on, 431.
special, of immovable property, how effected, 433.
beneficium ordinis does not hold in, 434.
—— may be retained for simple debts, when, 435.
—— preferred to prior general mortgage, 436, 447.
of securities, and how extinguished, 430, 432.
by, testator of property bequeathed, 336.
how imposed on a feud, 402.
duty of 2½ per cent., when payable, 427.
preference of, see *Preference.*
by *Schepen Kennissen*, how affected, 438.
cannot be sold without a judge's decree, 439.
tender of debt by a subsequent mortgagee, 441.
not extinguished by the bare knowledge of creditor that the property would be sold, 442.
prescription against, of a third party and of the debtor, 443.
must be discussed before the surety can be cited, 507, 508.
of a vessel or goods, where creditor does not undertake risks, is not a bottomry, 554.
of a debt, how effected, 538.

N

NAMPTISSEMENT, see *Provisional Payment.*

NATURALIZATION
letters of, 177.
—————— *ad honores, ib.*

NEGOTIORUM GESTIO
should be taken as gratuitous, 771.

NEIGHBOURING COUNTRIES
laws of, 7–24.

NORTH HOLLAND
law of, concerning the succession of natural children, 342.
—— succession *ab intestato*, 347, 348, 365.
election of succession may be made in, 363.
law of, concerning the succession to natural children, 368.

NOTARY
testament executed in presence of, not vitiated by a legacy to a witness, 291.
inserting anything in his own favour in a testament, 292.
testament attested by, beyond his place of admission, 295.

NOTES
payable to holder or *lawful* holder, 525.

NOVATION
when effected by a new written obligation, 522.
when it takes place, 835.
postponement of payment does not operate as, 836.

NUDUM PACTUM
action when maintainable on, 484.

O

OATH
contract of a ward, not valid, even if confirmed by, 128.
tendered by fidei commissary or legatee to the heir, 313.
in the action for dowry against a ravisher, 801.
suppletory, may be tendered, in what cases, 882.

OBLIGATIONS
may be acquired through an agent, without cession, 478.
verbal, 513.
written, defined, 521.

OBLIGATIONS (*continued*)
written, for a debt already due on good consideration, does not operate as a novation, 522.
—— how construed, *ib.*
—— force of, and when barred by the exception *non num. pecuniæ*, 523.

OFFENCES
prohibited by *lex loci*, 30, § 3.
compromise of, 520.

OLD-CLOTHES' MERCHANTS
things sold by, 184.

ORPHAN ASYLUM, see *Asylum.*

ORPHAN CHAMBER
when excluded, 116.
exclusion of, how guardians affected by, 120.
advice of, when necessary, 131.
may compel an inventory, when, 135.
if excluded, guardians should call for an inventory, 136.
may permit the surviving parent to administer the children's property, 143.
may insist upon assignment to the minor children, 144.
bound to make an inventory, when, 146.
has no right to retain property as against the heirs of a deceased ward, 159.
property of prodigal kept in custody of, 165, 167.
debts contracted in right of, not subject to the 2½ per cent. duty, 427.

OWNER
right of, against a possessor, 183.
when bound to restore price paid by a possessor, 184.
does not lose his right in a lost thing, 189.
of stranded goods, 193, 195.
—————— may collect or reclaim them, 196, 197.
of property sold, deposited, lent, &c., entitled to preference, 448.

P.

PACTUM DE NON PETENDO, 828.

PARATE EXECUTION
on debts due to a ward, 158.
right of, may be acquired by agreement, 480.

PARENT
consent of, to publication of espousals between minors, 76.
does not include grandparents, uncles, or guardians, 77.
need not state reasons of dissent to espousals of minor children, 79.
disputes between, and children, 80.
———————— suitors, 81.
of unsouud mind, 82.
not claiming guardianship punishable, 123.
not bound to explain reasons of dissent to the marriage of minor children, 125.
when bound to make inventory, 135, 136, 140.
cannot dispense with inventory, 137.
concealing property, forfeits his share therein, 139.
penalty against, on failure of division of common property, 142.
may be allowed the administration of the minor's property, 143.
not compellable to maintain or educate children, when, 151, 152.
when bound to educate and maintain children, 152.
succession of, under *Aasdoms* law, 308.
surviving cannot dispose of the portion of the heirs in a continued community, 320.
may determine the child's domicile, 341.
surviving, collation between, and heirs, 349, 350.

PARENT (*continued*)
how far liable for offeuces of children, 476.
promises made to, on behalf of the children, 509.
———————— by to children, *ib.*
———————— by, children to, *ib.*

PARTNERS
in action between, no cession or delivery of property necessary, 700.
liable for slight blame, 701.
right of third parties against, 702.
cannot acquire discharge by merely ceding their shares in the concern, *ib.*
liability of, on the contract of one, 703.
making cession before paying his contribution to the concern, 705.

PARTNERSHIP
every community of profit and loss does not constitute, 698.
where all profits are in common, and the losses attach to one only, 699.
en commandite, 704.
differs from the statutory community, 706.
between ship owners, 709, 710.
sailing company, see *Sailing Company*.

PATERNAL POWER
abuse of, 76.
in respect of inheritances devolving on children, 103.
how determined, 108, 474, 475.
contracts of children who are under, 474.
exceptions founded on, 475.
does not hinder donations to the children, 485.

PATRIA POTESTAS, see *Paternal Power*.

PAUPERS
not prohibited from taking under a will, 284.

PAWNBROKERS
stolen property pledged with, 184.

PAYEE
of a Bill of Exchange, may demand security or repayment, when, 579, 585.
———— ought to send the bill for presentment in due time, 581.
———— ought to pay value, when, 583.
———— when entitled to sue drawer for damages, 586.
when liable for re-exchange, 587.
when preferred to other creditors, 588.
may accept *supra protest*, 607.
may elect to sue between the drawer and the acceptor, 625.
may revoke the bill, when, 628.

PAYMENT
to one creditor, by insolvent, 200.
by a person on behalf of an unwilling party, 505.
of money lent on interest, cannot be made before the time agreed on, 542.
of a bill may be made *supra protest*, 613.
should be made to the true creditor, 822.
postponement of, 836.

PECULIUM, 104.

PECUNIA TRAJECTITIA, 556, 557.

PENALTY
against parent who does not claim the guardianship, 123.
against marriage of wards without consent, 125.
against parent failing to make inventory and assignment, 270.
stipulation of, in contracts, 481.
may not exceed the legal rate of interest, 637.

PERFORMANCE
action to compel, on espousals, 57.

PESTILENCE
testament of person suffering from, 301.

PIOUS FOUNDATIONS
not prohibited from taking under a will, 284.

PLANTS
rule at *Middelburg* concerning, 215.

PLEDGE
by testator, of property bequeathed, 336.
when exempt from the 2½ per cent. duty, 427, 430.
when extinguished by alienation, 432.
may be retained for simple debts, when, 435, 450.
when preferred to tacit mortgage, 437, 450.
may be sold without the authority of a judge, when, 439.
how effected, 536.
of immovables, 537.
of a debt, 538.
of the property of another, 539.
accident to, 540.
of movables, good without delivery, 830.

PORTION
Legitimate, of children preferred to *doarium*, 259.
———— may be left subject to condition, 305.
———— and *Trebellianic*, may be deducted by a child who has been passed over, when, 307.
Trebellianic, cannot be prohibited, 315.
———— and legitimate, more than half of the estate cannot be deducted on account of, 300.
Falcidian, how reserved, 324.
———— does not obtain as regards legacies *ad pias causas*, 327.

POSSESSION
interdict for retaining, 208.
bona fide, 212.
of the property mortgaged
prescribes the mortgage,
when, 443.

POSSESSOR
acquires the fruits by gathering, 205.
may recover useful expenses,
212.
entitled to *Benef. non num.
pec.*, 429.

PRACTICE
of the Court regarding the
construction of laws, 12,
23.

PREFERENCE
between two espousals, 58.
under *Kusting-brief*, 179.
of wife, upon exclusion of
community, 263.
in respect of money lent for
repairs, 417.
———————— funeral
expenses and last illness,
418.
of bleachers of linen for
wages, 424.
of principal as against an
agent, 426.
of mortgages, 436—438.
and *Concurrence*,
rules of, at *Amsterdam*, 438.
question respecting, by
whom entertained, 444, 445.
laws concerning, 446.
1. *general order* of, 447—473.
of special and general mortgages, 447.
2. *particular rights* as against
all creditors :
of owners, reclaiming their
own property, 448.
of persons having the right
of retention, or who have
made themselves liable on
the strength of bills of
lading received abroad,
449.
of creditors to whom goods
or notes have been pledged
and delivered, 450.

PREFERENCE (*continued*)
3. *general right* of, over the
entire estate ;
of the judicial expenses, 451.
of those who have lent
money for the funeral
expenses and the last illness, 452.
of lessors over things
brought and carried in, 453.
of domestic servants for
their wages, 454.
of the secretaries and marshals of the city, and of
auctioneers for the price
of goods sold, 455.
of the State and the city
for debts and taxes due to
them, 456—459, 464.
of married women, upon
exclusion of community,
460, 463.
of children in respect of
property left by a prede-
ceased parent, 461, 463.
of wards over the property
of the guardian, 462, 463.
of special mortgages, posterior in time, and general
mortgages, 465.
4. *special right* of, over *all the
immovables :*
of judicial expenses, funeral
expenses, and real taxes,
466.
for repairs done to immovable property, 467.
for rent imposed on wind-
mills, 468.
for emphyteutic rents,
ground rents, and perpe-
tual rents, *ib.*
of special mortgages and
Kusting brieven, 469, 470.
for the interest due on
mortgages, 471.
of persons placed in possession upon execution of a
judgment, 472.
of chirograph creditors, 473.
of bottomries, 564—567.
of payee against the estate
of the holder, 588.

PREMIUM
of Insurance, see *Insurance*.

PRESCRIPTION
of immovables and annual rents, 206, 875.
of actions *in personam*, and movables, *ib.*, 207, 874.
of hypothecary actions, 207.
of actions for injury, *ib.* 208.
of the exception *non num. pecuniæ*, *ib.*
of relief on the ground of minority, *ib.*
does not run against minors, 210.
of feuds, 405, 412.
of mortgages, 443.
of actions on insurance, and of relief against, 769.
of action for contribution in average, 795.
of advocates' fees and debts not due in writing, 876.

PRESENTMENT
of bill of exchange, when excused, 581, 582, and see *Bill of Exchange*.

PRICE
restitution of, 200.
payment of, necessary to pass the property in the thing sold, 203.

PRINCIPAL
tacit mortgage and preference of, as against agent, 425, 448.
bound to accept a bill drawn on him by his agent, 615.

PRIVILEGES
(charters) when promulgated, constitute the law, 2.
of debts due to wards, 158.
of testaments made *jure militari*, 299.
————————— during pestilence, 301.
————— of country-folks, 300.
of money lent for funeral expenses and last illness, 418.
of sureties and women, see *Beneficium*.

PROCLAMATIONS
of espousals, 76—80, 83, 125.
————————— debar a prior *sponsus*, 85.

PRODIGAL
may be interdicted, 165.
cannot bind himself when so interdicted, *ib.*
property of, kept in custody of Orphan Chamber, 165, 167.
when and how discharged from curatorship, 166.
wife of, cannot be appointed curator, 168.
testament of, 281.

PROFIT
what things included under, 253, 254.
and *loss*, community of, see *Community*.

PROMISE
consideration necessary, 484.
made to parent on behalf of children, 509.
—— by parent to children, *ib.*
—— by children to parent, *ib.*
—— to a third party who assents without authority, 510.
specific performance of, 512.
verbal, 513, 515.

PROMISSORY NOTES
defined, 603.
want of consideration, when pleadable, 603.
See further, *Chirographs*.

PROOF
of espousals, 86.
of a debt as against third parties, 528.
of value of goods, in an insurance, 738.
by suppletory oath, 882.

PROPERTY
regulated by *lex loci*, 30.
movable, supposed to be found in the place of domicile, 36.
————of wife may be alienated, 98.
————— of a ward, how disposed of, 129, 143.
————— belonging in common to a ward and another, 148.

PROPERTY (*continued*)
movable what things classed under, 181.
———— may be alienated by simple delivery, 201.
———— prescription of, 206, 207.
———— succession to, 339.
————pledge of, when exempt from the 2½ per cent. duty, 427.
———— when extinguished by alienation, 432.
———— if delivered to the creditor, is entitled to preference, 450.
immovable, of wife, cannot be alienated, when, 97.
———— of a ward how alienated, 130, 132.
———— what things classed under, 180.
————transfer of, how effected, 202, 203.
———— special mortgage of, how effected, 433.
———— prescription of, 206.
incorporeal, 37, 38.
———— not comprehended under movables or immovables, 178.
———— if required to be so referred, then, 179—181.
common, inventory of, when necessary, 136, 137.
———— division of, between surviving parent & children, 142.
———— belonging to several wards, 149.
———— profits promised to wife out of, 262.
———— mutual will of, how far revocable, 283.
community of, see *Community*.
of the wife, under the management of the husband, 91.
———— not subject to fines or confiscation for the husband's delicts, 94.

PROPERTY (*continued*)
of the wife, not subject to the husband's debts, when, 255.
acquired by children in service, 104.
———— by their own industry, *ib.*
adventitious, of minor children, 105.
devolving on minors, 140, 141.
division and assignment of, to the children, on dissolution of community, 142, 143, 274—276.
assignment not necessary, when, 144.
community of, between children and surviving parent, *ib.*, 266—276.
of wards, how disposed of after their death, 159.
———— disposition of, how restricted, 285, 286.
of prodigals, 167.
of absentees, 163, 167.
of persons incapable of managing their own affairs, 164.
administration of, granted to wife during husband's insanity, 101.
concealment of, in making an inventory, 139.
annual rents, 154.
inheritance does not pass *ipso jure*, 182.
owner's right, as against possessor, 183.
stolen, if pledged with public pawnbrokers, 184.
sold by old-clothes' merchant, 184.
gold or silver, sold to a goldsmith, *ib.*
lost, continues to belong to the owner, 189.
———— passes to the finder, when, *ib.*
in uninhabited lands, passes to the discoverer, 190.
in an enemy's ship, 191.
in ship captured by the enemy, 192.
in stranded goods, 193, 197.

PROPERTY (*continued*)
in treasure-trove, 198.
in a thing sold, does not pass
by mere delivery, 203.
purchase by insolvent shortly
before cession, 204.
possessor of, acquires fruits
by gathering, 205.
buildings upon another's, 212,
213.
in trees planted in a leasehold,
215.
merger of, on marriage, 216.
in money realised by sale of
a feud, 220.
subject to *fidei-commissum*,
does not become common,
221.
division of, upon dissolution
of marriage, 222.
brought in marriage, inventory of, 230.
separation from, 233.
succession to, of married
parties, 235—240.
——— of children 241
—243.
——— of strangers,
244—246.
——— of illegitimate
children, 368.
collation of, married parties
cannot sue each other for,
during marriage, 256.
——— between surviving
parent and heirs, 350.
exclusion of, includes accidental losses and necessary
expenses, 257.
omitted in antenuptial contract, 251.
purchased by married persons,
when considered as profits,
254.
of persons maintained in
charitable asylums, 280.
legacy of, is subject to annual rent, 325.
burthens of, attach to whom,
340.
mortgage of, see *Mortgage*.
may be acquired through an
agent, 478.

PROPERTY (*continued*)
in dispute may be alienated,
630.
risks and benefits of, attach
the purchaser, 639.
PROTEST
necessary to entitle an acceptor
supra protest to sue in cambial process, 607.
expenses of, payable by acceptor, 627.
for non-acceptance, 854.
for non payment, 855.
time of making, 856.
effects of not making in due
time, 857, 858.
when unnecessary, 858.
on refusal or concealment or
insolvency of drawee, 859
to whom sent, 861.
for non acceptance, security
may be demanded upon, 862.
PROVISIONAL PAYMENT
on instrument without just
consideration, 526.
in what cases allowed, and
how opposed, 527.
for interest, 549.
on a bill of exchange, not
prevented by the exception
contractûs non impleti, 602,
603.
not prevented by the mere
application for relief, 877.
PUBERTY
espousals between children
below, 54.
marriage of children below, 66.
PUNISHMENT
of *infamy*, 59, 63.
against bigamy, 62, 63.
under *lex hac edictali*, 69.
against adultery, 70.
of death or transportation,
ground for divorce, 89.
evasion of, by flight, *ib.*
of sailors, 687, 689—692.
PUPILLARY SUBSTITUTION,
See *Substitution*.
PURCHASER
who was privy to fraud not
entitled to restitution of
price, 200.

PURCHASER (continued)
  does not acquire property by
    mere sale and delivery, 203.
  risks and benefits of property,
    when they attach to, 639.
  bound to pay interest on de-
    fault, 640.
  knowingly purchasing the
    property of another, 641.

Q.

QUERELA INOFFICIOSI
  TESTAMENTI
  against successory contracts,
    236.
  when maintainable by a child
    who has been passed over,
    307.
  upon disinherison, 332.
  inofficiosi dotis, when main-
    tainable, 244.

R.

RAVISHMENT
  of a virgin, action for dowry,
    801.
RECLAIM, see *Retractus*.
REDEMPTION
  of annual rent-charge, 633,
    634.
  value of money in, 635, 636.
RE-EXCHANGE
  on bills, how recovered, 868.
  on bills, when recoverable
    and from whom, 587, 869.
RELEASE
  by donation, see *Acceptilation*.
RELIEF, see *Restitutio in Integrum*.
REMITTANT
  of a Bill, see *Payee*.
RENT-CHARGE
  jus retractus in, 662.
  may be sold, 632.
  redemption of, 633, 634.
  pact binding the vendor to
    redeem within a certain
    time, 633.
  value of money in redeem-
    ing, 635.
RENTS
  annual, prescription of, 875.

RES ALIENA
  purchaser of, cannot recover,
    when, 641.
RESCISSION
  of sale, on a latent defect in
    the thing sold, 642.
  ———— founded on fraud,
    666.
  of compromises, 896.
  of contracts and public sales,
    898, 899, 901.
RES LITIGIOSA
  may be alienated, 630.
RESPITE
  letters of, requisites, 890.
RESTITUTIO IN INTEG-
  RUM
  not necessary in the rescission
    of sales founded on fraud,
    606.
  against prescription in cases
    of insurance, 769.
  on the ground of minority,
    when prescribed, 900.
  not necessary in transactions
    which are *ipso jure* void, 877.
  applied for, but not yet
    granted, 878.
  to a widow under 25 years of
    age, 879.
  to a girl under 25, against a
    promise of dowry, 880.
  against assignment by a
    surviving parent, to the
    children, 897.
  against contracts and public
    sales, under Cod. iv. 44. 2,
    898, 899, 901.
  prescription of, 881, 900.
RETENTION
  right of, over goods saved, for
    average, 793.
  ———— over vessel and
    goods, for losses arising
    from collision, 813.
  ———— over merchandise,
    for freight, 882, 883.
RETRACTUS
  legal and *conventional*, 643, 646.
  right of, when it accrues, 645.
  ———— does not obtain in
    respect of public sales,
    when, 647.

RETRACTUS (*continued*)
  family, 644.
  —— when and by whom exercised, 648, 656.
  —— how lost, 654, 655.
  —— time of instituting, 657.
  —— price need not be tendered pending the suit, 658.
  —— how exercised, 659, 660.
  ——does not accrue to one posterior in order, on default of the prior, 661.
  —— of lands subject to rent-charge, and of personal debts, 662.

S.

SAFE CONDUCT
  how obtained, and when granted, 894.
SAILING COMPANY, 707, 708.
SAILOR
  just grounds of claiming discharge, 686.
  desirous of being discharged, 687.
  private merchandise of, 688.
  verbal injuries caused by, how punishable, 689.
  concealing his ignorance, 690.
  deserting or found drunk, 691.
  stealing goods or tackle, 692.
  may be retained, even upon an alteration of the destination of the vessel, 693.
  heirs of entitled to the wages, 695.
  when entitled to wages or salvage on loss of vessel, 694.
  wages of in case of delay in the voyage, 779.
  losses arising from disablement of, 782.
SALE
  and delivery do not pass the property, unless—, 203.
  rescission of, on a latent defect, 642.
  condition of forfeiture in, 637.

SALE (*continued*)
  when parties may withdraw from, to avoid a *retractus*, 645.
  in execution does not pass the risks, until cession, 639.
  on withdrawal from, a new sale takes place, 665.
  founded on fraud, how rescinded, 666.
  public, relief against, 899.
SALVAGE
  deduction of, when allowed, 681.
SATISFACTION
  signification of, 834.
SCHEPENDOMS LAW
  of succession, in respect of feuds, 389, 392, 393.
  See further *Succession*.
SECOND SPOUSE
  if appointed heir to the exclusion of children, 288.
SECURITIES
  public, belonging to a ward, 130.
  —— right of owner against possessor, 183.
  —— alienated by simple delivery, 201.
  —— disposition of, by a ward, 286.
  —— pledge of, not subject to the 2½ per cent. duty, when, 430.
  —— pledge of, when extinguished by alienation, 432.
SECURITY
  uncertain guardians bound to give, 119.
  when dispensed with, 120.
  to be given by guardians, 134.
  guardian bound to take for money lent, 155.
  to appear in court, 175.
  to be given by usufructuary, 371–373.
  to be given by a legatee or fidei-commissary, 511.
  payee of a bill may demand, when, 579.
  drawer may demand, when, 580.

SECURITY (*continued*)
bound to give, when, 585, 612.
may be demanded on non-
acceptance of a bill, 862.
SENATUS-CONSULTUM
MACEDONIANUM
exceptions under, 474, 475.
SENATUS-CONSULTUM
VELLEJANUM
exceptions under, 495.
renunciation of, 496.
SENTENCE
a person paying a just debt
after being absolved, 797.
set-off pleadable after, 827.
SEPARATION
from bed and board, 25, 90.
of property, *ib.*
from bed, board, and property
excludes community, 231.
SEQUESTRATION
necessary, when allowed, 534.
SERVANTS
preference of, in an insolvent
estate, 454.
master how far liable for
offences of, 477, 811.
domestic, may be dismissed
without compensation, 679.
SERVICE
property acquired by children
in, 104.
contract of, between master
and crew of a vessel, 685.
SERVITUDE
prædial, considered as immovable, 181.
———— how established, 369.
SET-OFF
in the payment of a bill of
exchange, when allowed,
623.
may be pleaded against an insolvent or against a person
who has *respite* or *surcheance*, 825.
of an agent's debt against the
principal in an insurance,
826.
may be pleaded even after
sentence, 827.
SEURETE DU CORPS, see
Safe conduct.

SHARES
of children, parent, and second
spouse, how determined,
274–276.
See further, *Portion.*
SHIP
in some places not subject to
division on dissolution of
community, 142.
enemy's, if captured by a private vessel, 191.
if captured by the enemy, 192.
how alienated, 201.
profits derived from, included
under community of profits,
253.
usufructary liable for neglecting to insure, 370.
money lent to build not entitled to tacit mortgage, 418.
right of master to discharge
himself by cession of, 684.
illicit goods cannot be shipped
without owner's consent,
696.
owners of, how far liable, 697.
sailing company, see *Sailing
Company.*
insurance of, 717, 719.—See
further *Insurance.*
majority of owners, may compel a public sale, 776.
putting into port in apprehension of the enemy, 783.
furniture of, 784.
master and owners of, when
liable for things thrown
overboard, 791.
losses arising from overloading,
ib.
goods deposited in an improper
place, 792.
master and owners, right of
tacit mortgage over goods
saved, 793.
neglect of attaching buoys,
805.
losses from fraud or fault of
master, 806.
——— in removing or neglecting to remove a vessel from
danger, 807.
——— from collision, 812—814.

2 B

SHIP (*continued*)
losses, by whom made good, 812, 815—821.
——and in what proportion, 816.

SHIPOWNERS
partnership between, and rights of the partners, 709, 710.

SHIPWRECKED GOODS
owner of, may collect or reclaim them, 196, 197.
may be sold by the Treasury, when, 197.
right of the Treasury to, 193.
jurisdiction over, 194.

SILVER
sold to a goldsmith, 184.

SLANDER, see *Defamation.*

SLAVE
found on Dutch soil, free, 46.
fugitives from the colonies, *ib.*

SOLDIERS
excused from acting as guardians, 42.
cannot be sureties, when, 497.
testament of, 299.

SOUTH HOLLAND
laws of, concerning the succession of natural, adulterine, and incestuous children, 344, 345.
——————— to illegitimate children, 365, 366, 368.
——————— of the Treasury, 365.
——————— succession *ab intestato*, 347, 348.

SPECIFIC PERFORMANCE, 512.

SPONSORS
gifts made by, to children, 104.

STATE
has a tacit mortgage over the property of its debtors, 419, 420.

STATUS
recognized by comity, 42.

STATUTES
personal, 27, 34, 42.
real, 28.
mixed, 29, 35.

STATUTES (*continued*)
mixed, how far controlled by comity, 39.
force of, *within* the territory, 30.
—— *beyond* the territory, 32, 33.
foreign, force of, 32.
may be departed from, when, 43, 44.
diversity of, in respect of antenuptial contracts, 228.

STEP-FATHER or MOTHER
when bound to make inventory, 135.
property of, how far liable in tacit mortgage, 422.
when entitled to collation, 223.

STOLEN PROPERTY
if pledged with a public pawnbroker, 184.

STUDENTS
from a foreign country, 30, § 1.

SUBSTITUTE
to an heir or legatee, in usufruct, 374, 375.
entitled to property, after deduction of the legitimate and Falcidian portions, 106.

SUBSTITUTION
Pupillary and *Quasi-pupillary*, 312.

SUCCESSION
ab intestato, regulated by *lex loci*, 33.
——————— of children legitimized by rescript, 172.
——————— of a parent under the *Aasdoms* law, 308.
——————— to movables, 339, 341.
——————— by the *Aasdoms* law, 346, 348.
——————— by the *Schependoms* law, 347, 348.
——————— Roman law called in, *in subsidium*, 359.
——————— in *Briel* and *Voorn*, 351.
——————— in *Curacoa, Surinam, Berbice,* and the Colonies, 352.

SUCCESSION (continued)
ab intestato, of ascendants and collaterals, 353, 354, 356.
———— of half-brothers, and surviving parent, 356.
———— of grandchildren and brothers, 357.
———— half brothers and the children of full brothers, 358.
———— not restricted, 364.
———— to illegitimate children, 368.
by antenuptial contract, to property of the married parties, 235, 240, 363.
———— of the children, 241—243.
———— of strangers, 244—246.
of a sole or a particular heir, 309.
election of, how effected and how it operates, 360.
———— by testament, and by devisory contract, 361, 362.
———— in Zeeland and Zierickzee, ib.
———— by antenuptial contract, 363.
of the Treasury, 365, 366.
by accretion in Zeeland, 367.
to feuds, 388, 389, 393, 403, 404, 407, 408.
agreements concerning, 479.
SURCHEANCE, see Suspension.
SURETIES
soldiers may not be, when, 497.
husband may give, for payment of the dowry, 498.
engaging for a larger sum than the principal debtor, 499.
may apply to be discharged, when, 500.
may engage himself without any solemn form of words, 501.
privileges of, how renounced, 502, 503.

SURETIES (continued)
privileges of, merchants selling goods on del-credere commission not entitled to, 504.
paying on behalf of an unwilling party, 505.
cession of action to, 506.
cannot be sued until the mortgage has been discussed, 507, 508.
how affected by granting time to principal, 836.
SURETYSHIP
of a third person in a married woman's contract, 96.
SURVIVOR
community between and children, 266—276.
may revoke a mutual will, when, 283.
SUSPENSION OF PAYMENT
when and to whom granted, 895.

T.

TAXES, 36.
farmers of, entitled to tacit mortgage, 419.
due to the State or Province, preference and conourrence of, 456—459, 466.
TENANT
extraordinary charges in an emphyteusis attach to, 668.
TESTAMENT
executed according to lex loci, 39.
wife may make without the husband's knowledge, 100.
executors of, need not allege excuse, 124.
alienations under title of, 202.
revocation of autenuptial contract by, 265.
mutual, community may be continued by, 266, 267.
———— how far revocable by the survivor, 283.
———— one party may recede from, 298.
right of making, 277.
of Roman Catholics, 278, 279.

TESTAMENT (*continued*)
of persons maintained in charitable asylums, 280.
of prodigals, 281.
of illegitimate children, 282.
of a ward, 285.
disinherison of son and appointment of second spouse as heir, 288.
distinction between, and codicil, 289.
without the appointment of an heir, 290, 375.
legatee may be witness to, 291.
one who inserts anything in his own favour cannot take, unless—, 292.
may be made orally, before 7 witnesses, 293.
disinherison, how effected, 294.
attested by a notary beyond his place of admission, 295.
———— a notary and witnesses, but not signed by testator, 296.
gros and *minut* defined, 297, *note.*
———— testator cannot prevent, being shown to the heirs, 297.
jure militari, how long valid, 299.
made during pestilence, 301.
ad pias causas, 302.
how far invalidated by the passing over of children, 306.
a son passed over may dispute, when, 307.
impossible conditions in, 310.
executors of, cannot debar the heirs from the inheritance, 323.
———— cannot alienate without the consent of the heirs, *ib.*
cassatory and *derogatory* clauses in, 320.
wherein the derogatory clause has not been inserted, 329.
revocation of, by destruction of the *gros*, 330.

TESTAMENT (*continued*)
of parent in favour of the children revoked by a subsequent testament, 331.
not rendered *ipso jure* void by a disinherison, 332.
election of succession by, 361, 362.
disposition of feuds by, 406.

TESTAMENTARY
dispositions by antenuptial contract, 236.

TESTATOR
cannot prohibit the testament being shown to the heirs, 297.
persons who have caused the death of, 334.

THINGS
placed or suspended in a dangerous position, 810.

TIMBER, see *Wood*.

TITHES
referable to immovables, 180.

TOLLS
abolished, 176.

TOWNS
tacit mortgage of, over the property of tax-collectors, 425.

TRADE
a married woman carrying on, 95.

TRANSACTION, see *Compromise*.

TRANSFER
of ships, how effected, 201.
of property without delivery of the instrument, 202.
of movables by delivery, 201.
of public securities, *ib.*
of legal mortgages, 202.
under title of dowry, community, antenuptial contract, testament, and division, 202.

TRANSPORTATION
of a husband or wife, 89.
of a father, 109.

TREASURE TROVE
found on one's own land, 198.
———— another's land, *ib.*

TREASURY
right of, to succeed *ab intestato*,
365, 366.
—— to stranded goods, 193,
195, 197.
TREBELLIANIC PORTION,
see *Portion*.
TREES
planted on a leasehold pass
with the land, 215.
TUTELAGE
determined by majority, 110.
children may be discharged
from, before majority,
when, *ib*.
of *Impuberes*, and *Cura* of
minors, 111.

U.

UNCLE
not included under the term
parent, 77.
UNINHABITED LANDS
pass to the discoverer, 190.
USUCAPION
of movables, 207.
USUFRUCT
benefits of, included under
community of profits, 253.
if left with power of alienation,
371—373.
if left to surviving spouse as
heir or *legatee*, with substitution of another, 374, 375.
is destroyed by cession to
another, 376.
of apparel, 377.
of money lent out on security, 378.
how charged on a feud, 402.
USUFRUCTUARY
of a ship liable for neglect to
insure, 370.
security to be given by, cannot
be dispensed with by the
testament, unless—, 371—
373.
UTRECHT, Treaty of, 13.
VASSALS, see *Feud*.
VENDOR
rights of preference of, 448.
See *Sale*.

VENIA ÆTATIS, 107, 110.
does not qualify a person to
act as guardian, 112.
requirements of, and how obtained, 161.
VIRGIN
ravishment of, action for
dowry, 801.
VOORN
rule of succession *ab intestato*
in, 347.

W.

WAGERS
causes rarely decided upon,
514.
WAGES
of sailor, on his death, should
be paid to his heirs, 695.
—— in case of delay, 779.
WARD
cannot appear in court without his guardian or curator,
127; excepting in criminal
causes, *ib*.
contracts of, invalid, even if
confirmed by oath, 128.
movable property of, may be
alienated, when, 129.
public securities belonging to
how alienated, 130.
property devolving on, 140.
—— assigned to, 143.
division between surviving
parent and, 145.
notes belonging to, kept in
custody of the Orphan
Chamber, 147.
—— how secured from alienation, *ib*.
—— belonging to several,
148.
property belonging to several
149.
how educated and maintained,
150—152.
money of, how invested, 153.
—— may be lent to the
States or Treasury, 155.
annual rents purchased for,
have certain peculiarities,
154.

WARD (*continued*)

money of, may be lent to private parties, or invested in country farms, 155.

debts due to privileges of, 158.

property of, how disposed of after death, 159.

discharge of, from guardianship, 160.

on continued absence of, property how disposed of, 163.

cannot institute his guardians or their children, or his own concubine as heirs, 285, 286.

right of preference for debts due by the guardians, 463.

contracts of, how far effectual, 529.

debt of, to whom payable, 822.

WIDOW

right of abandoning the common estate, 226.

under 25 years of age, whether entitled to relief, 879.

WIFE

power of husband over property of, 91, 92.

how far liable on contracts of the husband, 93.

property of, not subject to fines or confiscations for crimes of husband, 94.

WIFE (*continued*)

has no *persona standi in judicio*, 95.

how far liable on her own contracts, 96.

immovable property and notes of, 97.

movable property and notes may be alienated, when, 98.

action for indemnity by, 98, 99.

when not liable for debts contracted during marriage, 99.

when liable for things supplied on credit, *ib.*

may make testament or donation *causâ mortis*, 100.

may claim administration of property, during husband's insanity, 101.

cannot be appointed as curator over insane or prodigal husband, 168.

property of, cannot be taken in execution, when, 255.

father of, may be sued for dowry, 25.

not entitled to *morgen-gave* or *doarium*, until, when, 259, 260.

institution of as heir cancels, marriage-gift, when, 261.

www.ingramcontent.com/pod-product-compliance
Lightning Source LLC
Chambersburg PA
CBHW031350290326
41932CB00044B/864